Children of the Night

Children of the Night

A Study of Adolescent Prostitution

D. Kelly Weisberg
Hastings College of the Law

Lexington Books
D.C. Heath and Company/Lexington, Massachusetts/Toronto

Library of Congress Cataloging in Publication Data

Weisberg, D. Kelly.
    Children of the night.

    Bibliography: p.
    Includes index.
    1. Prostitution, Juvenile—United States   2. Prostitution, Male—United States.   3. Prostitutes—United States—Social conditions.   4. Prostitutes—Services for—United States.   5. Runaway youth—Services for—United States.

    I. Title.
HQ144.W44   1985   306.7'45'0973   82–48957
ISBN 0-669-06389-4 (alk. paper)

Third printing, February 1986

Published simultaneously in Canada
Printed in the United States of America on acid-free paper
International Standard Book Number: 0-669-06389-4
Library of Congress Catalog Card Number: 82-48957

To my husband,
George R. Blumenthal,
for his moral support
and encouragement

Contents

List of Figures and Tables

Figures

Tables

Preface

The focus of this book is adolescent prostitution—specifically, the etiology of the problem, the young prostitutes' lifestyles, and their involvement with the juvenile justice and social service delivery systems. Special attention is given to an examination of the relationship between adolescent prostitution and the factors of child abuse and neglect, and runaway behavior. The phenomena of both female and male adolescent prostitution are studied.

This book is based, in part, on research conducted from 1979 to 1981 pursuant to a contract awarded to Urban and Rural Systems Associates (a San Francisco–based consulting firm) by the Youth Development Bureau of the U.S. Department of Health and Human Services. The purpose of that study was to develop an in-depth demographic and descriptive knowledge base on adolescents involved in prostitution and to examine the relationship of that phenomenon to involvement in pornography and other forms of sexual exploitation, child abuse and neglect, and runaway behavior. Although the emphasis of that research was on adolescent male prostitution, all data on males were compared with existing data on adolescent female prostitutes.

The research involved multiple data collection efforts. First, a review of the literature on female and male adolescent prostitution was undertaken, in the course of which an annotated bibliography on adolescent prostitution was developed. The bibliography contained information on published and unpublished research on female and male adolescent prostitution and a list of related materials on child and adolescent abuse, sexual abuse, sexual delinquency, delinquency, runaways, and adult prostitution.

Second, the project staff conducted ethnographic research in two cities— San Francisco's Tenderloin and Polk Street areas and New York City's Times Square and Upper East Side. Field studies focused on daily interactions between prostitutes and their customers. By living in hotels frequented by young prostitutes, field researchers were able to formulate an ethnographic account of the daily lives of adolescent prostitutes and of the milieu in which their prostitution is conducted.

Next, the study team surveyed a range of existing social service programs that serve young prostitutes and runaway youth. An initial telephone survey was conducted with agencies throughout the country, and seven cities were selected for site visits. In these cities (Boston, Houston, Los Angeles, Minneapolis, New York, San Francisco, and Seattle), programs were identified that served adolescent prostitutes. Field researchers then visited the cities to conduct ethnographic observations in prostitution locales, to visit social service agencies, and to meet with local law enforcement authorities. In each city, the research staff sought to locate both youth agencies and community-based gay-identified agencies to discover if there were distinctions between these types of agencies that serve juvenile prostitutes.

A primary purpose of the site visits was to explore the nature of the agencies and the types and extent of programs and services offered to adolescent prostitutes and runaway youth. Data were collected about the agencies' creation, funding sources, staffing patterns, and range of services, and discussions were held with agency staff members to elicit their opinions regarding effective techniques for intervention with their client population. In the course of the research, a resource manual for service providers was prepared (see bibliography).

Finally, data collection involved the development of adolescent prostitute profiles. With the cooperation of agency staffs in several cities, the researchers were able to identify seventy-nine young male prostitutes and to collect data on several factors, focusing on the youth's background and family characteristics (race, socioeconomic status, family composition, child abuse and neglect histories); entrance into prostitution (age at onset, education and employment at onset, influence of significant others, drug use, residential situations, and motivations); prostitution lifestyles (relationships with and attitudes toward customers and other prostitutes, types of prostitution, attitudes about sexuality and sexual orientation, involvement in pornography, drug and alcohol use, physical and mental health); juvenile justice involvement (runaway histories, nature and extent of general arrest histories, and prostitution-specific offense histories); and social service involvement (interactions with the social service delivery system before and after entering prostitution, including the prostitutes' responses to service providers).

This data collection activity allowed field staff to compile descriptive profiles of each of these seventy-nine youth. Then, a comparative analysis of this population was undertaken, yielding the following demographic characteristics of the youth. These youth are primarily (85 percent) adolescents, from ages 12 through 18, with a small number over 18. Their mean age is 16.96. Sixty percent of the youth are either 16 or 17 years old, and 71 percent are between 16 and 18 years old.

Two-thirds of the youth are Caucasian; approximately one-fourth are black; 3 percent are Native Americans; and other racial groups combined account for 6 percent. In terms of socioeconomic status, a large proportion of the youth (38 percent) perceive their family's economic rank as middle class; an almost equal percentage (37 percent) rate their family's socioeconomic status as lower class; and 5 percent report an upper-class socioeconomic status.

Data on the level of education attained by the youth reveal that the mean grade completed is 9.6 ($\pm$0.2). More than 75 percent have not completed high school. Although a high noncompletion rate might be expected in a predominantly adolescent sample, age alone does not explain this finding. Indeed, almost one-third (29 percent) completed only the eighth grade or less. In addition, most of these youth are not currently employed; only 28 percent are employed in legitimate jobs in addition to their prostitution.

In terms of sexual identification, the majority of the prostitutes identify as a sexual minority—47 percent as homosexual, 29 percent as bisexual, 8 percent as transvestite, and 4 percent as transsexual. Only 16 percent of the youth identify as heterosexual. (The total sums to more than 100 percent because two transvestites and one transsexual also identify as homosexual.) Additional results of the data analysis of these prostitute profiles are incorporated into chapters 3 and 5, in which data on family backgrounds, entrance into prostitution, prostitution lifestyles, criminal justice involvement, and social service involvement are presented and compared with existing research on adolescent female prostitutes.

In the past decade, considerable knowledge has accumulated on the subject of female and male adolescent prostitution. It is hoped that the knowledge gained by this research will enable the criminal justice system and the social service delivery system to provide improved services to these youth.

The material in this book is not in any way related to the Hollywood, California institution called "Children of the Night", a charitable organization.

Acknowledgments

The assistance of the many persons and agencies who helped with this research project is gratefully appreciated. I wish to acknowledge the special contribution of the following programs: Project START, The Shelter, Seattle, Washington; Central City Hospitality House, San Francisco, California; Bridge Over Troubled Waters, Boston, Massachusetts; Steppingstone, Santa Monica, California; Gay and Lesbian Community Service Center, Hollywood, California; and New Bridge, Minneapolis, Minnesota.

I would like to thank the Youth Development Bureau (YDB), U.S. Department of Health and Human Services, for their financial support of the research upon which part of this book is based. The research, "Adolescent Male Prostitution: A Study of Sexual Exploitation, Etiological Factors, and Runaway Behavior," was completed pursuant to contract number HEW 105-79-1201, Youth Development Bureau, Administration for Children, Youth, and Families, U.S. Department of Health and Human Services. Darryl Summers, YDB project monitor, made several valuable contributions to the study design and data analysis.

I would also like to express my appreciation to the several Urban and Rural Systems Associates staff members who participated in this research: Toby Marotta and Toby Johnson, who contributed ethnographic research, Ernest Fazio, and project directors Noel Day and Bruce Fisher. Special thanks are also due to Robert W. Deisher, M.D., of the University of Washington, Seattle; J. Fred E. Shick, M.D., of the University of Illinois, Chicago Circle Campus, Chicago; and Victoria Wagner of Project START, The Shelter, Seattle, who served as consultants to the URSA research.

In addition, I express gratitude to the following research assistants from Hastings College of the Law: William J. Lafferty, Jan Lindberg, Lisa Rasmussen, Joanne Sakai, Margaret Schaus, Wendy Spector, and Elissa Warantz. I appreciate, too, the assistance in typing provided by Stephen R. Lothrop and Peggie C. MacDonald.

All case studies presented in the text are actual accounts, although all identifying data have been altered to protect the privacy of the youth involved. I am especially grateful to these youth for contributing to our understanding of this subject.

1
Adolescent Prostitution: Construction of a Social Problem

C hildhood prostitution has it roots in antiquity. Historian Lloyd deMause notes that children growing up in ancient Greece and Rome often were used sexually by older men, although the form and frequency of the abuse varied by geographic area and date. He writes: "Boy brothels flourished in every city, and one could even contract for the use of a 'rent-a-boy' service in Athens."[1] He notes, further, that some children were sold into concubinage by their parents. This sexual abuse of children and adolescents continued in ancient Greece and Rome even after the enactment of legislation to curb such practices.[2]

Despite evidence of childhood prostitution in antiquity, the labeling of this phenomenon as a pervasive social problem is relatively recent. Only since the mid-1970s has juvenile prostitution become a topic of widespread national interest. At that time, national concern was mobilized by newspaper and magazine articles and films.[3] Public response to the social problem was swift. In the spring of 1977, congressional hearings were held on the subject, culminating in the Protection of Children Against Sexual Exploitation Act.[4] Legal policy was quickly formulated on both the state and federal levels to address the problem.[5] Thus, in this period, the social problem of juvenile prostitution was "socially constructed."[6]

In exploring the construction of the social problem of juvenile prostitution, we must address the question of why adolescent prostitution came to the forefront of public attention at this particular time in contemporary history. Since childhood prostitution has its roots in antiquity, its labeling as a social problem is not attributable to its emergence as a new phenomenon. Rather, the answer appears to lie in a number of social movements and social forces in the 1960s and 1970s, including (1) the hippies and the counterculture movement of the 1960s, (2) the emergence of the problem of runaway youth in the late 1960s, (3) the recognition in the 1960s and 1970s of child abuse and sexual abuse of children, and (4) the children's rights movement. Each of these social movements or forces helped lay the groundwork for the subsequent recognition of juvenile prostitution as a social problem.

The Hippies

The Haight-Ashbury district—known as "the Haight"—is located near the geographic center of San Francisco. It is bounded on the west by Golden Gate Park and on the south by a hilly area called either Buena Vista or Ashbury Heights. Besides Golden Gate Park, two other parks are encompassed within the boundaries of the Haight: "the Panhandle"—a four-block strip of grass— and, at the other end, the much larger Buena Vista Park. Haight Street, the main thoroughfare of the district, runs from downtown Market Street across much of San Francisco into Golden Gate Park. The Haight-Ashbury district encompasses several schools, churches, a branch library, a boys' club, many neighborhood businesses, and two hospitals.[7]

In the 1940s the Haight was a working-class residential district with a somewhat paradoxical liberal and progressive atmosphere. Changes occurred in the district in the late 1950s and early 1960s. Redevelopment and relocation activity in adjacent ghetto areas resulted in a large influx of blacks. At the same time, the liberal residents provided a milieu for the development of radical political groups. Merged with the liberal tradition was a bohemian tradition; writers, artists, and actors had lived in the district for many years. With the dissolution of San Francisco's North Beach "beat scene" in the late 1950s and early 1960s, many residents were attracted to the diversified Haight-Ashbury district.

From 1966 to 1968, thousands of persons poured into this small urban area. This was the beginning of the hippie era in the Haight—the era of the "flower children." The predecessors of the hippies during the 1950s and early 1960s were the beatniks. The beatniks, having rejected the conformity and materialism of the middle class, began excursions into drugs, sexual experimentation, poetry, and music.[8] Many of the ideas of this bohemianism carried over, and it was rechristened "the hippie movement" in the mid-1960s.

The Haight became the symbolic center of the new social movement. It also became the mecca for white middle-class youth.[9] Before the summer of 1967, a headline in the *San Francisco Chronicle* threatened: "100,000 will invade Haight-Ashbury this Summer."[10] Although the 100,000 did not materialize, several thousand young people did inundate the region. The "Be-In" in Golden Gate Park, a gathering of 20,000, was followed by "the Summer of Love," and hippies became the subject of considerable media attention and scholarly interest.[11]

The hippie ideology was characterized by several beliefs, including (1) the power of innocence (flower power) before it is destroyed by society and by mechanical modes of teaching; (2) the importance of each person's self-expression (doing one's own thing); (3) the idea of living for the moment; (4) sexual permissiveness; (5) female equality; and (6) the importance of psychedelic drugs to transcend the confining reality.[12]

Much of the ideology of the hippie culture was not new. Sociologist Bennett Berger points out that many of the same ideas characterized bohemianism in the 1920s.[13] What was new about the hippies, however, were the numbers of adherents and their ages. Berger writes: "First, there is the unprecedented, colossal size of the cohort between, say 13 and 25, even a small percentage of which produces very large numbers indeed."[14] Second, he writes, the cohort of youth "has been further swelled by the group known as 'teeny-boppers'—preadolescents and early adolescents who have not, to my knowledge, previously played any significant role in bohemian movements."[15]

These thousands of young persons put a tremendous drain on urban social services. The youth wandered through the city streets, slept in Golden Gate Park, and ate wherever food was available. They were constantly in need of food, shelter, and money.[16] Furthermore, their ideology about sexual permissiveness and experimentation with drugs ultimately led to problems with venereal disease and drug abuse. A number of social service agencies sprang up to deal with the young people's problems—among them the Free Medical Clinic and Huckleberry House, the first shelter facility for young runaways.

The hippie community in the Haight died as quickly as it had begun. By 1968, most of the hippie residents had fled. Some left for North Beach, some went to Telegraph Avenue in nearby Berkeley, and many others began a migration to rural communes, especially in the counties of Sonoma and Mendocino, north of San Francisco. These migrants believed that the hippie morality and ideology could flourish only in the country. Their exodus contributed to the burgeoning communal movement in the United States.[17]

The Runaway Phenomenon

The hippies first focused national attention on the problems of runaway youth, although running away from home was not a new development in the late 1960s. Children who ran away from home had been a subject of occasional scholarly research in the 1930s and 1940s.[18] During these earlier decades, running away was associated with juvenile delinquency or with transiency prompted by the Depression.

Runaways began attracting considerable attention, however, during the latter half of the 1960s. During the era of the hippies and flower children, many juveniles ran away from home to specific urban destinations. In 1967, San Francisco was the first mecca. In 1968, San Francisco was replaced by Boston and then, in 1970, by Boulder.[19]

Articles began appearing in popular magazines about the young persons who ran away to these urban centers. *Newsweek* recounted the story of "Gentle Marcie: A Shattering Tale of a Runaway to Hippieland";[20] *Time* magazine also addressed the problems of teenagers who ran away to join the hippies;[21] *Look* and *Life* magazines focused on case histories of individual runaways;[22] and other popular magazines looked into the reasons runaways leave home.[23]

The runaways among this group of migrants constituted a new population of affluent suburban youth.[24] Moreover, they were running away from home in greater numbers. From 1967 to 1972, the literature cited "dramatic," "marked" and "staggering" increases in the numbers of runaway youth.[25] Estimates of the numbers of runaways were 600,000 in 1971 and 1,000,000 in 1973.[26]

In Houston, the largest mass murder in United States history further spotlighted the runaway problem.[27] Over a 3-year period, twenty-seven young persons were murdered, many of them runaway teenagers. The Houston police department, criticized for their failure to investigate the disappearance of so many young persons, responded that they were "overwhelmed by sheer numbers" of runaways.[28] The runaway problem was especially pronounced in large metropolitan areas such as Houston. In other cities, such as New York, the police department reported that there were 20,000 runaways in that city at any given time.[29] The police in Chicago dealt with 16,500 missing children in 1972, and Los Angeles reported 7,601 cases that same year.[30]

The trickle of accounts on runaways began to swell. In 1970–1971, additional magazines such as *Reader's Digest, Newsweek,* and *Today's Education* focused on the problems of runaway youth.[31] During the same period, several popular books were published on the subject of runaways.[32] One book intended for a general audience, Lillian Ambrosino's *Runaways*, described in detail the plight of runaway youth.[33] In 1972, articles also appeared in *McCalls, PTA Magazine, U.S. News and World Report, Seventeen* and *Time.*[34]

By 1972, the runaway problem was attracting such national concern that congressional hearings were held on the subject.[35] The public hearings culminated in the Runaway Youth Act, signed into law in 1974.[36] The purpose of the act was to make grants and provide technical assistance to communities and nonprofit private agencies to develop local facilities for dealing with the immediate needs of runaway youth outside the juvenile justice system.

The congressional testimony and the popular accounts highlighted the many serious problems facing young runaways. As runaways attracted public attention, their lifestyles on the metropolitan streets also came into focus. The hearings and popular accounts revealed that life on the city streets often turned out very different from what the youth had imagined. Since runaway episodes begin impulsively, the runaways seldom brought much money with them,[37] and they frequently found themselves without resources for food and shelter. They might find shelter with strangers, but such aid might well be conditioned on an exchange of services involving drug dealing or prostitution.[38] Counselors at runaway shelters testified at the congressional hearings that they witnessed many forms of deviant conduct inflicted upon runaways.[39] Rape and prostitution were only two of the practices experienced by runaway youth living on urban streets.

In the early 1970s, the congressional hearings on runaway youth first suggested the link between running away and prostitution. That link was further explored and documented in the years subsequent to the Runaway Youth Act hearings. In 1976, journalist Robin Lloyd published his popular book on boy prostitution in America.[40] The book's introduction was written by Senator Birch Bayh, chairperson of the Senate Subcommittee to Investigate Juvenile Delinquency and sponsor of the runaway youth legislation. Senator Bayh wrote of runaway youth:

> The children who run look for companionship, friendship and approval from those they meet. Many such youths are easy marks for gangs, drug pushers and pimps. Runaways often sell drugs or their bodies, and steal to support themselves.[41]

Lloyd's book recounts the tales of Jimmy on the East Coast and Scott on the West Coast, among others. The tales have a common thread—runaway boys turn to prostitution when they are in need of funds to survive. The book also suggests a link between runaway youth and pornography. Just as runaway youth often sell their bodies by engaging in prostitution, so also are they compelled to earn a livelihood by posing for pornographers. Scott on the West Coast, for example, ran away from Las Vegas to Los Angeles at age 14. There he met a man with whom he lived for several months. During the day, Scott was a student at a fashionable junior high school. In the evenings, he obediently kept appointments made for him by his adult roommate. Some of these appointments consisted of posing for photographers, occasionally with other young boys Scott recruited from his school.[42]

Lloyd's book was a best-seller. It was republished in paperback and quickly became a Book-of-the-Month Club alternate selection. It served to focus considerable attention on the problem. As child prostitution and pornography became a topic of popular interest, the media continued to highlight these forms of commercial sexual exploitation of children. *Time* magazine, the *Washington Star*, the *Chicago Tribune*, and the *Washington Post* carried stories of child pornography and prostitution.[43] Such attention by the media helped make commercial sexual exploitation of children a topic of national concern.

Child Abuse and Child Sexual Abuse

The recognition of juvenile prostitution as a social problem parallels the contemporary discovery of child abuse. Just as child prostitution has roots deep in history, so, too, does the physical abuse of children. As deMause writes:

> The history of childhood is a nightmare from which we have only recently begun to awaken. The further back in history one goes, the lower the level of child care, and the more likely children are to be killed, abandoned, beaten, terrorized, and sexually abused.[44]

Radbill notes that, throughout the centuries, children have been victims of mutilation by means of such practices as castration, footbinding, and cranial deformation.[45] Radbill and deMause point out that such maltreatment of children found legitimacy in the need to discipline, to transmit educational ideas, to please certain gods, or to expel evil spirits.

In the 1960s, physical abuse of children came to the forefront of public attention. An influential study was published in the *Journal of the American Medical Association* by a group of radiologists.[46] They revealed that significant numbers of children with unexplained injuries were actually being beaten by their parents and caretakers. The radiologists gave the condition a new medical term, "the battered child syndrome." At the same time these radiologists published their findings, several social workers also published results of their research and offered suggestions regarding how abused children, once identified, might be helped.[47] In January 1962, the Children's Bureau of the Department of Health, Education and Welfare (now the Department of Health and Human Services) convened a conference of professionals to formulate recommendations to address child abuse. The product of that conference was proposed mandatory reporting legislation,[48] and various other groups proposed additional legislation during the 1960s.[49] These legislative suggestions served as the model for statutes that were rapidly enacted into law in forty-nine states by 1966.[50]

While professionals were lobbying at the state level for legislation addressed to child abuse, efforts were also undertaken at the federal level. Prior to 1974, there had been no coordinated federal effort addressed to child abuse and neglect. In 1973, in response to increasing public concern about battered children, Senator Walter Mondale (D.-Minn.) introduced Senate bill 1191. Hearings were held on the legislation by the Subcommittee on Children and Youth in Washington, Denver, and New York, and also in Los Angeles at a joint hearing of the Special Subcommittee on Human Resources and the Subcommittee on Employment, Poverty, and Migratory Labor.[51] The proposed legislation received tremendous bipartisan support and was ultimately enacted in 1974 as the Child Abuse Prevention and Treatment Act.[52]

Although physical abuse was first labeled as a social problem in the 1960s, the recognition of sexual abuse as a social problem occurred somewhat later. The definition of child abuse first enacted into federal and state legislation characterized abuse as intentional physical injury. Early model legislation, proposed in the 1960s, defined abuse as "serious physical injury or injuries inflicted [by] other than accidental means," or alternatively as "serious injuries" as a result of abuse or neglect.[53] Several years passed before professionals began to view sexual abuse as a component of child abuse. By 1974, the recognition that sexual abuse was a growing social problem was finally enshrined in federal and state legislation. The federal Child Abuse Prevention and Treatment Act, enacted in 1974, included the new designation. The act provided that for states to qualify for federal monies for the prevention and treatment of abuse, the states must adopt a uniform definition of abuse to include "physical or mental injury, *sexual abuse,* negligent treatment, or maltreatment" (emphasis added).[54]

The expansion of the definition of child abuse in federal and state legislation to include sexual abuse appears to be due to the influence of several professionals. The definitional process of sexual abuse as a social problem was begun simultaneously by a psychologist and a social worker-lawyer.[55] In the early 1970s in Santa Clara County, California, a Juvenile Probation Department supervisor conferred with a consulting psychiatrist in reference to the growing incest caseload.[56] This psychiatrist turned to a psychologist—marriage and family counselor Henry Giarretto—and asked Giarretto to undertake a pilot effort limited to 10 hours of counseling per week for a 10-week period.

The pilot program, Therapeutic Case Management of Sexually Abused Children and their Families, later called the Child Sexual Abuse Treatment Program (CSATP), came into being in July 1971, with Giarretto as the principal therapist. From the beginning, CSATP advocated that more attention be paid to the child victim. The central notion was to deal not only with the offender but with the entire family, especially the victim.[57]

The new label of child sexual abuse, as Giarretto and his staff referred to it, was effectively marketed from its West Coast origins. The psychologist-director of CSATP published articles discussing the problem.[58] The program was the subject of considerable media attention, and staff members appeared on local and national television and radio programs. The staff disseminated information on child sexual abuse by sending information packets to interested persons and also conducted presentations and training seminars for members of professional groups. One of the secondary objectives of the psychologist-director was to have the Santa Clara program serve as a model for the formation of similar centers in other communities.[59] Thus, it is not surprising that, with such national publicity, similar programs were soon established to provide services to sexually abused children and their parents in Washington, Connecticut, Georgia, New York, and Pennsylvania.

The Santa Clara program had a direct impact on legal policymaking in the California legislature. The response of the legislature to the "new" social problem was prompt. Legislation was introduced in the 1975 session by Assemblyman John Vasconcellos of Santa Clara County.[60] This legislation ensconced the term *child sexual abuse* into law.

On the federal level as well, professionals were influential in encouraging recognition of the problem of sexual abuse. One social worker in particular, Vincent DeFrancis, played a prominent role. DeFrancis was responsible for broadening the focus of national attention on battered children to include sexually abused children. In 1954, DeFrancis, a lawyer with postgraduate training in social work, became director of the American Humane Association—a prominent child protection organization.[61] DeFrancis had long been interested in child protective services and had a special interest in child sexual abuse. In 1965, he became project director of a study on sexual abuse funded by the Children's Bureau of the Department of Health, Education and Welfare. The 3-year project explored the incidence and nature of sexual abuse in two New York counties.[62] That project resulted in several publications that brought added attention to the problem of sexual abuse. DeFrancis's associates, also social workers who disseminated the project's findings, further highlighted the problem of sexually victimized children.[63]

DeFrancis's influence reached the federal level. When Congress considered enacting national child abuse legislation, DeFrancis was called to testify before the Senate. He urged a broader definition of abuse to encompass other types of abuse in addition to child battering:

> First, let me begin by broadening our consideration. . . . We are concerned about the abused child, but children are abused in many ways, not purely the battered child, we have children who are sexually abused, we have children who are psychologically abused, we have children who are neglected in a host of ways. If we are going to address ourselves to the problems of children who need help we must address ourselves to the entire problem.[64]

DeFrancis then attempted to put the problem of battered children in its proper perspective by pointing to the lesser incidence of intentionally inflicted injuries compared to other types of abuse. He remarked:

> Putting this in perspective, based upon an estimate...there must be somewhere between 30,000 and perhaps 40,000 at the outside of truly battered children but there must be at least 100,000 children each year who are sexually abused and probably two or three times that number of children who are psychologically damaged.[65]

Largely as a result of the influence of DeFrancis, the federal definition of child abuse was broadened from physical injury alone to include sexual abuse and mental injury. With this expansion of the federal definition, sexual abuse finally became recognized as an important social problem, paving the way for the subsequent attention focused on juvenile prostitution.

The Children's Rights Movement

These developments took place against a backdrop of a movement to protect children's rights. The law on children's rights witnessed a dramatic growth from the mid-1960s to the mid-1970s, as the courts handed down a number of significant decisions concerning the rights of juveniles.

A number of important U.S Supreme Court decisions expanded the rights of juvenile offenders in the 1960s and 1970s. One such case was *In re Gault*,[66] in which the Supreme Court made a fundamental departure from juvenile delinquency law. The *Gault* case involved an adolescent who was committed to a state industrial school for 6 years after a conviction on a charge of making lewd telephone calls. The penalty for an adult convicted of the same crime would have been a fine of five to fifty dollars or imprisonment for not more than 2 months. Observing that "neither the Fourteenth Amendment nor the Bill of Rights is for adults alone,"[67] the Supreme Court held that juveniles are entitled to substantial due process protection, including the right to counsel, notification of the charge, confrontation and cross-examination, and warning of the privilege against self-incrimination. In a later decision, *In re Winship*,[68] the Supreme Court held that the standard of proof for juveniles, similar to the standard for adult defendants, is "beyond a reasonable doubt." In addition, in *Breed v. Jones*,[69] the Supreme Court held that the protection of the double jeopardy clause was applicable to juveniles.

In this same period, the Supreme Court also expanded children's rights in another area—freedom of expression. In *Tinker v. Des Moines Independent Community School District*,[70] several high school students publicized their objection to the Vietnamese war by wearing black armbands to school. After the high school principal became aware of the students' actions, he suspended them. When the case reached the Supreme Court, the Court ruled in favor of the students and their first amendment rights, holding that restrictions on expression are permissible only to preserve educational discipline. In its opinion, the Court stated: "It can hardly be argued that either students or teachers shed their constitutional rights to freedom of speech or expression at the schoolhouse gate."[71]

The significance of these decisions has been profound. These landmark cases contributed to the recognition that children are individuals who possess fundamental constitutional rights.

At the same time that the courts were expanding the rights of juveniles, a number of reformers were also advocating greater rights for children. Educator John Holt, for example, urged giving children the rights to vote, to hold a job, to choose their guardians, and to set up their own households.[72] Other psychologists and writers also urged increased rights for children.[73]

Several social events contributed to the emergence of the children's rights movement. During the 1960s, there were widespread mass protests against racism and exploitation at home and abroad. Rebellions developed in the urban ghettos, and the civil rights movement and the student, antiwar, and women's movements attacked inequality on several levels, drawing attention to minority groups. A degree of consensus arose to the effect that certain groups had suffered discrimination that needed to be remedied. The social climate focused on the plight of such minority groups as women, the aged, and the poor—and another of these minority groups was children.

National Focus and Research Funding

With the children's rights movement as the background, the social forces were set in motion to contribute to the recognition of juvenile prostitution as a social problem. After child abuse, sexual abuse, and running away came to the forefront of public attention, juvenile prostitution also became labeled a social problem. These social forces focused the national limelight on children—specifically, the manner of their victimization by adults and society.

This focus on the problem of juvenile prostitution culminated in congressional hearings on the protection of children from sexual exploitation, which addressed two forms of sexual exploitation: juvenile prostitution and pornography. The 1977 hearings and subcommittee investigations led to several conclusions, including (1) that the use of children as prostitutes or as the subjects of pornographic material is harmful to both the children and society and (2) that existing federal laws dealing with prostitution and pornography do not protect against the use of children in these activities, so that specific legislation in this area is needed.[74] In addition, the hearings also led to the conclusion that research on the phenomenon and increased services to its victims were essential.

The primary purpose of the congressional investigations, according to the opening statement of Representative John Conyers (D.-Mich.), chairperson of the Subcommittee on Crime of the Committee on the Judiciary, was to "attempt to establish the breadth and depth of the abusive practices sought to be proscribed by the bills before [Congress]."[75] An essential element of that inquiry, continued Representative Conyers, was "the quest for answers to a number of specific questions that need to be answered if we are to understand the true nature and extent of the problem and to make informed decisions on the need for additional legislation."[76]

Among the crucial questions before Congress, as framed by Representative Conyers, were the following:

Are these practices growing or is the appearance of increases due to public attention finally being focused on practices which have been long ignored?

If the practices are proliferating, what are the causal factors contributing to the increase of the sexual exploitation of youth?

Is the problem monolithic or three distinct and separable problems—sexual child abuse, prostitution and pornography?

What contribution do factors such as parental unemployment, the breakdown of families and marriages, and the physical or emotional abandonment of children have on their vulnerability to these practices, both as a victim and, later in life, as an abuser? and

How strong are financial and other material inducements and related factors in attracting children to these practices?[77]

Throughout the legislative hearings, professionals and legislators indicated the need for extensive study of child sexual exploitation to provide answers to these questions. Research was needed to better understand the dimensions of the problem and to explore the relationship of child sexual exploitation and child abuse, sexual abuse, and runaway behavior.

Following the clarion calls for further research throughout the 1977 hearings, several federal grants were awarded to study the sexual exploitation of children. An early federal research effort was funded by the Youth Development Bureau (YDB) of the Department of Health, Education and Welfare. (The YDB is the agency charged with responsibility for administering the Runaway Youth Act.) The bureau commissioned a consulting firm, Arthur Young and Company, to "examine the nature and extent of teenage prostitution, and to formulate intervention strategies whereby the Department of Health, Education and Welfare, through the Youth Development Bureau, can most effectively focus its resources on the problem."[78] The ensuing report, "Juvenile Prostitution: A Federal Strategy for Combatting Its Causes and Consequences," focused on several broad-based intervention strategies to deal with juvenile prostitution.

Over the next few years, the federal government awarded five additional grants for research on the sexual exploitation of children. The Office of Juvenile Justice and Delinquency Prevention, within the Department of Justice, awarded one grant to Tufts University's New England Medical Center Hospital to develop and analyze descriptive information on sexually exploited children from an individual, family, and community perspective. The research addressed several types of juvenile sexual exploitation, including intrafamilial and extrafamilial abuse, prostitution, pornography, and juvenile offenders. The medical center had been involved in treating emotionally and socially maladjusted children and adolescents, but only a few youths served by the program had been involved in prostitution or pornography.[79]

In addition to the Justice Department grant, several agencies within the Department of Health and Human Services awarded four grants to study various aspects of adolescent prostitution and child pornography. First, the National Center on Child Abuse and Neglect (NCCAN) awarded grants to study child pornography—one of them to the Washington School of Psychiatry to gather psychological and social profiles of the victims of child pornography.[80] Second, NCCAN also awarded funds to Boston University to develop profiles of sexually exploited children, pedophiles, and producers of child pornography and to identify the organizational and operational levels of child sex rings.[81] Third, the National Institute of Mental Health awarded funds to anthropologist Jennifer James, of the Department of Psychiatry and Behavioral Sciences at the University of Washington, to study the entrance of males and females into juvenile prostitution.[82] Finally, the Youth Development Bureau awarded a grant to Urban and Rural Systems Associates (URSA) of San Francisco, with which the author was affiliated. The focus of this research project was to develop an in-depth demographic and descriptive knowledge base of adolescent male prostitutes and to compare that knowledge to research findings on adolescent female prostitution. Research was conducted in seven cities during a two-year period. This book is the outgrowth, then, of the construction of juvenile prostitution as a social problem.

Notes

1. Lloyd deMause, "The Evolution of Childhood," in *The History of Childhood,* ed. Lloyd deMause (New York: Harper & Row, 1974), 43.
2. Ibid., 43–44. On the history of boy prostitution, see also Dennis Drew and Jonathan Drake, *Boys for Sale: A Sociological Study of Boy Prostitution* (New York: Brown, 1969), and Robin Lloyd, "The History of Boy Prostitution," in *For Money or Love: Boy Prostitution in America* (New York: Ballantine, 1976), 58–72. For bibliographic material on the sexual abuse of children in various historical epochs, see LeRoy G. Schultz, "The Sexual Abuse of Children and Minors: A Bibliography," *Child Welfare* 63(March 1979): 147–63, especially 148–49.
3. See, for example, George Bliss, "Child Sex: Square Block in New Town Tells It All," *Chicago Tribune,* 16 May 1977; Kirk Loggins and James Branscome, "Boys Farm Scandal: People in Rural Tennessee County 'Just Didn't Know' What Went On," *Washington Post,* 5 June 1977; Ted Morgan, "Little Ladies of the Night," *New York Times Magazine,* 16 Nov. 1975, 34–38+; Selwyn Raab, "Veronica's Short Sad Life— Prostitution at 11, Death at 12," *New York Times,* 3 Oct. 1977, p. 1, col. 3; Michael Sneed, "'Chicken' Makes $500 a Week, But at 17 He's Getting Too Old," *Chicago Tribune,* 16 May 1977; "Requiem for Tina Sanchez," WNBC-TV–produced documentary, 1976; "Youth for Sale on the Streets, *Time,* 8 Nov. 1977, p. 23, col. 1.
4. 18 U.S.C. §§ 2251, 2253, 2254 (1978). See also *Sexual Exploitation of Children: Hearings on H. 4571 Before the Subcommittee on Crime of the House Committee on the Judiciary,* 95th Cong., 1st sess., 1977 [hereafter cited as *Hearings on H. 4571*]; *Hearings on S. 1585 Before the Subcommittee to Investigate Juvenile Delinquency of the Senate Committee on the Judiciary,* 95th Cong., 2d sess., 1978.
5. For further discussion of the federal and state legislation pertaining to juvenile prostitution, see chapter 6. The role of legislation in the construction of social problems generally has been previously explored. See, for example, Howard Becker, *Outsiders: Studies in the Sociology of Deviance* (New York: Free Press, 1963): 121–63; John F. Galliher and Allynn Walker, "The Puzzle of the Social Origins of the Marijuana Tax Act of 1937," *Social Problems* 24(February 1977): 367–76; Stephen J. Pfohl, "The 'Discovery' of Child Abuse," *Social Problems* 24(February 1977): 310–23.
6. On the social construction approach to social problems, see Malcolm Spector and John I. Kitsuse, *Constructing Social Problems* (Menlo Park, Calif.: Cummings, 1977).
7. Sherri Cavan, *Hippies of the Haight* (St. Louis: New Critics Press, 1972), 42–45.
8. Keith Melville, *Communes in the Counter Culture: Origins, Theories, Styles of Life* (New York: Morrow, 1972). On the beatniks, see also Ned Polsky, "The Village

Beat Scene: Summer 1960," in *Hustlers, Beats and Others* (New York: Doubleday Anchor, 1969), 144–82.

9. Crystal and Gold report that a large number of hippies were Jewish middle-class teenagers. David Crystal and Irwin H. Gold, "A Social Work Mission to Hippieland," *Children*, 16, no. 1(1969): 28–32.

10. Cited in Melville, *Communes in the Counter Culture*, 66.

11. Melville (ibid.) writes that there were daily headlines about hippies in the *San Francisco Chronicle*. Numerous sociologists also studied the hippie movement. See, for example, Cavan, *Hippies of the Haight*; Bennett Berger, "Hippie Morality: More Old than New," in *The Sexual Scene*, ed. John H. Gagnon and William Simon (New Brunswick, N.J.: Transaction Books, 1973); Sherri Cavan, "The Hippie Ethic and the Spirit of Drug Use," and Fred Davis, "Focus on the Flower Children: Why All of Us May Be Hippies Someday," in *Observations of Deviance*, ed. Jack D. Douglas (New York: Random House, 1970); Fred Davis with Laura Munoz, "Heads and Freaks: Patterns and Meanings of Drug Use Among Hippies," *Journal of Health and Social Behavior* 9(June 1968): 156–63.

12. Berger, "Hippie Morality."

13. Ibid., 66.

14. Ibid.

15. Ibid., 71.

16. Cavan, *Hippies of the Haight,* 173.

17. By 1970, more than 2,000 communal groups were established across the country. Robert Houriet, *Getting Back Together* (New York: Avon Books, 1971), 8 (citing a *New York Times* survey of communes in 34 states). For more details on this social movement, see Rosabeth Moss Kanter, *Communes: Creating and Managing the Collective Life* (New York: Harper & Row, 1973).

18. See, for example, Clairette P. Armstrong, "A Psychoneurotic Reaction of Delinquent Boys and Girls," *Journal of Abnormal and Social Psychology* 32(October 1937): 329–42; Theodore Leventhal, "Inner Control Deficiencies in Runaway Children," *Archives of General Psychiatry* 11(1941): 755–82; Franklyn Newcomb, "Transient Boys," *The Family* (now *Social Casework*) 14(1933): 57–59; Morris D. Riemer, "Runaway Children," *American Journal of Orthopsychiatry* 10(July 1940): 522–28; Hugo Staub, "A Runaway from Home," *Psychoanalytic Quarterly* 12(1943): 1–22.

19. David E. Suddick, "Runaways: A Review of the Literature," *Juvenile Justice* 24(August 1973): 47–54. For further discussion of problems posed by the runaway population in Boston, see Jeffrey D. Blum and Judith E. Smith, *Nothing Left to Lose: Studies of Street People* (Boston: Beacon Press, 1972).

20. "Gentle Marcie: A Shattering Tale of a Runaway to Hippieland," *Newsweek*, 30 Oct. 1967, 88.

21. "Runaways—Teenagers Who Run Away to the Hippies," *Time*, 15 Sept. 1967, 46.

22. "Runaway Kid," *Life*, 3 Nov. 1967, 18; J. Whitehead, "Greenwich Village Case Histories," *Look*, 25 July 1967, 26.

23. S. Margetts and M.R. Feinburg, "Why do Executives' Children Run Away?" *Dun's Review*, January 1968, 40; W. Peters, "Riddle of Teenage Runaways," *Good Housekeeping*, June 1968, 88.

24. Crystal and Gold, "A Social Work Mission"; Runaways: A Million Bad Trips: How Youth Agencies Try to Help," *Newsweek*, 26 Oct. 1970, 67–68. For a study of affluent suburban runaways, see John Goldmeier and Robert D. Dean, "The Runaway: Person, Problem, or Situation?" *Crime and Delinquency* 19(October 1973): 539–44; Jerry J. Tobias and Jay Reynolds, "The Affluent Suburban Runaway," *Police Journal* 43, no. 10 (1970): 335–39.

25. "Runaways: A Non-Judicial Approach," *New York University Law Review* 49(1974): 110–30, 110; Suddick, "Runaways: Review," 47; Deborah Klein Walker, *Runaway Youth: Annotated Bibliography and Literature Overview*, Technical Analysis Paper No. 1 (Washington D.C.: Department of Health, Education and Welfare, May 1975), 1. One study was undertaken in a suburban county after the rate of juvenile runaways almost tripled over a five-year period. Goldmeier and Dean, "Runaway: Person, Problem, Situation," 539.

26. *U.S. News and World Report*, 3 Sept. 1973, 34.

27. *New York Times*, 14 Aug. 1973, p. 1, cols. 1–2.

28. *New York Times*, 17 Aug. 1973, p. 18, col. 3.

29. *New York Times*, 16 Aug. 1973, p. 17, cols. 1–2.

30. *Time*, 27 Aug. 1973, 57.

31. Lillian Ambrosino, "Runaways," *Today's Education* 60(December 1971): 26–28; "Runaways: A Million Bad Trips: How Youth Agencies Try to Help," *Newsweek*, 26 Oct. 1970, 67–68; B. Surface, "Case of the Runaway Teenager," *Reader's Digest*, May 1970, 143–46.

32. Lillian Ambrosino, *Runaways* (Boston: Beacon Press, 1971); Julia Sorel, *Dawn: Portrait of a Teenage Runaway* (New York: Ballantine, 1971); Bibi Wein, *The Runaway Generation* (New York: McKay, 1970).

33. Ambrosino, *Runaways*.

34. P. Brooks, "They Can Go Home Again," *McCalls*, June 1972, 57; R. Larsen, "Runaways," *PTA Magazine*, November 1972, 26–32; C. Remsberg and B. Remsberg, "How Teen Runaways Get Help: Huckleberry House, S.F.," *Seventeen*, June 1972, 122–23+; "Runaway Children," *U.S. News and World Report*, 24 Apr. 1972, 38–42; "White Slavery 1972: Teenage Prostitutes in Greenwich Village," *Time*, 5 June 1972, 24. By 1975, so much had been written on runaways that the Department of Health, Education and Welfare commissioned a bibliography of these materials. See Walker, *Runaway Youth*.

35. *Hearings on Runaway Youth Before the Subcommittee on Equal Opportunities of the House Committee on Education and Labor*, 93rd Cong., 2d sess., 1971 [hereafter cited as *House Runaway Hearings*]; *Hearings on Runaway Youth Before the Subcommittee to Investigate Juvenile Delinquency of the Senate Committee on the Judiciary*, 92nd Cong., 1st sess., 1972 [hereafter cited as *Senate Runaway Hearings*].

36. *Juvenile Justice and Delinquency Prevention Act of 1974*, Public Law No. 93-415, 8 Stat. 1109-43 (1974) (codified in scattered sections of 18 U.S.C. and 42 U.S.C.). The act consists of two separate measures, the *Juvenile Justice and Delinquency Prevention Act of 1972*, 42 U.S.C. § 5601 (Supp. 1975) and the *Runaway and Homeless Youth Act*, 42 U.S.C. §§ 5701-5702, 5711-5713, 5715-5716, 5731-5732, 5751 (Supp. 1978).

37. Robert Shellow, Juliana Schamp, Elliot Liebow, and Elizabeth Unger, "Suburban Runaways of the 1960's," in *Senate Runaway Hearings*, 218.

38. Ambrosino, *Runaways*, 13–14.

39. See *Senate Runaway Hearings,* 14 (testimony of William Treanor, Director, Special Approaches in Juvenile Assistance, Inc.), and 82–83 (testimony of Rev. Fred P. Eckhardt, Director, Operation Eye-Opener).

40. Lloyd, *For Money or Love.*

41. Ibid., x.

42. Ibid., 17–20.

43. See sources cited note 3.

44. deMause, *History of Childhood,* 1.

45. Samuel X. Radbill, "A History of Child Abuse and Infanticide," in *The Battered Child,* ed. Ray E. Helfer and C. Henry Kempe (Chicago: University of Chicago Press, 1968). On the history of physical abuse of children, see also R.H. Helmholz, "Infanticide in the Province of Canterbury during the Fifteenth Century," *History of Childhood Quarterly* 2(1975): 379–90.

46. C. Henry Kempe, Frederic N. Silverman, Brandt F. Steele, William Droegemueller and Henry K. Silver, "The Battered Child Syndrome," *Journal of the American Medical Association* 181(1962): 17–24.

47. See, for example, Elizabeth Elmer, "Abused Young Children Seen in Hospitals," *Social Work* 5(1960): 98–102; Helen F. Boardman, "A Project to Rescue Children from Inflicted Injuries," *Social Work* 7(1962): 43–51.

48. U.S. Department of Health, Education and Welfare, Children's Bureau, "The Abused Child—Principles and Suggested Language for Legislation on Reporting of the Physically Abused Child, 1963.

49. The Humane Association, Children's Division, "Guidelines for Legislation to Protect the Battered Child," Publication 22, 1963; American Medical Association, "Physical Abuse of Children—Suggested Legislation" (Mimeographed), 1956; Council of State Governments, "Suggested State Legislation," 1965; New York County Medical Society, "Suggested Penal Code," *New York State Journal of Medicine* 64 (1964): 215, 224; Committee on Infant and Preschool Child, American Academy of Pediatrics, "Maltreatment of Children—The Physically Abused Child," *Pediatrics* 37(1966): 377–82, cited in Alan Sussman and Stephan J. Cohen, *Reporting Child Abuse and Neglect: Guidelines for Legislation* (Cambridge, Mass.: Ballinger, 1975), 9, n.15, 16, 17, 18, 19.

50. Monrad Paulsen, "The Legal Framework for Child Protection," *Columbia Law Review* 66(1966): 711.

51. See *Senate Report No. 167,* 95th Cong., 1st sess., 1977, 27.

52. 42 U.S.C. §§ 5101–5106 (1974).

53. The Children's Bureau model act defined abuse as "serious physical injury or injuries inflicted [by] other than accidental means"; the American Medical Association and the Council of State Governments speak of "serious injuries" as a result of abuse or neglect. Cited in Sussman and Cohen, *Reporting Child Abuse,* 63.

54. 42 U.S.C. § 5102 (1978), originally enacted in 1974.

55. For further discussion on the labeling of sexual abuse as a social problem, see D. Kelly Weisberg, "The 'Discovery' of Sexual Abuse: Experts' Role in Legal Policy Formulation," *U.C. Davis Law Review* 18(forthcoming, 1984).

56. As cited in Henry Giarretto, "Humanistic Treatment of Father-Daughter Incest," in *Child Abuse and Neglect: The Family in the Community,* ed. Ray E. Helfer and C. Henry Kempe (Cambridge, Mass.: Ballinger, 1976), 143, 149.

57. See "Child Sexual Abuse Treatment Program" (Mimeographed), 2 Sept. 1975, 3.

58. See, for example, Giarretto, "Humanistic Treatment"; Henry Giarretto, "Treatment of Father-Daughter Incest: A Psycho-Social Approach," *Children Today* 5(1976): 2; Henry Giarretto, Anna Giarretto, and Suzanne M. Sgroi, "Coordinated Community Treatment of Incest," in *Sexual Assault of Children and Adolescents,* ed. Ann W. Burgess, A. Nicholas Groth, Lynda L. Holmstrom, and Suzanne Sgroi (Lexington, Mass: Lexington Books, 1978), 231–40.

59. Giarretto, "Humanistic Treatment," 150.

60. The proposed legislation, Assembly Bill 2288, was enacted into law that same year. Cal. Welf. & Inst. § 18275 et seq. (West 1975).

61. *Who's Who in the West,* 14th ed., 1974–75, 162–63. The American Humane Association, originally organized to protect animals, established a Children's Division in 1887 to coordinate the activities of the various voluntary protective service associations that developed in the last half of the nineteenth century. Alfred Kadushin, *Child Welfare Services* (New York: Macmillan, 1967), 206.

62. See Vincent DeFrancis, *Protecting the Child Victim of Sex Crimes Committed by Adults* (Denver: American Humane Association, 1969), iv.

63. See DeFrancis, *Protecting;* Vincent DeFrancis, "Protecting the Child Victim of Sex Crimes Committed by Adults," *Federal Probation* 35(1971): 15. See also Yvonne Tormes, *Child Victims of Incest* (Denver: American Humane Association, 1967); Wilson D. McKerrow, *Protecting the Sexually Abused Child,* Second National Symposium of Child Abuse, 1973.

64. *Child Abuse Prevention and Treatment Act; Hearings on S. 1191 Before the Subcommittee on Children and Youth of the Committee on Labor and Public Welfare,* 93rd Cong., 1st sess., 1973 (testimony of Vincent DeFrancis), 93.

65. Ibid.

66. 387 U.S. 1 (1967).

67. 387 U.S. at 13.

68. 397 U.S. 358 (1970).

69. 421 U.S. 519 (1975).

70. 393 U.S. 503 (1969).

71. 393 U.S. at 504.

72. John Holt, *Escape from Childhood* (New York: Dutton, 1974).

73. See, for example, Virginia Coigney, *Children Are People Too: How We Fail Our Children and How We Can Love Them* (New York: Morrow, 1975); Richard Farson, *Birthrights* (New York: Macmillan, 1974).

74. "Sexual Exploitation of Children—A Problem of Unknown Magnitude," Report to the Chairman, Subcommittee on Select Education, House Committee on Education and Labor, General Accounting Office (GAO), 20 Apr. 1982, 2.

75. *Hearings on H. 4571,* 2.

76. Ibid.

77. Ibid.

78. Arthur Young and Company, "Juvenile Prostitution: A Federal Strategy for Combatting Its Causes and Consequences," Report submitted to the Youth Development Bureau, Office of Human Development Services, Department of Health, Education and Welfare, June 1978.

79. "Sexual Exploitation of Children" (GAO report), 22.

80. Ibid.

81. Ibid.

82. Ibid.; see also Jennifer James, *Entrance into Juvenile Prostitution* (Washington, D.C.: National Institute of Mental Health, 1980); Jennifer James, *Entrance into Juvenile Male Prostitution* (Washington, D.C.: National Institute of Mental Health, 1982).

2
Portraits of Adolescent Male Prostitutes: An Ethnography of Adolescent Male Prostitution

Adolescent male prostitution appears to be shaped by various subcultures. Two distinct subcultures that characterize male prostitution in many major metropolitan areas—and that often are delimited by geographic area—are (1) the peer-delinquent subculture and (2) the gay subculture.

For youth in the first subculture, prostitution is an integral aspect of delinquent street life. These adolescents engage indiscriminately in prostitution, drug dealing, panhandling, and petty criminal activity.[1] They sell their sexual favors habitually as a way of making money, viewing prostitution as just one aspect of "hustling"—as the term is used to mean procuring more than one gives.[2]

Youth in the gay subculture engage in prostitution for different reasons. Prostitution is one outlet for their sexuality. They find in the gay male subculture a means of identification, and prostitution satisfies their needs for social interaction with gay persons and for sexual partners. Simultaneously, it provides a way of making money, since the purchase and sale of sexual activity is a product of the sexual mores of that community.

These two subcultures and their prostitute members may be found within specific geographic parameters in many major urban areas. In some cities, the two subcultures exist side by side; youth from both subcultures engage in prostitution in the same locale. In other cities, the two subcultures are demarcated more clearly by geographic locale. In these cities, youth in the peer-delinquent subculture engage in prostitution in the cities' "sex-trade zones," whereas, for youth in the gay subculture, prostitution is carried out predominantly in gay neighborhoods.

This chapter will explore these two subcultures within the context of one major metropolitan area—San Francisco—where the two subcultures are demarcated by separate geographic areas. In San Francisco, the sex-trade zone is commonly referred to as the Tenderloin.[3] It is located in a lower-class neighborhood in the downtown Market Street region near Hallidie Plaza. The gay neighborhood in which male prostitution occurs is located on several commercial and residential blocks of Polk Street.[4] The two subcultures that exist in these locales differ on several dimensions, including socioeconomic composition, prostitution lifestyles, the sexual orientation of the members, and the members' involvement with the juvenile justice system, among others.

Juvenile male prostitution in San Francisco may also be found, though to a lesser extent, in the Union Square region of the city's downtown luxury hotels, which is situated geographically on the periphery of the Tenderloin. The Union Square area has some commercial sexual establishments that cater to the upper class, but it is similar to the Polk Street gay neighborhood in that it attracts many gay men, both customers and prostitutes. Prostitutes here share characteristics with other members of the gay subculture.

At all these sites, and especially on evenings and week-ends, boys stand and lean and wait. They wait until a prospective customer approaches and engages a youth in conversation. Conversational approaches are varied, including requests for directions, for a match, or for the time. There is then a meeting of the eyes and a repeated and persistent "looking over" of each other, and an offer of a cup of coffee or a meal may follow. Soon, however, arrangements are made regarding time and place, the type of sexual services, and the fee. Such encounters most often occur in certain city streets in definite locales, but may occur anywhere—in movie theaters, while hitchhiking, or at the beach.

The Tenderloin: Prostitution in the Lower-Class Sex-Trade Zone

Just a 10-minute walk south and west from San Francisco's exclusive theater district is the deteriorating region commonly known as the Tenderloin. The Tenderloin, consisting of several blocks north of Market Street from the Powell Street cable car turntable to the Civic Center, is downtown San Francisco's lower-class sex-trade zone, where filmstrip arcades, pornographic shows and bookstores, strip joints, and massage parlors abound.[5] Its population primarily includes the aged on fixed incomes and the urban poor—especially blacks, Hispanics and recent immigrants who are Vietnamese and Cambodian. Along Market Street from Mason to Taylor Streets is the "Meat Rack." Here young male prostitutes congregate, making themselves available to customers.

Many of the people passing through Hallidie Plaza on the edge of the Tenderloin are businesslike in appearance and gait; suits and briefcases characterize the dress of many of the men and women hurrying along the streets. Many of these people are on their way to and from their jobs in the nearby financial district or in the city, state, and federal office buildings near the city's Civic Center. Some of the people passing quickly through the area are on their way to or from the nearby underground subway or the city bus stops on heavily traveled Market Street.

These passersby form a sharp contrast to other persons who occupy the Plaza. On any given day, a large number of "sitters" and "leaners" may be found in and near the Plaza. Some of those who sit on steps and stand on street corners are elderly; a good proportion are black; most of them are male. Many of them live in the cheap residential hotels that line the nearby streets.

The Tenderloin's population also includes numerous male homosexuals. Some come to the Tenderloin as tourists from other urban areas; others come from their homes in the suburbs. Some reside in the area's cheap hotels, and some live in the relatively inexpensive old apartment buildings found in the upper border of the area.

The adolescent male prostitutes who hang out in the Tenderloin are sometimes difficult to identify as prostitutes. They are often the slender boys standing in front of bus stations or the teenagers in tight jeans standing beneath movie marquees. These are the street hustlers who hang out in the late afternoon and evening hours in the hope of "turning a trick" or "making a score." The men who employ these hustlers are called "johns"; they are sometimes also referred to as "chickenhawks," because they are attracted to young boys ("chickens").

San Francisco reputedly has a long and colorful history associated with boy prostitution. The earliest large-scale boy prostitution in the United States, according to Drew and Drake, was in San Francisco during the Gold Rush.[6] Boy brothels, termed "peghouses," operated from 1840 through 1910.[7] From the mid-1800s, when San Francisco developed as a major port of entry and disembarkation for those in search of gold, downtown San Francisco served as a magnet for homosexuals. The downtown cheap hotels and apartment buildings and the bars, brothels, and other entertainment establishments provided shelter and recreation for the restless. Also, San Francisco's longstanding tolerance for diversity and deviant lifestyles, dating from the Gold Rush, contributed to the city's attraction for homosexuals.

Later, during World War II, San Francisco became a center for soldiers serving in the Pacific. By most accounts, it was then that a substantial number of local men began to identify as homosexuals. They developed distinctive methods of signaling, meeting, and interacting with each other; they developed language and institutions to accommodate these ways; and they began to speak of themselves and their mores as "gay." The homosexual subculture flourished side by side with a heterosexual sex-trade zone. With the subsequent emergence of San Francisco's North Beach as the major heterosexual sex-trade zone, the Tenderloin increasingly attracted a larger homosexual clientele.

Juvenile prostitution first attracted considerable public attention in San Francisco in the 1960s, during the hippie era. In the mid-1960s, the Tenderloin received the overflow from the Haight. Some of the hippies, those with homosexual feelings, went to the Tenderloin in search of the gay life. They were drawn by the inexpensive residential hotels and apartments and the excitement of downtown. To support their lifestyles and provide money for rent, food, clothes, movies, marijuana, and LSD, they performed odd jobs and panhandled. In addition, some discovered they could earn money by "turning tricks."

Some of these youth were heterosexual males who found that they could earn easy money by permitting homosexual customers to fellate them. Whenever these young men needed money, they would go to the Old Dog, a gay bar on Market Street. If they were over 21, they would have a beer or two. If they were younger and did not have false identification, they would hang out in front and wait for older men to ask if they wanted to "come home" with them. An older man knew from a youth's appearance, demeanor, and age, the locale, and the youth's response to the proposition, that such sexual activity would require a fee. The youth would agree shyly and accompany the man. After the sexual interaction, a more experienced youth would ask the homosexual for ten dollars; a shy amateur would ask for whatever he felt it was worth. The customer usually paid the fee and sometimes might supply a few more dollars, as well as articles of old clothing or food. Usually without spending the night, the youth would indicate that he wanted to leave. Sometimes, the customer returned the youth by car to the Tenderloin. There, he would congregate with friends, smoke marijuana, or drink wine until the early hours of the morning.

These young persons were primarily hippies, not full-time prostitutes. Many of them were heterosexual—when they closed their eyes and let the homosexual "do his thing," they pretended he was a girl. Most of these youth would be termed situational hustlers, who prostituted only on occasion, in certain situations, and who viewed their activity as temporary. Similar to most hippies of the 1960s, many of them moved on to other places. Some, however, remained in San Francisco's Tenderloin.

Those who remained tended to be young men with homosexual feelings who enjoyed prostitution as a dimension of the sexual promiscuity of the gay subculture. For many youth, prostitution became a vehicle for the enjoyment of their sexuality, for sociability with other gay men, and for a declaration of their own homosexuality. In addition to the easy money, the youth enjoyed "cruising" and being "cruised" and the adventure of interacting sexually with a stranger. They enjoyed receiving remuneration for something they would have done for nothing. Many of these gay-identified young men who engaged in prostitution were also situational prostitutes. They turned tricks only when they wanted or when circumstances required; they, too, viewed prostitution as a temporary interlude.

Many of these youth discovered that prostitution could be depressing employment if they were tired, wanted more time to themselves, or desired a more meaningful relationship. For this reason, the more attractive gay prostitutes found lovers or older men ("sugar daddies") who would support them. Others found employment in gay bars, bathhouses, restaurants, and pornographic enterprises, or they moved into jobs where their homosexuality would be accepted—such as hairdressing or design.

Departure from the Tenderloin was a symbol of upward mobility. Those left behind were the misfits—those who were too effeminate or who liked to cross-dress ("drag queens"), those who felt too conflicted about their homosexuality, and those who were unattractive, unintelligent, or unskilled. By and large, they viewed prostitution as an activity to engage in regularly; hence, they may be termed habitual hustlers. To the extent that a problem population came to be recognized among the Tenderloin youth, it consisted of these young persons.

In 1965, the Tenderloin's Glide Memorial Church, long known for its interest in social problems, became interested in adolescent prostitution. A group of people who were concerned about the hippies inundating the downtown area wrote a report identifying juvenile prostitution as a major problem. That report estimated that "200 or more young men are hustling in the Tenderloin areas as a means of earning money and obtaining some sort of adult affection, some as young as 12 and 13, the median age around 17."[8] The report's authors noted that "a young physically attractive hustler may earn over \$60.00 per week" but that "most of the hustlers are always in desperate need of money."[9] The root of the hustler's problem, according to the report, was that he

> ...is generally without satisfying emotional relationships and seldom experiences self-fulfillment in any of his endeavors. Moreover, as the hustler gets older (past his early twenties) it becomes increasingly difficult for him to make money by selling his body. His well established pattern of hustling, his lack of a trade, of work experience, of education and his psychological problems make it very difficult for him to obtain and then sustain himself in satisfying employment. These difficulties are so overwhelming that their only recourse seems to be to criminal activity, such as pimping, pill pushing, shoplifting, robbing and rolling.[10]

The authors of this report were primarily concerned with the young people who began engaging in prostitution when certain circumstances dictated (situational hustlers) but who were soon drawn into lower-class Tenderloin life and found it difficult to escape. They then moved rapidly from situational to habitual prostitution. The authors recommended that a committee of citizens be appointed to facilitate the development of social services directed at these needy youth. At the beginning of 1967, the Tenderloin Committee set up Hospitality House to provide services to the youth on the street.

In the past decade, prostitution and the prostitute population in the Tenderloin gradually changed. Although the Tenderloin continues to attract "long hairs," they tend to be more aggressive, less attractive, and more likely to be on drugs than the former hippie prostitutes. Most of them are habitual prostitutes and older youth in their twenties. These young men present themselves as heterosexual in appearance, language, and behavior—not only because they are comfortable this way, but also because customers prefer it. Some customers find a "macho" man attractive, and some alleviate conflicts about their own masculinity by having sex with "real" men. Like many of their customers, many of these youth wrestle with doubts about their sexual identities. Those who are more comfortable with their homosexuality prefer to engage in prostitution in a locale where, reportedly, fees are higher and the customers are less likely to be dangerous. Increasingly, the adolescent homosexual and situational prostitutes in San Francisco have relocated to the gay neighborhood of Polk Street.

Bobby

Bobby is a Tenderloin habitual prostitute. For the most part, he works in the Tenderloin, although he occasionally works on Polk Street. Bobby was born in a small town in Arizona. He was known as a "bad boy" from his earliest years. With each punishment administered by his father, his behavior worsened; and, as Bobby's behavior worsened, the punishments became more severe. Long periods of confinement in a juvenile home followed foster home placements. He also spent time in reform school and jail.

Perhaps as a result of his chaotic early life, Bobby found it difficult to stay in any locale for any length of time. In his mid-teens, he met a gay man from Los Angeles who offered to take Bobby with him to Alaska. Before the trip, however, Bobby got angry one day and walked out. He hitchhiked to San Francisco and survived by living with a lesbian and engaging in prostitution in the Tenderloin. One day, Bobby was picked up by the police and taken to the police station for not having identification. He was identified through police records on an outstanding warrant for his participation in a car robbery, and was returned to Arizona and to jail.

Bobby completed his sentence and his term of probation, and, on his eighteenth birthday, he took a bus to Los Angeles. He had dreams of making it big in "tinseltown." His fantasy was to become successful by writing his life story. To survive, he planned to prostitute on Santa Monica Boulevard—the way he had survived each time he had run away from home.

The day he arrived in Los Angeles, however, his fate was changed by an encounter with a gay man named Constantine. Constantine was in L.A. on a trip from San Francisco. Bobby eagerly accepted Constantine's suggestion that the two spend the night together. Only when the sex was over did Bobby mention money. He brought up the subject not by insisting that Constantine pay for the sex, but rather by complaining that he was broke. Constantine took the hint and gave Bobby twenty dollars.

The next morning, Bobby wanted to spend another day and another night at Constantine's place. After his second night with Constantine, Bobby no longer said anything about expecting payment. When Constantine suggested that Bobby return with him to San Francisco, Bobby appeared genuinely excited by the invitation; he said he was pleased because he would have the chance to see his many good friends on Polk Street. When their relationship had persisted for about a month, Bobby told Constantine that he was the first person who had been nice to him in a year and a half.

Bobby seemed to enjoy his time at Constantine's house in San Francisco. He brought his friends to enjoy the pleasant surroundings, and he called Constantine whenever he was in a jam. He was often angry and distant, however, when Constantine talked intimately or was affectionate with him in front of Bobby's friends, especially when Bobby was hanging out with some of his friends on Polk Street. Bobby did not want any of his friends to think that he and Constantine were lovers. More and more, privately as well as publicly, Bobby insisted that he was straight. He told everyone that he had sex with men only for financial reasons.

A short time after returning with Constantine to San Francisco, Bobby met Connie and became interested in her. As his relationship with Connie developed, his relationship with Constantine started to deteriorate. Finally, Bobby rented a room in a Tenderloin hotel and moved there, but continued to see Constantine from time to time. During this period, Bobby, with Connie and two other boys, involved the unwitting Constantine in the theft of some marijuana plants. Later, the two boys who were accomplices, in turn, ripped off Bobby and Connie. When Bobby became aware that he had not made any money dealing in marijuana, he returned once again to street prostitution.

All of life was a hustle to Bobby—panhandling, drugs, prostitution, and larceny were part of his lifestyle. Each time he was approached by the interviewer, he asked for a buck, telling the interviewer that he should consider it part of his down payment for talking to him.

Bobby's relationship with Constantine continued on-again, off-again for some months. The end of the relationship was marked by Bobby's going to Constantine's home one day when Constantine was out. Bobby stole Constantine's marijuana, two suitcases, and some clothes, including an expensive leather jacket. Constantine believed that the relationship ultimately came to this ending because Bobby was so conflicted about his sexual identity. "He needed to see me as a bad guy," Constantine said, "because he needed to find an explanation for our homosexual intimacy. He needed to put me in the role of the dirty old man whose only interest in him was sex . . . that I was using him. That was a good reason for him to be angry at me and to punish me by ripping me off."

Lisa/John

John is a special type of Tenderloin habitual prostitute—he engages in prostitution dressed as a woman and calls himself Lisa. As a child, John was mistreated by his working–class father and mother. His father abandoned the family when John was young, and John's mother continued to abuse him during his adolescence. John remembers that he first "had sex" at the age of 6, with his older brother. At 14, John started hustling in New Orleans, where, in the French Quarter, he learned about "drag" prostitution. After he discovered that he attracted more attention when he was dressed as a girl, John began to prostitute as Lisa. By the time he was 17 years old, John felt more comfortable facing the world as Lisa than as John.

John came to San Francisco when he was 17. Much of his time was spent with friends in the Tenderloin. Every afternoon, John and his friends would begin their day by meeting at a drag bar on Geary Street, about six blocks west of the Prince Edward Hotel.[11] Some of the patrons at the bar were attracted to transvestites, some came because they had transvestite friends, and others were there merely because they enjoyed offbeat scenes.

Often, John and his friends managed to "score" by 10 or 11 P.M. If they were unlucky on a particular night, however, they would walk toward Union Square until they reached another well-known drag bar. The Union Square bar featured romantic music and dim lighting, in contrast to the Tenderloin bar's loud rock music. Patrons at the Union Square bar included potential customers as well as gay men who were not interested in paying for sexual activity. Straight women were discouraged from entering the bar, however, because the men in drag viewed them as competition.

If John and his friends failed to find a customer in the city's two main drag bars by closing time, they would cruise the streets of the Upper Tenderloin looking for customers. Occasionally, they crossed paths with the female street-walkers who also were looking for customers.

Partly because they are reluctant to belie their role playing, the drag hookers rarely knew whether the men who picked them up realized they were hiring transvestites. Most of the customers presented themselves as heterosexual. One reason that the work of drag hookers is especially draining is that they have to offer intimacy and affection while avoiding the process of self-revelation, which includes maintaining their female disguises at all times. Interactions with customers are fraught with anxiety, because an unsuccessful management of the process may result in a negative, even violent, reaction from rudely awakened customers.

John, like other drag hookers, found that he was able to please most customers without running the risk of self-disclosure by limiting his sexual activities to performing fellatio. The men with whom he engaged in more extensive sexual involvement, including those he serviced at their homes, tended to be customers who made known their attraction to transvestites.

John characterizes his interactions with each potential customer and each actual customer as "hard work." He maintains that his work requires a great deal of fortification with drugs and alcohol. His profession is not so glamorous or entertaining as he, and many drag hookers, had imagined. One common aspiration of drag hookers is to be professional drag entertainers, enabling them to be creative and self-expressive without the constant worry of self-disclosure. In reality, however, such jobs are few and far between. The only employment left for those who prefer to appear to the world in drag is prostitution.

Discouraged because business was slow, John enrolled in a vocational program established by a San Francisco runaway center. Upon completing the program, John found a job cleaning a vacant apartment building in the Tenderloin. John usually appeared at work in drag, but, because the building was vacant, his employer did not object. Nonetheless, John abruptly quit his first regular job. His reason was not that the work was too demanding or the pay too low; rather, it was that "I just couldn't stand climbing all those stairs in my high heels." Eventually, John decided to return to New Orleans. He later reported to a friend in San Francisco that the work in New Orleans was much better. The friend suspected that "work" meant prostitution.

Jago

At the age of 17, Jago was another Tenderloin hustler who had dreams of social mobility. Jago had hitchhiked from New Jersey to Hollywood. After being arrested by an undercover police officer for prostitution on Santa Monica Boulevard, he decided to move to San Francisco. He took a bus and, after arriving at the bus station, hurried to the gay scene at the Liberty Baths. His first prostitution experience was on Polk Street, because of its proximity to the gay bathhouses.

Jago was not comfortable on Polk Street, however; he said he did not identify with the crowd. He felt most comfortable with other delinquent types. In Jago's eyes, it was safer for a prostitute to operate in the Tenderloin than on Polk Street. Also, he preferred the Tenderloin because the youth on Polk Street were very visible and flirtatious in their prostitution, almost daring the police to arrest them. Jago was not comfortable flaunting his sexuality so openly. He maintained, that was fine for someone whose only goal was to engage in prostitution, perhaps, but not for someone who really wanted to move up in the world—someone like Jago. Jago was interested in doing something significant; he wanted "to make money." He was into "many, many businesses": he was advertising his TV for sale and negotiating to buy marijuana for resale, and he was also talking about giving up street hustling to become a call boy, advertising in the gay newspapers and developing a regular clientele.

Jago preferred hustling in the Tenderloin because it was "so easy to blend in." He admitted that there were many more "speed freaks" in the Tenderloin. In his judgment, the profits were lower in the Tenderloin than on Polk Street because speed freaks let people fellate them for as little as ten or fifteen dollars, which kept the price low. The price was higher on Polk Street—thirty, forty, or fifty dollars—because the customers and prostitutes were more selective. Nonetheless, Jago still preferred to hustle in the Tenderloin.

When he first came to the Tenderloin to hustle, Jago engaged in prostitution at the back of the movie arcade. He was anxious about the police arresting him. At present, he is aware of the pace of his life—its intensity and its costs. He refers to himself as a "businessman," as someone who trades his sex appeal, his body, and drugs for a profit. When he moved into a Tenderloin hotel, Jago was offered a small room. Seeing that a few larger rooms were being readied for occupancy, he offered to paint the bathroom if he could have one. Later, he traded some psychedelic mushrooms for some expensive shaving lotion. He used fine shampoos on his hair, and he thought about getting another phone. Jago also talked about forming an organization of hustlers called "Enterprise"; the organization would serve male and female clients.

When asked, however, Jago indicated that women did not cruise him. They used male prostitutes who operated out of exclusive hotels. Jago said that he would work from these hotels if he had the chance—first, for the money and, second, for the experience. He insisted that he was not homosexual but that he was "a horny guy" who could give sexual pleasure. He insisted repeatedly that he was not homosexual.

Jago recognized that prostitution has its bad moments. He spoke of the extraordinary loneliness he felt on certain occasions, but he believed that most of his clients helped him forget his loneliness. Despite the occasional loneliness, he estimated that he relished 75 percent of his sexual experiences. Jago's credo was: "Remember, all of life is a hustle."

A certain professionalism set Jago apart from other habitual Tenderloin prostitutes. Prostitution for Jago was not done simply for survival but was an activity pursued as "enterprise." Jago conceptualized his "work" similarly to the way which a professional would, and he pursued prospects in the same manner. For him, prostitution was a vocation. Many of his attitudes showed the same professionalism as some of the gay prostitutes of Polk Street. They were better dressed and more well groomed, but both he and they spoke of developing regular clientele through advertisements and call-boy services.

Jago apparently lacked the wherewithal to realize his dreams of success, however. He could not surmount nor exit from the Tenderloin's lower-class lifestyle. The last we heard of Jago, he had started shooting speed and had been evicted because he could not pay the rent.

Polk Street: Prostitution in the Gay Neighborhood

There are three gay ghetto zones in San Francisco—Castro Street, Folsom Street south of Market, and Polk Street. The Castro area at the base of Twin

Peaks is a five to six block region that has developed within the past ten years from a quiet, unassuming neighborhood to an openly gay ghetto lined with restaurants, bars and shops catering to a gay clientele. Although gay men openly cruise for sexual partners here, prostitution is minimal in the Castro district.

Scattered among warehouses and industrial buildings is the second gay ghetto, located on Folsom Street south of Market. Here, bathhouses, "leather bars," and sex parlors cater to those gay men who affect a rough style—men who are more masculine in appearance than those who cruise Castro and who are seeking other adult men with extensive sexual repertoires. The threat of violence is an integral aspect of the "turn on" for this group. Youth has little place here.

The third ghetto is Polk Street, now consisting of a fashionable strip of shops and restaurants. In the late 1970s, gay youth increasingly began to hang out on Polk Street. A few of the Polk Street bars had liberal age verification policies and when a juice bar opened nearby, the youth found still another place to congregate. By 1977 the merchants on Polk Street began complaining about the large influx of street youth, the drug trafficking, vandalism, and street fights. After the merchants' complaints reached the police department and the mayor's office, the neighborhood began to lose some of its distinctive gay identity.

The youth who now frequent Polk Street range from a few Tenderloin prostitutes who feel more safe working on Polk Street, to gay youth from the suburbs, to street youth in general. The community's response to the problems of the late 1970s was successful—not in terms of driving the hustlers away, but in reducing the vandalism and ambience of violence on the streets. Here, during evening and week-end hours, the hustlers are still able to make "easy money."

Gene

Gene is a prostitute who gravitates to Polk Street. He was the youngest of five children reared by bellicose, alcoholic parents. When Gene was 10, his father ran off with another woman, and his parents were divorced soon after. Gene's mother tried but failed to shake her alcoholism. She went on welfare when her ex-husband ceased child support payments. Another source of family funds was disability insurance, for which Gene's mother became eligible as a result of injuries she received in a physical fight with her then-husband.

Gene's family resided in a small California town. Early in his life, Gene decided that hometown life was boring. Television, newspapers, and magazine articles made him yearn to be a "city person." During his adolescent years, Gene ran away from home on several occasions, each time to nearby San Francisco. Gene's runaway experiences began shortly after his fourteenth birthday. One day, when Gene's mother had passed out on the sofa and her boyfriend was drunk, the boyfriend offered Gene a six-pack of Pepsi if Gene would engage in sexual activity with him. Not being able to handle his mother's continuing relationship with this man, Gene ran away.

Gene's final runaway episode was precipitated by his mother's discovery of his homosexuality. Upon finding a sexually explicit letter Gene had written to a boyfriend, his mother insisted that Gene "go straight." The resulting turmoil at home contributed to Gene's running away. Following this episode, Gene lived briefly with his lover before moving into an older sister's apartment in San Jose, California, close to an area known as San Jose's Tenderloin district. Gene began working in one of the area's theaters. He quickly became friends with several of the drag queens who spent time in front of the theater. His newfound friends told Gene he could easily earn more money by "turning tricks" as they did. Since Gene did not want to dress as a woman, however, and since he mistakenly believed that this was essential to prostitution, he failed to act on his friends' suggestion.

One day, while Gene was passing time with his friends, an adult man approached Gene on the street. The man offered twenty-five dollars if Gene would engage in sexual activity with him, and Gene decided to accept the offer. At that time, Gene was not aware that he was engaging in hustling. He did not know the meaning of the term, nor did he know how to find customers or negotiate with them. Gene discovered the trade of prostitution merely by being in the right place at the right time, in the company of known prostitutes.

Gene's second experience with prostitution occurred several months later. Gene and several homosexual friends decided to spend a week's vacation in San Francisco. While there, Gene discovered the Castro district, one of San Francisco's major gay neighborhoods. At first, Gene mistakenly thought that all the gay men who were standing and cruising for sexual partners were prostitutes. Since Gene's funds were beginning to run low, he asked one of the more friendly men standing on the street to tell him how to prostitute. The man told Gene that if Gene wanted to earn good money, he would have to go to the Prince Edward Hotel in downtown Union Square.

After asking how to get there, Gene took a bus and proceeded downtown, carrying all his possessions in a backpack. He found the hotel and stood in front. Within minutes, a good-looking man invited Gene to his hotel room, where the man fellated Gene. After Gene gave the man "a little hard luck story" about needing money to return home to his small town, the man slipped a fifty-dollar bill into Gene's pocket.

Later that week, Gene again joined his friends "to party." This time, his friends introduced him to Polk Street. He discovered that Polk Street, rather than the Castro district, is the primary setting for homosexual prostitution in San Francisco. While on Polk Street, Gene was approached by two customers. That day, Gene earned ninety dollars.

From the other prostitutes on Polk Street, Gene began learning the rules and norms of prostitution. He learned to avoid uniformed police. He learned that as soon as someone spread the word that the police were approaching, he should begin walking casually in the opposite direction. He learned to identify the two regular undercover police. In addition, he learned the fee schedule for different sexual acts. He learned to negotiate with customers—the price varying according to his own tastes, the time of day, the mood, sexual attractiveness and potential of any given customer, the pace of business, and the competition.

Gene discovered many types of hustlers while he was working on Polk Street, including the older professional prostitutes, some of whom traveled frequently to Hollywood and occasionally flew to New York,·Boston, Miami, and other coastal Florida resorts. Gene also became acquainted with part-time prostitutes, and these were the prostitutes with whom Gene felt most comfortable. "Part-timers" engaged in prostitution only when they desired money to buy clothes or "to party" in the Castro district. Some of these part-time prostitutes lived at home, while others lived with older admirers whom they referred to as sugar daddies. (A youth and a sugar daddy entered into a form of quasi-contractual arrangement, usually involving sexual activity in exchange for room and board.) Still other young prostitutes resided in Tenderloin apartments and hotel rooms that they shared with male intimates they referred to as sisters, boyfriends, or lovers. Gene also met drug dealers and drug users on Polk Street. He met people who sold only marijuana and people who dealt in pills, speed, and acid. Gene, too, began to use drugs.

Before long, Gene had earned enough money to rent a room in the Hotel El Toronado, which was just off Polk Street on the Tenderloin side. He continued prostitution on a regular basis. He found prostitution anxiety-provoking at the cruising and negotiating stage, but he found the actual "work" easy and pleasant. Gene's introduction to prostitution was relatively easy—as a "pretty new face" on the street, he attracted customers readily.

Gene never felt pressured to have sexual activity with any customer he found personally unattractive, and never felt coerced to perform sexually in ways he found unpleasant. He found that he enjoyed most of the sexual activity and would have engaged in it with many of his customers without demanding a fee. The late hours, the constant partying and the frequent opportunities to drink and use drugs began to take their toll, however. Because Gene felt that the life he was leading was too much "in the fast lane," he began thinking about other alternatives.

This motivation contributed to Gene's finding his lover, Ted. Ted was well known on the streets as someone who dated young boys but never paid for sexual activity. When a mutual friend introduced them, Ted invited Gene home for a joint and some wine. They ended up spending the night together, and Ted invited Gene to stay. Eventually, because Gene liked Ted's attitudes and the way Ted "looked at life," he moved in with Ted. Gene was sure that

Ted never viewed him as a prostitute in search of a sugar daddy. Gene was also certain that Ted would have thrown him out if he had had any indication that Gene's interest was not entirely romantic.

Gene had had several prior opportunities to move in with sugar daddies. At different times, three of Gene's regular customers had invited him to move in with them. Each time, Gene's friends urged him to take advantage of the opportunity—to "Get as much as he could in a short time, then leave." Once, Gene did move in with a regular customer for a short time. Gene felt so uncomfortable professing to love the man when he did not, however, that he moved out precipitously and refused to see the man again. Gene asserted that, unlike his friends, he could not accept a sugar daddy because he found it impossible to fake affection. He maintained that he felt only repugnance when he heard friends talking about how to "work" older men who expressed interest in them. Whenever Gene believed a customer was beginning to desire a more sustained relationship, he severed all further contact. Gene managed to convey the message that he was no longer interested in any sexual relationship by standing up the customer.

Gene began to wean himself from prostitution because of his relationship with Ted. Ted was aware that Gene engaged in prostitution from time to time, and he was eager for Gene to stop. Ted's concern was not the sexual promiscuity—they both agreed to maintain an "open" relationship and to have sexual activity with other persons they met. Ted objected, however, to many aspects of prostitution, particularly the constant exposure to and involvement with drug dealers—especially those dealers who sold unhealthy merchandise (meaning, according to Ted, drugs other than marijuana, LSD, mushrooms, and amyl nitrate). Ted also objected to the debilitating late-night hours and the constant partying; unreliable friends; the risk of arrest; the contact with other prostitutes and their jaded, cynical attitudes about love, sex, and relationships; and the failure to develop discipline, skills, and habits that held some hope for financial security and professional fulfillment.

For some months, Ted had been urging Gene to find a legal and steady job so that they could share the expenses of an apartment and move out of the Polk Street area. Gene was not happy at the thought of moving away from his Polk Street friends. To please Ted, however, he began looking for legitimate employment.

Jack

Jack's parents were divorced when he was an infant. His father was an alcoholic who graduated to heroin. Jack and his younger brother were raised for a time by their mother, but the mother soon became addicted to heroin herself, and later abandoned the two boys. They then went to live with their father for a short time. The boys were treated abusively by their father and his second wife, and both of them were seduced by their paternal grandfather.

The grandfather, a "closet homosexual" who was an Italian steelworker, began seducing Jack when he was 4. When the grandfather came to visit, he would fellate Jack, and he also taught Jack to fellate him. Jack describes "being scared to death" of his grandfather when he was a young boy. He remembers hiding in trees whenever his grandfather came to visit.

Jack also engaged in sexual activity with his uncle (his father's brother). The uncle, whom Jack now calls "a real queen," was married and the father of two. When Jack was about 10 years old, the uncle began making sexual advances. After his experiences with his grandfather, Jack was no longer afraid. The uncle forced Jack to engage in anal sex, which Jack did not enjoy.

While Jack was in elementary school, one of his best friends introduced him to an older man in the neighborhood, Al. Al paid the boys to engage in sexual activity with him. Several days per week, for about a 2-year period, Jack went to Al's apartment, and Jack enjoyed the relationship with Al. Al gave Jack money any time he asked for it. If Jack wanted clothes, Al bought them for him. Jack now describes Al as "a really nice guy...actually he was a sugar daddy. I would say that now because I know what a sugar daddy is. Then I didn't know what it was."

When Jack was 12, he and his brother were sent by their father and his second wife to live with their paternal grandparents. After continual forced sexual activity with his grandfather, Jack decided he had had enough. One night when the grandfather was drunk and making sexual advances, Jack called the police. That same night, Jack told his grandmother about the molestation. The police arrested the grandfather on a charge of child molestation, and several months later the grandmother divorced the grandfather.

In the midst of the divorce, Jack was sent to a foster home, from which he ran away. Over the next few years, Jack shuttled between group homes and juvenile hall. At age 17, after passing a qualifying exam at juvenile hall and saving $800 from employment as a nurse's aide, he was declared an "emancipated minor" by the court. Jack moved in with his first girlfriend's family. Three months later, however, after discovering that his girlfriend was a "two-timer," he decided that he was gay.

Now Jack believes that he probably was always homosexual, although he suspects that the early sexual activity with his grandfather had something to do with it. He remembers feeling attracted to older males as early as his grammar school days and being drawn to other boys while in junior high school. In addition to the sexual activity with his grandfather, his uncle, and Al, Jack had also engaged in sexual activity with his peers. He and his younger brother "did things" when they were growing up and he also engaged in sexual activity with some of his friends. Jack now believes that the early sexual activity with his grandfather was exploitative, if only because, at age 4, he was "too young to be forced to decide if you like it."

After he moved out of his girlfriend's house, Jack accepted employment in a convalescent home. He moved into the house of a friend he had met at a disco he was frequenting. For the next 4 months, Jack was what he calls a "sleaze," trekking off with his roommate to explore the cruising scenes at the local park and beach, the public toilets in Capitola, and the baths in San Jose. He had numerous "one-night stands." The experience of sleeping with perhaps a dozen men, however, quickly influenced him to become "rather picky." He decided to become more selective about those he allowed to relate intimately to him.

Jack and his roommate decided to change their residence. They moved in with two other persons from the disco—Jack's first boyfriend, Bob, and a lesbian named Angel. Jack learned much about female prostitution from Angel. He had first learned about male prostitution from the disc jockey at the disco who had told him that any young, gay male could survive in San Francisco by working Polk Street. Angel had previously been employed as a prostitute by several local massage parlors. At present, she was advertising herself as a masseuse in a local Santa Cruz newspaper.

Jack decided, "almost for the hell of it," to try the same type of prostitution as Angel. Angel told Jack she charged $60 for men to visit, $70 for outcalls, and $150 to stay the night. Jack decided to adopt the same price schedule. He drafted an ad that paralleled Angel's and placed it in the same newspaper. The ad elicited a tremendous response from approximately 150 men and two women. Jack attributes his success to the fact that his was the only male masseur advertisement. About twenty-five of the men, "the ones who sounded nice on the phone," Jack invited over to his house. When they approached, he watched through the window. Most he eluded by pretending no one was at home, and he provided sexual services to only three: a gay man who also wanted a massage and two bisexual men who wanted only sex. He charged one of the bisexual customers $60. He charged the other $150, although he felt uncomfortable demanding this fee because the customer first took Jack to dinner and to a film.

After a particularly enjoyable weekend in San Francisco on his nineteenth birthday, Jack decided to move to the city permanently. He planned to continue working at the nursing home until he saved $2,000 and then relocate. A turn of events upset his plans, however. His boyfriend Bob was arrested by an undercover police officer for soliciting, and he left for Los Angeles. Angel suggested that she and Jack resettle immediately in San Francisco for safety's sake. Their second night in San Francisco, their car was burglarized. Jack lost the $800 he had brought to finance his relocation.

Thus, when a local friend, Wally, told them he had been supporting himself by prostitution and was sure they could do likewise, Jack and Angel decided on the spur of the moment to go to the Prince Edward Hotel to turn tricks. Wally quickly explained the techniques to Jack. He told Jack to dress well, to look sweetly at any man who looked him straight in the eyes, and to ignore anyone who asked him into a car. That last request, at the Prince

Edward Hotel though not on Polk Street, meant that the interested customer was probably an undercover agent. Wally scored shortly after they arrived at the hotel. Jack met an older man, who invited him to dinner and then rented a room in a nearby motel, where Jack earned the sixty-dollar fee for which he earlier bargained. The three friends met later that night, as previously arranged. Angel reported that she had met a customer immediately after Jack did and had earned $150.

Wally taught them both more about the local prostitution scene. The prices on Polk Street were lower than those on Union Square, he informed them, although prostitution there was more safe and more social. There were so many gay youth hanging around Polk Street that the police merely attempted to keep them walking. Also, Wally noted, a degree of safety came from operating among so many gay men who were openly cruising.

The idea of socializing with many other gay men appealed to Jack. He went to Polk Street "to hang out." There, the men were more attractive, and the idea of prostitution seemed more enjoyable. From other prostitutes who were also "working Polk," Jack learned more techniques. He learned how to act when uniformed police approached him ("Walk!"). He learned how to recognize the two undercover police officers. He learned how to ensure that a customer is not a police officer "by asking suspicious-looking customers if they are police officers," by remaining silent until the customer makes a proposition and suggests a price, and by determining if the customer is comfortable when touched. Jack was also told that the younger he looked, the more he could charge. He shaved his faint mustache with regret.

Since their friend Wally had a regular clientele (five "all-nighters," which guaranteed him $250 per week), Jack and Angel often went to Polk Street with each other or with their friend Jason, who recently had come to the city from Santa Cruz. Business was best on Friday and Saturday nights between 7:30 and 9:30 or after midnight, when people began to leave the discos. During the month of December, Jack turned about ten tricks. Each of these customers requested oral sex, and each paid him twenty dollars. Several of his customers wanted him to perform additional sexual acts; and some wanted to perform sexual acts on him. Jack refused, however, to engage in more than fellatio for several reasons; he stated that he did not feel attracted to the men, nor did he find the idea of sexual activity in a car pleasant.

Furthermore, Jack was finding that he did not enjoy being a prostitute. The customers who were willing to pay were less appealing than the gay men who were merely cruising. Often, Jack thought that instead of standing around waiting for the right customer, he would rather have been dancing. Instead of spending time being intimate with strangers, he preferred to share his life with friends and lovers. He believed that his friends Angel and Wally had profited from prostitution—Angel had her high-priced customers, and Wally had his regulars—but Jack could not dispel the feeling that engaging in sexual activity for money was not an honest day's work. Jack wanted to earn his money, to have a steady and reliable income, to keep his personal life and his professional life separate. Not that Jack believed prostitution should be against the law; not that he believed he was hurting anyone by prostitution—it just wasn't his thing.

Therefore, at the same time that Jack was engaging in prostitution, he was also looking for legal employment. He wanted to find a job in which he could earn money without hiding his homosexuality. He searched the help-wanted advertisements in the gay press, made inquiries through the Gay Switchboard, and asked everyone he met on Polk Street for leads. Someone mentioned seeing a poster advertising Hospitality House, a community organization with a job-training program. At first, Jack was reluctant to attend the program because he did not like the idea of going to a social service agency for help.

While he was considering whether to approach the social service agency, Jack's employment as a prostitute came to an abrupt end the night before New Year's Eve. On Polk Street, Jack agreed to go home with a "very macho dude" who was a sadist searching for a masochist to participate in an elaborate sado-masochistic fantasy. Not having understood the meaning of "S & M," Jack was quickly reduced to tears, and he begged to be taken home. The customer drove Jack back to Polk Street, paid him thirty dollars, and said he would look for him again. Jack spent the money on a gala New Year's Eve with Angel, and at midnight he resolved never to hustle again.

Union Square: Prostitution in the Upper-Class Sex-Trade Zone

The northeast periphery of the Tenderloin is demarcated by an exclusive district of apartments, theaters, restaurants, clubs, and hotels. Because of its many luxury hotels catering to tourists and businessmen, the Union Square area in San Francisco has long supported a population of male prostitutes. Beginning with World War II, the dominant cruising scene extended from the Prince Edward Hotel southward to the Tenderloin. The prostitutes of Union Square live and work in geographic proximity to the lower-class prostitution subculture of the lower Tenderloin, but over the years, these two populations have increasingly differentiated themselves.

The attitudes, interests, and styles of the Union Square prostitutes differ significantly from those of the prostitutes who work in the lower Tenderloin sex-trade zone. The prostitutes who use the Prince Edward as their base of operation are older, more attractive, more self-confident, personable, better-dressed, and middle-class—attributes they share with some of their Polk Street counterparts. Also, Union Square prostitutes tend to be more professional in conducting their work than Tenderloin prostitutes. Some Union Square prostitutes are artists who engage in prostitution to support their careers; they view prostitution as an avocation and hence may be termed avocational prostitutes.

In the 1940s, younger homosexual men with an interest in earning money in this manner met older men in the posh bars of San Francisco's fine hotels, in restaurants known to cater to gay clientele, and at private parties. In the 1950s and 1960s, they populated the first gay bars and bathhouses. By the end of the 1960s, prostitution became more commercial, as some young men accepted employment with certain "escort services" and "modeling agencies" that dispatched prostitutes in exchange for a percentage of the fee. In the early and middle 1970s, young men increasingly operated as independent free-lancers, advertising their services in gay periodicals or working more openly in discos and on the streets of selected neighborhoods. Male prostitution was gradually becoming more visible.

Concomitant with the burgeoning of the gay male subculture in San Francisco in the 1970s, prostitution developed as a manifestation of subcultural assumptions about the value of youth, beauty, sexual prowess, interpersonal skills, and entertainment. These qualities, cherished in the subculture, reflected not only middle-class ideas about money, taste, and style but also countercultural attitudes about self-expression, pleasure, and homosexuality. Many gay men thought it reasonable to pay for assets they valued; hence, they became customers of male prostitutes.

For a long time, upper-class male prostitution passed virtually unnoticed. It first attracted attention when young prostitutes from the Tenderloin tried to "muscle in" on business. Tenderloin prostitutes were "undesirable elements," as one Union Square prostitute described, because they were "into real heavy drugs, bad appearances, and survival." Tenderloin prostitutes worked for considerably less money, "for unseemly five dollar sexual encounters," and often terminated services by stealing from customers ("rolling johns"). Hotel officials, passersby, and merchants found it easy to overlook the attractive young men who worked the Prince Edward; the police rarely received complaints about them, and political pressure was nonexistent. With the arrival of "toughs" from the Tenderloin, however, complaints proliferated, and police surveillance and interrogation of passersby increased. Undercover police began to work the streets, forcing many prostitutes who formerly had worked the Prince Edward to change their mode of operation. Some of the older, more independent, and more professional youth became call boys. Those who were less able or less willing to engage in any forms of prostitution other than street hustling migrated to Polk Street, the commercial heart of the middle-class gay neighborhood.

Rafael

Rafael is an upper-class Union Square prostitute with an upper-class background. Rafael's family are Mexican-Americans with roots deep in the Southern California Chicano community. His father, educated at Stanford, served on numerous posts in San Francisco's social service and mental health communities at both the state and federal levels. Until age 12, Rafael lived with his grandparents. This placement followed a court order after his father's divorce from his mentally incompetent mother shortly after Rafael was born. The judge refused to award the father custody of the infant until the father had established a "stable household."

His father finally established such a household in San Francisco when Rafael was 12, and Rafael moved in with him. For the next few years, Rafael mingled with the upper-class offspring of wealthy San Franciscans and attended a progressive school. His father, meanwhile, enjoyed a series of relationships with wealthy women until he permanently selected two of them, a wife and a mistress. Rafael loved his father and felt great respect for him, but Rafael's father never felt comfortable talking with his son about sex. The father's laissez-faire attitudes about parenting made Rafael feel that coming of age sexually was his own responsibility.

At age 14, Rafael accepted an invitation to have sex with a local rock star, who subsequently asked Rafael to join his entourage. Rafael was so overwhelmed that he quickly severed the relationship, but the sexual encounter had been so pleasurable that it led Rafael to believe he was homosexual. To test this belief, Rafael entered into a sexual relationship with a girl at his school. When this relationship turned out to be unsatisfying, Rafael came to the conclusion that he was homosexual.

Rafael's self-discovery occurred in the middle of the 1970s, when the gay subculture in San Francisco was becoming commercial. A number of major discos opened in the city—an entertainment complex in North Beach and several on Polk Street. The disco clientele was not the ragged gay counterculture members who had danced in the 1960s and early 1970s at discos in the lower-class area south of Market Street. Rather, the clientele consisted of avant-garde adolescents who identified with rock stars, such as Janis Joplin and David Bowie. They wore sparkly shirts and socks, experimented with makeup and the androgynous look, used marijuana, and called themselves "the glitter scene." The gay life in San Francisco fascinated many of the teenagers at Rafael's school. Several of his classmates, including Rafael, were open about their homosexuality and their involvement in unconventional relationships. Although he was candid about his homosexuality at school, Rafael hid the truth from his father. One day, his father stumbled upon him with a lover at home. After that, their emotional estrangement grew. For support, Rafael turned even more to his peers at school.

When Rafael was a junior, his father decided that his son's formal education was inadequate, and he insisted that Rafael transfer from the progressive school to a local public high school. If Rafael refused to attend, his father threatened to terminate his allowance. Rafael was receiving sixty dollars per week from his father, an allowance that, though generous by some standards, was insufficient in light of the life Rafael was leading. The Polk Street discos attracted a smart set, and being well groomed and well dressed cost money.

Shortly after his transfer to a public high school, Rafael chose a lover who had an apartment in the upper Tenderloin. It was while spending time there that Rafael first discovered prostitution. He noticed the rough-looking street prostitutes of the Meat Rack, and he also took note of the better-dressed prostitutes who worked on the south side of the Prince Edward Hotel. One day, outside a disco, an adult admirer offered to pay him twenty dollars for sex. Rafael decided it would be stupid to refuse; he needed the money. It was then that Rafael decided to supplement his weekly allowance by regular prostitution.

Rafael decided to go to the Prince Edward to find customers. He determined to double the price he had quoted to his first paying customer, feeling that he was worth at least that much. He waited for an attractive older man to approach him and engaged him in pleasant conversation and then in more explicit negotiation. He discovered that his price was accepted readily. After learning from other prostitutes at the Prince Edward that the standard price was twenty-five dollars, Rafael raised his regular price to fifty dollars. He believed the men he hoped to attract could well afford his price.

Rafael found his business successful. His customers, who consisted of hotel clientele—businessmen and tourists—invited him for drinks and dinner. They told him about their professions and, often, about their families. His "clients," as Rafael referred to them, entertained Rafael before he entertained them sexually. They treated him genteelly, paid him dutifully, and sometimes returned.

Rafael engaged in prostitution at the Prince Edward for more than a year. He worked three or four evenings a week, usually Thursdays through Sundays. He made friends with perhaps six to twelve peers who worked in the same locale. He and his friends had cocktails together before work and went on shopping sprees to spend their money after work. Rafael spent much of his money on clothes and entertainment for himself and his lover. He continued to use his lover's Tenderloin apartment occasionally, although he never used it for business. His professional encounters took place in his clients' hotel rooms.

Rafael's career as an upper-class prostitute came to an abrupt end. One day, just before he turned 18, Rafael arranged for a client to phone him at home—that is, at his father's house. When the client telephoned early, the father answered to the name Rafael, since he was Rafael, Senior. The father quickly gleaned from the conversation that the caller was arranging to meet his son for pay.

Rafael's father demanded an explanation. During the confrontation, he insisted that the occupation reflected Rafael's lack of self-esteem. Rafael argued that it was a way to make easy money and to obtain attention and excitement. He tried to explain that he enjoyed prostitution—getting dressed up, going downtown to meet friends, and being entertained. He explained that prostitution was only a temporary means of employment. Partly because Rafael felt it was time to move on, however, and partly because of his respect for his only parent, Rafael followed his father's orders and never prostituted again.

Summary

The youth described here, and others, are members of the two distinct subcultures that characterize adolescent male prostitution: the peer-delinquent subculture and the gay subculture. The subcultures differ on several dimensions. First, the Tenderloin prostitutes, such as Bobby, John, and Jago, are more likely to come from lower-class origins, and are more likely to define themselves as heterosexual. They are also more likely to be involved in prostitution simultaneously with other petty criminal activity.

In contrast, the youth of the gay subculture engage in prostitution in gay neighborhoods such as Polk Street and in the area near the downtown luxury hotels. These prostitutes are somewhat more likely than peer-delinquents to be from the middle class. Youth such as Gene, Jack, and Rafael are more likely to define themselves as either homosexual or bisexual. They engage in prostitution for the opportunity for social interaction with other gay persons, and they enjoy the sense of community they gain from spending time in the gay neighborhood. Prostitution satisfies their need for sociability and for sexual gratification, as well as constituting a method of making money. Thus, prostitution serves a different function for the youth of these two subcultures.

Several categories of prostitutes can be identified that cross-cut these two subcultures:

Situational prostitutes—young men who engage in prostitution only under certain circumstances or in some situations and who view prostitution as an occasional activity.

Habitual prostitutes—young men involved in inner-city street life for whom prostitution is an integral aspect of a street lifestyle that also includes such acts as drug dealing, petty theft, and robbery.

Vocational prostitutes—young men who view prostitution as a career, or as a steppingstone in a career, and who regard themselves as professionals.

Avocational prostitutes—vocational prostitutes who regard their work as part-time employment.

Situational prostitutes turn to prostitution when opportunity knocks or when they are in need of money. Some engage in prostitution when they come to the central city for a weekend night to explore the night life. The motivation for engaging in prostitution may be material (for rent, food, or entertainment) or adventure-seeking. Over time, some of these young men become habitual prostitutes. They become "addicted" to the life and to the lifestyle, which includes drug use, alcohol use, and petty theft as well as prostitution. They become involved to the extent that they become street people and earn their living from the street by whatever methods they are able.

The lives of situational and habitual prostitutes differ from those of vocational or avocational prostitutes. Some prostitutes who work on the streets become more professional about their prostitution. Some of these also work as escorts or masseurs, operating from agencies or advertisements. Others work as call boys and develop regular clientele. For situational and habitual prostitutes, prostitution is a means of participating in street life—it finances the drugs and partying. The situational or habitual prostitute rarely takes care of himself physically or emotionally; he rarely thinks beyond the present. For the vocational or avocational prostitute, however, his appearance and wardrobe are the tools of his trade. To succeed, he must take care of himself. He works to establish and cultivate a clientele, and he is usually more sophisticated, better looking, and more well groomed than his situational or habitual counterpart.

These categories of prostitutes are found among the prostitute subcultures. Further similarities and differences between adolescent prostitutes from the two subcultures will be explored in the next chapter.

Notes

1. The norms of the peer-delinquent prostitute were first explored in Reiss's sociological classic. See Albert J. Reiss, Jr., "The Social Integration of Queers and Peers," *Social Problems* 9(Fall 1961): 102–20.

2. As English and Stephens note: "The use of the term hustle has not been operationalized by sociologists in any consistent fashion." Definitions of hustle or hustling have been applied to specific actors. In addition to prostitutes, hustler has been used to refer to pimps, pool sharks and drug dealers. Clifford English and Joyce Stephens, "On Being Excluded: An Analysis of Elderly and Adolescent Street Hustlers," *Urban Life* 4(July 1975): 211, n. 3.

3. The area was christened, so it is said, by a corrupt police captain who exclaimed that the bribes paid by the owners of the illicit enterprises would be sizable enough to afford him the best cuts of meat—hence "the Tenderloin."

4. San Francisco has a number of prominent gay neighborhoods, the most well-known being Polk Street and the Castro. Male prostitution appears to be carried on primarily in the Polk Street neighborhood.

5. San Francisco has another sex-trade zone located near Broadway and Columbus streets. This area also contains some strip joints and massage parlors, in addition to many topless bars. Businesses here command much higher prices, however, and the establishments in the Broadway area are frequented more commonly by tourists and by heterosexual persons than are those in the downtown sex-trade zone.

6. Dennis Drew and Jonathan Drake, *Boys For Sale: A Sociological Study of Boy Prostitution* (New York: Brown, 1969), 141.

7. The term originates, according to Drew and Drake, from a custom in Middle Eastern and Mediterranean ports, whereby brothel boys were required to sit on greased pegs on benches. The pegs had two functions: to keep the anus dilated for easier penetration and to enable prospective customers to gauge the penis size a boy was capable of encompassing. Ibid., 142.

8. Reverend Edward Hansen, M. Forrester, and Reverend F. Bird, *The Tenderloin Ghetto: The Young Reject in Our Society* (San Francisco: Glide Urban Center, 1965), 7.

9. Ibid., 7–8.

10. Ibid.

11. The name of this commercial establishment and others referred to in the text have been altered.

3
Adolescent Male Prostitutes: Backgrounds, Lifestyles, and Juvenile Justice Involvement

P rostitution as a social phenomenon has been the subject of considerable research. The literature is so extensive, in fact, that bibliographies have been published on the subject.[1] The majority of this literature focuses on adult female prostitution, since adult male prostitution has been the subject of much less research.[2] Literature focusing exclusively on juvenile male prostitutes is virtually nonexistent.

Studies of adult male prostitutes do yield some insight into the situation of juveniles, but the literature on adult males also has several shortcomings. First, few studies are based on samples that include large numbers of juveniles, and only two studies are drawn from exclusively juvenile samples.[3] Second, most of the research has been limited to studies on small samples in only one locale.[4] Only an occasional study has included a larger sample, based on an examination of male prostitution in, at most, two locales.[5] Thus, because such studies are not truly national in scope, it is difficult to extrapolate their findings to the country as a whole.

In addition, much of the research on male prostitution has been limited to studies based on one type of prostitute. Some research, for example, focuses on hard-core street hustlers,[6] and an occasional study explores the male house of prostitution[7] or the prison prostitute.[8] This research misses those youth who engage in other common forms of prostitution, such as call boys, or those prostitutes who secure customers by advertisements or in gay neighborhoods or gay bars. Many studies fail to recognize the inherent diversity that characterizes this population.

Furthermore, many of these studies were conducted in the 1960s,[9] when the hippie movement and the counterculture were influencing youth lifestyles. Because of this frame of reference, most of the studies fail to address the relationship between juvenile prostitution and more current social problems, such as running away and sexual and physical abuse.

The study of adolescent male prostitutes reported here has attempted to address some of the shortcomings of prior research. As explained earlier, the study is national in scope, encompassing research on adolescent prostitution in seven major metropolitan areas (Boston, Houston, Los Angeles, Minneapolis, New York, San Francisco, and Seattle). The sample consists of youth contacted through social service agencies as well as youth contacted on the street. The majority (85 percent) of the youth were adolescents between the ages of 12 and 18. Numerous topics were included in the discussions with seventy-nine juvenile male prostitutes, including each youth's family background, education, prior employment, history of child abuse and neglect, entrance into prostitution, prostitution experiences, and interactions with the juvenile justice system (including runaway involvement) and the social service delivery system. The findings are presented here and compared with the findings of prior research on male prostitution.

Family Backgrounds

> Gene: I'm a native Californian. I lived in Modesto with my mother, brothers and sisters. My mother and father were divorced when I was 10. They just couldn't hit it off together. They were both alcoholics; they used to fight all the time.

> Larry: My father's been dead since I was 4 years old. When I was 12 I lost my mother. I lived with my brother for about a year. My brother was 10 years older than me. My brother didn't understand a lot of things about me. We just didn't get along, so I left.

These two young men reveal family backgrounds typical of many adolescent male prostitutes. As noted in his case study in chapter 2, Gene is the youngest of five children. He grew up with his mother, father, two older brothers, and two older sisters. His parents, both alcoholics, fought often. When Gene was 8 or 9, his father began leaving home for weeks at a time in response to family conflicts. These conflicts eventually led to his parents' divorce when Gene was 10. Gene's father, an airline mechanic, moved to another state and soon remarried. Gene and his brothers and sisters remained with their mother in California.

Larry grew up in a large family. He was raised by his mother after his father died when Larry was 4. Like Gene, he was the youngest of several siblings. When Larry was 12, his mother died. Larry moved in with his 22-year-old brother, who had recently married, but the brothers did not get along. After one fight, Larry left home and stayed with friends, but he returned several days later. After another fight when Larry was 13, Larry left for good. He lived temporarily with a customer he had met. When that brief relationship ended, Larry moved in for a time with an older sister who was single and working.

The family backgrounds of Gene and Larry are characteristic of many adolescent male prostitutes. A substantial number of these youth come from homes that have been dissolved by death or divorce. When the seventy-nine prostitutes in our sample were asked to name the primary person or persons

Table 3-1
Primary Persons Who Raised Youth

Primary Caretakers	Number of Youth (n = 79)	Percentage[a]
Mother and father	27	34
Parent and stepparent	8	10
Mostly mother	28	35
Mostly father	7	9
Foster parents	5	6
Institutions	3	4
Other	1	1

[a]Percentages do not total 100 percent because of rounding.

who raised them, only 34 percent of the youth named both their mother and father. Commonly, these youth have resided in family arrangements that differ from the traditional nuclear-family model. In many cases, the youth have shifted from one residential arrangement to another.

A large number of these youth were raised by only one primary caretaker; almost half of the sample report being raised by single parents. Thirty-five percent of the prostitutes identified their mother as primarily responsible for their upbringing, and another 9 percent indicated that their father was their primary caretaker—giving a total of 44 percent of the youth raised primarily in a single parent family. The experience of growing up in a reconstituted family—a parent and a stepparent, is noted by an additional 10 percent of the youth. In addition, a surprising percentage of the youth (10 percent) were raised primarily by foster parents or in institutions. Table 3-1 shows the numbers and percentages of youth raised by the various constellations of caretakers.

Prior research on male prostitutes emphasizes several similar characteristics of their home life, including a high frequency of broken homes, a lack of affection, and indifferent or hostile mothers, fathers, and stepfathers.[10] Allen notes that only eighteen of ninety-eight youth in his study have an intact family, with both parents present and "reasonably effective."[11] Slightly over half of the youth in Allen's study have an inadequate, nonfunctional family or no family. Even when an apparently intact family exists, Allen found poor family relationships.

Most studies concur that fathers of male prostitutes, more often than mothers, are either absent or ineffective.[12] In Allen's study, only one-fourth of the fathers are present and functional, compared to almost half of the mothers. Forty percent of the fathers are absent; another 13 percent are replaced by stepfathers who often do not get along with the stepson; another 14 percent are classified as inadequate because of alcoholism; and a final 4 percent are abusive.[13] Ginsburg also notes many of these characteristics in the family pattern of male prostitutes:

The parents, almost always the father, were either not present, or present but nonsupportive or unstable. Disinterest, aloofness, hostility and rejection were in one form or another continually registered toward the youth from his earliest years outward.[14]

Prior research has failed to highlight the number and varieties of family arrangements that the youth experience. Larry, for example, appears to be typical of a large number of boys. After his mother's death when he was 12, he went to live with an older brother, then moved out at age 13 to live with friends, then with a customer, and then with an older sister until he struck out on his own. Another youth, for example, reported that he was raised by his mother till age 8, then by "relatives" until, at age 12, he was sent to a youth home. Still another youth lived with his mother and father till he was 9, with his mother till age 15, and finally with his aunt till he was 16. Because he began to "feel like an intruder" in his aunt's home, he left.

Many youth live with several different caretakers, but the reasons for these continuous disruptions of the family system are often external to the youth. Sometimes, the death of a parent triggers alterations in the family structure, and these alterations may culminate in the youth's desire to leave home. Such was the case with Frank, who ran away from home at 15 because "I lost my mother and she was the only one I really cared for." Thus, the death of a parent my result in changes in the family structure that then become unbearable for the youth. One youth describes what occurred in his case: "I left home at 16 when my mother died. Then I lived with my stepfather but he hassled me so much, I finally left."

More often than not, these youth's family arrangements begin with an intact nuclear family. When divorce, separation, or death dissolves that arrangement, the youth lives with the remaining parent for a time, but the new arrangement may be of brief duration. The youth may leave that parent (or be thrown out in some cases) to live with other family members.

In a small number of cases, the youth's living arrangements include institutional care; that is, a youth may live with a parent or parents, but when that arrangement is changed, he may spend time in an institution. One youth recounted that he was raised by his mother "till age 5, then in an orphanage till 12, then I was adopted." Still another related that he was raised by "my mother, when small, then my father, then institutions." Often, the institution is a mental health facility. One respondent lived with his mother till age 10; after several foster care placements, he was admitted to a psychiatric hospital at age 15. Another youth lived with his father, then in an orphanage, then in a residential mental health center.

Physical and Emotional Abuse

Little prior research information is available on physical abuse in the family backgrounds of adolescent male prostitutes. In our study of seventy-nine adolescent prostitutes, twenty-seven (34 percent) report physical abuse by family members. Among these youth, seven report being physically abused by a step-parent, five by a father, four by a mother, and two by an older sibling. (In the remaining cases, the youth either refused to specify the perpetrator or, based on professional judgment, the interviewer did not probe.) For some youth, the abuse could be characterized as severe. One youth reports being beaten repeatedly by his stepfather with fists, phone cord, and jump rope. For several youth, the act of leaving home was precipitated by such recurrent physical abuse.

In addition, 38 percent of the youth experienced considerable emotional abuse in their families. Again, primary caretakers are most often responsible for this form of abuse. Among the family members frequently mentioned as perpetrators of emotional abuse are, first, fathers, then mothers. Brother, stepfathers, and stepmothers are also named.

Two primary types of emotional abuse are mentioned most frequently. In the first type, the youth reports a parent "putting him down" constantly. As one youth describes it: "My father keeps running me down as a failure." The second most frequently cited type of emotional abuse involves negative comments about the youth's homosexuality. This abuse is perpetrated by various family members, including mothers, fathers, brothers, stepparents, and foster parents. In one case, the youth felt he was driven out of the house by his stepmother: "When I told her I was gay, she was afraid I would cause her two sons to be gay by [my] influence." Another youth, describing constant emotional abuse by his father, cites an incident following disclosure of his homosexuality. When a friend told his father that the youth was gay, his father told all the youth's friends and his employer and revoked the youth's car privileges.

The backgrounds of many of these youth also evince histories of neglect. Although queries were directed at the discovery of abuse rather than neglect, the youth's responses nonetheless reveal the presence of neglect. One type of neglect that several youth mention is abandonment. A number of youth report they were "kicked out" by their parents at some time during their adolescent years. One youth, when asked by whom he was raised, explains: "my mother and my father, but I've lived on the streets on and off since I was 9." Another youth reports that he was kicked out of the house at the age of 11 by his mother and grandfather, with whom he was then living. Still another notes that he left home at age 16, the reason: "My mom moved. She tole [sic] me I'm on my own." This type of treatment occurs even with young adolescents. One youth describes the situation of a 13–year-old acquaintance (another prostitute):

> Some of them [hustlers], their parents can't give a shit what happens to them. Like there's one that I know, his name is Timmy, he's 13. Maybe he'll pull a trick four times a week, just to keep him provided for. He stays with friends, or whatever, it doesn't matter where he stays. He says he lives with his mother, but he only goes back maybe once a week if that. From what I hear his mother's an alcoholic. ... I think his life is really confused.

In our study, we found no substantial correlation between the incidence of any form of abuse and the variables of race or family composition.

In an attempt to compare our findings with other research, we discovered that little prior research explored specifically the extent of physical abuse, emotional abuse, or neglect within the families of prostitutes, although a few studies do mention the presence of physical abuse in youth's family backgrounds. Allen, for example, notes that 4 percent of the fathers of the youth in his study were "abusive."[15] Caukins and Coombs note the presence of "authoritarian" and "punitive" fathers.[16] One study, also conducted in San Francisco, notes the presence of physical abuse,[17] finding an incidence somewhat higher than ours (47 percent compared to 34 percent). Those researchers also found that most young prostitutes who are physically abused are abused by a male parent or stepparent.[18] The phenomenon of abandonment by parents of juvenile prostitutes also has not been well researched, although one early study does note that five youth (among forty-one who left home) left because they were "ordered out by parents."[19] This topic clearly merits further research.

Sexual Abuse and Early Sexual Experiences

Sexual abuse is another common characteristic in the family backgrounds of many adolescent male prostitutes. Twenty-nine percent of our sample report having been sexually abused by a family member. (These are self-reports of victimization, for which no specific acts are designated.) The family members include fathers, siblings, and other male relatives. An additional 15 percent of the sample report being sexually abused by nonfamilial assailants, including mothers' boyfriends, sisters' boyfriends, and others. One youth, for example, admits being "raped" at age 9 by a minister, and another youth describes being sexually abused by a babysitter (sex unspecified) when the youth was 8 years old.

We also solicited data about the age at which adolescent male prostitutes had their "first sexual experience." Again, we elicited self-reports of first sexual experiences for which no specific acts were suggested. Some of these early sexual experiences take the form of sexual experimentation. One youth, for example, recounted sexual encounters at age 6 with an older brother; another reported consensual sex with several cousins. Some of these early sexual experiences, however, are clearly abusive. We suspect that the low incidence of childhood sexual abuse reported here (29 percent) may well be attributed to the fact that many youth characterized such incidents as early sexual experiences rather than as sexual abuse.

Table 3–2 displays the prostitutes' reported ages of their first sexual experiences. The frequency of sexual experiences at very young ages is surprising. Three youth report their first sexual experiences at age 5 or younger. Another three youth note early sexual experiences at age 6. Eleven youth recount their

Table 3–2
Age at First Sexual Experience[a]

Age (years)	Number of Youth (n = 79)	Percentage[b]
3	1	1
4	1	1
5	1	1
6	3	4
7	1	1
8	2	3
9	8	10
10	2	3
11	3	4
12	16	20
13	12	15
14	11	14
15	5	6
16	4	5
17	1	1
Unknown	8	10

[a]First sexual experience includes both sexual abuse and consensual sexual activity.
[b]Percentages do not total 100 percent because of rounding.

first sexual experience at ages 7 to 9. Thus, seventeen youth, or twenty percent of the sample, report their first sexual experiences prior to age 10. From table 3–2, we see that the mean of this age distribution for first sexual experience is 11.8 years (± 0.4), while the median and mode are both 12 years of age.

Little prior research exists on the extent of sexual abuse in the family backgrounds of prostitutes, but our tentative findings on sexual abuse appear to be consistent with the findings of the few studies to explore this variable. In Shick's subsample of 57 hustlers with whom he conducted in-depth interviews, 10 percent report familial sexual abuse by fathers, brothers, uncles, and cousins.[20]

Two other studies shed some additional light on this variable. Sexual abuse among the family backgrounds of juvenile male prostitutes is reported by James, whose data reveal that of 44.7 percent of adolescent male prostitutes who had their first sexual experience with another male, this experience was incestuous for many; for 25.6 percent of the prostitutes, their first sexual experience was with a relative.[21] Furthermore, for many of the youth, this first sexual experience was coerced; 10.6 percent report being physically coerced, and 12.8 percent felt emotionally coerced to participate.[22] An extrapolation from James's data reveals a median age at first sexual involvement closely approximating that of our sample (11 years).[23] The Huckleberry Project research also notes a high percentage of youth who were sexually abused (53 percent). Of these youth, 37 percent were raped or molested either at home or on the street, and another 17 percent received unwanted sexual advances.[24]

That study does not differentiate, however, between intrafamilial sexual abuse, extrafamilial sexual abuse, and sexual abuse experienced during acts of prostitution. Hence, the extent of sexual abuse specifically by family members is impossible to determine.

One respondent in our sample provided details about the extent of his early sexual abuse. Jack, whose story was given in detail in chapter 2, reports being abused sexually by his paternal grandfather:

> My grandfather was screwing with me when I was four years old. ... I cannot say how it started or why it started. All I know is that he screwed with me when I was four. I can remember living in fear when I was four years old. I can remember hiding in trees when he'd come to visit me.

When asked whether the abuse was rape, Jack responds with denial at first:

> No, I don't think so. I protested quite a bit. ... I remember telling him no, but he would force himself on me. I don't know what you would call it today, but he did force himself on me.

The sexual abuse ceased one day when Jack at the age of 9 or 10, decided he had had enough:

> I turned him in. I got fed up one night. He tried to force himself on me again and he was drinkin' and I didn't want nothin' to do with him. ... I didn't go for it any longer so I told my grandmother the same night. The cops came. They arrested him. "Child molesting" they called it.

While in elementary school, Jack was also "recruited" by his grandfather to engage in sexual activities with one of the grandfather's friends. Jack says: "He wanted me to do something with both of them. I told him, no, I would not do it."

Jack's history of sexual abuse by his grandfather supports the notion of the transmissibility of abuse.[25] Jack also reports being sexually abused by an uncle (one of Jack's grandfather's four sons):

> My uncle was a different story. My uncle didn't do anything with me when I was younger ... [but] he did when I was maybe 10 or somewhere's up. ... I think after my grandfather's experience and everything else, it wasn't so scary anymore. I knew what was going on. ... He went a little bit further than what my grandfather was doing. ... I didn't like, you know, messing with the back area at all. I didn't like it. It hurt. But whatever else, I didn't enjoy it. But when he would force himself on me I'd tell him "no way, stop." But he'd keep going.

Jack's grandfather also abused Jack's older brother; then, some time later, the brother and Jack became involved in sexual experimentation with each other. When asked if he was involved sexually at a young age with peers, Jack replies:

> Well, yeah, my brother and I did something too. See, my grandfather screwed with my brother too, when he was younger. My brother and I did quite a few things together. You know, oral sex. ...

The duration of the abuse in this case is noteworthy. The abuse by Jack's grandfather did not cease when it was discovered by the authorities. The grandfather was not incarcerated, and the abuse persisted. Jack notes:

> My grandfather called me two weeks ago and asked me to go with him again. And I'm now 19! I told him, "no way." I said, "I charge you!" That's what I told him.

Jack also reports other sexual encounters with nonfamily members. His first paid sexual encounter, when Jack was in elementary school, occurred with an older man, "perhaps 45 or so." As Jack describes it:

> I met him through a friend of mine. One of my best friends started coming to him. He paid me, so I would go to bed with him.

Jack's experiences appear to be characteristic, to some extent, of those of many adolescent male prostitutes. For many youth, sexual experiences occur from an early age, and the participants include both family members and persons external to the family.

Prostitution Experiences

Onset of Prostitution

The early sexual experiences of these youth teach them the value of their body as a commercial asset; they begin at an early age to realize that sexual encounters can be a source of money. As Jack describes his first paid sexual encounter, when he was in elementary school:

> It wasn't just for sex. He'd give me money anytime I'd ask for it. Actually he was a sugar daddy. But I would say that now because I know what a sugar daddy is. Then I wouldn't know what it was. He was a sugar daddy. I'd ask for five bucks and he'd give it to me. If I wanted clothes, he'd buy them for me. You know, it was just that kind of thing. He was just a super guy, a really nice

guy. I mean, I have nothing against him. I'm sorry I lost contact with him. It would have been handy today [laughs].

For seven boys in our sample, the first time they were paid for sexual acts occurred before they were 11 years old. Two boys were first paid at age 6, another at age 9, and four at age 11. The number of boys first paid for sex at age 12 or 13 reflects a significant increase. Nine boys (11 percent of the sample) were first paid at age 12, and ten boys (13 percent) at age 13. The numbers continue to increase throughout mid-adolescent years—fifteen boys (19 percent) were first paid for sex at age 14, and fourteen boys (18 percent) at age 15. The payment for these sexual activities included money and other considerations.

Some youth, like Jack, are introduced to prostitution by their friends. Other youth learn of it inadvertently. Certain locales that naturally attract adolescents may facilitate their acquisition of knowledge since potential customers know to patronize these settings. The beach appears to be one such locale.

Larry was first introduced to prostitution at the beach. He reports spending considerable time at the beach at Venice, California, one summer when he was 12 or 13. One day, he was hitchhiking from the beach and was given a ride by a 35-year-old airline pilot. The man asked if Larry wanted to earn some money, and Larry quickly agreed. That is how Larry first found out about hustling. The relationship continued for a time until the man found someone else—"younger, blonder, tanner [*sic*]." The relationship ended "gentle-like," says Larry, "he set me up with some friends."

Other locales that facilitate youth's learning about prostitution are the gay sectors of an urban area and the heart of the downtown section—"the Meat-Rack" or "the Tenderloin" which attracts young runaways when they first arrive in a city because of its abundance of inexpensive accommodations. Hal's account illustrates the influence of these settings.

Hal moved away from home at 17 because of conflicts with his mother about his homosexuality. He arrived in San Jose, and settled into the downtown area:

I was there for, like, 7 months or so. When I moved there, things were kind of hard for me, because I was first starting out. ...

The people he met and associated with in that downtown locale tended to be prostitutes. One day, when he was "just kind of hanging around with them," a man approached him. As Hal describes his first hustling experience:

Then this man came up and he offered me $25 if I would do his little thing with him. And I said "sure." That was the first one I ever did. I thought, "that was great for 20 minutes of my time, to get that and then go party or something."

For most youth, the realization that they possess a salable asset comes as a surprise. The ease with which they acquire payment influences some to decide to utilize that asset on a more regular basis. These youth often become full-time professional prostitutes.

A distinction must be made, however, between engaging in an occasional sexual act in exchange for money and becoming a full-time prostitute. Many youth participate in sexual acts for money on an occasional basis for several years before they begin turning tricks on a regular basis. Some youth, in fact, engage in sexual acts at such an early age that they are still unaware of the significance of their acts; that is, they may not be aware it is "hustling" or even that it is "sex". When many youth first engage in sexual acts for remuneration, they may think of it as an isolated incident—a neighbor, a friend of the family, or a stranger may approach them and offer some item or money in exchange for sexual acts.

Other youth realize the salability of their skills at quite a young age. Larry, for example, now 17, became aware of prostitution as a means of employment at age 12. He notes:

> I've been out there quite a while. I got turned out real young, 'bout 13. I ran away from home ... and I realized I had something I could sell because I was young and I was cute and there was a lot of old perverts out there that paid for it.

For a few youth, considerable time elapses between the initial payment for sex and the time of their entrance into prostitution. Seven youth report first being paid for sex by age 11. One youth notes he was first paid for sex at age 8; he began hustling regularly at age 11. Another youth's first sexual experience at age 4 (by an unspecified person) was also the first time the boy was paid for sex; that youth began hustling regularly at age 15.

A significant proportion of youth, however, begin prostitution on a regular basis a short time after their first paid sexual encounter. The overwhelming majority of the sample (74 percent) began prostitution on a full-time basis within the same year as their first prostitution experience; and 91 percent became regular prostitutes within 1 year after their first paid sexual encounter.

Table 3-3 shows the ages at which the youth's first prostitution experiences occurred and the ages at which they began regular prostitution. *Regular prostitution* is defined as engaging in prostitution several times per month: *first prostitution experience* is defined as the first time a youth is paid for sexual activity. The mode and median ages at which the youth began prostitution regularly are 16 and 15.5 respectively; the mean is age 14.8. This signifies that most of the youth began prostitution on a regular basis at age 16. The asymmetric distribution, skewed toward younger ages, indicates, however, that, although 16 is the most probable age for the onset of regular prostitution, more prostitutes begin full-time prostitution earlier than age 16 than begin later than age 16.

Table 3–3
Age at First and Regular Prostitution Experiences

Age (years)	First Prostituted	Began Prostitution Regularly
6	2 (1%)	—
7	—	—
8	—	—
9	1 (1%)	—
10	—	—
11	4 (5%)	4 (5%)
12	9 (11%)	8 (10%)
13	10 (13%)	9 (11%)
14	15 (19%)	9 (11%)
15	14 (18%)	11 (14%)
16	13 (16%)	21 (27%)
17	9 (11%)	11 (14%)
18	2 (3%)	2 (3%)
19	1 (1%)	1 (1%)
Unknown	—	3 (4%)

Onset variables do not appear to correlate with racial or sexual identification. They do correlate, however, with family composition and first sexual experience; that is, male prostitutes raised in a nontraditional family begin their first prostitution experience and regular prostitution about one year earlier (at age 14) than those raised in two-parent families. As previously stated, onset variables also appear to correlate with first sexual experience, as illustrated in figure 3–1. The rapidity of the shift from first act to regular prostitution signifies that the youth quickly realize the value of their body as an asset. The allure of easy money soon attracts them to street life on a more full-time basis.

Once the youth realize that prostitution is a ready source of funds, they still must learn the rules and norms. They have to learn the locations in which to prostitute, the best times of day, the way to approach a customer or encourage a customer to approach them, how much to charge, and how to negotiate.

Some youth learn the norms of prostitution from friends. Gene describes how a friend taught him:

> I met a friend Matt. ... We were driving around to go to Polk Street. He was the first hustler I knew. I was asking him "How do you do this?" And he goes, "It's not how you do it, you just do it. You just stand around and look pretty, and have somebody pick you up." ... This was about maybe three in the afternoon. It was really bright and sunny and I was in a pair of cut-offs and a ripped T-shirt, and he said I was dressed perfect for it.

The two boys then went to a corner in front of a restaurant. Gene continues:

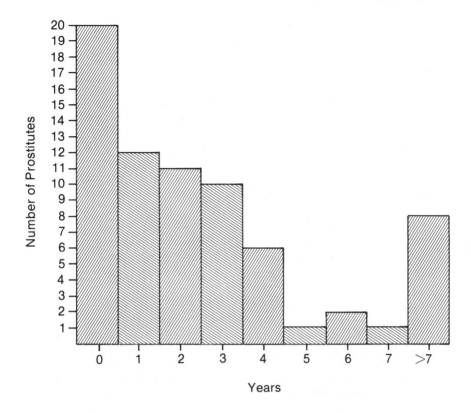

**Figure 3–1. Time between First Sexual Experience and First
Prostitution Experience**

He [Matt] was sitting on a fire hydrant. I was just kinda hanging onto a pole,
just kinda posing. He said, "You've got to pose if you want to get a trick"; so
I'd just be sitting out there posing and trying to look pretty.

Some of this learning process takes place on the job, as some would-be
prostitutes learn about prostitution from customers. George describes his learning process when he first began prostitution in the downtown area of
Minneapolis:

One man was quite helpful. He had picked up quite a few hustlers. We devel-
loped quite a relationship. He told me how [to hustle], you know, and where
… gave me a few pointers. It was really great. We ended up going to Europe
together.

Table 3-4
Primary Reasons for Engaging in Prostitution

Reason	Number of Times Cited[a]	Percentage[a]
Money	69	87
Drugs	2	3
Sex	21	27
Fun/adventure	15	19
Ego boost/attention	4	5
Sociability	9	11
Other	1	2

[a]Since many of the youth gave multiple motivations for engaging in prostitution, the total numbers exceed the sample size of seventy-nine, and the total percentages exceed 100 percent.

Gene also learned some of the rules about prostitution from a customer. He describes his first encounter, relating how he learned how much to charge for prostitution:

> I was wearing a pair of cut-off Levis and the slits were like all the way up to the beltline. I had on a holey T-shirt just to be like punk rock of last summer. I met this guy and he wanted to have sex with me while I was wearing all this little raggedy get up. ... So that was O.K. ... We went up to his place. He had a hotel room. ... I asked him what do people usually charge whenever they're hustling. ... he told me he'd give me $50. I told him that'd be fine. Then we just went up and did our thing and then I left.

Motivations for Prostitution

Adolescent male prostitutes engage in prostitution for many reasons. The primary reasons are listed in table 3-4. As expected, money was the primary motivation (cited by 87 percent of the sample). Sexual gratification was a motivating factor for 27 percent of the prostitutes, fun and adventure for 19 percent, and sociability for 11 percent. For a few youth, drugs were the primary reason for engaging in prostitution.

Many youth are impressed with the amount of money they are able to earn in prostitution. For adolescents who are unable to find employment or barely able to earn the minimum wage in low-skilled jobs, the possibility of earning thirty to forty dollars for 20 minutes' work is enticing. As George describes his experiences:

> I came back to Indianapolis ... and I had to put together a home. I thought the fastest way to make some money would be to try that [hustling]. Well, I found myself making $40 a night—$45 or so—in just a couple of days. I was doing well. That was the most I'd ever made. I was only getting $2 to $2.50 doing something else [unspecified employment]. And I didn't have to spend much time at it. It was exciting.

Other youth enjoy the sociability aspects of prostitution. They enjoy spending time "hanging around" in prostitution locales with their peers and receiving the attention of older males who find them attractive. This can be seen in Larry's characterization:

> I came here. ... I was just going to get a job. I had every intent of getting a job. I got picked up by this guy and I stayed with him and his lover for close to 3 months ... then I hit the streets. They introduced me to Polk Street and I saw the hustle going on. And I said, "Ooh, baby, it's in my blood." I got to make some money. I got turned on by that. I like material things ... I love the hustle. I liked it because I was out there with friends partying.

Larry's primary enjoyment, however, is the money:

> I mean, everybody turns a trick if the opportunity comes on. Everybody. It's in your blood after a while. ... I enjoy the money. ... Sometimes, the sex is good too. I can get off on it. But, basically, it's the money.

The youth stress that prostitution is "easy money," with "easy" referring to the short duration of the sexual encounter as well as the lack of difficulty in performing such employment. The youth also like the absence of fixed working hours, leaving them time to "do their own thing."

When we explored other associated factors, we found that the primary reasons for engaging in prostitution do not correlate significantly with the variables of age, race, or family composition. There does appear to be a strong correlation, however, between homosexual identification and sexual gratification as a motivating factor; that is, those prostitutes who define themselves as homosexual are more likely to point to sexual gratification as a primary reason to engage in prostitution.

Another reason some youth engage in prostitution is to secure funds for purchasing drugs. This motivating factor can be seen from Larry's account of the first time he was arrested. Larry became a prostitute at age 14. He was living with his married sister and "hanging out" in Los Angeles on Santa Monica Boulevard when an older man (who happened to be a law enforcement official) approached him:

> He picked me up ... asked me how much I wanted for me to suck his dick. I was stupid enough to say "thirty bucks." I was desperate. I needed some drugs. I was really spaced in those days.

Few studies appear to have asked the youth their reasons for engaging in prostitution. Only James interviewed youth on this topic. Her data reveal that many youth engage in prostitution for economic necessity (36.2 percent). Almost as many others (25.5 percent) are willing to prostitute for money and material goods, and much smaller percentages engage in prostitution for curiosity

(8.5 percent), for excitement and adventure (4.3 percent), or to secure money for drugs (2.1 percent).[26]

Shick also arrived at some tentative hypotheses based on his research in Chicago. Although he did not query the youth directly on motivations, Shick suggests that youth engage in prostitution because they do not have to work very hard or every day, can spend a lot of time socializing, and have power over adults. The prostitution milieu satisfies their emotional needs by providing them with a supportive peer group. In addition, Shick found that prostitution provides a form of entertainment.[27] The Huckleberry House study suggests, however, that most youth hustle for money and survival needs,[28] although the Huckleberry findings may result from the composition of the research sample (primarily runaways).

Drug Use

Adolescent male prostitutes frequently use drugs while they are engaged in prostitution. Seventy-two percent of the youth in our study report using drugs while engaging in acts of prostitution. The reason most often given for taking drugs while prostituting is the enjoyment of "being high"—a view expressed by 88 percent of the users. Another reason given for using drugs while engaging in prostitution is to mitigate the "upsetting" or "scary" nature of their work (reported by 20 percent of the users), and some prostitutes use drugs to help them handle the tension of their work. As Jack notes:

> The thing I like the most is Quaaludes because they're a very strong downer. Whenever I take a Quaalude or a half a Quaalude, and then go out to hustle, it really calms me down. Because when I go out to hustle, it makes me really super nervous. I get really scared because no telling what these guys could do to you. They could come up with a knife or try to beat you up.

Drugs or alcohol are also employed to help the youth handle the loneliness engendered by the casualness of their encounters. This is aptly described by Larry:

> **Larry:** I try and block it out. The drugs had a lot to do with it. I think I could have made a career of hustling if I wanted to. But it's not really what I wanted. I drink too much. I had to have a little something to drink for every trick I had.
>
> **Interviewer:** So that drugs are really a way of making hustling pleasant?
>
> **Larry:** It can. That's why I don't think I'm cut out for it.
>
> **Interviewer:** But what was it about hustling that you found unpleasant?
>
> **Larry:** I was kinda lonely, because after a while it came to be like everybody was paying for it. I didn't have really anybody to hold on to. I got very lonely.

Drug use as a way of life accompanying prostitution often takes its toll on the youth. As Jack notes:

> Hustling gets really tired fast because there's so much [drugs] … you're so close to drugs, and junkies and speed freaks and everything. …

Some prostitutes learn better than others to manage their drug use while working. These youth learn to avoid drugs that interfere with their sexual performance and, conversely, to select drugs that maximize their performance. As Jack reports:

> Like when I'm on a Quaalude or something, then I have no problems like, getting a hard-on or telling them what the facts are, and how much they're going to have to pay me. Like when you're on MDA, you can get the trick and you can get him off in like a half an hour because you're so speeded. You can do just anything really fast. And then, some of them [drugs] are really fun to party on. But like with some stuff, from the speed in it, it can keep you from getting an erection. So that's not really very good to hustle with.

Several earlier studies have explored drug use among prostitutes;[29] however, they all report general usage patterns as opposed to usage specifically while engaged in acts of prostitution. Two studies indicate that male prostitutes are not significantly involved in drug or alcohol use,[30] but numerous other studies reveal contrary findings. Allen's study found that 29 percent are regular users of hard drugs (other than marijuana) and 42 percent are heavy drinkers or alcoholics.[31] In Allen's subsample of full-time street and bar prostitutes, he notes a high incidence of poly-drug abuse and drug dealing among one-third of these youth. He writes: "Prostitution was used by some to support their drug use, and, as their ability to earn money as a prostitute waned with age, drug-dealing became their major source of income."[32] From the Shick study, it becomes apparent that prostitutes are moderately frequent users of a variety of drugs—most often, on a daily basis, marijuana and alcohol. Furthermore, 24 percent of Shick's sample—but only 10 percent of the juveniles—had tried at least one drug intravenously; 10 to 15 percent are frequent users of intravenous drugs, commonly amphetamines and heroin.[33] Shick reports relatively few daily users of drugs other than marijuana and alcohol. Sedative hypnotics, amphetamines, PCP, and psychedelics are generally confined to recreational, periodic use.[34]

Similarly, in the Huckleberry House population of male prostitutes, the majority (83 percent) have tried marijuana, and most (77 percent) still use it.[35] Thirty-seven percent have tried psychedelic drugs, about 20 percent have tried stimulants, 33.3 percent have tried depressants, but only one had tried heroin.[36] Both the Shick and Huckleberry Project studies find that although many youth use considerable amounts of drugs, they do not identify themselves as having a "drug problem."[37]

Table 3–5
Number of Times per Week Prostitute Is Paid for Prostitution

Times per Week	Number of Youth (n = 79)	Percentage
Less than 1	7	9
1–3	27	34
4–7	27	34
8–14	8	10
15–30	5	6
More than 31	3	4
Do not know	2	3

Frequency and Duration of Prostitution

Data on the frequency with which adolescent male prostitutes engage in prostitution are generally unavailable from prior research. Our data reveal that more than two-thirds of the male prostitutes are paid for sex between one and seven times per week (see table 3–5). Only seven youth in the sample (9 percent) engage in prostitution less than once a week, and sixteen youth (20 percent) engage in prostitution more than once a day.

James also acquired some data on this variable by asking the youth how many days per week they work. She reports that most youth work often: 25 percent work daily, another 25.5 percent work 4 to 7 days per week, and 17 percent work 1 to 3 days per week. Most earn less than a hundred dollars per night. She also found that most have prostituted quite a long time: 27.7 percent for 2 or more years, 23.4 percent for more than 1 year, and 17 percent for 6 months or more.[38]

Frequency of prostitution depends on several variables, including the season of the year. Youth engage in prostitution more frequently during the summer months. This seasonal variation appears to be more marked in colder climates, but it is also apparent, though to a lesser extent, in climates without much seasonal variations. As one prostitute comments about July in San Francisco:

> For the past couple weeks it's been kind of hard. ... There's like hustlers stealing other hustlers' tricks. It gets funny out there. ... Hustlers are out there chasing each other [and saying] "Well, I'm gonna get this one. I want this one, you get to pick this one." There's more hustlers than tricks! 'Cause in the summer so many people come up from Hollywood and the suburbia towns. They figure, "Well, since everybody else is doing it, why don't I do it?" Pretty soon, you've got 500 people out there for three tricks.

This seasonal variation also affects the price. According to the principle of supply and demand, the greater the supply of prostitutes is, the less each prostitute can charge. Another factor affecting price is recent entrance to prostitution. Newer prostitutes are more eager for money and will undercharge regulars. In some cases, this undercharging occurs intentionally; in other cases, it occurs unintentionally because the newer prostitutes are still learning the price system.

Prior research has generally failed to study frequency—the number of times per week the youth actually engage in prostitution (rather than merely the days they are out on the street trying to attract customers). Only one other study, the Shick study, collected data on this variable. That study, which found average earnings per week of $200 to $300, estimates that the youth prostitute an average of eight to twelve times per week,[39] somewhat more often than the youth in our sample. Our observations and discussions with agency personnel who are familiar with the prostitution milieu indicate that the average income of the Shick sample is high. Perhaps the seasonal factor explains, in part, the higher frequency found in that study, since the data were collected during the summer in Chicago.

One problem that must be noted in any study of frequency is that prostitutes tend to hustle anyone, including interviewers. They may tend to magnify the number of customers and the number of times they engage in sexual encounters. Thus, self-reported frequency data must be viewed with caution. We attempted to minimize this problem by verifying findings through observational data and interviews with personnel of social service agencies that serve juvenile prostitutes.

Prostitution Locations

The majority of adolescent male prostitutes are street prostitutes. Virtually our entire sample (seventy-four prostitutes, or 94 percent) use the street as a primary business location. Street settings tend to be either in the downtown regions of metropolitan areas or in the gay neighborhoods. The youth hang out in these areas in front of restaurants or on street corners and wait for customers to approach them. Other popular locales for prostitution are parks and hotels. In resort communities, the beach, with its public toilets and game arcades, is also a prime site. Prior research has provided details of the cruising techniques used in these locations by adult male prostitutes.[40] The same techniques appear to be used by adolescents.

Restaurants also serve another purpose as a prostitution locale, as they may be frequented by prostitutes intermittently between acts of employment. Thus, they provide a place to rest and to gain sustenance when business is slow. One feature that many of these locations have in common is that waiting is a central activity; that is, at bus stops people wait for a bus, and at restaurants people wait to meet other people. Thus, these locations are conducive to youth hanging around for long periods of time without being conspicuous or coming to anyone's attention.

Learning the prime locations is one of the first items of knowledge a prostitute must master. Often, this process requires some trial and error. One youth described his entrance into prostitution while socializing with friends who are drag hustlers. Over a period of perhaps 7 or 8 months, he occasionally turned tricks (about three). Being on a downtown street corner and spending considerable time with friends who are prostitutes facilitated the acquisition of his first client. This youth slowly acquired the necessary knowledge. At first, the youth thought that "going in drag" was an essential aspect of attracting business:

I didn't think I'd be able to do it [hustling] because I wasn't into going in drag. I didn't know how to wear a dress or high heels or anything. And, I figured that since I was so young and everything, that nobody would want me. I used to just sit around and watch people. One day an old man came up to me and that was the first trick I ever pulled.

Early in his prostitution career, the youth was told by other teenagers that a local pornographic bookstore was a prostitution locale. At first, he considered this site as a possible location, but he abandoned the site after he decided the tip he had received must be an error. Some time later, when he needed money to return home following a runaway episode, the youth had better luck finding the right business location. He was told to frequent a major hotel in a wealthy section of the downtown:

I started hanging around Castro [Street] and then I ran out of money. I was talking to some people that I knew kinda well, and I was saying, "Well, now I'm stuck in the city and I don't have any money and I need to get back to Modesto, so how could I hitchhike back to Modesto?" They said "The best thing to do is go in front of the Prince Edward Hotel and go out and pull a trick and then you'll have enough money to go back to Modesto and come back to the city five or six times!" I asked them where is the Prince Edward, and they gave me directions. So I went down to the Prince Edward.

While there, the youth attracted a customer. The ease with which this transaction was accomplished made him say to himself, "... well, I could do this and stay here in the city and not have to go back [home] 'cause I made $50 just for that."

Knowledge about the best locations for prostitution can be acquired intentionally, when the youth specifically seek this information, or unintentionally. One youth described how he acquired this knowledge inadvertently:

[One day] when I was on Castro [Street], some of my friends drove by. ... They called me over to the car ... and they told me to hop in ... we was going to Polk Street. ... I had my little backpack with me and I was walking around

Polk Street and I was saying, "Well, why is everybody just standing around doing nothing?" And they said, "Well, we're making money dear." And I said, "Well, how do you do that? Show me how you make money." I go, "Am I dressed for it?" I was dressed fine for it, they said. I had my little backpack and they said, "You look like a little runaway," and [they] said, "That's fine." That's how I got introduced [to hustling].

Certain bars are also settings in which prostitutes can find customers. Twenty-seven percent of the youth in our sample prostitute in bars and discos. For juvenile prostitutes, this often means waiting in front of the bars, unless they have false identification to gain entry. Other methods of conducting business include advertising, using an agency or service, calling regular customers, and using a madam. These other means of prostitution are used by no more than 5 percent of the prostitutes.

When we attempted to correlate prostitution location with other factors, we found that youth who identify as heterosexual prostitute less in bars and discos than do gay or bisexual youth. Black prostitutes have a higher frequency of prostitution in bars and discos; twelve of the nineteen black youth in our sample are bar or disco prostitutes. Also, older prostitutes are more likely than younger prostitutes to prostitute in bars, undoubtedly because they have an easier time gaining admission to such settings. Younger prostitutes tend to congregate outside the bars in hopes of attracting customers.

A principle of graduation becomes apparent in juvenile prostitution; that is, some prostitutes graduate from street hustling to more organized forms of prostitution—such as becoming call boys. This principle of graduation has also been noted by the author of another study:

In the social hierarchy of the subculture, the street prostitute occupies the lowest level. It is on the street that most of these young men begin their activities in the world's oldest profession. Paradoxically, it is also where they end up—when youth has gone. The best hustlers are quickly graduated into the easier ranks of prostitution (call-boys or kept boys).[41]

These "graduates" become what we term vocational or avocational prostitutes, many of whom regard prostitution as a vocation and take a certain degree of pride in their work. They view their work as a profession, and they conduct business more professionally than street hustlers. They have regular customers who contact them, and they cultivate and service these customers in a manner similar to the cultivation of relationships in other business contexts.

Some vocational prostitutes work as call boys—a category that has received some attention in the literature on adult male prostitutes.[42] Caukins and Coombs note that these young men are usually the more successful prostitutes. They maintain that call boys are generally "good looking, well built, easy going, sexually versatile, dependable (a rare trait in male prostitutes), and well hung."[43] Adolescent call boys, like adult call boys, differ from other types of adolescent prostitutes in several ways: they command higher prices, their range of sexual acts is generally broader, and they tend to be less prone to violence.

In addition, call boys are able to avoid the dangers of the streets—police sweeps and potentially dangerous customers—as well as erratic work hours and unstable income. Being a call boy requires a certain amount of conscientiousness and organization, however, which many young prostitutes lack. The youth must keep records of phone numbers and client preferences, which often means keeping a notebook and not depending on memory. These skills are not consistent with the free-wheeling present orientation of many street prostitutes.

Jack, for example, is just beginning his career as a call boy. He has two regular clients, whom he met in the gay neighborhood. He did have a third regular customer, but his lack of organization led to the loss of this client. As Jack describes it: "I had another one [regular customer]. He's a taxi driver. But I lost his phone number. ..."

Call boys do run one occupational hazard that street prostitutes can avoid: regular customers sometimes become too intimate. A tenet of the profession is the maintenance of a certain psychological distance, and the youth must manage the dilemma of cultivating customers but maintaining this distance during the course of the relationship. If a youth cannot do this, he must make a decision—to enter into a more stable relationship with the customer (move in, or adopt the customer as a sugar daddy, for example) or to end the relationship. Young prostitutes generally are reluctant to terminate a relationship, as this means losing a customer, but they will take this step if necessary. As one youth recounts this occupational dilemma:

> I'm kind of hesitant about going with this priest again because he keeps saying "Well, when are we going to get married?" and "When are you going to move in with me?" I don't know what to do about him. I stood him up the other day. Usually after I stand them up once, they usually get the hint. But this guy isn't getting the hint very well. So I don't know what to do.

One feature that leads some prostitutes to become more professional is dissatisfaction with the lack of selectivity in regard to customers. When adolescents first become prostitutes, they accept any customer who approaches them, but some have difficulty engaging in sexual acts with unpleasant or unattractive customers. Jack describes his reactions after deciding to engage in prostitution.

> I went home with a guy. He was an older man. Disgusting! I walked around for two hours [afterwards]. I was disgusted. I mean I was sick, I really was. I didn't know what to think of myself. I really can't explain the feeling ... because I went home with this man, plus he was disgusting! Just to think about him ... he was a troll ... had a nice yacht. Gotta say he had money. That's about it. ... I felt disgusted. I think mainly because he was ugly. He told

me he wanted me to live with him and take me on this trip around the world. I told him, "No way." I said to myself, "Just get me out of here." So when he fell asleep, I just split. ... I like older men. I don't like someone around my own age. I like them about 25 to 35. I've been to bed with people 40 and 42, 45, but they have to have something ... not money or anything like that ... they have to have the looks, the personality. That's the number one factor I look at, and a nice body.

This desire for increased selectivity leads some youth to seek means other than street prostitution to locate customers. One method is placing advertisements, which sometimes enables them to choose the customer rather than having the customer choose them. One youth, for example, received numerous responses to his advertisement as a masseur. He winnowed out some customers through telephone conversations, and eliminated others when they presented themselves at the appointed hour.

The objective of a call boy is to maintain a supply of regular clients. Larry graduated to being a call boy after several years of part-time prostitution on the streets of Los Angeles. He decided to become more professional when he moves to San Francisco. He describes how he acquired his first customers in the new city:

I establish regulars, you know. When I stayed at the National [Hotel], I never really went out to Polk Street to hustle. I'd go out there and party and pick up tricks that way. Then I'd call 'em. For the first three months that I was here, that's the first thing that I established—my datebook.

If Larry is approached by a potential customer while he is "out partying," he tells the customer, "Look, you know, I'm out partying now with my friends. If you want to make it with my wallet, let's go [later], but don't insult me [now]." At the time of the initial contact, Larry asks for a business card or phone number. Later, he telephones the customer and negotiates the price and when and where to meet.

Call boys make contact with new clients either by being approached in social settings or by obtaining referrals from their friends. The latter method is preferred, since it minimizes the risk of dangerous customers as well as the potential of arrest. Larry describes how he is contacted by one of his current regulars, Rick:

... he called me because Ron, my friend, was tricking. He called me one night because he couldn't get in touch with Ron. Ron had been living at my place ... So Rick called me ... and I got a message and I didn't know who the hell Rick was. ... I was looking through my datebook and there were no Rick's in there. So I called him and he asked me if I did the same thing Ron did. I said, "Yes, of course. That's my sister." (Laughs) He set up an appointment with me and I said, "I'm a little more expensive than Ron ... The first time it's fifty bucks."

Larry now defines himself as a call boy, laughingly referring to his business as "Dial-a-trick." He arranges his schedule so that he engages in prostitution 3 days each week—enough to pay rent for the month. Then he spends the rest of the week partying.

Call boys have internalized certain professional values, one of which is that street prostitution is demeaning. As one youth comments:

> I cannot go out there anymore. I can't bring myself to go standing out there and be embarrassed by a bunch of idiots driving around in cars gawking at me. It's a waste of time, waste of energy, mental energy.

The necessary attributes of a call boy, in addition to good looks, organizational skills, and conscientiousness, also include the ability to cultivate clients—including cultivation of the mental as well as the sexual elements of the relationship. As one call boy noted: "You have to make them happy ... be pleasant company, don't rush them."

For call boys, success is equated with having clients who are "repeat tricks"—customers who call the youth regularly to ask for sexual services. Only if business is slow, or if it is part of the arrangement, do the youth contact the customer. The more professional call boys proudly say, "I never call a client!"

As mentioned earlier, another common method of prostitution is acquisition of customers through advertisements. One youth decided to place an ad together with two friends who were also prostitutes. Two of the three young men lived in the same apartment, so they placed an advertisement from which all three eventually obtained customers.

Some prostitutes place advertisements as a temporary means of prostitution. These youth place ads occasionally to secure customers "as a lark," rather than as a steady source of customers. As noted in chapter 2, Jack learned about this method of prostitution from a female friend. He drafted an ad offering services as a masseur and placed it in a small-town newspaper. He attributes his large response to the fact that he was the only male masseur listed. Despite acquiring customers this way, however, Jack continues to engage in prostitution on the street. In fact, he acquires most of his customers from the street and in bars.

For some youth, working from advertisements is a mark of professionalism. George, for example, graduated from street prostitution in Indianapolis to hotel prostitution in San Francisco and finally to advertisements. He began placing advertisements after finding hotel prostitution too time-consuming. He also abandoned hotel prostitution because he wanted to be more selective about customers. He notes:

I had some pretty good luck there. [But] I couldn't be picky enough. I couldn't pick out my clients like I wanted to and a lot of them did not treat me very well. Actually it was taking too much time. I got bored standing there for an hour before somebody finally, you know, got interested.

Also, George disliked the competition; he believes that he was more professional than many other prostitutes at the hotel.

Right in front of the Prince Edward where the men would stand on the corner ... they didn't seem to have a whole lot to offer someone. Too many seemed to be doing it just for the affirmation that they were worth something. It didn't seem like they were professional. It wasn't like they knew what they were doing. There were some that knew what they were doing and they seemed a little jaded to me. ... They were too "off the wall." They still had not much respect for their clients. In the many prostitutes that I've run across, there have only been a couple that I knew of, that I felt had a good attitude about it. I always thought the profession needed somebody like me!

Thus, after a few "dates" at the hotel, George decided advertisements would be less time-consuming, and he began placing ads in several gay newspapers. At first, a number of customers contact him. After several failed to arrive for prearranged appointments, however, he decided to improve his success rate by improving the advertisement. He decided to include a photograph in the advertisement and to elaborate on his hobbies. After trial and error, he chose one ad to run on a regular basis, which gives him "plenty of business."

Living Arrangements

Adolescent male prostitutes reside in a variety of living arrangements, but the majority live apart from their families. Only 18 percent of the youth in our sample live with their families. Most of the prostitutes live alone (35 percent) or with roommates and friends (29 percent); another 8 percent live with a male lover; and 3 percent live with a female lover. Black prostitutes appear more likely to live alone than do white prostitutes (58 percent versus 26 percent). Thirty-six of the prostitutes (46 percent) live in either houses or apartments, while 21 (28 percent) live in hotels.

Shick acquired comparable data on this variable by inquiring both where and with whom the youth live. Shick found that 19 percent of the youth live in a hotel, 23 percent with their families, 4 percent with a same-sex lover, and 3 percent with an opposite-sex spouse.[44] The only significant difference occurs in regard to the percentage of youth living alone; Shick reports a somewhat lower percentage than our findings (21 percent versus 35 percent).[45]

In addition, the prostitutes in both the Shick sample and our sample indicate that housing is the most costly of their various expenses.[46] It is also the most difficult need to satisfy. By and large, few adolescent prostitutes have long-term housing arrangements; the majority live in short-term arrangements with friends or customers. When they are desperate for a place to stay, many go home with a customer for the night.

Despite the prevalence of short-term arrangements, many prostitutes aspire to having a more stable residence, and many voice a desire for an apartment of their own. To obtain an apartment, however, they need to demonstrate to a landlord a stable source of employment. This may be an ineluctable obstacle for many young prostitutes; as one prostitute jokes, "You know, you can't put 'employment: hustler' on your [apartment] application!"

Involvement in Pornography

Much recent literature refers to the interrelationship between pornography and juvenile prostitution,[47] but there is no empirical research demonstrating such a relationship. Therefore, we attempted to discover the nature of the relationship between adolescent prostitution and the use of juveniles in pornography. To measure the extent of prostitutes' involvement in pornography, we sought information on whether the prostitutes have ever been photographed by a customer. We found that twenty-one youth (27 percent) have been so photographed, and thirty-three (42 percent) have not. (Information on the remaining youth is unknown.) No correlations are apparent between involvement in pornography and age or sexual identity.

One youth describes his experience of being photographed by a customer:

> I've had this one [customer]. He comes to see me every once in awhile. He's from New York, I think. All he likes to do is take 3 or 4 nude pictures of me. They're from these cameras where the picture comes out the bottom ... Polaroids. ... He gives me $40 for that. He says they're for his own personal use. He picks up other hustlers and does the same thing. He doesn't want to have sex, just wants some nude pictures.

Of those prostitutes photographed by customers, sixteen said they were photographed primarily for private collections, and seven indicated that the photographs were to be circulated among friends of the customer. Only nine of the prostitutes have been photographed by a "professional"; all nine were photographed for pornographic magazines. Five other prostitutes were photographed for movies. Three prostitutes first became involved in pornography at age 14; the others ranged in age up to 21 at the time of first involvement.

Several of the youth who have been approached by individuals to be in pornography have refused. Their reasons for refusing vary: the pay is insufficient; they find it "unprofessional"; they fear they will be identified back home; or they worry that they will not be able to sustain a sexual performance before a camera. Larry, for example, notes that he has been approached "a million and one times," to be in pornographic movies, but he has never accepted. When asked why, he replies:

> I don't know. It's kind of cheap. It's not a very tactful thing. ... There are a lot of cheap ones [operations] around. There are a lot of them that are just real tacky.

Nonetheless, the youth are often impressed by the amount of money that can be made. As Larry comments:

> I know a couple of people who've done it. And been well paid for it. They did it the right way. ...

The only other data on prostitutes' involvement with pornography was collected by James, who found that 10.6 percent of the prostitutes in her sample had participated in making pornography on one occasion, 4.3 percent on more than one occasion, and 2.1 percent several times. The largest category (42.6 percent) had never participated in pornography.[48] According to James's data and our data, it appears that involvement in pornography is not pervasive among adolescent male prostitutes.

Runaway Behavior

A subject of considerable interest in the literature is the relationship between runaway behavior and prostitution. Various studies have hypothesized a link between these two phenomena,[49] but empirical research has not explored this subject fully. Some attention has been paid to the relationship between adolescent female prostitution and running away,[50] but empirical research on adolescent male prostitutes has been nonexistent for the most part.

In exploring the relationship between these two social problems, we found a high correlation between running away and adolescent male prostitution. For purposes of this study, a runaway was defined as a youth under the age of 18 who is living away from home without parental permission. Data were gathered on the ages at which the youth left home. For nonrunaways, this age signifies the establishment of a residence away from home.

Table 3-6
Age at Which the Youth Left Home

Age (years)	Number of Youth ($n = 79$)	Percentage[a]
5–8	1	1
9–10	2	3
11–12	9	11
13–14	12	15
15–16	31	39
17	9	11
18–20	4	5
Unknown	11	14

[a]Percentages do not total 100 percent because of rounding.

Table 3-7
Reasons for Leaving Home

Age (years)	Number of Times Cited[a]	Percentage of Youth Citing this Reason
General family conflict	22	28
Family conflict over homosexuality or sexuality	19	24
Desire for freedom/adventure	18	23
Abusive family	12	15
Other	17	22

[a]Since some respondents gave multiple reasons for leaving home, the total numbers exceed the sample size of seventy-nine, and the total percentages exceed 100 percent.

As shown in table 3–6, sixty-four of the youth (81 percent) left home permanently before age 18. The average age at which they left home is 14.8; the median age is 15; and the mode of the distribution is 16 years of age. Thus, this distribution is skewed toward lower ages.

In attempting to determine whether age at leaving home could be correlated with other variables, we found that black prostitutes leave home slightly later than the population mean (at age 15.3). In correlating with sexual identification, it appears that heterosexual prostitutes leave home considerably earlier (at age 13.1).

We also explored the relationship between running away and certain demographic characteristics. One interesting correlation pertains to family composition: two-thirds of the runaways come either from homes with only one parent present or from institutions, whereas less than one-third (31 percent) of the nonrunaway prostitutes were raised under such circumstances.

We also examined the interrelationship between running away and such demographic characteristics as education and employment history. We found that runaways complete an average of one year less education than nonrunaways (9.4 versus 10.4). When running away history was correlated with previous (legal) employment, it appeared that runaways are significantly less likely than nonrunaway prostitutes to have been legally employed (23 percent versus 50 percent).

We also explored the reasons the youth gave for running away from home. As shown in table 3–7, general family conflict and family conflict over the youth's sexuality are the most frequently cited reasons for leaving home (25 percent and 22 percent, respectively). A number of youth cite a desire for freedom or adventure, while many left home, at least in part, because of an abusive family situation. It is not surprising that those youth who cited family conflicts over their sexuality are all nonheterosexual (gay or bisexual). Also, over one-third (35 percent) of the sexual minority subsample are runaways.

One surprising discovery of our research was the extent of the youth's involvement with prostitution before leaving home. Based on a prior literature review, we hypothesized that many runaways began turning tricks to be able to survive on the streets. On the average, we found that runaways experienced their first act of prostitution 1.5 years earlier than nonrunaways (age 14.1 versus age 15.6). The runaways in the sample also began regular prostitution at an earlier age than the nonrunaways (age 14.6 versus age 15.9). This correlation almost certainly results from the runaways' need for support—prostitution becoming the chosen method. This relationship is illustrated graphically in figure 3–2.

Our data reveal, however, that some prostitutes have prior experience with prostitution—that is, experience before leaving home. As figure 3–2 indicates, almost half of the prostitutes (43 percent) first began prostitution during the same year in which they left home. Of the remaining youth, over two-thirds had their first prostitution experience before leaving home. This suggests that a number of prostitutes have some initial experience with prostitution that precedes running away.

The relationship between runaway behavior and prostitution also emerges as well in the Huckleberry House study. A full 85 percent of the male prostitutes in that sample first started prostituting when they "were on the run, broke and needed money for food and shelter."[51] Only 10 percent of these youth started prostitution at a time when they already had a job and housing. On this basis, the Huckleberry House report concludes that, for most youth, hustling is "for survival, not luxuries."[52] The Huckleberry House findings on these issues must be viewed with caution, however, because they lack data on the age of the first act of prostitution and the age of the first runaway episode. Also, it must be remembered that the Huckleberry House sample was drawn from a runaway population, so that the correlation between prostitution and running away would naturally be high.

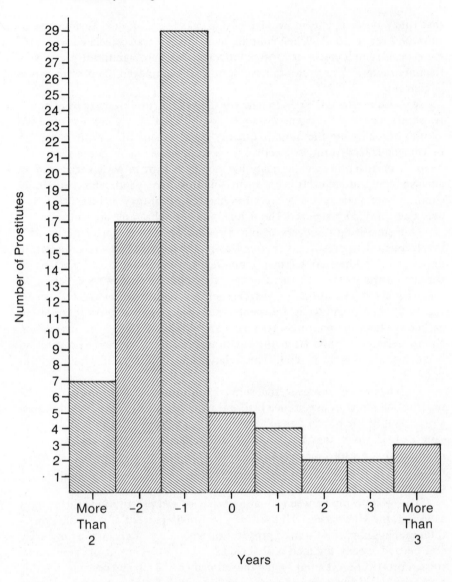

Figure 3–2. Time between First Prostitution Experience and Youth's Leaving Home

Several other interesting findings on runaways emerge from our study. We determined that runaways are more likely than nonrunaways to live in hotels (38 percent versus 18 percent). The hotels in the downtown sex-trade zones offer inexpensive lodging on a day-to-day basis, and these factors of low cost and immediacy of occupancy more easily satisfy the needs of runaways.

We also found that runaways are more likely than nonrunaways to say they use drugs while engaging in acts of prostitution because hustling is an upsetting or scary experience. Perhaps this is because runaways are somewhat younger than nonrunaways and thus less equipped psychologically to handle the occupational stress.

A comparison of our findings on runaway history with those of earlier studies yields interesting similarities and differences. Allen reports that approximately one-third of the male prostitutes in his study are or were runaways.[53] In Shick's subsample of nineteen male hustlers between the ages of 14 and 17, eight (42 percent) admit to being current runaways.[54] This figure is considerably lower than our findings (77 percent) and those of the Huckleberry House research (which indicates that "most" male prostitutes are either runaways or lack a stable living stiuation, with no percentages specified).[55] In another comparison, the mean age for the first runaway episode of our sample is slightly higher than that reported by Shick (14.8 versus 13.1), as is the median age of our sample compared to the Huckleberry House sample (15 versus 14).[56]

Our findings on the reasons youth leave home may also be compared with those of other studies. Family conflicts appear to be a common motivating factor cited by other studies. In the Deisher study, at least 42 percent of the youth left home because of some family conflict (assuming that the youth gave only one reason for leaving home).[57] The primary reason for running away given by the young male prostitutes in the Huckleberry House study is family tension (59 percent), followed by wanting to be with friends or their "own people" (18 percent).[58] Like our study, the Huckleberry research emphasizes that the two factors of family conflicts and the desire to be with people similar to themselves are related to the youth's sexual identification.[59] The Allen study, which also reveals a high percentage of runaways (one-third), does not provide a detailed breakdown on the factors precipitating the youth's departure from home.[60] That study does, however, note the presence of physical abuse and rejection as a result of the families' discovery of the youth's homosexuality.[61]

Gene's story illustrates the problems faced by many runaway prostitutes. Gene first ran away from home at age 14, taking a bus from his small hometown to the big city, and staying away from home for 3 days. As is typical of many runaways, Gene's runaway episode was impulsive and unplanned.[62] He left home with little money and only a few possessions packed in a suitcase. As he describes it:

> I had $35 of money that I'd saved up from babysitting for my sisters and everybody. I figured, well, "I have enough to support me until eternity."

Gene had few plans regarding where to stay on his arrival in the city:

I didn't know where anything was or which way to go . . When I got in the city, I was asking people how I could get to the beach, 'cause the beach is my favorite part of anyplace. And this black guy told me, "You mean the water?" And I go, "Yeah, the beach, the sand and sea shells, and stuff like that." He goes, "Just walk all the way down to the end of that street." And I walked all the way down to the end of the street and all that was there was the docks and ships, and no sand or sea shells or nothing, just all this black grease and some ugly dogs. So I figured, "Well, if I follow this water, I could find the beach." I walked for hours. ...

Some adolescent prostitutes also run away from foster home placements. Jack, for example, after being sent to live with his grandparents when his mother abandoned him, was sent to a foster home when his grandmother divorced his grandfather. Jack ran away from the foster home and spent the next few years shuttling between various group homes and juvenile halls.

The mere possibility of a foster home placement can trigger a runaway episode, especially if the youth has been in foster placements before. One youth who had previously been placed in a foster home had witnessed the foster mother physically abusing her two children, although she never beat him. His second runaway episode occurred when his mother told him she was going into the hospital to give birth and discussed with him the plans for his temporary foster home placement. Because of his prior unhappy experience in foster placement, he decided to run away.

Sometimes a youth stays with people he knows after he runs away. After Larry's mother died, for example, Larry want to live with his older brother. Because of conflicts with this brother, however, Larry left his brother's home to stay with friends for a time.

Some youth run away to live with a lover, or they may move in temporarily with a customer. Once they are on the run, the youth may encounter persons who attempt to use them sexually. Gene reports two such experiences he had during two different runaway episodes:

The first time I ran away I met this guy. ... He must have been gay or something. ... He asked me if I'd like to come over to his house to talk about why I ran away. ... He had a small hotel room and it was just, it was really nasty looking. It was the first time that I had ever seen a hotel room. It had a sink and a closet and this squeaky old bed. He had pornographic pictures of little boys that looked like they were about 12 years old on the walls. I just kind of looked around and said, "yuck." I figured, "Well, this guy's obviously gay or perverted or something." It made me have some suspicions but whenever I first came here, I figured, "Well, this guy can help me do something, and he was pretty nice when I was talking to him. ..."

We went to bed and I was just laying there and I couldn't sleep. He started putting his hand down my pants. I was sleeping with my pants on. ... I just acted like I was asleep and I ignored him. Then he just kind of rolled over and went back to sleep himself.

The sexual encounter Gene experienced during a later runaway episode was more violent:

> Another time, when I ran away, I was walking [down this street] and this guy in a triple-A truck, those trucks that help people when their car's all messed up, his truck was parked at the side of the road. He was in a phone booth, this was like four in the morning. He was like 6 foot and looked like he weighed about 300 pounds. I asked him where the nearest restaurant or bathroom was because I had to go to the bathroom really bad and he goes, "Well, hop in and I'll show you where it is." He took me to the Doggy Diner and then they said that the bathrooms were out-of-order or locked. We went driving around looking for another restaurant. We wound up driving by the park. ... Then he parked and we just sat there. I go, "Why did we park?" You know, it was all dark, just pitch-black, and I started getting scared. I had a little stick pin of a fairy in my coat. Then he grabbed me. He grabbed me by the neck and he goes, "Give me head, you fucking little white punk." I started screaming and I said, "No, no." He grabbed me by my head and he started forcing me down and then I just grabbed my little stick pin in my hand and I hit him with it. I lost the little bottom of it, but I still had the stick pin part. Then I hit him and then I opened the door with this hand and then I kicked it open with my foot and I jumped out. I started screaming and yelling and screaming and everything. He stayed parked there for a little while, but I started running. ...

Such sexual exploitation appears to be a common problem faced by many runaway youth.[63]

Involvement with the Juvenile Justice System

A significant number of adolescent male prostitutes are involved with the juvenile justice system. Approximately two-thirds of the youth in our sample (fifty-two prostitutes) have been arrested at least once. Among their offenses, prostitution-related acts were (33 percent) the second most frequent offense category for which they had been arrested. These findings are similar to those of the Huckleberry House and Shick studies. Seventy percent of the Huckleberry House sample report being arrested at least once, and 29 percent of these were arrested for prostitution.[64] Two-thirds of the Shick sample report being arrested at least one time, 5 percent of the arrests being for prostitution.[65]

It appears from our data that the younger the prostitute, the more likely he is to be arrested. Of the prostitutes 15 years of age and younger, eleven of twelve (92 percent) have been arrested. Only thirteen of twenty prostitutes aged 18 or older (65 percent) have been arrested.

Table 3–8
Offenses for Which Prostitutes Have Been Arrested

Offenses	Number of Times Arrested
Theft/shoplifting/robbery	29
Prostitution-related offenses	18
Status offense (runaway/truancy)	10
Assault	6
Drugs	5
Other	8
Unknown	1

Younger adolescents are more inexperienced in regard to learning the rules of prostitution. Specifically, they are less aware of methods of avoiding arrest; for example, they are not yet able to identify undercover officers by sight to determine whether a potential customer is a law enforcement official. Hence, they are more likely than older prostitutes to be arrested. (Although young prostitutes are more prone to arrest, their age does yield some advantages. Younger prostitutes are able to charge more than older prostitutes. In fact, youth is such an asset that many prostitutes attempt to look younger than their age. One youth reluctantly decided to shave his moustache to appear younger. Another youth, when asked his age, responded: "Lots of kids try to look really young so that they can ask for more money; I'm *really* 17.")

This susceptibility to arrest also applies to runaways. They, too, are generally newer arrivals on the scene, and are more inexperienced in the rules of the game—specifically, methods of avoiding arrest. Hence, it is not surprising that runaways also appear to have a higher risk of arrest (72 percent) than nonrunaways (46 percent).

Adolescent prostitutes are also involved in several other offenses. As shown in table 3–8, the most common crimes for which the young male prostitutes in our sample were arrested are theft, shoplifting, or robbery (accounting for 56 percent of those who have been arrested). Eighteen prostitutes (33 percent of those arrested) were arrested for prostitution-related offenses, ten for status offenses (running away, truancy), six for assault, and five for drug-related charges. Interestingly, all prostitutes arrested for prostitution are runaways. We also found that, of those prostitutes arrested, thirty-eight (73 percent) have spent time in juvenile hall and sixteen (31 percent) have spent time in adult jails. This latter finding may result because some prostitutes lie about their age to police because they believe they will receive shorter and more determinate confinement from criminal justice processing as an adult.

Our findings on offense type are somewhat similar to those of the Shick and Huckleberry House studies. Property offenses are the second most common crimes for which youth have been arrested (after drug offenses) in the

Shick study[66] and in the Huckleberry research (after status offenses).[67] Arrests for assault and drug-related offenses are roughly comparable for the youth in our study and those in the Huckleberry House sample. Shick finds a significantly higher percentage (16%) of arrests for drug-related offenses—16 percent,[68] compared to 6 percent in our study and 3 percent in the Huckleberry House research.[69]

Involvement with Social Service Agencies

Adolescent male prostitutes have a number of service needs, the most crucial of which are food and shelter. (This is especially true for the prostitutes who are runaways.) Their other service needs include medical care, drug treatment, job training, employment, and counseling for personal problems.

Although many prostitutes evidence a need for social services, the extent of their utilization of such services was unclear at the beginning of our research, so we attempted to explore this variable. We found that a high proportion of the youth had received services from a social service agency at some time in the past: fifty-one of the male prostitutes in our sample (64 percent) had received services from a social service agency, whereas only twenty-six (33 percent) had not. This large percentage may be attributed in part to sample bias, because many of the youth in our sample were contacted with the aid of agency personnel.

We also found that runaways are more likely than nonrunaways (70 percent versus 46 percent) to receive services from agencies. Younger prostitutes are somewhat more likely to be aided by social service agencies: 91 percent of the prostitutes under the age of 16, compared to 79 percent under the age of 17, had received services.

This greater utilization of services by younger prostitutes and runaway prostitutes may be explained by the increased vulnerability of these youth to street life and their inability to handle stress. It may also be that their youth and runaway status (that is, carrying all their possessions on their backs) makes them more visible to social service outreach personnel and to law enforcement officials who might refer them for social service intervention.

In correlating social service involvement with other variables, we determined that 65 percent of the white prostitutes received services from an agency, compared to 56 percent of the black prostitutes. In addition, a greater percentage of heterosexual male hustlers (83 percent) use a social service agency than do gay (61 percent) or bisexual prostitutes (52 percent).

Of the prostitutes who utilize a social service agency, most (54 percent) are served by a runaway shelter. Sixteen of the youth used a state department of social services, eight used an employment service, six used gay agencies, and ten used other agencies, such as clinics, church groups, or drug abuse centers.

Twenty-seven youth said they sought agency assistance to find housing, sixteen for job training and employment, twelve for counseling, and sixteen for other reasons, such as food, money, and drug rehabilitation.

We also asked about the youth's satisfaction with agency intervention. Overall, thirty-two youth (63 percent) report that they are satisfied with the services they receive, eleven (22 percent) are not satisfied, and eight (16 percent) are uncertain. As a group, the homosexual prostitutes tend to be more satisfied with the assistance they receive than are the heterosexual or bisexual prostitutes. Finally, 62 percent maintain that they would return to the agency if they needed assistance again, but 20 percent say they would not (another 18 percent are uncertain).

Our findings on social service involvement differ from those of research conducted in the 1960s but coincide with those of more recent research. Deisher's research, conducted in the 1960s, found virtually no male prostitutes who had any knowledge of, or contact with, public or private agencies.[70] In contrast, all of the youth in the Huckleberry House sample had contact with social services—seeking crisis housing (83 percent), employment counseling (69 percent), or individual counseling (55 percent).[71] This finding of a high degree of social service involvement is not surprising since the Huckleberry House study reflects the same sample bias as our study—that is, drawing respondents through social service agencies. Such respondents would be more likely to reveal a history of social service involvement.

Analysis by Prostitute Typology

Adolescent prostitution may also be explored by reference to the prostitute typology discussed in chapter 2. The typology categories are (1) situational prostitutes, (2) habitual prostitutes, (3) vocational prostitutes, and (4) avocational prostitutes. Situational prostitutes engage in prostitution only in certain situations; habitual prostitutes engage in prostitution as an integral aspect of street life; and vocational and avocational prostitutes regard prostitution as a profession and consider themselves professionals.

The majority of adolescent prostitutes in our sample can be classified as either situational or habitual prostitutes. Of the seventy-nine prostitutes, thirty-three can be classified as situational, thirty as habitual, ten as vocational, and six as avocational. Thus, 80 percent of the youth are situational or habitual prostitutes; and 20 percent are vocational or avocational prostitutes.

Although there was no significant correlation between the category of prostitute and the current age of the youth, a correlation can be noted between a given category and sexual identification. Most youth who define themselves as heterosexual may be classified as situational or habitual. The majority of vocational and avocational prostitutes identify as homosexual (a small number of these as bisexual). Some homosexual youth are also found among situational prostitutes.

These categories are also useful in analyzing the youth's family backgrounds, prostitution experiences, and criminal justice involvement. The young men categorized as vocational and avocational prostitutes come from higher socioeconomic backgrounds. Although family composition does not appear to correlate with prostitute category, a correlation with education is apparent. Habitual prostitutes complete fewer years of education than either situational or vocational/avocational prostitutes.

At the time of their first sexual experience, vocational and avocational prostitutes are generally older (13.1 years) than are situational prostitutes (11.8 years) or habitual prostitutes (10.2 years). Moreover, whereas 33 percent of the situational prostitutes and 36 percent of the habitual prostitutes were sexually abused at home, only 8 percent of the vocational or avocational prostitutes were so victimized. Similarly, more of the situational and the habitual prostitutes were physically abused at home than the vocational/avocational prostitutes (44 percent of the situational and 43 percent of the habitual versus 33 percent of the vocational/avocational prostitutes).

In terms of prostitution experiences, the habitual prostitutes begin fulltime prostitution at an earlier age (13.8 years) than do situational prostitutes (14.7 years) or vocational (14.5 years) prostitutes. Money is the primary motivation for engaging in prostitution among all categories of prostitutes. Whereas situational and habitual prostitutes more often are street prostitutes exclusively, vocational and avocational prostitutes are more likely to use informal networks to obtain customers. The incidence of drug use while prostituting is similar among all categories of prostitutes.

The typology also has utility in terms of the youth's runaway history and criminal justice involvement. Those who are classified as habitual prostitutes leave home at an earlier age (14 years) than do those in the other categories (15 years). A much smaller percentage of habitual prostitutes cite family conflicts over the youths' sexuality as a reason for leaving home (undoubtedly because a larger proportion of habitual prostitutes identify as heterosexual). Vocational and avocational prostitutes appear to be somewhat less likely to be runaways than are habitual or situational prostitutes; 67 percent of the vocational and avocational prostitutes were runaways, compared to 81 percent of the situational prostitutes and 87 percent of the habitual prostitutes.

In addition, habitual prostitutes are more likely to have arrest histories than are situational or vocational prostitutes; 80 percent of the habitual prostitutes have been arrested at least once, compared to 61 percent of the situational prostitutes and 56 percent of the vocational and avocational prostitutes.

Both situational and habitual prostitutes are more likely to have used a social service agency (67 percent) than are vocational or avocational prostitutes (50 percent). In addition, a higher percentage of situational prostitutes (84 percent) and vocational/avocational prostitutes (71 percent) report that they are satisfied with the assistance they receive from an agency than do habitual prostitutes (53 percent). The low satisfaction level expressed by habitual prostitutes mirrors the reports of agency staff that this population of prostitutes is especially difficult to serve.

Conclusion

Several characteristics emerge from this study of adolescent male prostitutes. Typically, the home situations of these prostitutes are unstable, their backgrounds often involving a considerable variety of caretakers and living situations. The youth are likely to experience physical abuse and, to a lesser extent, sexual abuse by family members. Family conflicts, particularly over the sexuality of gay-identified youth, contribute to many youth running away from home, and the unstable family situations and physical abuse also prompt many runaway episodes.

Thus, it is not surprising, given their relative lack of education and employment skills, that most adolescent prostitutes turn to prostitution within 1 to 3 years of running away. By age 16, most youth are prostituting regularly—between one and seven times a week. They engage in prostitution primarily for the money. Some, especially the gay-identified youth, also engage in prostitution for sexual gratification. Most of these youth are employed as street prostitutes, and those who can gain entry also work in bars and discos. Experimentation with drugs and regular use of alcohol and marijuana characterize their lifestyle. Involvement in pornography, though evident, is not pervasive.

Most adolescent male prostitutes have some contact with both the juvenile justice system and the social service delivery system. A majority, particularly runaways under age 15, have been arrested for theft offenses and, to a lesser extent, for prostitution-related and status offenses. Those prostitutes who contact social service agencies—again, primarily the younger prostitutes—have crucial social service needs for food, housing, and legitimate employment.

Notes

1. See, for example, Vern Bullough, *A Bibliography of Prostitution* (New York: Garland, 1977); Harry Benjamin and R.E.L. Masters, "Bibliography," in *Prostitution and Morality* (New York: Julian Press, 1964).

2. Allen notes that a survey of the *Cumulative Medical Index* for a 10-year period reveals that only 10 of more than 100 published papers on the subject of prostitution refer to males. In addition, he adds that a bibliography on male prostitution prepared by the Institute for Sexual Research at the University of Indiana (Kinsey Institute) lists only fourteen English-language references to male prostitution from the scientific literature. Donald M. Allen, "Young Male Prostitutes: A Psychosocial Study," *Archives of Sexual Behavior* 9, no. 5(1980): 400.

3. Michael Craft's research investigated thirty-three boys aged 15 and below who practice male prostitution. All subjects were drawn from the author's psychiatric practice in Wales. See Michael Craft, "Boy Prostitutes and Their Fate," *British Journal of Psychiatry* 122, no. 492(1966): 1111–14. Albert Reiss, a sociologist, studied 200 boys between the ages of 12 and 17. His sample was drawn largely from youth incarcerated in the Tennessee State Training School for Boys. The Reiss study focused on one type of adolescent prostitute—the juvenile delinquent who engages in prostitution as an aspect of a delinquent lifestyle. See Albert J. Reiss, Jr., "The Social Integration of Queers and Peers," *Social Problems* 9, no. 2(1961): 102–20.

4. For example, research was conducted by Caukins and Coombs ($n = 33$) in Los Angeles, by Ginsburg ($n = 30$) in San Francisco, and by MacNamara ($n = 37$) in New York City. Sivan E. Caukins and Neil R. Coombs, "The Psychodynamics of Male Prostitution," *American Journal of Psychotherapy* 30 (July 1976): 441–51; Kenneth N. Ginsburg, "The 'Meat-Rack': A Study of the Male Homosexual Prostitute," *American Journal of Psychotherapy* 21, no. 2(1967): 170–85; D.E.J. MacNamara, "Male Prostitution in an American City: A Pathological or Socioeconomic Phenomenon?" Paper presented at the 42nd Annual Meeting of the American Orthopsychiatric Association, New York, 1965.

5. Deisher's research on sixty-three prostitutes was conducted in San Francisco and Seattle. See Robert W. Deisher, Victor Eisner, and Stephen I. Sulzbacher, "The Young Male Prostitute," *Pediatrics* 43, no. 6(1969): 936–41; Patrick Gandy and Robert Deisher, "Young Male Prostitutes: The Physician's Role in Social Rehabilitation," *Journal of the American Medical Association* 212, no. 10 (1970): 1661–66. One study explored male prostitution in several cities, but the findings of that research have only been summarized in an abstract. See D.E.J. MacNamara, "Male Prostitution in American Cities: A Socioeconomic or Pathological Phenomenon?" *American Journal of Orthopsychiatry* 35(1965): 204 [hereafter cited as MacNamara, "Male Prostitution in American Cities"].

6. See, for example, Ginsburg, "Meat-Rack"; Deisher, Eisner, and Sulzbacher, "Young Male Prostitute" (interviews with street prostitutes in San Francisco's Tenderloin and Seattle's Skid Row area).

7. David J. Pittman, "The Male House of Prostitution," *Trans-Action* 8 (March-April 1971): 21–27.

8. Margaret Southwell, "Counseling the Young Prison Prostitute," *Journal of Psychiatric Nursing and Mental Health Services* 19, no. 5(1981): 25–26.

9. See, for example, Deisher, Eisner, and Sulzbacher, "Young Male Prostitute"; Gandy and Deisher, "Young Male Prostitutes"; Ginsburg, "Meat-Rack."

10. Allen, "Young Male Prostitutes," 401; Ginsburg, "Meat-Rack," 179.

11. Allen, "Young Male Prostitutes," 401.

12. Ibid. See also Ginsburg, "Meat-Rack," 179.

13. Allen, "Young Male Prostitutes," 401.

14. Ginsburg, "Meat-Rack," 179.

15. Allen, "Young Male Prostitutes," 409.

16. Caukins and Coombs, "Psychodynamics," 442.

17. Sparky Harlan, Luanna L. Rodgers, and Brian Slattery, *Male and Female Adolescent Prostitution: Huckleberry House Sexual Minority Youth Services Project*

(Washington, D.C.: U.S. Department of Health and Human Services, Youth Development Bureau, 1981), 12.

18. Ibid.

19. Deisher, Eisner, and Sulzbacher, "Young Male Prostitute," 939.

20. J.F.E. Shick, Personal communication, 11 May 1980.

21. Jennifer James, *Entrance into Juvenile Male Prostitution* (Washington, D.C.: National Institute of Mental Health, 1982), 43 [hereafter cited as James, *Male Prostitution*].

22. Ibid.

23. Ibid., 54 (based on an analysis of data on age at first sexual experience).

24. Harlan, Rodgers, and Slattery, *Male and Female*, 19.

25. On the intergenerational nature of abuse, see, for example, Robert M. Barehal, Jill Waterman, and Harold P. Martin, "The Social Cognitive Development of Abused Children," *Consulting and Clinical Psychology* 49, no. 4(1981): 508–16; R.J. Gelles, "Violence toward Children in the United States," *American Journal of Orthopsychiatry* 48 (1978): 580–90; R.S. Hunter, N. Kilstrom, E.N. Kraybill and F. Loda, "Antecedents of Child Abuse and Neglect in Premature Infants: A Prospective Study in a Newborn Intensive Care Unit," *Pediatrics* 61(1978): 629–35; Murray A. Straus, "Family Patterns and Child Abuse in a Nationally Representative American Sample," *Child Abuse and Neglect* 3(1979): 213–25.

26. James, *Male Prostitution*, 115.

27. Shick, Personal communication.

28. Harlan, Rodgers, and Slattery, *Male and Female*, 31–33.

29. Patrick Gandy, "Environmental and Psychological factors in the Origin of the Young Male Prostitute," Paper presented at the American Anthropological Association Meeting, New York, November 20, 1971; Harlan, Rodgers, and Slattery, *Male and Female;* MacNamara, "Male Prostitution in American Cities"; J.F.E. Shick, "Service Needs of Hustlers," Unpublished manuscript, Chicago, 1980.

30. MacNamara, "Male Prostitution in American Cities"; Gandy, "Environmental and Psychological Factors."

31. Allen, "Young Male Prostitutes," 416.

32. Ibid.

33. Shick, "Service Needs," 16–17.

34. Ibid., 18, table 6.

35. Harlan, Rodgers, and Slattery, *Male and Female*, 22.

36. Ibid.

37. Shick, "Service Needs," 18; Harlan, Rodgers, and Slattery, *Male and Female*, 22. (Only 13 percent felt they had a problem.)

38. James, *Male Prostitution*, 98.

39. Shick, Personal communication.

40. See, for example, Donald W. Cory and John P. LeRoy, *The Homosexual and His Society: A View from Within* (New York: Citadel Press, 1963); Martin Hoffman, "The Male Prostitute," *Sexual Behavior* 2(1972): 16–21.

41. Caukins and Coombs, "Psychodynamics," 442.

42. Ibid. See also Allen, "Young Male Prostitutes," 405–406; Shick, Personal communication.

43. Caukins and Coombs, "Psychodynamics," 444.

44. Shick, "Service Needs," 10–11.

45. Ibid., 10.

46. Ibid., 26.

47. Judianne Densen-Gerber, "Child Prostitution and Child Pornography: Medical, Legal, and Societal Aspects of the Commercial Exploitation of Children," in *Sexual Abuse of Children: Selected Readings* (Washington, D.C.: U.S. Department of Health and Human Services, National Center on Child Abuse and Neglect, November 1980), 77–81; Judianne Densen-Gerber and Stephen F. Hutchinson, "Sexual and Commercial Exploitation of Children: Legislative Responses and Treatment Challenges," *Child Abuse and Neglect Clearinghouse (NIMH)*, 3, no. 1(1979): 61–66; U.S. Senate, Committee on the Judiciary, *Protection of Children Against Sexual Exploitation Act of 1977. Report on S. 1585* (Washington, D.C.: Government Printing Office, September 16, 1977), 5.

48. James, *Male Prostitution,* 125.

49. Harlan, Rodgers, and Slattery, *Male and Female*; Shick, "Service Needs."

50. Enablers, *Juvenile Prostitution in Minnesota: The Report of a Research Project* (St. Paul: The Enablers, 1978); Diana Gray, "Turning-Out: A Study of Teenage Prostitution," *Urban Life and Culture* 1, no. 4(1973): 412; Harlan, Rodgers, and Slattery, *Male and Female,* 29; Jennifer James, *Entrance into Juvenile Prostitution* (Washington, D.C.: National Institute of Mental Health, 1980), 50; Frances Newman and Paula J. Caplan, "Juvenile Female Prostitution as Gender Consistent Response to Early Deprivation," *International Journal of Women's Studies* 5, no. 2(1981): 131; Mimi H. Silbert, *Sexual Assault of Prostitutes: Phase One* (Washington, D.C.: National Institute of Mental Health, National Center for the Prevention and Control of Rape, 1980), 92.

51. Harlan, Rodgers, and Slattery, *Male and Female,* 31.

52. Ibid., 32.

53. Allen, "Young Male Prostitutes," 410.

54. Shick, "Service Needs," 21.

55. Harlan, Rodgers, and Slattery, *Male and Female,* 27.

56. Shick, "Service Needs," 22; Harlan, Rodgers, and Slattery, *Male and Female,* 27.

57. Deisher, Eisner, and Sulzbacher, "Young Male Prostitute," 939.

58. Harlan, Rodgers, and Slattery, *Male and Female,* 27.

59. Ibid.

60. Allen, "Young Male Prostitutes," 410.

61. Ibid., 410–11.

62. James D. Orten and Sharon K. Soll, "Runaway Children and Their Families: A Treatment Typology," *Journal of Family Issues* 1, no.2(1980): 252.

63. Ibid.

64. Harlan, Rodgers, and Slattery, *Male and Female,* 25.

65. Shick, "Service Needs," 13.

66. Ibid., 13, table 5.

67. Harlan, Rodgers, and Slattery, *Male and Female,* 25.

68. Shick, "Service Needs," 13, table 5.

69. Harlan, Rodgers, and Slattery, *Male and Female,* 25.

70. Deisher, Eisner, and Sulzbacher, "Young Male Prostitute," 940–44.

71. Harlan, Rodgers, and Slattery, *Male and Female,* 43.

4
Adolescent Female Prostitution: A Review of Research Findings

lthough adult female prostitution has been the subject of considerable research,[1] less attention has been devoted to juvenile female prostitution. There has been some discussion of juvenile prostitution in research investigating the early lives of adult prostitutes and their entrance into the profession,[2] but such research typically provides accounts of only a small number of juvenile prostitutes. Thus, our knowledge of adolescent female prostitution has remained limited.

This gap in the literature has been partially remedied by a number of recent studies that focus on adolescent female prostitution. In the past decade, empirical studies in Houston,[3] Minneapolis,[4] New York,[5] San Francisco,[6] and Seattle[7] have explored the backgrounds and lifestyles of juvenile female prostitutes. A few additional studies have involved clinical investigations of young women engaged in prostitution.[8] These recent research efforts are based largely on interviews with prostitutes themselves, although an occasional study includes an analysis of official police and court records.[9] Respondents are drawn primarily from samples of prostitutes who have interacted with the criminal justice system[10] or the social service delivery system.[11] A few other studies rely on these respondents to some extent but also include prostitutes contacted on the streets.[12] Several of these studies include samples exclusively composed of juvenile prostitutes;[13] others contain mixed samples of adults and juveniles.[14] The research, all of which was conducted in major metropolitan areas, reflects a predominantly urban sample.

A review of the findings of these recent studies—both published and unpublished—provides a profile of adolescent female prostitutes along a number of dimensions, including the following:

1. *Background and family characteristics:* age, parents' socioeconomic status, race, family composition, history of sexual abuse and physical abuse.
2. *Entrance into prostitution:* age at onset, influence of significant others, feelings upon turning out, drug usage, residential situation, level of education at onset, employment at onset, motivations.
3. *Prostitution lifestyles:* relationships with pimps, relationships with and attitudes toward customers, violence, types of prostitution, attitudes about prostitution, attitudes about money, sexuality and sexual orientation,

physical and mental health, drug and alcohol use, future expectations and exit from prostitution.

4. *Juvenile justice system involvement:* runaway history, nature and extent of general arrest history, prostitution offenses (number and frequency), police and court dispositions, responses to incarceration.

5. *Social service agency involvement:* interaction with the social service delivery system before and after entering prostitution, service utilization patterns, prostitutes' perceptions of their service needs and service utilization.

Backgrounds and Family Characteristics

Age

Adolescent female prostitutes range in age from 12 to 18 years. James reports that the mean age for juvenile female prostitutes is 16.9 years,[15] but further data on age are scarce. It is particularly difficult to gather specific data on age distribution from the literature. MacVicar and Dillon, for example, state only that their sample includes ten adolescent and young female prostitutes,[16] but no age breakdown of the sample is given. Bracey states that a total of thirty-two prostitutes under age 18 were interviewed in her study,[17] but the reader must analyze case histories to determine the age breakdown of the sample. Even such an analysis reveals data on only one-third of the sample, however (five girls were 15, four were 17, one was 18); the ages of the remaining adolescents cannot be determined.

In some studies, the reader is able to glean information on the ages of the adolescent females indirectly by an analysis of other data. James's data on current grade level, for example, provide some insight: almost 7 percent of the sample ($n = 136$) is in grade seven (therefore, approximately 12 to 13 years old); 5 percent in grade eight (approximately 13 to 14 years old); 15 percent in grade nine (approximately 14 to 15 years old); and 18 percent in grade ten (approximately 15 to 16 years old).[18]

Regrettably, only three studies furnish a detailed age breakdown of their juvenile female samples. The Enablers research reveals that of fifty-two women aged 18 and under, six were 14 years old at the time of the interview, nine were 15, twelve were 16, fifteen were 17, and ten were 18.[19] In the Huckleberry House study, 3 percent of the adolescent prostitutes ($n = 30$) were 12 years old, 3 percent were 13, 10 percent were 14, 20 percent were 15, 27 percent were 16, and 37 percent were 17.[20] In Crowley's study of twenty runaway prostitutes, none were at either end of the age continuum (12 or 17), three were 13, three were 14, nine were 15, and five were age 16.[21]

One important question that the literature addresses but leaves unresolved is the youngest reported age for adolescent female prostitutes. The youngest prostitute found in any empirically based study is one 10-year-old respondent in Silbert's study.[22] Views on this issue are conflicting, however. Although Silbert interviewed one 10-year-old girl, another researcher maintains that, although it is not uncommon to find 10- and 11-year-olds attempting to "rip off" people in some fashion, these juveniles are not actually involved in prostitution.[23] Some findings that emerge conclusively from the limited data are that most juvenile prostitutes are older adolescents (ages 15, 16, and 17)[24] and that few adolescent female prostitutes are under 14.[25]

Socioeconomic Status

Adolescent female prostitutes come from all socioeconomic classes. Various studies report a predominance of different socioeconomic ranks, but this probably reflects the sample bias of the studies. Two studies note a prevalence of lower- and working-class backgrounds,[26] but both of these studies had small samples of twenty to thirty juveniles. Other research with larger samples reflects a more middle- and upper-class composition. In the Enablers sample (under age 20, $n = 57$), at least 26 percent of the respondents note that their father's occupation is "professional" or "proprietor."[27] Silbert reports that over two-thirds of her sample of 200 prostitutes are from families with average or higher incomes.[28] Slightly more of her juvenile sample (70 percent) are from families with average or higher incomes.[29] The families of James's respondents are also characterized by average or above-average income levels.[30]

Some studies note a new phenomenon—the presence of many affluent juvenile prostitutes. As James points out: "A group of juvenile prostitutes we have labeled as 'affluent and overindulged' is phenomenal in its rate of increase."[31] She explains that the inducements of prostitution for these juveniles are distinct from those for others:

> Along with succumbing to intense social pressure to be sexual and to measure self-worth in a direct relationship with money-making ability, middle-class life yields other conditions that make prostitution alluring. ... It appears that for them it is basically entertaining to dress up with your friends and go down on the street and con, cajole, and be the aggressor. The extravagant sensations from the illegality, projected immorality, and danger of prostitution is a relief from the neutrality of suburbia. ... It is like being offered your first joint of marijuana or trying out meditation. It is just something to do—another high.[32]

Race

Juvenile prostitutes come from many racial groups, but researchers overwhelmingly concur that the majority are Caucasian.[33] Of the prostitutes interviewed by James ($n = 136$), 61.8 percent are white, compared to 80 percent in the Enablers sample, 80 percent in the Huckleberry House sample, 69 percent in

Silbert's sample, and 50 percent in Crowley's sample.[34] Blacks comprise the second largest racial group for juvenile prostitutes. Estimates of black prostitutes include 25 percent in James's sample, 18 percent in Silbert's sample, and 12.1 percent in the Enablers sample.[35] The highest proportions of black prostitutes are found by Crowley (40 percent of her sample) and Gray (eleven of twenty-one prostitutes, or 52 percent).[36] These data appear to contradict the literature on adult female prostitutes, which finds a disproportionate number of black prostitutes.[37]

Native American and Hispanic juveniles sometimes engage in prostitution, but studies disagree regarding which of these two groups constitutes the third largest subcategory of juvenile prostitutes. In James's study, 11 percent of the female prostitutes are Native Americans, and 1.5 percent are Hispanic.[38] Silbert's findings are the converse: 2 percent of her sample were Native American and 11 percent were Hispanic.[39] This disagreement probably stems from the different population bases from which the two studies were drawn.

Apparently, Asian juveniles seldom prostitute. James and the Enablers report no Asians in their samples, and only 1 percent of Silbert's sample is Asian.[40]

Family Composition

Studies of adult female prostitutes report that broken homes characterize the women's family backgrounds,[41] and research on juvenile prostitutes has noted a similar finding. Researchers concur that about two-thirds of the prostitutes come from nonintact nuclear families.[42] James, for example, notes that 70 percent of her sample report the absence of one or more parents during their childhood.[43] The Huckleberry House research reports a similar finding: 53 percent of the females have divorced parents, and an additional 17 percent lived with mothers who have never married or lived with their fathers.[44] Sixty-seven percent of the Enablers study respondents (under age 20) report that their natural or adoptive parents are no longer together at the time of the interview.[45] In three-fourths of the cases in Silbert's study, one parent was absent from the household at least part of the time the girls were growing up.[46] Specifically, 39 percent were raised by their mother only; 4 percent by an adoptive guardian or foster home, 2 percent report by themselves, and 7 percent by a sibling, grandparent, father, or other relative (exact percentages for these last categories are unspecified).[47] Newman and Caplan report that, in their small sample of ten juvenile prostitutes, only one set of parents remains married. The fathers of eight of the ten girls and the mothers of six have been absent for all or significant portions of their daughters' childhoods, and four of these juveniles lived without both parents for substantial portions of their childhoods.[48] Bracey also finds that most juvenile prostitutes come from nonintact nuclear families. Six juveniles in her sample lived with a natural parent and a stepparent, another nine in single-parent families, three with relatives other than parents, and two in foster homes.[49] The highest percentage of juvenile prostitutes from broken homes—85 percent—is reported by Crowley.[50]

The studies differ regarding which parent is more likely to be absent. Whereas James finds that the absent parent most often is the father,[51] MacVicar and Dillon conclude that prostitutes are more likely to have experienced separations from the mother.[52]

There is evidence that parental absence in these cases is of long duration. In the Enablers sample, for example, 49 percent of those from broken homes report that the absence of one parent began when the respondents were age 5 or younger.[53]

Furthermore, large numbers of juvenile prostitutes report poor relationships with one or both parents. Gray notes that 75 percent of her subjects describe their home situations as "poor" or "very bad."[54] Silbert reports that only 19 percent of her subjects had a positive relationship with their fathers while growing up, and only 32 percent had a positive relationship with their mothers.[55] In Crowley's study, 25 percent of the juvenile prostitutes had a poor relationship with their fathers, and 42 percent had a poor relationship with their mothers.[56] The Huckleberry House research also finds that few female prostitutes have positive feelings toward their parents.[57]

Research suggests that the male parental relationship is more likely to be experienced as negative. Silbert, for example, found that 32 percent of the prostitutes in her sample report a positive relationship with their mothers, compared to 19 percent who report such a relationship with their fathers.[58] James concurs, finding that the juveniles in her study report more problems with the male parent;[59] 59.1 percent claim to have a positive relationship with their mothers, but only 30.9 percent report such a relationship with their fathers.[60] The Huckleberry House research found that almost half of the adolescents have negative feelings toward their father, whereas only 10 percent have negative feelings toward their mothers.[61] The Enablers research also notes that more females admit feeling closer to their mothers than to their fathers,[62] and the literature on adult prostitution has reported more negative and conflictual relationships with fathers.[63]

The literature presents different views regarding the influence of male versus female parental figures. Some sources suggest that the juveniles' relationships with their mothers are crucial. MacVicar and Dillon, for example, espouse the view that female prostitutes' mothers are inadequate and inappropriate role models, causing their daughters difficulties in development.[64] They suggest that the young prostitute idealizes her mother, forming an intense attachment with both preoedipal and oedipal features, denying the mother's defects, and retaining her as a good object. This idealization of the mother tends to break down in early adolescence, when the girl's increasing cognitive capacity makes the mother's defects more apparent. The girl then begins to be "bad" herself, while maintaining the mother's "goodness" and avoiding the feelings of depression, helplessness, and rage that loss of this image would entail.[65] Gibbens, however, notes that a common feature of juvenile female prostitutes is a strong attachment to the father, even if the father does not deserve or support such attachment.[66]

The problem with basing conclusions on the young prostitute's relationship with her father, as Newman and Caplan point out, is that little research attention has been devoted to the role of fathers in their prostitute daughters' development.[67] Newman and Caplan suggest that this issue is omitted in the literature partly because most prostitutes' families are headed at one time or another by a single female parent. After discovering that many of the juvenile prostitutes' fathers are absent, criminal, alcoholic, rigid, or disturbed, Newman and Caplan argue that the male parent is at least as important a role model as the inadequate female parent. They suggest that juveniles turn to prostitution in an attempt to obtain available, though inappropriate, father surrogates. In psychoanalytic terms, these juveniles have not worked through their unresolved oedipal issues, which typically reemerge during early adolescence; therefore, their adult psychosexual development is not successful.[68]

Another issue omitted in the literature is the influence of a mother who is a prostitute. A few studies reveal that some juvenile prostitutes have prostitute mothers. Newman and Caplan, for example, note that three of ten juvenile prostitutes in their study have mothers who are prostitutes.[69] James mentions, by way of anecdotal evidence, the case of a juvenile whose prostitute mother was subsequently murdered.[70] MacVicar and Dillon also note that one of the juveniles in their sample ($n = 10$) has a prostitute mother; they also note that other juveniles' mothers are promiscuous.[71] Promiscuity of the juvenile's mother has also been noted previously as associated with the development of prostitution behavior.[72] MacVicar and Dillon suggest an explanation of how such a mother may influence a daughter's choice of prostitution as an occupation; they theorize that the daughter's prostitution may be an acting out of the parent's prostitution fantasies or, in some cases, identification with actual parental promiscuity.[73]

The influence of a prostitute mother does not appear to have been given the attention it deserves, and it is an area that merits further research. Especially interesting would be an examination of situations in which mothers actually "turn out" their daughters, since some evidence of this phenomenon exists.[74]

An interesting conclusion that can be drawn from several studies is that the families of some adolescent female prostitutes show considerable instability. The data reveal that some of these juveniles experience many shifts in caretakers during childhood. Gray reports that several of the juveniles in her sample were raised by relatives when young, then reclaimed by their parents at puberty.[75] In the Enablers study, of the respondents whose natural parents were not together at the time of the study, most absences of a parent occurred when the children were 10 years old or younger; for almost half, the absences of one of the parents occurred when the children were 5 or younger.[76] The Huckleberry House research concurs that the vast majority of adolescent female prostitutes experienced shifts in caretakers during childhood; more than one-third of the group experienced caretaker instability before age 5.[77] Davis found that more than half of the prostitutes in her sample ($n = 30$) spent one year or more before the age of 12 separated from their nuclear family.[78]

Tragically, some juveniles have not had an important caretaker during their lives—neither mother nor father. The Huckleberry House project, for example, cited three adolescents in the sample who never had an important caretaker.[79] Newman and Caplan note that four juveniles in their study lived without both parents for substantial portions of their childhood.[80] A similar conclusion can be drawn from Silbert's findings that 2 percent of her respondents (five prostitutes) report raising themselves.[81] Further research is necessary to shed more light on this aspect of the family backgrounds of adolescent prostitutes.

Sexual Abuse

The literature contains numerous references to the correlation between prostitution and early sexual abuse, suggesting that one effect of incest or child molestation may be subsequent prostitution.[82] Most of this research focuses on adult female prostitutes through the use of retrospective analyses, but a few recent studies report data based on mixed samples of juveniles and adults.[83] Even fewer studies report data based exclusively on juveniles.[84] Because so little research has dealt exclusively with juveniles, the findings summarized here are drawn from the few studies of juveniles alone and the studies of mixed samples of adults and juveniles.

The literature focusing on this variable includes information on intrafamilial and extrafamilial abuse, rape, and first intercourse, in terms of incidence, perpetrators, duration, frequency, and short- and long-term effects. Whereas, until recently, research was limited to studies of samples of incest victims (revealing prostitution as one of the long-term effects),[85] research now exists that is based on samples composed exclusively of prostitutes. These studies of prostitutes have found that early sexual abuse is a common feature of their backgrounds.[86] The Huckleberry House study, for example, estimates that 90 percent of female prostitutes have been victims of sexual abuse.[87] This estimate includes both familial and extrafamilial victimization.

It appears that the most common form of early sexual abuse is incest. All studies report high estimates of incestuous experiences for prostitutes. In the Enablers study, for example, 31 percent of the respondents experienced early incestuous abuse.[88] Most perpetrators of familial abuse are father figures, including both natural fathers and stepfathers.[89] Other male perpetrators include foster fathers, brothers, uncles, cousins, and mothers' boyfriends.[90] Although researchers concur that father figures are the most frequent familial perpetrators, there is no consensus on whether the natural father or the step-father is the more frequent perpetrator.[91]

Little information is available on the frequency and duration of sexual abuse of young prostitutes. The few available studies support the notion that such sexual abuse begins at an early age, occurs with some frequency, and continues over a considerable period of time. Silbert found that the average age at which the abuse started was age 10, with some cases starting as young as age 3, 4, 5, or 6.[92] The Enablers study, reporting similar findings, notes that for nearly half the respondents, the abuse began at age 10 or younger, and in all instances by age 14. One-third of the young women who reported incestuous experiences admit being victimized more than three times.[93]

The sexual abuse of these children is often of long duration. The Huckle-berry House project notes that one of every three juveniles who are victims of incest was abused from age 7 until she ran away from home.[94] Silbert found that the abuse was repeated over an average of 20 months,[95] and she concurs that, in some cases, the abuse lasted until the subject ran away from home.[96]

Researchers have also pointed out that juvenile female prostitutes first experience intercourse at an early age. The mean age for first coital experience is approximately 12.5 years old,[97] and almost all juvenile prostitutes experienced first intercourse at age 14 or younger.[98] The age when regular intercourse began is approximately a year later.[99] In correlating first coital experience with race, Gray found that white juvenile prostitutes were more likely than blacks to have their first coital experience with a stranger or a casual acquaintance,[100] whereas black juvenile prostitutes were more likely to have had this first coital experience with a boyfriend within 5 years of their own age.[101] For some prostitutes, the first coital experience is with a pimp; for many, it is with a family member.[102]

One interesting conclusion to be drawn from Silbert's research is the existence of multiple perpetrators of sexual abuse. Silbert reports that the prostitutes in her study were abused by an average of two people each.[103] Elsewhere, she points out that two-thirds of the women were abused by a father figure, one-half by a relative, one-fourth by an acquaintance, and one-tenth by a stranger,[104] noting, significantly, that "the total percentage is more than 100% because of abuses by different people."[105]

Most research that explores the relationship between prostitution and sexual abuse concentrates on familial abuse, but prostitutes also experience early sexual exploitation by other acquaintances and by strangers. One study found that about 25 percent of the prostitutes had been sexually abused by acquaintances and a smaller percentage (10 percent) by strangers.[106] James found that 20.6 percent of her sample experienced early sexual advances by strangers and

42.8 percent by friends or acquaintances.[107] Such evidence confirms the commonly held notion about child sexual abuse—that the perpetrator is most often a member of the child's household.[108]

Research also reveals that physical force was a factor in a large percentage of sexual abuse incidents. Silbert found that some force was used in more than 80 percent of the incidents of juvenile sexual abuse[109] —physical force in one-fourth of the cases, emotional force in less than one-fourth (either threats or promises), and both physical and emotional force in over one-third of the cases.[110] Silbert notes that an average of four acts of forceful sexual abuse are reported per victim: in 61 percent of the cases, the girl was held down; in 48 percent, the man promised love or implied that the abuse was a show of love; in 44 percent, the man told the girl it was her duty and she should do it if she loved him; and in 31 percent of the cases, the abuser hit or beat the girl.[111]

James also notes the frequency of forceful sexual abuse, reporting that juvenile prostitutes are disproportionately the victims of physical force at the time of first intercourse.[112] Furthermore, she notes that, among adolescent prostitutes, 65 percent report a "forced/bad sexual experience" (sexual experience is defined as intercourse),[113] with most such experiences occurring at age 15 or younger. These experiences were perpetrated by fathers (23 percent), by other relatives (15 percent), by strangers (15 percent), and by more than one man at a time (23 percent).[114] In addition, James notes that more than half of her sample report being raped at least once in their lives. Of these, 36.2 percent were raped more than once, and 7.5 percent were raped by multiple assailants.[115] Data on adult prostitutes also reveal abusive childhood sexual experiences, including a younger age at first intercourse than for nonprostitutes and a higher frequency of rape during first intercourse.[116]

Some caution is necessary in interpreting the foregoing findings. Sexual abuse of children typically includes a range of sexual misconduct, from fondling to intercourse.[117] Ideally, to effect comparisons, researchers should use the same definitions of sexual abuse, but problems arise in interpreting findings because some studies fail to define the term *sexual abuse*[118] and others use differing definitions. James, for example, defines sexual abuse as sexual play by a significantly older person, whereas Silbert defines it as sexual activity forced on a juvenile.[119] Such definitional problems make it more difficult to generate meaningful comparisons.

Physical Abuse

Child abuse and neglect are widely considered common childhood experiences of female prostitutes. Two-thirds of the Enablers sample of prostitutes under age 20 admit being beaten by a family member,[120] and estimates in other studies are as high. Both James and Silbert report that 62 percent of their respective samples of prostitutes were physically abused, compared to 70 percent in the

Huckleberry House sample and 73 percent in Crowley's sample.[121] Slightly lower estimates are found in other research—for example, approximately 50 percent in Bracey's study.[122] Some studies mention that the juveniles also experience other forms of abuse; for example, 70 percent of Silbert's subjects report emotional abuse.[123]

A few studies provide data on duration and extent of abuse. The Enablers research reveals that 27.5 percent of those young prostitutes who were physically abused admit being beaten until they left home.[124] In James's sample, 21.3 percent report being abused "regularly."[125] Silbert reports that the physical impact of such abuse is severe: 47 percent were seriously injured (including broken bones, cuts, bruises, and concussions), over 90 percent lost their virginity as a result of the abuse, 68 percent received bruises, 51 percent suffered cuts, 5 percent became pregnant, and 10 percent acquired a venereal disease.[126]

The reported physical abuse was perpetrated by both fathers and mothers.[127] Some research also notes severe neglect by parents or guardians,[128] but none of the terms used by the researchers to describe a pattern of neglect are operationally defined.

Entrance into Prostitution

Age at Onset

Adolescent prostitutes first become involved in prostitution at an early age. Most researchers agree that the vast majority of juvenile prostitutes are under age 16 when they first engage in prostitution[129] and that the average age for the first act of prostitution is 14.[130]

Since age 14 is an average, it is apparent that some juvenile girls experience the first act of prostitution at quite an early age. The Enablers found that 11.1 percent were age 12 at the time of first involvement, 22.2 percent were 13, and 28.9 percent were 14.[131] Few data are available, however, on the involvement of juveniles younger than these ages. Silbert merely notes that "a number [of respondents] were under 9, 10, 11 and 12," without providing further details.[132] James's study provides some data on initial involvement of preadolescents, but these findings are not helpful since they are based on research exploring the age at which the juveniles "were asked to prostitute," without clarifying whether the juveniles did, in fact, start prostitution at that time.[133]

Data are also scarce on the period between the initial act of prostitution and the time the juvenile began engaging in regular (that is, full-time) prostitution. In one study that has explored the lag between age at initial act and regular prostitution, Silbert reports an 8-month difference between the average age at the initial act of prostitution and the average age of working regularly.[134] These data support the notion that not all prostitutes are innocent runaways; if this were the case, one would expect the initial act and the beginning of regular prostitution to occur at approximately the same age. Further evidence on this period between initial and regular prostitution would be most illuminating. If a time delay indeed exists, intervention at that point would be helpful.

Influence of Significant Others

The literature mentions the influence of numerous persons in the juvenile's entrance into prostitution, including friends, relatives, other prostitutes, pimps, and customers. The influence of these persons has been analyzed in terms of (1) making the female aware of prostitution and (2) introducing the female to prostitution ("turning out"). Most of the research concerns the latter aspect, but two studies have explored the influence of others in making the young female aware of prostitution. Having asked respondents how they first "heard about" prostitution, Silbert found that 14 percent mentioned friends, 7 percent cited "kids at school," 6 percent cited a neighbor, 13 percent cited a family member, 9 percent cited a husband or "old man," 11 percent cited other prostitutes, and 32 percent mentioned movies, books, and magazines.[135] James asked her respondents a similar question, and her findings are remarkably similar to Silbert's: 13 percent mentioned girlfriends and 12 percent cited other prostitutes; however, James notes a higher percentage of relatives as the influential persons.[136]

Friends. Friends play an important role in the juvenile's entrance into prostitution. In the Enablers study, 16 percent of the sample reported that, at the time they became involved in prostitution, they had friends who were already involved in prostitution.[137] In James's study, 13 percent responded that they first learned of prostitution from a girlfriend.[138] Bracey also provides data on this variable, finding that for 60 percent of the juveniles, the decision to become a prostitute was influenced by schoolmates, neighborhood friends, former friends who had left home, and new acquaintances (the exact percentage for each category was unspecified).[139] The Huckleberry House project reveals that 19 percent of juvenile female prostitutes learn about prostitution from friends or other youth on the street.[140] Silbert reports that 14 percent of the prostitutes in her study claimed they first heard about prostitution from friends; an additional 7 percent mentioned a related response, "kids at school."[141]

Relatives. For some juveniles, relatives are influential in the decision to enter prostitution. James notes that 23 percent of her sample first learned of prostitution from a relative,[142] and, surprisingly, 4 percent reported that they were with a family member at the time of their first act of prostitution.[143] Silbert reports a smaller percentage of prostitutes who first learned of prostitution from family members—13 percent.[144] For 4 percent of her sample, it was a family member who turned the woman out as a prostitute.[145]

The relationship of these family members to the juvenile is unclear from the literature. Gray notes one case of a juvenile whose sister-in-law was a prostitute,[146] and a few researchers report cases in which a mother introduced the juvenile to prostitution—MacVicar and Dillon[147] and Barclay and Gallemore.[148] Further research clearly is needed on this variable.

Pimps. The literature on adult female prostitution, as well as that on juvenile female prostitution, has emphasized the importance of the pimp in the entrance into prostitution. A large number of juvenile female prostitutes are influenced to turn out by a pimp; in fact, virtually all of the prostitutes in James's sample had been approached at some time by a pimp and asked to prostitute.[149]

Initial contact with the pimp occurs in various ways. Most frequently, the pimp initiates the contact. A less frequent method of contact is meeting a pimp through friends or relatives. In the Enablers sample ($n = 44$ prostitutes under age 20) 25.9 percent met their pimps through a friend or relative; in 2 percent of the cases, the girl initiated the contact; and in 35.3 percent of the cases, the pimp initiated the contact.[150]

Pimps use both psychological and physical coercion to persuade young girls to become prostitutes. James points out that the suggestion of prostitution and the attendant flattery by pimps affects a young girl's image of herself and her ultimate decision to engage in prostitution.[151] Bracey points out that the pimp's charm, flattery, and the promise of money, protection, companionship, and emotional closeness are enough to initiate girls into the world of prostitution.[152] Similarly, many respondents in the Enablers study reported being "conned" or "sweet-talked" into prostitution. A few indicated that they started prostitution because they were in love with the pimp and felt prostitution was necessary to maintain their relationship with him.[153]

Sources differ on the extent of actual physical coercion used by pimps to turn out young women. Case histories suggest that this method of entrance is common,[154] but empirical evidence fails to support this. The Enablers research notes that most women do not consider themselves forced into prostitution;[155] only 5 percent claim they were turned out because of a physical threat by a pimp.[156] Another study reports that only 4 percent of the subjects became involved in prostitution because they were threatened physically.[157] (It can only be surmised from this study that a pimp was the perpetrator of the threats, since the method of entrance is not broken down according to the persons who turned out the prostitutes.) Bracey is even more forthright in claiming that physical coercion is used infrequently: "Although we have heard stories of kidnappings and of totally innocent girls being raped and then 'turned out,' none of the girls interviewed claimed to know anyone who had been started in prostitution in these ways."[158]

Some research suggests that juveniles' involvement with pimps may differ from adult prostitutes' involvement with pimps, but the sources are not in agreement concerning the nature of these differences. Some researchers indicate that juveniles are more likely than adults to have pimps and more likely to be influenced by pimps to start prostitution. Bracey, comparing her findings on juveniles with those of a study of adult prostitutes, notes that only 10 percent of her juvenile sample claimed they had never worked for a pimp, compared to 28 percent of the adult sample.[159] Silbert found that in "almost all" cases of juvenile prostitutes, as opposed to "many" cases of adult prostitutes, a pimp or a woman recruiting for a pimp enticed the subject into prostitution.[160]

Some researchers report, however, that comparatively few adolescent females are involved with pimps. Newman and Caplan, for example, note that only five of the ten juveniles in their study work for pimps.[161] In James's sample, only one in three adolescent female prostitutes is involved in a relationship with a pimp.[162] James notes that a majority of the juveniles have been approached and asked to prostitute by a pimp, but most refuse—electing independence and rejecting the servility of the status as suitable only for "dummies."[163] James comments that this is an interesting reaction from young women who are "pursuing an antifeminist life with all the zealous ideals or independence associated with feminism."[164]

One possible explanation for this discrepancy in the reported extent of juveniles' involvement with pimps may be definitional problems. It is not clear from the research whether the interviewers use a uniform definition of *pimp* or, indeed, whether they define the term to their respondents. Moreover, comparisons are made more difficult because, as the Enablers discovered, some prostitutes do not perceive their present man as a pimp, even though evidence suggests otherwise.[165]

Other Prostitutes. Other prostitutes also play a role in a young female's entrance into prostitution, sometimes working as recruiters for a pimp. Thus, pimps influence the entrance into prostitution indirectly as well as directly, since one way for a prostitute to ingratiate herself with her pimp is to recruit other girls. Silbert found that in 20 percent of the cases in her study, the prostitutes were recruited by other women who were working for a pimp or a madam.[166] James notes the same method of recruitment, but she reports a smaller percentage who are asked to prostitute in this manner.[167]

Bracey explains why a pimp might use other women recruiters. She suggests, first, that this indirect method of recruitment is more safe (in terms of avoiding legal sanctions). Second, the pimp can thus save himself considerable time. Third, he can depend on an experienced prostitute to recruit girls who have the necessary qualities for prostitution. Fourth, experienced prostitutes are often more effective than the pimp could be, especially in recruiting young girls. Finally, the promise of friendship and companionship with other girls, more than romantic interest in a pimp, often makes joining a pimp's "stable" attractive to some recruits.[168]

Prostitutes who are not working for a pimp also influence some young women to turn to prostitution. Silbert found that for 7 percent of her respondents, the person who involved the female in prostitution was another prostitute (distinct from the women who were recruiting for a pimp or madam).[169] Also, it is possible that the influence of other prostitutes is even greater than the research indicates, because most researchers neglect to clarify the nature of the relationship when interviewees respond that "a friend" or "a woman" introduced them to prostitution.[170] The friend or woman may have been another prostitute.

Although we know that other prostitutes influence some women to engage in prostitution, the setting in which this recruitment occurs is not well studied. One setting is suggested by James, who points out that almost 21 percent of the adolescent girls in her study learned about prostitution after being picked up for running away and placed in detention or in a court-appointed home. While under court jurisdiction, the new recruits learned the fundamentals of prostitution from others who had prostituted or who had pimping experience.[171]

Customers. A few studies mention that customers influence some juveniles to turn to prostitution. The Huckleberry House project reports that 10 percent of the juvenile female respondents were introduced to prostitution by customers.[172] Silbert also notes that some of the women in her study—though fewer (3 percent)—were introduced to prostitution by customers.[173] She adds that the customer's usual mode of influence is to offer the juvenile money in return for sexual services.[174]

The Juveniles Themselves. It is important to note that, despite the emphasis in the literature on the influence of other individuals in the decision to enter prostitution, many young women enter prostitution on their own initiative. Silbert found that in 21 percent of the cases, the women become involved on their own.[175] In Gray's sample, eight of seventeen prostitutes reported that they turned themselves out.[176] In the Enablers sample, 13 percent claim they were introduced to prostitution by "self,"[177] and the same percentage in James's sample responded that they began prostitution on their own initiative.[178]

Feelings upon Turning Out

Several studies have explored the prostitutes' general psychological state just before they entered prostitution, and negative feelings are reported by many prostitutes. In the Enablers under-age-20 sample, 58 percent state that they felt "depressed," "unhappy," "lonely," "insecure," "not good," or "ashamed" at the time they first became involved in prostitution. Only 21 percent felt "good," "ok," or "neutral" about themselves.[179] Silbert's respondents also mention general psychological and emotional problems.[180] In addition, Silbert reports, 94 percent had very negative feelings about themselves: 21 percent felt depressed or unhappy; 16 percent felt rejected, isolated, and lonely; 15 percent felt inadequate or insecure; 14 percent felt confused, ashamed, degraded, or embarrassed; and 14 percent felt afraid.[181] Silbert adds:

> In addition to problems at home, almost total lack of positive social supports, and a strong push into prostitution via survival needs and deviant social networks, entrance into prostitution is marked by an extremely negative self concept and a depressed emotional state.[182]

Research has also explored the more specific issue of the prostitute's psychological state at the first act of prostitution, as opposed to her general psychological state at the time of involvement in prostitution. Most juveniles admit they felt "scared" or "nervous" when they turned their first trick. Some report having felt "degraded," "dirty," "bad," "terrible," or "sick." Fewer reflect that they "liked the money they got" the first time they engaged in prostitution.[183] James also studied prostitutes' feelings upon turning out. When asked about their mood during their initial act of prostitution, many adolescents (47 percent) responded that they felt fearful and scared, 10 percent admitted that they felt "happy/good," and another 10 percent said that they felt "sad/depressed."[184] These findings lead to the conclusion that most prostitutes have negative feelings about themselves prior to their first act of prostitution and that their feelings upon turning their first trick are generally fearful. The most positive feeling reported is an enjoyment of the money thereby acquired.

Drug Use During Initial Involvement

Although some literature exists on the relationship between adult prostitution and drug use,[185] little research has explored the use of drugs at the time of the initial act of prostitution, and findings in the few existing studies are contradictory. A majority (78.3 percent) of the prostitutes in the Enablers study (under age 20) admit using drugs at the time they started prostitution. Of those, 66 percent admit they were smoking marijuana, 42.6 percent were drinking alcohol, and 40.4 percent were taking amphetamines.[186] Silbert also found high levels of drug and alcohol involvement just prior to initial involvement in prostitution: 43 percent of the prostitutes were drinking alcohol, and 70 percent were using drugs. Of this 70 percent, 47 percent report using heroin; 50 percent marijuana and derivatives; 36 percent stimulants, amphetamines, "uppers," or speed; 26 percent cocaine; 12 percent LSD, mescaline, or other hallucinogens; 7 percent methadone, and 4 percent angel dust, or THC/PCP.[187] James's findings reveal considerably less drug use during initial involvement: 7 percent of her respondents said that they were high on drugs and another 1 percent were high on alcohol during their first act of prostitution.[188] Again, it is possible that the discrepancy may be explained by the nonuniform definition of drug use upon initial involvement; that is, initial involvement may mean the initial act of prostitution or the more general time frame of entrance into prostitution.

General Situation Before Starting Prostitution

Many juvenile prostitutes turn to prostitution as an answer to a variety of problems. At the time of initial involvement with prostitution, the living situations of many of these juveniles are unstable. Many have problems with school and are not otherwise employed. Since many are runaways, they are also plagued by financial problems involving food and shelter.

Living Situation. When the respondents in the Enablers study were asked about their general situation just before turning out, 13.3 percent stated that they were having problems regarding their living situation, and another 38.3 percent cited problems regarding running away.[189] Most reported that they were not living at home at the time they started prostitution: some were living in licensed residential facilities, and most others were staying with friends or relatives. The majority of these respondents under 20 (65 percent) and those under 18 (66.7 percent) admit they were runaways, either just before they started prostitution or at the time they were becoming involved.[190] Silbert reports an even higher percentage of runaways just prior to the start of prostitution (96 percent).[191] Gray also found that most juveniles had unstable living situations at the time they made the decision to engage in prostitution. She, too, notes that most were runaways from home or from a juvenile institution, and that a few were under parole supervision after spending time in a juvenile institution or were living on their own or in a foster home.[192]

As a result of their unstable living situations, some juveniles became involved in prostitution because of financial pressure. In the Enablers sample, 13.3 percent mentioned that they were having money problems before starting prostitution.[193] Significantly more women in Silbert's sample (68 percent) report having had money problems before their involvement in prostitution.[194]

Employment. It might be surmised that one reason prostitutes have financial problems is that they are not otherwise employed at the time they enter prostitution, and the data bear this out. Eighty-four percent of James's sample and 73 percent of the Enablers sample were not working at the time they started prostitution.[195] When the Enablers respondents were asked if they felt they had other options at the time, 71.7 percent stated that they felt they had no other ways of supporting themselves at that time.[196]

For the few females who are employed, prostitution is nonetheless an attractive occupational choice, since the other types of employment in which these women are engaged are neither glamorous nor highly remunerative. Silbert found that 62 percent of those women (juveniles and adults) who were employed before entering prostitution worked as domestics, salesgirls, or waitresses; another 10 percent worked as clerks and secretaries; 10 percent worked as models (mostly in the nude); 3 percent worked in nursing fields; 6 percent worked in social services; and 6 percent were housewives.[197] When the Enablers asked their respondents whether they would have started prostitution if they had been able to obtain a good job, 48 percent claimed they would not have started prostitution in that case.[198]

Education. Research data also reveal that most respondents, even though of school age, were not in school prior to starting prostitution. Although 78 percent of Silbert's sample were of school age at the time they became involved in prostitution, only 19 percent were attending school at that time.[199] The Enablers research reports high levels of truancy at the time of initial involvement in prostitution: 40 percent of the juvenile prostitutes either were not in school at the time they started prostitution or, if they were in school, were not attending regularly (20 percent).[200]

Motivations for Entrance into Prostitution

The literature on adult prostitutes provides a retrospective view of motivations for entrance into prostitution. James differentiates three categories of motivations discussed in the literature: psychoanalytic, conscious, and situational.[201] A variety of psychoanalytical motivations are mentioned. Early theories stressed the neurotic aspects of prostitution, such as the acting out of oedipal conflicts and the need to defy parental and societal standards.[202] Both Choisy and Greenwald have commented on the role of masochism in the psychology of the prostitute,[203] and Choisy points to unconscious atonement for guilt produced by incestuous fantasies.[204] Both Maerov and Hollender see homosexuality as a neurotic component of the motivation to enter prostitution,[205] and Greenwald views prostitution as an attempt to deny homosexual feelings.[206] Maerov attributes the motivation to engage in prostitution to frigidity,[207] whereas Greenwald cites the need to prove physical attractiveness through sexual contact with many men.[208]

Other psychoanalytic writers have claimed that the prostitute has a disturbance in her sense of self. Both Deutsch and Agoston discuss the "pseudopersonality" of the prostitute—her feeling that the role of prostitute is not her true self and her subsequent fabrication of a romantic story about herself, which she communicates to customers.[209] Hollender examined the two identities of the prostitute—the good and the bad—theorizing that they result from conflicting early identifications with two important objects.[210]

The conscious motivating factors are generally referred to by the literature as the economic circumstances that predispose women to prostitution. James says that "virtually all of the literature" mentions money as a motivating factor.[211] She cites two views of money as a motivating factor: (1) prostitutes are wretched creatures forced into prostitution by extreme economic deprivation, (2) prostitution is an occupational alternative that women freely choose because it affords them the highest attainable standard of living.[212] Some researchers suggest that prostitution offers alternative working conditions to so many "routine and confining jobs" in our culture.[213]

Finally, the category of situational motivations includes such factors as parental abuse, physical abuse, neglect, and poor relationships with parents.[214] According to several researchers, early life experiences, such as early sexual experience and traumatic events (for example, rape and incest), play an important role in causing women to turn to prostitution.[215] Low-status service occupations that reflect traditional female service roles, such as waitressing or tending bar, are also found to influence some women to enter prostitution.[216]

Psychoanalytic Motivations. Research studies on adolescent female prostitutes also discuss psychoanalytic, conscious, and situational motivations. Two studies examine juvenile prostitution from a psychoanalytic perspective, and two additional studies provide psychological analyses of juvenile prostitutes in other cultures. These last two studies yield data remarkably similar to the findings of the psychoanalytic research on prostitutes in our culture.

In their study of ten juvenile girls, Newman and Caplan present a detailed psychodynamic picture of stunted development at an infantile stage as a result of emotional deprivation, in which omnipotent rage coexists with a sense of hopelessness and a fear of abandonment.[217] With respect to ego development, the juveniles have few coping mechanisms, and those that exist are childlike. Feelings of emptiness and depression underlie boredom and anger. The need to avoid confronting the emotional abyss within themselves manifests itself both by keeping constantly busy and by runaway behavior. The juveniles' chaotic and emotionally impoverished early lives leave them insatiable for goods with which to fill their emptiness.[218] They are prey to pimps, whose praise reinforces the sense that their worth comes from being a sex object. In response to the pimp's praise, the girls adopt even more stereotypically feminine, passive ways, which do not help them find alternatives to prostitution and which reinforce their alienation from other women who might provide support to change their lives.[219]

MacVicar and Dillon conducted a clinical investigation of ten adolescent and young adult prostitutes. Three of these women were psychotic, with schizophrenic psychoses, and the remaining seven were nonpsychotic, with borderline character structures.[220] MacVicar and Dillon also found these women to be emotionally deprived. The defense mechanisms utilized by the women, such as splitting, projection, idealization, and devaluation, stemmed from impoverished and inadequate parental relationships, especially with their mothers.[221] The women manifested severe splits in the world of self and object; when idealization of the mother began to break down in adolescence, the juveniles began to be "bad" themselves, thus maintaining the mother's "goodness" and avoiding the feelings of depression, helplessness, and rage that loss of this image would entail.[222] Their entry into prostitution came soon after encountering a pimp, at a time when they were threatened with the loss of an important love object (the mother or a lover/spouse). Not being able to tolerate separation or feelings of emptiness and desperation, they formed a relationship with the pimp. This relationship was characterized by masochistic submission to an idealized object, manifesting a transferral to the pimp of longings for a union with the all-good mother.[223]

In his psychological study of juvenile prostitutes in Singapore, Wilson reveals several psychological traits of prostitutes in that culture that are similar to the foregoing findings. He notes, for example, that the juveniles feel inadequate, uncertain, and hostile, that they have difficulty establishing rapport and have a tendency to withdraw emotionally, that they are uneasy and suspicious and unwilling to take responsibility, and that they feel an emotional emptiness in their lives.[224] Whereas some manifest withdrawal and alienation, others manifest denial.[225] Many are overtly hostile, expressing resentment and dislike toward parental and authority figures.[226]

In his study of eighteen institutionalized juvenile prostitutes in England, Gibbens also explores the psychological makeup of juvenile female prostitutes, classifying the adolescents into three types: (1) intelligent but unstable girls, (2) borderline-defective wayward immigrants, and (3) girls who are normal in intelligence and stability but have some psychopathological characteristics in common.[227] Among those in the largest group (the first category), he found hostility and resentment. Among those in the third group, he reports a strong attachment to an inadequate father and some degree of unconscious homosexuality.[228]

Several noteworthy similarities appear among the foreign prostitutes in the Wilson and Gibbens studies and those in the studies conducted by MacVicar and Dillon and by Newman and Caplan. All of these sources comment, for example, on the juveniles' difficulties in relating to parental or authority figures; their hostility, rage, and resentment; their strong mistrust of human relations; their feelings of emptiness; and their childlike and inadequate coping mechanisms.

Economic Motivations. In addition to psychological or psychoanalytic motivations, research has also explored economic motivations. Research on adolescent prostitutes, like that on adults, points to the importance of economic circumstances; several sources note that financial problems often plagued the juveniles before they started prostitution.[229] Some researchers claim that many juveniles prostitute not only for luxuries but for economic survival. The Huckleberry House project, for example, found that most female prostitutes (75 percent) first started prostitution when they were on the run and in need of money to survive.[230] James writes: "The apparent reason for prostitution among adolescents is for economic survival and to meet other needs."[231] Undoubtedly, the economic motivations are especially applicable to runaways, who constitute a large percentage of prostitutes.

Not all juveniles engage in prostitution for survival, however. As noted earlier, some juvenile prostitutes are affluent, and some live at home and engage in prostitution even though their financial needs are being met. The Huckleberry House research, for example, discusses two juveniles who began turning tricks to make extra money even though they had a stable living situation,[232] and Bracey found a sufficient number of juveniles of this type to term them "weekend warriors."[233] James notes an increase in the number of affluent juveniles who engage in prostitution.[234] Thus, these affluent juveniles choose prostitution for other than economic motivations.

Situational Motivations. The majority of the research findings on adolescent prostitution concern situational motivations, including physical abuse and neglect[235] as well as poor relationships with parents.[236] Many sources point to the influence of early sexual experience and such traumatic events as incest and rape,[237] and a few sources mention early exposure to prostitution during childhood as playing a role in entrance into prostitution.[238] Truancy and school problems are noted by some researchers,[239] and a few studies mention problems with peers.[240] Finally, several sources cite running away as an important factor in motivating many juveniles to engage in prostitution.[241]

Prostitution Lifestyles

Once a young woman becomes involved in prostitution, her socialization begins, and she must learn to abide by certain norms and rules. These rules concern interactions with customers, such as obtaining the fee before providing services; interactions with the police, such as learning to recognize police officers and to avoid arrest; relationships with pimps, such as not dealing with other pimps and not showing disrespect to her pimp; and relationships with other prostitutes, such as warning other women about the police and not stealing another woman's customers. The rules also specify not interacting with "straight" people while working.[242]

A young woman measures her success in prostitution according to several indicators, including how much fashionable clothing and fine jewelry she has acquired, how few hours she must work, the amount of her earnings, and the type of prostitution in which she engages. Other indicators of success are related to the status of her pimp—his resources, his car, and the number of women in his employ.[243]

Relationships with Pimps

Pimps play an important and continuing role following adolescents' entry into prostitution. Although the literature on adult female prostitution contains considerable data on the adult prostitute–pimp relationship,[244] comparatively little information is available on juveniles' relationships with their pimps. Most studies of juvenile prostitutes have not interviewed the adolescents' pimps,[245] so the existing data are based primarily on the prostitutes' reports.

Pimps perform several functions for juvenile prostitutes: providing security, managing money, providing shelter and clothes, making them feel important, and furnishing protection.[246] According to prostitutes, the pimp also is "someone who cares about me," "someone who provides respect," "someone who makes an economic contribution," and "someone who provides drugs."[247] Gray agrees that adolescents feel they need a man to take care of business and to give them social status.[248] She comments that although, paradoxically, the prostitute is the financial provider, the prostitute–pimp relationship shows many similarities to conventional marital behavior. The pimp serves as the major decision maker, authority, and controller of the funds.[249] In return, the women provide him with emotional support and earn money for him.[250] An interesting finding that emerges from Silbert's research is that only 4 percent of her sample describe the pimp as someone they love. Furthermore, when she asked the prostitutes to name the advantages of having a pimp, a surprising percentage (41 percent) replied that there are no advantages.[251]

Pimps are particularly influential during the "apprenticeship" period, when the juvenile prostitutes are learning the rules of the game. Two-thirds of the adolescents in Gray's sample were explicitly briefed by the pimp (or by another prostitute—respective numbers are unspecified) on how to wash the customer, examine him for venereal disease, and persuade him to wear a condom. Approximately another one-third report being instructed by pimps (or other prostitutes) in techniques for avoiding the police, protecting against pregnancy, attracting customers, and locating "trick houses."[252]

One of the first lessons a young prostitute learns from her pimp is to turn over her earnings to him. Most juvenile prostitutes are expected to turn over all their earnings to their pimps, and in most cases the pimp expects the prostitute to bring in a certain amount of money each day.[253] Few juveniles report that they retain all their earnings; a few receive an equal share with the pimp, but most turn over all or a substantial portion of their earnings.[254] In return, the pimp buys them clothes and entertains them, telling them, in some cases, that he is saving for their future.[255]

Despite the importance of the pimps, most adolescent prostitutes do not maintain permanent attachments with them. Some juvenile females report working for more than four different pimps.[256] Sixty-two percent of prostitute–pimp relationships last 3 months or less, and 90 percent last less than 1 year.[257] Not only are these relationships short-lived, but they also are fraught with conflict. Although mutual attraction and affection often mark the commencement of the relationships, these feelings are soon replaced by hostility and fear,[258] some of which may be attributed to the violence pimps inflict on the prostitutes, as we will discuss later.

When the prostitutes in Silbert's study were asked to name the advantages and disadvantages of having a pimp, significantly more respondents reported disadvantages: 85 percent described the pimp as someone who takes money; 68 percent described him as someone who abuses them physically; 64 percent mentioned a loss of independence; 48 percent felt he makes them work too hard; 26 percent stated that he sets a quota; 21 percent mentioned the fact that he has other women as a disadvantage; and 13 percent claimed he is absent too often to provide protection.[259]

Various reasons are given to explain why juvenile prostitutes remain with pimps. Silbert maintains they do so because they feel they have no one else—no other place to go—and do not have a sufficient sense of control over their lives to move.[260] A primary reason prostitutes leave their pimps is that there are problems with the relationship. Another frequent cause is that they get arrested.[261]

Research on juvenile prostitutes notes several differences between juveniles' relationships with pimps and adults' relationships. Some research suggests, for example, that the pimp–prostitute relationship may be of shorter duration for juveniles than for adults.[262] The data also suggest that juveniles have different reasons for having a pimp. Bracey, comparing her data with James's data on older prostitutes, found that juveniles more often cite emotional reasons rather than business reasons for having a pimp.[263] Bracey suggests that this difference may exist because adolescent prostitutes are less concerned with their futures than their older counterparts are.[264]

Data on differences in the juvenile versus adult prostitute–pimp relationship may also be gleaned from pimps' attitudes toward working with juveniles and adults. Bracey found that pimps are more reluctant to work with juveniles, not only because they face more severe legal penalties by employing juveniles, but also because they feel the juveniles are not worth their time. Pimps feel that adolescents are volatile, undependable and troublesome: "Because they distrust the youngsters' judgment, pimps must check and follow these girls more closely than they do older women."[265] Therefore, they generally prefer working with adult prostitutes.

Customers

Our knowledge about customers of juvenile prostitutes stems from the adolescents' accounts. To date, no researcher has collected data by interviewing customers of juvenile prostitutes, although such data do exist on customers of adult prostitutes.[266]

The encounter with the customer (the "trick" or "john") is generally brief, usually taking less than 30 minutes from the pickup to the end of the transaction.[267] First, the girl attracts a customer on the street, and the pair agree to a sexual encounter (a "date") and reach an understanding on price and the services to be provided. They then proceed to a location usually designated by the prostitute (such as a hotel near the pickup site, sometimes termed a "trick house"). Often, the sexual acts take place in cars.[268] The prostitutes prefer to use taxis for transportation and to choose locations themselves to minimize the possibility of assaults by customers.[269]

When a prostitute and her customer arrive at the chosen location, the girl first washes the customer and examines him for venereal disease before having sexual intercourse. Generally, neither party disrobes completely. Afterward, they part company; often, one or both will return to the place where the encounter began.[270]

Young prostitutes just entering the profession work erratically and irregularly;[271] once they are committed to prostitution, however, they may work 5 to 7 days per week. Peak working hours are after 6 P.M., particularly on weekends, or after dark until 2 or 3 A.M.[272]

The prostitute's services are not confined to sexual intercourse. Other services requested are fellatio, cunnilingus, anal sex, intercourse with multiple partners, homosexual contact (with more than one female prostitute), sadomasochistic activities, urination or defecation, or use of obscenity.[273]

Adolescent prostitutes tend to prefer older rather than younger customers. This preference stems from their belief that older men pose less danger and are easier to rob.[274] Also, juveniles prefer foreign customers, especially Asian men and foreign sailors—again, because they believe these customers pose less danger and treat them better. Both black and white juvenile prostitutes are reluctant to become involved with young customers or black customers. They fear abuse from these customers and are afraid they will not obtain their fees.[275] Pimps sometimes warn them against accepting black customers, because the pimps are afraid of losing their prostitutes to another pimp.[276]

Juveniles who have engaged in prostitution for any length of time generally develop a clientele of a few regular customers (sometimes called "steadies"). In Gray's study, eleven of seventeen juveniles reported having at least one steady.[277] The prostitutes usually make contact with their regular customers by being at the same place at a certain time each week so that the customer can find them. The prostitute never initiates contact with these regular customers.

Adolescent prostitutes generally have negative attitudes toward their customers. When the Enablers study respondents were queried on their opinions of their customers, the most frequent responses were "don't like them, sick, weird," "fools, suckers," and "repulsive, hate them, pigs."[278] Few of the young prostitutes had positive responses.[279] It is interesting that adolescents' responses are considerably more negative than those of adult female prostitutes.[280] Gray reports that the juveniles are even reluctant to volunteer descriptions of their customers. She notes that the juvenile prostitutes give the impression that the customer is merely incidental or, at best "a necessary evil."[281]

These views of customers are frequently used by the prostitutes to rationalize robbing a customer, which appears to be a common occurrence. Almost half of the juvenile prostitutes in the Enablers study stated that they rob customers regularly or on every possible occasion.[282]

MacVicar and Dillon provide a psychoanalytic explanation for prostitutes' views of their customers. They theorize that the prostitutes view customers as debased and all-bad, having projected onto them the negative images once projected onto the women's fathers. Thus, customers are objects to be used and discarded. The prostitutes gain satisfaction from being admired, and they delight in having control over the man, in being able to trick him and take advantage of him (even, at times, by robbing him). The possibility of liking a customer or obtaining sexual satisfaction from him is unlikely, since this would threaten the prostitutes' conception of customers as bad, which helps the women hold on to their "good" self images.[283]

Violence

Violence from Pimps. Studies reveal that young prostitutes' lives are characterized, to some extent, by violence, which consists of physical abuse of the prostitutes by pimps and by customers. The Enablers report that in more than half of the prostitutes' relationships with pimps (often involving more than one pimp), the prostitutes claim to have been beaten.[284] Silbert reports that 66 percent of the prostitutes in her study admit physical abuse by pimps.[285] Bracey finds that of 23 adolescents, only three claim that their pimps would never use violence; the others assert that, given provocation, any pimp would beat a prostitute.[286]

Such physical abuse by pimps may be frequent. Silbert, for example, reports that more than half of her respondents are beaten regularly or constantly.[287] In the Enablers study, although beatings occur one or two times for most prostitutes, one-fifth report constant or regular beatings.[288] Physical abuse perpetrated by pimps may also be quite brutal. Gray reports that one juvenile was beaten with a 6–foot bullwhip, and another was tied to a car and forced to run behind it.[289]

Various factors precipitate the physical abuse, the most frequent being that the prostitute is disrespectful to the pimp.[290] Other factors include violation of prostitution rules, failure to earn enough money, departure or threatened departure, and expressions of jealousy.[291] Unfortunately, many prostitutes report being beaten by their pimp for no reason at all.[292]

Most prostitutes accept the violence as a way of life or feel they deserve it. Some are even flattered by it or accept it as evidence that the pimp cares for them.[293] Many juveniles accept the abuse with passivity because they are convinced that violence is the acceptable standard by which men and women relate. Since they grew up in families in which violence is a way of life, the prostitutes accept physical abuse as an intrinsic aspect of close personal relationships.[294]

Despite the verbal and physical abuse, many prostitutes feel that their relationship with the pimp is satisfactory. Gray found that some young prostitutes justify the abuse by considering it a necessary part of their training. These juveniles rationalize that being beaten by their pimp helps them learn the skill of hiding their anger when they are being taken advantage of by customers, so that they do not precipitate problems with the police.[295]

MacVicar and Dillon posit a psychoanalytic explanation for the prostitutes' acceptance of abuse by pimps, suggesting that masochism plays a role. Masochistic tendencies involve turning anger toward the self in order not to see the object (the pimp) as defective. In the prostitutes' longings for a union with the pimp, any defects, such as his sadism, are minimized and seen as irrelevant.[296]

Violence from Customers. Juvenile prostitutes also run the risk of being victimized by customers. One author suggests that the juvenile, who often is smaller and more vulnerable than an adult, is especially prone to this type of victimization.[297] A significant number of juveniles who have spent time on the streets have had frightening experiences with clients. The Enablers study found that most juvenile prostitutes have been abused or beaten by a customer: 40 percent admit it has occurred once, 25 percent "a couple of times," and 28 percent three times or more.[298] Besides physical assaults, victimization by customers includes nonpayment, robbery, and forcing the prostitute to perform noncontractual sexual acts.[299] The most common factors precipitating such abuse are mutual misunderstandings regarding sexual acts to be performed, failure to satisfy a customer, and refusal to perform requested sexual acts. In some cases, an assault of a prostitute is precipitated by her robbery of the customer.[300]

Prostitutes learn to take precautions against the possibility of such assaults; they learn to avoid traveling alone with the customer in his automobile and to avoid accompanying him to his residence. They prefer to do "car tricks" or to choose the designated site themselves and travel with the customer by taxi to the agreed location. Even experienced prostitutes may take chances, however, if a considerable sum of money is promised.[301]

Violence from Other Sources. Prostitutes are also vulnerable to violence from other sources. Being in possession of large sums of money makes the prostitute a potential target. Also, many prostitutes are subject to rape in incidents unrelated to their work, and these incidents often involve extreme violence.[302] The high incidence of rape among prostitutes occurs because many prostitutes work and live in high crime areas and work during evening and early morning hours, when they are prime targets.

One source suggests that juveniles may be especially vulnerable to such victimization. Bracey theorizes that muggers, especially drug addicts, see the young prostitute as a source of funds:

> Her youth and comparatively small stature indicate to robbers that she will probably not be able to fight them effectively. ... Any prostitute will hesitate to make a complaint to the police; a juvenile who may be a runaway will be more reluctant than an adult.[303]

Violence by Prostitutes Toward Customers. Not all acts of violence associated with prostitution are perpetrated by pimps and customers. Violence perpetrated by prostitutes toward customers is also a common feature of prostitution, and a significant number of juvenile prostitutes engage in such acts of violence. Half of the juvenile prostitutes in one study admit they rob customers regularly,[304] and many others report they rob customers "sometimes or often."[305] Many juvenile prostitutes exploit customers to increase their earnings. Acts such as accepting payment and then failing to perform requested services or stealing additional money from a customer after performing requested services (called "taking" a customer) are common among street prostitutes. Moreover, some juveniles are not averse to "cutting" a customer to get his wallet; this is done in reaction to a supposed insult or merely for the excitement involved.[306] From a psychoanalytic perspective, the prostitutes' view of their customers as debased and hypocritical makes it easier to take advantage of them.[307]

Types of Prostitution

Adolescents engage in several different types of prostitution, but most are streetwalkers.[308] Streetwalking appears to be both the type of prostitution in which the juveniles are first involved and the type they prefer.[309] Other types of prostitution in which juveniles are engaged, though to a lesser extent, are prostitution by phone and prostitution in bars, hotels/casinos, and saunas.[310] Sometimes, they are involved in several of these types of prostitution at once.

Attitudes about Prostitution

Several studies have examined prostitutes' attitudes about prostitution by asking them (1) what they like and dislike about prostitution, (2) what the advantages and disadvantages of being a prostitute are, and (3) what the positive and negative effects of being a prostitute are. Prostitutes feel there are both positive and negative effects of being in the life, and the primary attractions are material and social. For juveniles, social reasons are mentioned almost as frequently as material reasons, which lends support to Gray's hypothesis that the girls seek social reinforcement that is unobtainable in other realms of their lives.[311]

Most prostitutes report that money and material goods are the most attractive aspects of being a prostitute.[312] Prostitutes' attitudes about money clearly reveal its importance as a motivating factor, and prostitution becomes the means to fulfill the dream of the good life. As one prostitute comments:

> There is one thing about prostitution that I figured out by myself and this is most of the prostitutes are addicted to prostituting. I was living in a receiving home and then in a foster home. ... I needed the money ... when I saw all the money coming, I wanted to be so bad. ... I loved to look at it [the money] that was something.[313]

Another notes: "I said to myself how can I do these horrible things and I said money, money, money."[314] These views are not surprising in light of research on adult prostitutes, which commonly cites high income as the primary attraction.[315] Clothes and cars are additional material goods that the money can provide.

Among the other factors that attract prostitutes to prostitution are the chance to meet interesting people and broaden life experiences; excitement, adventure, and independence; and sexual knowledge.[316] They also cite the opportunity to become more experienced about people and life, to be more mature and responsible, to learn the value of money and how to handle money, to develop self-confidence, and to be loved by a pimp.[317]

Prostitutes are even more aware of the unattractive aspects of prostitution,[318] including both psychological and physical costs. They dislike the potential danger from customers, physical or sexual abuse on the job, venereal disease, and police harassment, jail, and legal expenses.[319] Prostitutes also recognize the psychological disadvantages of prostitution, citing lowered self-esteem and feelings of self-worth, feelings of shame and guilt, loss of respect, social stigma, rejection by society, becoming negative toward men and toward sex, negative effects on family relationships, bad working conditions (long hours, hard work), no future, and being controlled by pimps.[320]

The foregoing findings are based on studies of mixed samples of juvenile and adult prostitutes. In the few studies that explore juveniles' attitudes alone, differences emerge between adult and juvenile prostitutes; for example, adolescents are more likely than adults to dislike the physical nature of their employment. Gray's adolescent sample cited having intercourse with the customer as the most unappealing feature about prostitution,[321] whereas adults appear to bear this aspect of their work better.[322]

Juveniles' responses include considerable shame and fear, as evidenced by comments such as the following: "I don't like to talk to anyone about that"; "I don't want people to know"; "It's nothing I'm proud of"; and "I have no self respect, I feel like meat, but it's money fast."[323] Pimps often cause the experience to be especially frightening for juveniles. Furthermore, many juveniles fear what might happen to them if they remain in prostitution, especially beatings and drug abuse. They also fear the effects of continued prostitution on their physical and mental health. One juvenile commented that because of the "strange head trips people have," she wanted to stop prostitution before it got to her and before she "flipped out";[324] and a 14–year-old stated:

> The movies and television and books make you think it's glamorous. But you don't feel independent and wanted. You feel like a piece of hamburger meat— all chopped up and barely holding together.[325]

Juveniles apparently have a fatalistic attitude toward prostitution; "once a prostitute, always a prostitute" typifies their feelings of entrapment in the profession.

The longer a juvenile has been in the life, the more likely she is to become realistic about the unpleasant aspects of prostitution, whereas younger juveniles, and those who are new to the occupation, are more likely to report positive attitudes toward prostitution. This difference results because increasing involvement also increases the likelihood of arrest, incarceration, and assaults from pimps and customers.[326]

Money

As mentioned earlier, money and material goods are the primary attraction of prostitution to young girls. The juveniles are impressed with the amount of money they are able to earn and with the fact that they need little skill, training, and time to earn it. As they say, it is "easy money." Young prostitutes can earn from fifteen to fifty dollars per sexual encounter,[327] and some young prostitutes report earning an average of twenty-five dollars per customer, with four to eight customers per night.[328] Moreover, they are paid immediately and do not have to wait to receive a weekly paycheck.

It is ironic that money is such an important motivating factor for juveniles who engage in prostitution, because few prostitutes retain their money for long. Although their total earnings are large, most (if not all) of the earnings are turned over to the pimp. In addition, juveniles fail to accumulate money or assets; few have bank accounts, and they spend their earnings quickly. Most streetwalkers are constantly on the edge of financial crisis; they often are forced to rely on others for such things as bail money if they are arrested.[329]

MacVicar and Dillon present a psychoanalytic explanation of the young women's views of money, attributing the squandering of money (giving it to the pimp or spending it on entertainment, drugs, or clothes) to their need to rid themselves of the money:

> It seems that if it were put to more permanent use, its source, the customer, would have to be regarded as having some good attributes, as being worthwhile in some ways. This is a threatening idea since it would arouse intolerable feelings of rage, envy, and worthlessness in the woman.[330]

Sexuality

One disadvantage juveniles mention is the negative attitudes they develop as a result of prostitution. They come to mistrust people in general—especially men—and they become frightened of men.[331] Other attitudes engendered by prostitution are ambivalence and neutrality about sex.[332] One striking finding from Bracey's study is the young females' neutral attitude toward the sexual act; they neither like nor dislike it but view it only as a way of making money.[333] Although adult prostitutes are sometimes reported as neutral toward sex with a customer but positive with a pimp or boyfriend, juveniles seem to be consistently neutral about sex.

These attitudes of neutrality and ambivalence toward sexuality are evident in the following accounts. One 15-year-old spoke about the effect of prostitution on her attitudes: "Sex doesn't mean anything to me now. I'm not interested in guys or girls right now. Sex is boring."[334] Another young woman commented, in response to a question about her feelings toward sex, "It's ok, I don't like it all the time." When asked, "When don't you like it?" she answered, "When I'm not high."[335]

Some juvenile prostitutes recognize that they were not ready for their early sexual activity, stating that they did not want to become involved sexually as early as they did but that they felt pressure from their peers. Some juveniles admit that they really disliked having sexual intercourse when they began. As one juvenile commented, "First, when I started off with sex at 12 or 13 I didn't like it, I hated it."[336]

First Sexual Experience. One of the most significant findings about juvenile prostitution is the early age at which the juveniles had their first coital experience. The mean age for first coitus is 12.8,[337] which appears to be earlier than that experienced by the adolescent female population as a whole.[338] Also, entry into prostitution occurs about two years after this first coital experience.[339]

Juveniles face numerous problems in regard to their early sexuality. Sexual activity is often a factor in adolescents' family conflicts,[340] and subsequent events, such as venereal disease, pregnancy, or abortion, contribute to family tension.[341] The juveniles' sexual activities also bring them to the attention of the juvenile justice system and contribute to their being labeled as criminals. James notes that 50 percent of young prostitutes have been reported to the juvenile authorities because of their sexual activity.[342]

One consequence of this early sexual activity is pregnancy, which results because of the juveniles' erratic and infrequent use of contraception. Contraception by juvenile prostitutes follows a cyclical pattern of disuse, use, and misuse, and more than one-fifth of juvenile prostitutes fail to take any precautions against pregnancy.[343] When contraceptives are used, their use is so erratic as not to be effective. As is true for adolescents in general, this pattern of contraceptive use reflects an ignorance of physiology, an avoidance of the self as a sexual being, and emotional distancing from sexual activity.[344] Most adolescent prostitutes who do use some form of contraception take birth control pills,[345] but those who use the pill rarely are conscientious enough to ensure its effectiveness. Other forms of contraception, such as the diaphragm, are shunned because of the juveniles' reluctance to touch themselves in the manner required for insertion.[346]

Juvenile prostitutes reveal a shocking ignorance about sexuality, contraception, and venereal disease. Such comments as the following are typical: "If I don't have rubbers or other birth control I just sit down and push on my stomach and relax at the same time and 90 percent of the sperm comes out" and "I take two aspirins at night before I go to bed and that keeps me from getting pregnant."[347] More than one-quarter of juvenile prostitutes take no precautions against venereal disease, such as examining the customer or using condoms.[348] The remainder use condoms for protection, but only some of the time.[349] Also, some juvenile prostitutes do not know what an orgasm is or even that it is part of the sexual experience.[350]

As a consequence of their ignorance and haphazard approach to birth control, many adolescent prostitutes become pregnant. Half of juvenile prostitutes have been pregnant at least once, a significant number have been pregnant more than once, and almost one-fifth have been pregnant more than twice.[351] The average age at first pregnancy is 14.5.[352]

Some adolescent prostitutes have babies when they are little more than children themselves. One 13-year-old said she started prostitution because her pimp "offered to care for the baby. I needed money for the baby."[353] Early pregnancies occur in a surprising number of cases, one study reporting that 2 percent of juveniles were pregnant at age 12, almost 10 percent at age 13, and another 10 percent at age 14.[354]

Most adolescent prostitutes are aware of the possibility of pregnancy but seldom comprehend its reality. When they find themselves pregnant, they respond as if the pregnancy were happening to someone else or as if it would "go away by itself." Many of these juveniles become more realistic after one experience with pregnancy, but some still refuse to use contraception and believe that pregnancy could not happen to them.[355]

Homosexuality. A number of juvenile prostitutes have had some experience with homosexuality before they enter prostitution. In Gray's study, three girls reported homosexual experiences; these experiences were occasional contacts rather than sustained relationships. The juveniles' mean age at the time of the first homosexual contact was 13.7.[356] Only one of the three girls reported continuing homosexual contacts; the other two abandoned such contacts upon release from the correctional institution in which the homosexual experiences took place.[357]

In some cases, homosexual contact occurs as a part of prostitution. To excite a customer, some prostitutes, for example, engage in sexual activities with another woman at the customer's request.[358] The prostitutes tend to regard these activities as "business," however. The majority of prostitutes define themselves as heterosexual; few describe themselves as homosexual or bisexual.[359]

A history of juvenile sexual exploitation and rape appears to have a marked effect on prostitutes' sexual orientation.[360] As Silbert reports, of the 8 percent of her subjects who are homosexual, 60 percent were sexually exploited as juveniles.[361] Undoubtedly, these experiences also explain why some prostitutes describe themselves as asexual. Silbert notes that even more significant than the relationship between homosexuality and juvenile sexual exploitation is the relationship between asexuality and juvenile sexual exploitation. In her study, 14 percent of the respondents report that they are asexual; of these, 96 percent were victims of juvenile sexual abuse.[362]

Homosexuality and frigidity in the sexual relationships of adult prostitutes have been noted in the literature, and some clinical researchers describe frigidity as a typical attribute of prostitutes.[363] Several authors explain this frigidity as stemming from either denied or unconscious homosexual feelings.[364] Hollender hypothesizes that the homosexual orientation of two prostitutes observed during psychoanalysis results from an eroticized and dependent relationship with the mother.[365] The prostitute, he believes, remains in a homosexual position with the mother out of a fear of emotional, sexual intimacy with the father—the oedipal struggle subsequently being generalized onto adult relationships. Maerov's clinical study of twenty prostitutes also explores homosexuality, finding that the women tend not to experience orgasm with customers or pimps;[366] however, almost half of the women report that they can achieve orgasm more frequently in lesbian relationships.[367]

Some empirical evidence, however, contradicts the general assumptions about homosexual behavior and frigidity in prostitutes. Exner's study of ninety-five prostitutes and a nonprostitute control sample found no significant difference between prostitutes and nonprostitutes with respect to the incidence of homosexual experiences or the frequency of orgasm.[368] That study also notes a higher frequency of orgasm by prostitutes with noncustomers than with customers.[369] Fields suggest that since the single empirical study (Exner's) on these aspects of interpersonal functioning contradicts clinical observations, there is a danger in attaching too much credence to these observations. She cites a need for additional research in this area.[370]

Physical Health

Adolescent prostitutes suffer from various health problems. Their health is often damaged by exposure to inclement weather, inadequate diet, and contagious illnesses, especially colds and flu. A primary cause for frequent illness is inadequate clothing.[371] Although prostitutes tend to work less in winter than in summer, many adolescents do work during the winter months, and they find themselves inadequately clothed against the weather, especially since streetwalkers in coats, hats, and waterproof boots are unlikely to attract many customers.[372]

Poor diet and poor nutrition also plague young prostitutes. They devour junk foods, such as pizza, french fries, and shakes, not merely as occasional snacks but as the bulk of their diet. Rarely do the juveniles cook for themselves; they eat their meals and drink coffee in restaurants, often eating on the run.[373]

Venereal disease, another occupational hazard, is the prostitutes' most prevalent health concern;[374] half of the women have contracted venereal disease at some point.[375]

In case of illness, the adolescents rarely care for themselves properly. Staying indoors and resting while recovering from a cold is not an option, especially if they work for a pimp. One frequent source of prostitute–pimp disputes is the pimp insisting that the prostitutes work the streets despite their poor physical condition.[376]

Mental Health

Mental health data on adolescent prostitutes are scarce, and the limited data that are available generally refer to the incidence of suicide or suicidal attempts. Adolescent prostitutes have high rates of suicidal thoughts and suicide attempts. In one study, ten of seventeen prostitutes report having had suicidal thoughts at one time or another, and half of these ten actually made suicide attempts.[377] It has been suggested that, although these rates of suicidal ideation are high, they do not differ significantly from a delinquent nonprostitute sample.[378]

The prostitute is isolated and has few social supports. She has few interpersonal ties to people who can be relied on to provide emotional sustenance, assistance, and resources in time of need. Most prostitutes report having no friends.[379] Of those who do have friends, many of them are also involved to some extent in prostitution. The majority of people who are most important to the prostitutes are dependent on them financially and also are involved in various forms of deviant behavior (such as addiction).[380] The prostitutes' relationships with such friends are often of short duration, lasting about a year or less.[381]

Psychoanalytic studies of juvenile prostitutes reveal further information about their mental health. Newman and Caplan note that the juveniles struggle against feelings of worthlessness, that they feel helpless and unloved, and that they behave in submissive, passive-aggressive, and self-destructive ways, making suicidal gestures or expressing suicidal fantasies, using drugs, and running away from difficult situations.[382] With respect to ego development, these young prostitutes have few coping mechanisms; they alternate between challenging, demanding, imperious behavior, on the one hand, and tears, pleading, and childlike bids for attention, on the other. They also reveal intense feelings of emptiness and depression.[383]

In a psychoanalytic study of ten prostitutes, three of the prostitutes were psychotic and seven were nonpsychotic, although the nonpsychotic women had borderline character structures in which masochistic tendencies played a prominent part. The psychotic women's practice of prostitution could be distinguished from that of the others. These women prostituted themselves at the height of their psychosis, (schizophrenia with evidence of a thought disorder). The study concurs that prostitutes experience intense feelings of abandonment and emptiness. The resultant rage is often turned against the self in the form of depression and suicide attempts.[384]

Additional data on the mental health of prostitutes may be drawn from self-report data on the negative effects of prostitution. As mentioned earlier, the prostitutes most frequently cite such negative effects of prostitution as lack of self-worth, loss of respect, social stigma, feelings of shame and guilt, and development of negative attitudes toward self and others. One study solicited data by asking prostitutes to rate their self-concept according to a series of Osgood Semantic Differentials. The lowest scores the prostitutes gave themselves were for insecurity and for femininity.[385]

Drug and Alcohol Use

Drug use is common among adolescent prostitutes, and few can say they never use drugs.[386] They experiment with a variety of drugs. Most have tried marijuana;[387] and many are frequent marijuana users.[388] Half have experimented with psychedelic drugs, and many have used narcotics at some time.[389] In addition, most of these young prostitutes use alcohol, at least occasionally,[390] and a substantial number have been drunk frequently.[391]

Marijuana, rather than alcohol, is the first drug used by a majority of prostitutes, and getting high for the first time is a significant social event for these adolescents. Marijuana smoking is usually done with friends—at someone's home, on the street, or at school. The reasons for trying marijuana include curiosity and the influence of friends or relatives. Research has found that the prevailing mood of these young people at the time of initial involvement with drugs is depression or sadness.[392]

The frequency of drug use among young prostitutes is high; studies reveal that from one-fifth to one-half of them use drugs all the time.[393] A considerable number feel they have drug problems.[394] Another indicator of the seriousness of drug use among these juveniles is the length of involvement with drugs; the average is over 5 years.[395]

Estimates of juvenile prostitutes who use drugs while they work range from about one-fifth to two-thirds.[396] The prostitutes indicate that drugs relax them and make their work more bearable. They claim, for example, that drug use "takes your mind off what you're doing," "makes it bearable," "calms me down so I can go through with it," "makes me feel less miserable," and that "otherwise I'd kill myself."[397]

When asked who turned them on to drugs, most prostitutes mention their friends, but a surprising number of young women, particularly those from wealthier backgrounds, report being turned on by family members.[398]

One study of juvenile prostitutes reports that although they use drugs while working, they do not usually use hard drugs, because they feel more relaxed and outgoing if they use alcohol or speed. These young prostitutes are more likely to use cocaine and heroin for recreational purposes than while they are working. The exceptions to this pattern of drug use are the few adolescents who become heroin addicts and use this drug even while working.[399]

Bracey's findings on drug use differ from those of the preceding studies; she contends that the incidence of drug usage among juvenile prostitutes is low, since less than 20 percent of her sample report using drugs other than marijuana and none report alcohol.[400] Based on interviews with prostitutes and pimps, she disagrees with the view that prostitutes use drugs while working, and she maintains that drugs hamper rather than help a girl in her performance as a prostitute:

> An effective street prostitute has to "hustle" and she cannot work if she is "spaced out." Because most girls have developed an emotional neutrality towards sex, they do not need drugs to endure distasteful sexual experiences.[401]

The pimps Bracey interviewed (the number is unspecified) were unanimous in insisting that a good pimp does not need to use drugs to control young prostitutes, claiming that psychological coercion, combined with the threat of violence, is sufficient. One pimp claimed that any girl on drugs would be eliminated from his stable, because drugs are a drain on finances and reduce a prostitute's ability to earn money.[402] It is possible that Bracey's findings are different from those of the other studies because she does not make as fine a differentiation between types of drugs used. Also, her findings of low drug usage may be a result of her use of an open-ended interview, rather than a structured questionnaire administered to the entire sample, as in other research studies.

Only one study has compared the drug use of adolescent prostitutes with that of adult prostitutes, concluding that adolescents exhibit less drug involvement than adults, based on age and length of exposure to prostitution.[403] The study also compared adolescent prostitutes and a control sample of delinquents not involved in prostitution, concluding that the prostitutes are more likely than the other delinquents to have tried heroin, although none were addicted.[404] This study also contends that, for the most part, drug use follows, rather than precedes, involvement in prostitution. As a result, the researcher concludes, many juveniles may experience additional problems with drugs as their usage increases with their greater involvement in prostitution.[405]

Future Plans and Expectations

Some researchers have found that juvenile prostitutes tend not to think of the future. Bracey, for example, notes that "their lack of concern with the future was reflected in comments often made by the girls themselves; they neither do nor desire to plan for their futures."[406]

Although these juveniles may be present-oriented for the most part, some studies find that they do harbor future expectations. When asked what type of life they want eventually, the most frequent response (63.3 percent) was getting a good job; the next most frequent response was having children, followed by getting married and having a nice home or apartment.[407]

Data on future expectations may also be found in terms of the features prostitutes want to change in their lives. It is interesting that only a small percentage of the young women mentioned that they would like to stop prostitution. The most frequent responses were that they wanted to learn to deal with their feelings, to live on their own, and to have better family relationships.[408] When asked how long they had thought they would be involved in prostitution when they first started, 20.3 percent claimed "forever"; 20.4 percent said "I didn't think about it" or "I didn't know"; 54 percent stated that they no longer wished to be involved in prostitution; 27.1 percent said they wanted to stay in prostitution for a limited time or until a particular goal was met; and 6.3 percent said they would be involved indefinitely. Some admitted that prostitution would always be a possibility as a last resort during hard times.[409]

Bracey's findings are similar to some extent. For the adolescents in her study, the most common aim is job-related, such as owning a boutique or a beauty salon, and many expect their pimps to be saving money for them to be able to start such a business.[410]

Silbert's study reports a difference in how juveniles and adult prostitutes perceive their options, reporting that juveniles are more likely to express a sense of entrapment in a hopeless situation. More juveniles than adults feel that they have no way to support themselves because of their lack of education; they see no options because they are runaways or have a criminal record or because they are addicted to drugs.[411] Silbert concludes: "It appears from these data that the juvenile prostitutes, feeling trapped in their degrading life, are simply afraid to hope."[412]

Exit from Prostitution

Exit from prostitution is difficult, and research has explored the factors that enable a prostitute to leave the profession. Silbert asked current prostitutes which factors would enable them to stop and also asked former prostitutes which factors actually enabled them to stop. Current prostitutes mentioned increased alternatives—especially adequate employment—as a factor that would enable them to stop. They view the obstacles to their exit as being outside themselves (for example, economic need, lack of education).[413] In contrast, former prostitutes reported that a change in self and self-determination was the factor most often responsible for their leaving prostitution. In short, former prostitutes tend to take credit for their success, whereas current prostitutes attribute the failure to their environment.[414]

Involvement with the Juvenile Justice System

Prior research on juvenile prostitution, and indeed on prostitution in general, has focused almost entirely on entrance into prostitution. Early family experiences and motivating factors are subjects of considerable attention, but little or no attention has been given to the involvement of prostitutes with the juvenile justice system. Unanswered questions concern the nature and extent of prostitutes' criminal records, the nature and extent of their involvement in status offenses (especially runaway behavior), and the nature of police and court dispositions. Especially interesting is the relationship between delinquency, such as prostitution, and the commission of status offenses (such as running away and truancy), which is a much debated issue in the juvenile justice literature.[415]

Research on the arrest histories of juvenile prostitutes is complicated because of the multiplicity of charges involved. Juveniles who are arrested for prostitution are not always charged with prostitution, since police frequently use a variety of other charges in cases of suspected prostitution, including (1) loitering with intent to solicit, (2) soliciting to vice, (3) escape from custody, (4) violation of curfew, (5) absenting, (6) disorderly conduct, and (7) some violations of the health and welfare code (such as engaging in behavior considered to be detrimental to the health and welfare of the individual).[416]

A few recent studies have collected information on prostitutes' involvement with the juvenile justice system. These studies have utilized both self-report data and official records,[417] and several findings emerge from an analysis of these data.

Running Away

The considerable body of literature on runaways[418] suggests a relationship between running away and prostitution.[419] This relationship has been explored further in recent research on prostitution, which has focused on the incidence, frequency, age at initial episode and at successive episodes, and reasons for running away.

Studies of juvenile female prostitutes reveal that the majority are runaways, and researchers concur that incidence figures are high. Some studies report that all juvenile prostitutes in their sample are runaways. All respondents in the Enablers study (age 19 or younger), for example, ran away from home at least once;[420] Newman and Caplan report that all ten of the juveniles in their study have histories of running away from home, school, or foster homes;[421] and Silbert reports that 96 percent of the juvenile prostitutes in her sample are runaways.[422] Some studies report lower, though still dramatic, estimates. More than 75 percent of the prostitutes in James's sample report involvement in runaway episodes,[423] and Gray claims, based on James's data, that eleven of seventeen girls (or 64 percent) are runaways, either from home or from an institution, at the time they begin prostitution.[424] In short, even the lowest reported incidence figures are rather high.

Frequency of Running Away. Less information is available on the frequency of running away for adolescent prostitutes. Newman and Caplan, for example, report only that most juvenile prostitutes they studied are in detention because of "frequent running away."[425] More information is provided by James's study, in which she reports that almost 17 percent of her sample run away once or twice; 31.2 percent run away occasionally; and 52.9 percent run away regularly.[426] James's statistics on juveniles who run away most frequently approximate the incidence figures in the Huckleberry House research, which reports that 63 percent of prostitutes run away "frequently"—defined as three times or more.[427]

Age upon Running Away. All runaway prostitutes in the Enablers study (age 19 or younger) had left home once by age 16. The vast majority (80 percent) had left home by age 14 or younger.[428] Silbert reports that the average age of leaving home permanently is 14, and many of the runaway youth are as young as 9 or 10.[429] Some evidence suggests that runaway behavior begins at a very young age. The Huckleberry House project found that 62 percent of runaway prostitutes run away at age 13 or younger.[430] Early ages for involvement in running away are also reported by James, who reports that 11 percent are "involved" in running away before age 12, 15.4 percent at age 12, and 23.5 percent at age 13.[431] Her data do not clarify, however, whether involvement signifies the initial episode.

Some data are available concerning the duration of runaway episodes and the distance traveled. Crowley found that most juvenile prostitutes are away from home 1 to 6 months during their runaway episodes, compared to most runaway nonprostitutes, who are away from 10 days to 1 month.[432] The Huckleberry House study notes that 57 percent of the young females in their sample have been away from home more than 1 month, and half have spent a cumulative time of more than 6 months on their own.[433]

Crowley also collected data on the distance the juveniles traveled during their latest runaway episodes, finding that the majority of the runaway prostitutes, as well as the nonprostitute runaways, traveled locally upon running away[434] and that 20 percent traveled interstate.[435] These findings contradict those of the Huckleberry House project, which reports that 57 percent of female prostitutes travel out of their guardian's state of residence when they run away.[436] More research is needed on this variable.

Where They Stay. Some data are available on the juvenile prostitutes' living situation following runaway episodes. The Enablers research reveals that when these adolescents leave home, the majority stay with friends; 12 percent stay in residential facilities; 7.7 percent stay with a relative; and 9.6 percent stay with a stranger.[437] Crowley found, similarly, that most runaway prostitutes stay with friends, but she also notes that a significant number stay with strangers. After comparing runaway prostitutes with a sample of nonprostitute runaways, Crowley asserts that prostitutes are more likely than nonprostitute runaways to reside with strangers during runaway episodes.[438]

Data on running away are also available from research findings on juvenile justice involvement, since many youth first come into contact with the law because of their running away. In the Enablers study, 27.9 percent report that their first arrest was for running away.[439]

Reasons. Research on adolescent prostitution suggests several factors that contribute to a young girl's running away from home. James cites "dispute with family" as one of two major reasons for leaving home,[440] and more than 75 percent of the Enablers sample mentioned some type of family conflict as a reason for leaving home;[441] 52 percent cited general conflict, 25 percent noted a

specific conflict, and another 8.3 percent mentioned a related reason—
"fighting."[442] Crowley's data reveal that nine of nineteen juvenile prostitutes
(47 percent) cited "personality conflicts" as a major reason for running away
from home.[443] These findings are not surprising in view of other data on the
quality of the relationships experienced by prostitutes with their parents.[444]

Abuse is the second major reason for juvenile prostitutes to leave home.
Silbert, for example, notes that 8.3 percent of the prostitutes in her study left
home because of physical abuse.[445] Crowley concurs, finding that ten of nineteen juveniles in her study ran away because of physical and sexual abuse (the
respective percentages are unspecified).[446]

Some runaway prostitutes are "throwaways" rather than runaways. In
noting the difference between the terms, Bracey says that "throwaway" does
not apply to a juvenile who no longer lives with her family because the family
no longer exists;[447] rather, in a surprising number of cases, the juvenile's family
has abandoned her or has thrown her out of the house. Silbert reports that 9
percent of the prostitutes in her study left home because they were rejected.[448]
Bracey also reports several juveniles whose families disintegrated around them;
in six cases, the remaining parent or other guardian left home or died without
making adequate provision for the child, and in two additional cases, the juvenile was told that she was in the way or that she caused too much trouble and
should leave. One juvenile was told to leave the foster home in which she
resided for five years because the foster parents would no longer be paid.[449] In
other cases, in Bracey's sample, juveniles who left home were sometimes told
not to return. When an officer of a runaway unit telephoned one juvenile's
mother to notify her that he had apprehended her daughter, the mother
evaded questions about the girl's return and refused to make financial
arrangements to enable the girl to return home.[450] Unfortunately, little
research has explored the aspect of throwaways in general or among juvenile
prostitutes in particular.

Much of the research on adolescent prostitutes confirms prior findings in
the runaway literature regarding reasons why youth run away from home.
Numerous studies mention that family problems are the primary reason for
running away.[451] Ambrosino contends that family problems constitute the most
prevalent reason for juveniles to run away;[452] and Goldmeier and Dean found
that runaways are more likely than nonrunaways to feel less warm toward their
mothers and fathers, to feel that neither mother nor father is warm to them, and
to be less at ease in their homes.[453] Similarly, Regel mentions disturbed parent-
child relationships among the factors that precipitate running away,[454] and
Libertoff notes an almost warlike atmosphere in runaways' homes.[455]

In Walker's summary of the literature,[456] she points to a considerable body
of research reporting that a large proportion of runaways come from broken
homes,[457] have poor home environments,[458] and/or have troublesome parent-
child or sibling relationships.[459] Walker concludes:

It is important in a discussion of predisposing factors to note that numerous articles point out that runaways often have more inadequate parent–child relationships and more unhappy or problem home environments than non-runaways. This general recognition of family or parent problems for a large number of runaways is true across multiple sample bases, varying definitions of runaways, and differing orientations towards the reasons for running away.[460]

The literature on runaway behavior also confirms that child abuse is a common precipitant for running away. Libertoff finds a high incidence of beatings, forcible restraint, and sexual abuse.[461] Goldmeier and Dean report that runaways, more than nonrunaways, tend to feel that they are punished excessively and undeservedly.[462] Walker also notes in her review of the literature that numerous studies have found physical abuse to be a causative factor in running away.[463]

Criminal Activity Prior to First Arrest

Prostitutes begin criminal careers at an early age. According to self-report data, they are involved during their early adolescence in both criminal and noncriminal misbehavior. The variety and frequency of their delinquent activities and status offenses prior to first arrest are considerable, including the following offenses, in rank order: truancy (91.2 percent of prostitutes), nonprescription drug use (83.1 percent), running away (80.1 percent), drinking (79.4 percent), curfew violations (72.8 percent), shoplifting (71.3 percent), prostitution (65.4 percent), fighting (53.7 percent), joyriding (53.7 percent), larceny (27.9 percent), and vandalism (25 percent).[464] This pattern of criminal involvement for prostitutes does not appear to differ significantly from that of a nonprostitute control population, except in regard to the involvement in prostitution.[465]

First Arrest

Most juvenile prostitutes have been arrested at least once. Some research suggests that about three-fourths of adolescent prostitutes have been arrested or apprehended by police.[466] Gray places the number of juvenile prostitutes who have been arrested even higher, reporting that all juveniles she studied in one jurisdiction ($n = 21$) had a record of arrest and commitment to the Juvenile Division of the Department of Institutions.[467] This finding may result, however, from sample bias.

The first arrest generally occurs at an early age, with almost 60 percent of the prostitutes experiencing their first arrest at age 14 or below.[468] The first arrest offense is most likely to be either running away or shoplifting, rather than prostitution. Silbert, for example, found that 41 percent of the prostitutes were first arrested for running away and 13 percent for shoplifting, compared to 2 percent for prostitution.[469] The percentage of prostitutes whose first offense is running away is similar in the Enablers study, which is based on official data; the study reveals that 41.9 percent of the juvenile girls referred to court for prostitution offenses in Hennepin County were first arrested for running away.[470] In James's study, however, 32 percent of the prostitutes were first arrested for shoplifting and 27 percent for running away, but the percentage difference between these two first offenses may not be significant.[471] Two conclusions can be drawn from these studies: first, the majority of juvenile prostitutes are initially arrested for a nonprostitution offense; and second: the most frequent first offense is either running away or shoplifting.

Subsequent Offense History

Many juveniles charged with prostitution have incurred several additional charges before their first prostitution arrest, and some have records encompassing a significant number of prior offenses. In the Enablers study, for example, forty-one juveniles with prior offense histories in Hennepin County juvenile court incurred a total of 256 charges before being charged with prostitution,[472] and ten of forty-one juveniles in Ramsey County court files had prior offense histories, with a total of forty charges before their first prostitution charge.[473]

An examination of the distribution of all offenses incurred before the first prostitution charge indicates that running away occurs more frequently than all other offenses.[474] This finding is confirmed by both court records and police records. In the Hennepin County court files, nearly 40 percent of all offenses prior to the first prostitution charge are runaway offenses. In the Ramsey County juvenile court files, running away accounts for 63 percent of all prior offenses; and for the Minneapolis and St. Paul Police Departments (combined), it accounts for 25 percent of all prior offenses.[475] Escape from custody—a form of running away—also occurs frequently, according to police records.[476] Running away from home often begins the process of enmeshing juvenile girls in the juvenile justice system. Adjudication for this offense may result in detention and/or placement in foster homes. When the juveniles have difficulty conforming in these settings, they often run away again, thereby continuing the cycle.

Running away is also a frequent offense following the juvenile's first prostitution offense. According to Hennepin County court records, twenty-four of the sixty-two prostitutes on record were charged with other offenses after their first prostitution charge.[477] These twenty-four persons incurred a total of eighty-five nonprostitution offenses after their first prostitution charge. In that county, the charge that occurs most frequently after the first prostitution charge is running away—a finding that is also true according to the Ramsey County court files.[478] Furthermore, an examination of police records, rather than court files, reveals that escape from custody is a frequent offense, even after the first prostitution offense.[479]

According to self-report data, the juvenile prostitute's second arrest is most likely for running away,[480] but the third arrest is most likely to be for prostitution.[481] The most common age at third arrest is 15 or 16,[482] signifying that all three arrests are likely to occur within approximately a 2-year period.

In summary, juvenile prostitutes tend to be involved in a variety of both delinquent and status offenses prior to their first arrest. Both self-report and official data indicate considerable and consistent involvement in running away, and self-report data reveal that a large number of prostitutes tend to be involved in prostitution prior to their first prostitution arrest. Both self-report and official data on arrest histories suggest that some degree of escalation occurs from status offense to delinquency. Juveniles are first arrested for running away and only later are arrested for prostitution. Further research on the escalation phenomenon would be valuable.

Number and Frequency of Prostitution Offenses

A significant number of prostitutes incur arrest specifically for the offense of prostitution. One study reports that 63.2 percent of juvenile prostitutes are arrested for prostitution.[483] A similarly high percentage, again in research on a juvenile sample, is reported by Gray; ten of seventeen prostitutes in her study were charged with prostitution or prostitution-related offenses.[484] In another study, 27 percent of the juvenile prostitutes who had arrest histories were arrested at some time for prostitution.[485]

Both court and police records reveal that a large percentage of juveniles arrested for and charged with prostitution have multiple prostitution offenses. The court and police records show that of a total of 198 cases, 27 percent of the juveniles had two prostitution arrests.[486] According to police records for St. Paul, almost 27 percent of these young prostitutes had four or more prostitution offenses.[487] Gray found that the longer a girl works the streets, the greater the likelihood is that she will be arrested for prostitution.[488]

Race as a Factor in Arrest

The racial composition of the juvenile prostitute sample has also been examined, and both court records and police records reveal that Caucasians represent the largest racial category among juvenile prostitutes, constituting about 55 percent of the total.[489] Blacks are the second largest racial category, constituting slightly more than 30 percent of both court and police records.[490]

This finding of an association between race and arrest has also been reported by Gray.[491] She suggests that the cause of this correlation is the white girls' greater visibility in a predominantly black neighborhood, where the center of prostitution in Seattle is located. She notes:

> A black girl on 14th and Jackson can claim that she is walking home or on her way to the store. ... The white girl is less able to explain her presence and may be arrested for loitering.[492]

Dispositions

Data are also available on court and police dispositions for first and subsequent prostitution offenses. The majority of first and subsequent prostitution offenses are referred to court intake by police in both St. Paul and Minneapolis, and of those juveniles arrested for prostitution, 81.4 percent are referred by police to court intake in Minneapolis.[493] Juveniles who are arrested again on subsequent prostitution charges are even more likely to be referred to court.[494]

Variations do occur in police handling. In St. Paul, for example, fewer juveniles are referred to court than in Minneapolis. In addition, more youth in St. Paul are released to their parents following their first prostitution offense,[495] but this home-release disposition is not utilized in St. Paul or in Minneapolis for subsequent prostitution offenders.

When examining juvenile court intake decisions for one county, certain patterns emerge. Some prostitution cases are closed at intake (29.3 percent). In other cases, some juveniles are detained at the juvenile center (18.9 percent), others are referred to court (20.7 percent), and some are referred to another jurisdiction (20.7 percent)—the last signifying a large number of nonresidents. In a few cases, the juveniles are placed in a diversion plan or ordered to undergo counseling.[496] Of cases that are referred to court and for which a detention hearing subsequently occurs, most youth are ordered detained at the juvenile center (ten of eleven youth). Infrequently at this stage, a youth is released to home curfew.[497]

Loitering is another charge used by police when they arrest a suspected prostitute. Loitering may be charged, rather than prostitution, when the arrest has not been obtained by solicitation by a law enforcement official. Police may merely see a juvenile loitering in a place of prostitution or loitering in the association of known prostitutes. According to Minneapolis police records, a significant number of the juveniles charged with loitering are also referred to court intake. Seventy-five percent of those charged by police with their first loitering offense are referred to court intake, and the same number of those charged with subsequent loitering offenses are referred to court.[498] A small number of juveniles initially arrested by police for prostitution and loitering are reprimanded and released, but this police disposition does not occur for subsequent offenders.[499]

Adult versus Juvenile Processing

Juveniles attempt to avoid being arrested as juveniles, preferring (if they have to be arrested at all) to be processed as adults. Criminal justice processing as an adult has one primary advantage: it results in minimal incarceration, often resulting in only one night in jail.[500] A prostitute who is charged as an adult can post bail and, for a first offense, probably will receive probation, a fine, or a short jail term. A juvenile, however, would be placed, without bail privileges, in the youth detention center, to remain there until a hearing is held. If adjudicated and found guilty of a prostitution offense in a specific jurisdiction, the juvenile is likely to remain in detention until she is transported to a diagnostic center, where she may spend 3 to 6 weeks until her subsequent incarceration in a correctional institution.[501] To avoid juvenile processing, the underage girl obtains (or is provided by her pimp) false identification, with a false name and age. This difference in treatment between juvenile and adult prostitutes has been noted previously in the literature.[502]

Responses to Incarceration

Data are also available on juvenile prostitutes' responses to their incarceration. One of the juveniles' complaints is that institutional staffs lack knowledge about prostitution.[503] This leads the juveniles to feel that caseworkers do not understand them and that the institutions fail to address the problems of street life. As one girl commented:

> I knew my caseworker didn't know nothing about prostitution and I didn't bring it up. But she brought the whole section [*sic*] up, 'cause I was always talking about "the game." And so one of those days, I told her and she brought me here and we talked about it. She don't know nothing about the game. Well, she looks at you so strange. She won't take her eyes off you. She just stares at you.[504]

In addition, juveniles may misunderstand the diagnostic psychological evaluation they must undergo, resenting the "childish games" that are part of the psychological testing. One juvenile bitterly reported:

> These people in this place. ... It makes you mad 'cause these people think you're crazy. Like my caseworker for instance. She comes up to me giving me all these little baby things to do, like I'm crazy. She goes and asks me these stupid questions about this picture-missing game. She asked me to tell her what was missing in the picture and she knows damn good and well what's missing![505]

In interactions with institutional staffs, the juveniles take pride in being able to outsmart staff members just as they delight in outsmarting their customers.

They may attempt to manipulate caseworkers in ways that help them survive on the street.

Occasionally, the juveniles develop meaningful social and emotional attachments to a staff member in an institution.[506] Such an attachment may facilitate the development of conventional behavior within the institutional setting, but conformity to the norms of the institution is no guarantee that the juveniles, once paroled, will not return to prostitution.

Involvement with the Social Service Delivery System

Prior research has explored, to a limited extent, the juvenile female prostitute's involvement with the social service delivery system. A few studies reveal some data on this involvement because their research samples consist of respondents who have approached a psychologist or psychiatrist for mental health problems.[507] More extensive studies of this issue were conducted recently by two agencies. The Enablers questioned prostitutes about their involvement with social service agencies both before and after they started prostitution, and data on social service involvement are also available in the Huckleberry House research, with a sample consisting of adolescent prostitutes and nonprostitutes who voluntarily sought services from the Huckleberry House runaway shelter. Admittedly, the data furnished by these studies represent a biased sample, since the sampling process of the studies guarantees a preponderance of persons most likely to manifest some degree of involvement with social service agencies.

Extent of Involvement

Juvenile prostitutes report considerable involvement with the social service delivery system, both before and after their entry into prostitution. In the Enablers study, 80 percent of the prostitutes under age 20 reported one or more contacts with social service agencies before they started prostitution. These contacts (in rank order) are most likely to be with probation officers; social workers; family counselors, school counselors, or other counselors; youth service workers; and medical personnel. Fifty-two percent of the prostitutes reported that they had seen probation officers or social workers; 29.2 percent had seen a school counselor and 20.8 percent a family counselor; 18.8 percent received individual counseling; 12.5 percent contacted youth service agencies; and 10.4 percent contacted medical centers.[508]

About half of the prostitutes spent time in out-of-home residential or shelter facilities before they started prostitution. The number of such facilities resided in by any one juvenile ranges from one to eight, with a median of three placements.[509] About half of these placements are made by social workers, probation officers, or welfare workers.[510]

Half of the respondents in the Enablers study reported having contact with a welfare worker, probation officer, or social worker after starting prostitution.[511] Over 50 percent report contact with medical centers, about 20 percent mention contact with youth service agencies, and 78 percent reside in a foster or group home, residential facility, or residential treatment program.[512]

Reasons for Referrals

Prostitutes have also been asked the reasons for their referrals to social service programs after they have become involved in prostitution. The most common reasons for referral of juvenile prostitutes to such programs are drug use, counseling, and shelter. In the Enablers sample, almost 19 percent of the respondents reported that they were referred for chemical dependency, 17 percent for counseling, and 13.2 percent for shelter.[513] Fewer are referred for parole problems (7.5%), prostitution (5.7%) or suicide (1.9%).[514]

One reason that a large number of youth have contacts with medical centers is their concern about venereal disease. Half the women admit having venereal disease, and all of these have received medical care for it.[515] Almost half of the young prostitutes visit a doctor monthly,[516] with most preferring clinics to private doctors.[517]

Additional data on social service involvement are available from the Huckleberry House project, which gathered information on services requested and received by adolescent prostitutes, on additional service needs and areas of concern, on the contact period with the Huckleberry House program, and on the youth's evaluation of the service delivery.[518] At intake, female prostitutes most frequently request crisis housing, employment counseling, and individual counseling,[519] which suggests that these are the service needs that bring them to the agency. Medical services and school counseling are the next most frequently requested services at intake. Fewer prostitutes request placement counseling, family counseling, and food.[520] Still fewer (7 percent or less) request alternative housing counseling, legal assistance, peer relationship counseling, or transportation to parent/guardian's home.[521] Significantly, none request sexuality counseling, family relationship counseling, or drug and alcohol counseling upon initial contact with the agency. (Family relationship counseling, as opposed to family therapy, is individual counseling that focuses on concerns about family relationships and conflicts.)

As the juveniles have more contact with the agency, most request additional services. These additional requests are for individual counseling, peer relationship counseling and family relationship counseling, alternative housing counseling, placement counseling, medical services, school counseling, sexuality counseling, employment counseling, and legal counseling.[522] (Placement counseling provides information about, or facilitates, out-of-home group or foster home placement; housing counseling explores housing options other than placement, such as housing with a relative, in a boarding house, or in a shared rental situation.) Medical requests most often are for birth control information and for tests for pregnancy and venereal disease.

Differences Between Prostitutes and Nonprostitutes

In comparing female prostitutes and a nonprostitute sample, the Huckleberry House project found that, at intake, female prostitutes require a wider variety of services than nonprostitute females. More prostitutes request crisis housing, employment counseling, and medical and school counseling. The only area in which more nonprostitutes initially request services is legal counseling.[523] Furthermore, as prostitutes continue to interact with the agency, they remain more in need of most services than nonprostitutes do. This is especially true in terms of alternative housing, school counseling, medical counseling, legal assistance, individual counseling, and sexuality counseling. The only area in which more nonprostitutes than prostitutes show an interest is family relationship counseling and family counseling.[524] In summary, the study concludes that programs serving adolescent female prostitutes should emphasize employment counseling, alternative housing, and school counseling, and should provide medical services, especially birth control and gynecological services, and more crisis housing.[525]

Prostitutes' Perceptions of their Service Needs

Some research has focused on the prostitutes' own assessment of their need for social services. Silbert specifically queried adult and juvenile respondents on services they would recommend for prostitutes who are rape victims. Most cited the need for a 24-hour switchboard, group counseling, individual counseling, social supports and advocacy, rap groups and prevention techniques, and legal services.[526] Silbert also notes the desirability of acquiring staff members who are ex-prostitutes and who are experienced with street life and victimization as well as with ways to cope with sexual assault.[527]

The Huckleberry House project also concluded that far more female prostitutes indicate a need for sexuality counseling than those who specifically request such services. For almost half of the females, this need for counseling stems from considerable distress about sexual abuse.[528] Another need is relationship counseling, especially concerning a male friend or lover. For some, bisexuality or homosexuality is a concern, and some youth are concerned about their general sexual functioning.[529] As might be expected, compared to an adolescent nonprostitute control sample, more female prostitutes are concerned with almost all categories of sexuality, sexual relations, sexual functioning, and attitudes. This obviously indicates a greater need for sexuality counseling in programs designed to meet the needs of this population[530] and a need for staff who are trained to deal with the problems of adolescent sexuality.

Notes

1. James H. Bryan, "Occupational Ideologies and Individual Attitudes of Call Girls," *Social Problems* 13(Spring 1966): 441–50; James H. Bryan, "Apprenticeships in Prostitution," *Social Problems* 12(Winter 1965): 287–96; Maryse Choisy, *Psychoanalysis of the Prostitute* (New York: Philosophical Library, 1961); Nanette J. Davis, "The Prostitute: Developing a Deviant Identity," in *Studies in the Sociology of Sex*, ed. James M. Henslin (New York: Appleton-Century-Crofts, 1971); T.C. Esselstyn, "Prostitution in the United States," *Annals of the American Academy of Political and Social Science* 376(March 1968): 123–35; Paul H. Gebhard, "Misconceptions About Female Prostitutes," *Medical Aspects of Human Sexuality* 3(March 1969): 24–30; Harold Greenwald, *The Elegant Prostitute: A Social and Psychoanalytic Study* (New York: Walker, 1970); Harold Greenwald, "The Call Girl," in *Deviant Behavior and Social Process*, ed. William A. Rushing (Chicago: Rand McNally, 1969); Harold Greenwald, *The Call Girl: A Social and Psychoanalytic Study* (New York: Ballantine, 1958) [hereafter cited as Greenwald, *Psychoanalytic Study*]; Travis Hirschi, *Cause of Delinquency* (Berkeley: University of California Press, 1969); Travis Hirschi, "The Professional Prostitute," *Berkeley Journal of Sociology* 7(1962): 33–49; Norman R. Jackman, Richard O'Toole, and Gilbert Geis, "The Self-Image of the Prostitute," *Sociological Quarterly* 4(April 1963): 150–61; Wardell B. Pomeroy, "Some Aspects of Prostitution," *Journal of Sex Research* 1, no. 3 (November 1965): 177–87; Charles Winick and Paul M. Kinsie, *The Lively Commerce: Prostitution in the United States* (Chicago: Quadrangle, 1971).

2. See, for example, Bryan, "Occupational Ideologies"; Bryan, "Apprenticeships"; Greenwald, *Elegant Prostitute*; Greenwald, "Call Girl"; Greenwald, *Psychoanalytic Study*.

3. Crowley's sample of juvenile girls under age 17 (twenty-five runaways who had had no involvement in prostitution and twenty who had been involved in prostitution during a runaway episode) was selected through five agencies in Houston, one agency in Galveston, one in Huntsville, and one in Dallas. Maura G. Crowley, "Female Runaway Behavior and Its Relationship to Prostitution," Master's thesis, Sam Houston State University, Institute of Contemporary Corrections and Behavioral Sciences, 1977.

4. Enablers, *Juvenile Prostitution in Minnesota: The Report of a Research Project* (St. Paul: The Enablers, 1978).

5. Dorothy H. Bracey, *"Baby-Pros": Preliminary Profiles of Juvenile Prostitutes* (New York: John Jay Press, 1979).

6. Mimi H. Silbert, *Sexual Assault of Prostitutes: Phase One* (Washington, D.C.: National Institute of Mental Health, National Center for the Prevention and Control of Rape, 1980); Mimi H. Silbert and Ayala M. Pines, "Sexual Child Abuse as an Antecedent to Prostitution," *Child Abuse and Neglect* 5, no. 4(1981): 407–11; Sparky Harlan, Luanna L. Rodgers, and Brian Slattery, *Male and Female Adolescent Prostitution: Huckleberry House Sexual Minority Youth Services Project* (Washington, D.C.: U.S. Department of Health and Human Services, Youth Development Bureau, 1981).

7. Diana Gray (Hilton), "Turning-Out: A Study of Teenage Prostitution," Master's thesis, University of Washington, 1971 [hereafter cited as Gray, "Turning-Out I"]; Diana Gray, "Turning-Out: A Study of Teenage Prostitution," *Urban Life and*

Culture 1, no. 4(1973): 401– 25 [hereafter cited as Gray, "Turning-Out II"]; Jennifer James, *Entrance into Juvenile Prostitution* (Washington, D.C.: National Institute of Mental Health, 1980); Jennifer James and Jane Meyerding, "Early Sexual Experience as a Factor in Prostitution," *Archives of Sexual Behavior* 7, no. 1(1977): 31–42 [hereafter cited as James and Meyerding, "Early Sexual Experience as a Factor"]; Jennifer James and Jane Meyerding, "Early Sexual Experience and Prostitution," *American Journal of Psychiatry* 134, no. 12(December 1977): 1381–85 [hereafter cited as James and Meyerding, "Early Sexual Experience"].

8. Katherine MacVicar and Marcia Dillon, "Childhood and Adolescent Development of Ten Female Prostitutes," *Journal of the American Academy of Child Psychiatry* 19, no. 1(1980): 145–59; Frances Newman and Paula J. Caplan, "Juvenile Female Prostitution as a Gender Consistent Response to Early Deprivation," *International Journal of Women's Studies* 5, no. 2(1981): 128–37; Kathryn Barclay and Johnny L. Gallemore, Jr., "The Family of the Prostitute," *Corrective Psychiatry and Journal of Social Therapy* 18, no. 4(1972): 10–16.

9. The Enablers and Silbert's samples, for example, include current and former juvenile prostitutes.

10. See, for example, Bracey, *"Baby-Pros"*, 3–4; Gray, "Turning-Out II," 404; James, *Entrance*, 9. Bracey also interviewed juveniles on the street.

11. See, for example, Enablers, *Juvenile Prostitution*, 8; MacVicar and Dillon, "Childhood and Adolescent Development," 146; Newman and Caplan, "Juvenile Female Prostitution," 128; Crowley, "Female Runaway Behavior," 41–42.

12. See, for example, James, *Entrance*; Silbert, *Sexual Assault*.

13. See, for example, Bracey, *"Baby-Pros,"* 11 (thirty-two prostitutes under the age of 18); Gray "Turnout-Out II," 404; Crowley, "Female Runaway Behavior," 41 (the sample includes forty-five juvenile girls under age 17); Harlan, Rodgers, and Slattery, *Male and Female*, 7 (thirty youth between ages 12 and 17); James, *Entrance*, 10, 16; (136 prostitutes from ages 13 to 17).

14. See, for example, Enablers, *Juvenile Prostitution*, 14; MacVicar and Dillon, "Childhood and Adolescent Development," 145; Silbert, *Sexual Assault*, 10.

15. James, *Entrance*, 17. Some of the adolescent subjects in James's research were interviewed by Gray and analyzed in her master's thesis, which may explain the same mean age in the two studies. See Gray, "Turning-Out I," 16. See also James and Meyerding, "Early Sexual Experience as a Factor," 33, n. 2.

16. MacVicar and Dillon, "Childhood and Adolescent Development," 145.

17. Bracey, *"Baby-Pros,"* 11.

18. James, *Entrance*, 20.

19. Enablers, *Juvenile Prostitution*, 14.

20. Harlan, Rodgers, and Slattery, *Male and Female*, 7.

21. Crowley, "Female Runaway Behavior," 58.

22. Silbert, *Sexual Assault*, 10.

23. James, *Entrance*, 17.

24. This conclusion is based on the few studies that furnish an age breakdown. In the Huckleberry House research, 84 percent of the adolescent female sample ($n=30$) is 15, 16, and 17. Harlan, Rodgers, and Slattery, *Male and Female*, 7. In the Enablers research ($n=80$), forty-six of the adolescent prostitutes are ages 15 through 18, compared

to six in the 12- to 14-year-old category. Enablers, *Juvenile Prostitution,* 18. In addition, Crowley interviewed fourteen juvenile females aged 15 and 16 but only six aged 14 and under (*n*=52). Crowley, "Female Runaway Behavior," 58.

25. This conclusion is based on the few studies that either furnish an age breakdown or provide data from which such a breakdown can be deduced. James, for example, reports that approximately 7 percent of her sample is in grade seven (signifying that they are approximately 12 or 13 years old). James, *Entrance,* 20. The Enablers sample includes no respondents younger than 14 years old. Enablers, *Juvenile Prostitution,* 18. In the Huckleberry House research, only 6 percent of the juvenile females are under age 14. Harlan, Rodgers, and Slattery, *Male and Female,* 7.

26. See Bracey, *"Baby-Pros,"* 19; Gray "Turning-Out II," 405.

27. Enablers, *Juvenile Prostitution,* 21.

28. Silbert, *Sexual Assault,* 15.

29. Ibid.; Silbert and Pines, "Sexual Child Abuse," 408.

30. James, *Entrance,* 18.

31. Jennifer James, "Entrance into Juvenile Prostitution: Progress Report, June 1978" (Washington, D.C.: National Institute of Mental Health, 1978), 53 [hereafter cited as James, "Progress Report"].

32. Ibid.

33. The exception is Gray, whose sample includes a higher proportion of black adolescents than is found in other studies. Her sample of twenty-one girls includes eleven blacks and ten whites. Gray, "Turning-Out I," 16.

34. Crowley, "Female Runaway Behavior," 60; James, *Entrance,* 19; Harlan, Rodgers, and Slattery, *Male and Female,* 7; Enablers, *Juvenile Prostitution,* 18; Silbert, *Sexual Assault,* 10.

35. James, *Entrance,* 19; Enablers, *Juvenile Prostitution,* 18; Silbert, *Sexual Assault,* 10. Compare, however, the Huckleberry House sample, in which Hispanic females constitute the second largest group, slightly outnumbering black females (13 percent to 10 percent). Harlan, Rodgers, and Slattery, *Male and Female,* 7.

36. Crowley, "Female Runaway Behavior," 60; Gray, "Turning-Out I," 16. See also note 33.

37. Gray, "Turning-Out I," 16.

38. James, *Entrance,* 19.

39. Silbert, *Sexual Assault,* 10.

40. Ibid.

41. Jackman, O'Toole, and Geis, "Self-Image"; Greenwald, *Psychoanalytic Study;* Davis, "The Prostitute."

42. Bracey, *"Baby-Pros,"* 40; Enablers, *Juvenile Prostitution,* 22; Harlan, Rodgers, and Slattery, *Male and Female,* 14; James, *Entrance* 17; Silbert, *Sexual Assault,* 95.

43. James, *Entrance,* 88.

44. Harlan, Rodgers, and Slattery, *Male and Female,* 14.

45. Enablers, *Juvenile Prostitution,* 22.

46. Silbert, *Sexual Assault,* 95.

47. Ibid., 13.

48. Newman and Caplan, "Juvenile Female Prostitution," 131.

49. Bracey, *"Baby-Pros,"* 40.

50. Crowley, "Female Runaway Behavior," 63.

51. James, "Progress Report," 59. James also reports that 35.5 percent of her respondents characterize their early relationships with their natural fathers as primarily "no relationship." James, *Entrance*, 88.

52. MacVicar and Dillon, "Childhood and Adolescent Development," 148.

53. Enablers, *Juvenile Prostitution*, 22.

54. Gray, "Turning-Out I," 25.

55. Silbert, *Sexual Assault*, 91-92.

56. Crowley, "Female Runaway Behavior," 73-74 (tables 11 and 12).

57. Harlan, Rodgers, and Slattery, *Male and Female*, 15.

58. Silbert, *Sexual Assault*, 91-92.

59. James, "Progress Report," 59.

60. Ibid. In a smaller sample, however, Crowley finds that more prostitutes report a poor relationship with their mothers than with their fathers; 42 percent (seven of seventeen) report a poor relationship with their mothers, whereas 25 percent (four of sixteen) report a poor relationship with their fathers. Crowley, "Female Runaway Behavior," 73-74.

61. Harlan, Rodgers, and Slattery, *Male and Female*, 15.

62. Enablers, *Juvenile Prostitution*, 23.

63. See, for example, Pamela J. Fields, "Parent–Child Relationships, Childhood Sex Abuse, and Adult Interpersonal Behavior in Female Prostitutes," Ph.D. dissertation, California School of Professional Psychology, 1980, 83.

64. MacVicar and Dillon, "Childhood and Adolescent Development," 148.

65. Ibid., 149-50.

66. T.C.N. Gibbens, "Juvenile Prostitution," *British Journal of Delinquency* 8, no. 1(July 1957): 6.

67. Newman and Caplan, "Juvenile Female Prostitution," 133.

68. Ibid.

69. Ibid., 131.

70. James, *Entrance*, 69.

71. MacVicar and Dillon, "Childhood and Adolescent Development," 148.

72. Arnold S. Maerov, "Prostitution: A Survey and Review of 20 Cases," *Psychiatric Quarterly* 39(January 1965): 675-701.

73. MacVicar and Dillon, "Childhood and Adolescent Development," 148-49.

74. Ibid., 148.

75. Gray, "Turning-Out I," 31.

76. Enablers, *Juvenile Prostitution*, 22.

77. Harlan, Rodgers, and Slattery, *Male and Female*, 14.

78. Davis, "The Prostitute," 303.

79. Harlan, Rodgers, and Slattery, *Male and Female*, 14.

80. Newman and Caplan, "Juvenile Female Prostitution," 131.

81. Silbert, *Sexual Assault*, 13.

82. Gray, "Turning-Out II"; Greenwald, *Psychoanalytic Study*; Jennifer James, "Motivations for Entrance into Prostitution," in *The Female Offender*, ed. Laura Crites (Lexington, Mass.: Lexington Books, 1976); James and Meyerding, "Early Sexual Experience as a Factor"; Jennifer James and Peter P. Vitaliano, *Multivariate Analysis of the Relationship Between Prostitution and Initial Sexual Activity* (Washington, D.C.: National Institute of Mental Health, 1977); Joseph J. Peters, "Children Who Are

Victims of Sexual Assault and the Psychology of Offenders," *American Journal of Psychotherapy* 30(1976): 398–421; Paul Sloane and Eva Karpinski, "Effects of Incest on the Participants," *American Journal of Orthopsychiatry*, 12(October 1942): 666–73; Irving B. Weiner, "On Incest: A Survey," *Excerpta Criminologica* 4(1964): 137–55; Narcyz Lukianowicz, "Incest I: Paternal Incest," *British Journal of Psychiatry* 120(1971): 301–13.

83. James, *Entrance*, 1, 5; MacVicar and Dillon, "Childhood and Adolescent Development," 146–47; Silbert, *Sexual Assault*, 1.

84. Enablers, *Juvenile Prostitution*, 5; Gray, "Turning-Out II," 404.

85. Several studies have reported that some incest victims become prostitutes. See, for example, Sloane and Karpinski, "Effects of Incest"; Lukianowicz, "Incest I"; Peters, "Children Who Are Victims."

86. See note 82.

87. Harlan, Rodgers, and Slattery, *Male and Female*, 21. James and Meyerding, however, note that 46 percent of their respondents answered affirmatively to the question: "Prior to your first intercourse, did any older person [defined as more than ten years older] attempt sexual play or intercourse with you?" James and Meyerding, "Early Sexual Experience," 1383. Silbert's estimate is 60 percent. Silbert, *Sexual Assault*, 84.

88. Enablers, *Juvenile Prostitution*, 22–23.

89. The Enablers note that 26 percent of the incest experiences were perpetrated by a father and the same percentage by a stepfather. Enablers, *Juvenile Prostitution*, 23. Silbert reports that two-thirds of her respondents were abused by a father figure. Silbert, *Sexual Assault*, 85.

90. Silbert, *Sexual Assault*, 85; Enablers, *Juvenile Prostitution*, 23.

91. In noting that two-thirds of the women in her study were abused by a father figure, Silbert adds that one-third were abused by their natural fathers and the others by stepfathers, foster fathers, or mothers' common law husbands (exact percentages are unspecified). Silbert, *Sexual Assault*, 85. Whereas a conclusion could be drawn from these data that natural fathers are more often the abusers, a contrary conclusion could be reached from the Enablers and from James's research. The Enablers study claims that stepfathers are abusers as frequently as natural fathers, and James's research supports the view that stepfathers are the more frequent perpetrators. Enablers, *Juvenile Prostitution*, 23; James and Meyerding, "Early Sexual Experience," 1383.

92. Silbert, *Sexual Assault*, 85.

93. Enablers, *Juvenile Prostitution*, 23.

94. Harlan, Rodgers, and Slattery, *Male and Female*, 21.

95. Silbert, *Sexual Assault*, 84.

96. Ibid., 85.

97. Gray, "Turning-Out II," 407; James, *Entrance*, 29; Enablers, *Juvenile Prostitution*, 38.

98. Enablers, *Juvenile Prostitution*, 38.

99. James, *Entrance*, 29.

100. Gray, "Turning-Out II," 408.

101. Ibid., 407.

102. Enablers, *Juvenile Prostitution*, 40 (table 33). For 10 percent of the prostitutes first coitus occurred with a pimp; for 5 percent, it was with a family member.

103. Silbert, *Sexual Assault,* 84.

104. Ibid., 85.

105. Ibid.

106. Ibid.

107. James and Meyerding, "Early Sexual Experience," 1383.

108. DeFrancis found that the sexual abuser is a member of the child's household in 27 percent of the cases, a relative in eleven percent, a friend or acquaintance of the family in 37 percent, and a stranger in only 25 percent. Vincent DeFrancis, *Protecting the Child Victim of Sex Crimes Committed by Adults: Final Report* (Denver: American Humane Association, 1969), 217.

109. Silbert, *Sexual Assault,* 86.

110. Ibid.

111. Silbert and Pines, "Sexual Child Abuse," 409.

112. James, *Entrance,* 62.

113. James and Meyerding, "Early Sexual Experience," 1383.

114. James and Meyerding, "Early Sexual Experience as a Factor," 37.

115. James and Meyerding, "Early Sexual Experience," 1383.

116. Fields, "Parent–Child Relationships," 108.

117. Suzanne M. Sgroi, Linda C. Blick, and Frances S. Porter, "A Conceptual Framework for Child Sexual Abuse," in Suzanne M. Sgroi, ed., *Handbook of Clinical Intervention in Child Sexual Abuse* (Lexington, Mass.: Lexington Books, 1982), 10–12.

118. Bracey, *"Baby-Pros,"* 44.

119. James and Meyerding, "Early Sexual Experience," 1383; Silbert and Pines, "Sexual Child Abuse," 409.

120. Enablers, *Juvenile Prostitution,* 22.

121. Crowley, "Female Runaway Behavior," 63; Harlan, Rodgers, and Slattery, *Male and Female,* 15; James, *Entrance,* 48; Silbert, *Sexual Assault,* 91.

122. Bracey, *"Baby-Pros,"* 44.

123. Fields, "Parent-Child Relationships," 112; Silbert, *Sexual Assault,* 91.

124. Enablers, *Juvenile Prostitution,* 22.

125. James, *Entrance,* 48.

126. Silbert and Pines, "Sexual Child Abuse," 410.

127. Fathers may be the more likely perpetrators. See James, *Entrance,* 48.

128. Bracey, *"Baby-Pros,"* 44; MacVicar and Dillon, "Childhood and Adolescent Development," 148.

129. According to the Enablers research, all those prostitutes in the sample under age 18 started by age 16, and 58 percent of those under age 20 started by age 14. Enablers, *Juvenile Prostitution,* 52. Silbert found that 62 percent of the prostitutes in her study were under age 16 when they first engaged in prostitution. Silbert, *Sexual Assault,* 39.

130. Enablers, *Juvenile Prostitution,* 52; James, *Entrance,* 29; Gray, "Turning-Out I," 412. Silbert, however, reports a mean age of 13. Silbert, *Sexual Assault,* 39.

131. Enablers, *Juvenile Prostitution,* 54.

132. Silbert, *Sexual Assault,* 39.

133. James, *Entrance,* 78. She notes that 4 percent were under age 12, 7 percent were 12, 13 percent were 13, 23 percent were 14, 27 percent were 15, 19 percent were 16, and 6 percent were 17.

134. Silbert, *Sexual Assault,* 39.

135. Ibid.

136. James found that 23 percent of her respondents were influenced by relatives, compared to Silbert's 13 percent. James, *Entrance,* 77.

137. Enablers, *Juvenile Prostitution,* 53.

138. James, *Entrance,* 77.

139. Bracey, *"Baby-Pros,"* 20.

140. Harlan, Rodgers, and Slattery, *Male and Female,* 34.

141. Silbert, *Sexual Assault,* 39.

142. James, *Entrance,* 77.

143. Ibid., 82.

144. Silbert, *Sexual Assault,* 39.

145. Ibid., 40.

146. Gray, "Turning-Out II," 410.

147. MacVicar and Dillon, "Childhood and Adolescent Development," 151–52.

148. Barclay and Gallemore, "Family of the Prostitute," 10–16.

149. James, *Entrance,* 68. In the Huckleberry House research, 57 percent of the juvenile females were first taught about prostitution by pimps. Similarly, many of the respondents in the Enablers study report the influence of a pimp in their initial involvement in prostitution. In describing how they were turned out, 58.3 percent report they were turned out by a man, and 31.6 percent specifically state that they were first turned out by a pimp. In Silbert's sample, 25 percent report that a pimp was the person who influenced them to become active in prostitution. Harlan, Rodgers, and Slattery, *Male and Female,* 34; Enablers, *Juvenile Prostitution,* 56; Silbert, *Sexual Assault,* 40.

150. Enablers, *Juvenile Prostitution,* 72 (table 68).

151. James, *Entrance,* 68.

152. Bracey, *"Baby-Pros,"* 23.

153. Enablers, *Juvenile Prostitution,* 516.

154. See, for example, Ted Morgan, "Little Ladies of the Night," *New York Times Magazine,* 16 Nov. 1975, 42; Mark Schorr, "Blood Stewart's End," *New York Magazine,* 27 March 1978, 53–58 (an account of kidnapping, rape, and beatings precipitating a juvenile's involvement in prostitution).

155. Enablers, *Juvenile Prostitution,* 59.

156. Ibid., 57.

157. Silbert, *Sexual Assault,* 40.

158. Bracey, *"Baby-Pros,"* 23.

159. Ibid., 33.

160. Silbert, *Sexual Assault,* 94.

161. Newman and Caplan, "Juvenile Female Prostitution," 133. Their statistics may be low, however, since they also note that in at least two additional cases, the juvenile has a boyfriend who may be considered a pimp; he does not make his living in this manner, but he does offer her sexual services to other men. For a discussion of the difference between a "boyfriend" and a "pimp", see Bracey, *"Baby-Pros,"* 32.

162. James, "Progress Report," 58.

163. Ibid.

164. Ibid.

165. Enablers, *Juvenile Prostitution*, 69. This discrepancy of opinion between the interviewer and the respondent occurs in 29.2 percent of the cases.

166. Silbert, *Sexual Assault*, 40.

167. James, *Entrance*, 78. In her study, 3 percent of the prostitutes report being asked to prostitute by a "pimp's woman."

168. Bracey, *"Baby-Pros,"* 23–24.

169. Silbert, *Sexual Assault*, 40.

170. The Huckleberry House research merely reports that 19 percent of the juvenile females learned about hustling from friends or other youth on the street, without specifying whether these friends or street youth were also prostitutes. See Harlan, Rodgers, and Slattery, *Male and Female*, 34. The Enablers queried prostitutes about individuals who introduced them to prostitution, but the study failed to ask respondents who answered "a woman" whether this woman was another prostitute. See Enablers, *Juvenile Prostitution*, 57.

171. James, "Progress Report," 68.

172. Harlan, Rodgers, and Slattery, *Male and Female*, 34.

173. Silbert, *Sexual Assault*, 40.

174. Ibid.

175. Ibid.

176. Gray, "Turning-Out I," 88.

177. Enablers, *Juvenile Prostitution*, 57.

178. James, *Entrance*, 78.

179. Enablers, *Juvenile Prostitution*, 53.

180. Silbert, *Sexual Assault*, 41.

181. Ibid., 42.

182. Ibid.

183. Enablers, *Juvenile Prostitution*, 58.

184. James, *Entrance*, 83.

185. Enablers, *Juvenile Prostitution*, 88; James, *Entrance*, 60; Jennifer James, "Prostitution and Addiction: An Interdisciplinary Approach," *Addictive Diseases: An International Journal* 4(1976): 601–18; Jennifer James, C. Gosho, and R. Watson, "The Relationship between Female Criminality and Drug Use," in *Drug Use and Crime* (Washington, D.C.: National Institute on Drug Abuse, 1976); Silbert, *Sexual Assault*, 48–50.

186. Enablers, *Juvenile Prostitution*, 53.

187. Silbert, *Sexual Assault*, 41.

188. James, *Entrance*, 83.

189. Enablers, *Juvenile Prostitution*, 55.

190. Ibid., 52.

191. Silbert, *Sexual Assault*, 40.

192. Gray, "Turning-Out I," 88.

193. Enablers, *Juvenile Prostitution*, 52.

194. Silbert, *Sexual Assault*, 41.

195. James, *Entrance*, 79; Enablers, *Juvenile Prostitution*, 53. Gray, however, found that two-thirds of her adolescent sample held legitimate jobs prior to their entrance into prostitution. Gray, "Turning-Out II," 406.

196. Enablers, *Juvenile Prostitution,* 53.

197. Silbert, *Sexual Assault,* 41.

198. Enablers, *Juvenile Prostitution,* 53.

199. Silbert, *Sexual Assault,* 40.

200. Enablers, *Juvenile Prostitution,* 52.

201. James, *Entrance,* 5.

202. See, for example, Helene Deutsch, *The Psychology of Women,* Vol. I (New York: Grune & Stratton, 1944); Edward Glover, "The Psychopathology of Prostitution," in *Selected Papers on Psycho-analysis, The Roots of Crime,* Vol. II (New York: International Universities Press, 1st ed. 1943, 1960); J. S. Kasanin, "Neurotic 'Acting Out' as a Basis for Sexual Promiscuity in Women," *Psychoanalytic Review* 31(1944): 221–32.

203. Choisy, *Psychoanalysis of the Prostitute,* 6, 42, 62; Greenwald, *Elegant Prostitute,* 6.

204. Choisy, *Psychoanalysis of the Prostitute,* 43.

205. Maerov, "Prostitution," 686–87, 693–94; Marc H. Hollender, "Prostitution, the Body, and Human Relatedness," *International Journal of Psychoanalysis* 42(1961): 404–13.

206. Greenwald, *Elegant Prostitute,* 178.

207. Maerov, "Prostitution," 692.

208. Greenwald, *Elegant Prostitute,* 144, 201–202. See also Winick and Kinsie, *Lively Commerce,* 27, 29.

209. Deutsch, *Psychology of Women;* Tibor Agoston, "Some Psychological Aspects of Prostitution: The Pseudo-Personality," *International Journal of Psycho-Analysis* 26(1945): 62–67.

210. Marc H. Hollender, "The Prostitute's Two Identities," *Medical Aspects of Human Sexuality* 2(January 1968): 45–51.

211. James, "Progress Report," 49.

212. Ibid. For research in the latter tradition, see Greenwald, *Elegant Prostitute,* 199; Wardell B. Pomeroy, "Some Aspects of Prostitution," *Journal of Sex Research* 1, no. 3(November 1965): 184; Harry Benjamin and R.E.L. Masters, *Prostitution and Morality* (New York: Julian Press, 1964), 93; Esselstyn, "Prostitution," 129; Kingsley Davis, "The Sociology of Prostitution," *American Sociological Review* 2(1937): 750–51.

213. Greenwald, *Elegant Prostitute,* 202; Winick and Kinsie, *Lively Commerce,* 38.

214. Tage Kemp, *Prostitution: An Investigation of Its Causes, Especially with Regard to Hereditary Factors* (Copenhagen: Levin and Munskgaard, 1936); Choisy, *Psychoanalysis of the Prostitute;* Maerov, "Prostitution"; Jackman, O'Toole, and Geis, "Self-Image"; Esselstyn, "Prostitution"; Greenwald, *Elegant Prostitute;* Davis, "The Prostitute."

215. D.E. Carns, "Talking About Sex: Notes on First Coitus and the Double Sexual Standard," *Journal of Marriage and the Family* 35(1975): 677–88; Choisy, *Psychoanalysis of the Prostitute;* Davis, "The Prostitute"; DeFrancis, *Protecting the Child Victim;* James and Meyerding, "Early Sexual Experience," 1384; Maerov, "Prostitution."

216. Esselstyn, "Prostitution"; Marshall Clinard, *Sociology of Deviant Behavior* (New York: Rinehart, 1959).

217. Newman and Caplan, "Juvenile Female Prostitution," 132.

218. Ibid.

219. Ibid., 135.

220. MacVicar and Dillon, "Childhood and Adolescent Development," 145.

221. Ibid., 149.

222. Ibid., 150.

223. Ibid., 151–52.

224. V.W. Wilson, "A Psychological Study of Juvenile Prostitutes," *International Journal of Social Psychiatry* 5, no. 1(1959), 69.

225. Ibid., 69–70.

226. Ibid., 71.

227. Gibbens, "Juvenile Prostitution," 5–6.

228. Ibid., 5–7.

229. Silbert, *Sexual Assault*, 41; James, *Entrance*, 68–69.

230. Harlan, Rodgers, and Slattery, *Male and Female*, 34.

231. James, *Entrance*, 68.

232. Harlan, Rodgers, and Slattery, *Male and Female*, 34.

233. Bracey, *"Baby-Pros,"* 58–59.

234. James, "Progress Report," 53.

235. Harlan, Rodgers, and Slattery, *Male and Female*, 15; Enablers, *Juvenile Prostitution*, 22–23; Bracey, *"Baby-Pros,"* 44; James, *Entrance*, 48.

236. Harlan, Rodgers, and Slattery, *Male and Female*, 15; MacVicar and Dillon, "Childhood and Adolescent Development," 148–49; Newman and Caplan, "Juvenile Female Prostitution," 132; Fields, "Parent–Child Relationships"; Gray, "Turning-Out II," 404; Enablers, *Juvenile Prostitution*, 21.

237. See, especially, James and Meyerding, "Early Sexual Experience as a Factor," 38–39; Silbert and Pines, "Sexual Child Abuse"; Fields, "Parent–Child Relationships," 113–26.

238. Gray, "Turning-Out I," 78.

239. Newman and Caplan, "Juvenile Female Prostitution," 131; Crowley, "Female Runaway Behavior," 76–77; Gray, "Turning-Out I," 33–35; Gray, "Turning-Out II," 406; Harlan, Rodgers, and Slattery, *Male and Female*, 17–18.

240. Harlan, Rodgers, and Slattery, *Male and Female*, 18; Newman and Caplan, "Juvenile Female Prostitution," 131.

241. Enablers, *Juvenile Prostitution*, 52; Gray, "Turning-Out II," 411–12; Harlan, Rogers, and Slattery, *Male and Female*, 29–34; Crowley, "Female Runaway Behavior," 33; Newman and Caplan, "Juvenile Female Prostitution," 131.

242. Enablers, *Juvenile Prostitution*, 60.

243. Ibid.

244. See, for example, Benjamin and Masters, *Prostitution and Morality*, 215–39; Choisy, *Psychoanalysis of the Prostitute*; Greenwald, *Call Girl*; Winick and Kinsie, *Lively Commerce*, 109–20; Susan Hall, *Gentleman of Leisure: A Year in the Life of a Pimp* (New York: Signet, 1972).

245. Bracey does not specify how many pimps of juveniles she interviewed, but an occasional account of an interview with a pimp appears in her book. See Bracey, *"Baby-Pros,"* 38–39. Another study, focusing on juvenile prostitution in Mineapolis–St. Paul,

specifically mentions interviewing pimps, although, again, the number is not specified. See Michael Baizerman, Jacquelyn Thompson, Kimaka Stafford-White and "An Old, Young Friend," "Adolescent Prostitution," *Children Today* 8, no. 5(September–October 1975): 21.

246. Enablers, *Juvenile Prostitution*, 69.
247. Silbert, *Sexual Assault*, 54.
248. Gray, "Turning-Out II," 417.
249. Ibid.
250. Enablers, *Juvenile Prostitution*, 69.
251. Silbert, *Sexual Assault*, 54.
252. Gray, "Turning-Out I," 90–92, 107.
253. Enablers, *Juvenile Prostitution*, 70.
254. Gray, "Turning-Out I," 110.
255. Ibid., 100; Bracey, *"Baby-Pros,"* 48.
256. Enablers, *Juvenile Prostitution*, 70.
257. Ibid., 69.
258. Gray, "Turning-Out I," 121.
259. Silbert, *Sexual Assault*, 55.
260. Ibid.
261. Enablers, *Juvenile Prostitution*, 70.
262. Ibid., 69. Sixty-two percent of the relationships (of those under age 20) last 30 months or less, and 90 percent last less than 1 year. The relationships of respondents aged 20 and older tend to be longer; 63 percent last 1 year or longer, and 19 percent last 3 months or less.
263. Bracey, *"Baby-Pros,"* 35.
264. Ibid., 36.
265. Ibid., 30.
266. See, for example, Charles Winick, "Prostitutes' Clients' Perception of the Prostitutes and of Themselves," *International Journal of Social Psychiatry* 8(1961): 289–97.
267. Gray, "Turning-Out II," 420.
268. James, *Entrance*, 73.
269. Gray, "Turning-Out I," 133.
270. Ibid., 129-30. See also Gray, "Turning Out II," 420–21.
271. James, *Entrance*, 74.
272. Ibid.
273. Gray, "Turning-Out II," 421.
274. James, *Entrance*, 74.
275. Ibid., 75.
276. Ibid.
277. Gray, "Turning-Out I," 130.
278. Enablers, *Juvenile Prostitution*, 76.
279. Ibid. Only 5.6 percent claimed that the customers are "nice, liked them." Another 16.9 percent indicated a mixed response.
280. Ibid., 76.
281. Gray, "Turning-Out II," 420.
282. Enablers, *Juvenile Prostitution*, 75.

283. MacVicar and Dillon, "Childhood and Adolescent Development," 153–54.

284. Enablers, *Juvenile Prostitution,* 70.

285. Silbert, *Sexual Assault,* 60.

286. Bracey, *"Baby-Pros,"* 37.

287. Silbert, *Sexual Assault,* 60.

288. Enablers, *Juvenile Prostitution,* 70.

289. Gray, "Turning-Out I," 117–18.

290. Silbert, *Sexual Assault,* 60; Enablers, *Juvenile Prostitution,* 70.

291. Ibid.

292. Silbert, *Sexual Assault,* 60.

293. Ibid.

294. Bracey, *"Baby-Pros,"* 37.

295. Gray, "Turning-Out I," 118–20.

296. MacVicar and Dillon, "Childhood and Adolescent Development," 152–53.

297. Bracey, *"Baby-Pros,"* 61.

298. Enablers, *Juvenile Prostitution,* 75.

299. Silbert, *Sexual Assault,* 60–61.

300. Gray, "Turning-Out I," 133.

301. Ibid.

302. Silbert, *Sexual Assault,* 62; Bracey, *"Baby-Pros,"* 61–62. On the general subject of victimization of adult and juvenile prostitutes, see Debra K. Boyer and Jennifer James, "Prostitutes as Victims," in *Deviants: Victims or Victimizers?,* ed. Donal E.J. MacNamara and Andrew Karmen (Beverly Hills: Sage, 1983), 109–46.

303. Bracey, *"Baby-Pros,"* 61–62.

304. Enablers, *Juvenile Prostitution,* 75.

305. Gray, "Turning-Out II," 416.

306. Bracey, *"Baby-Pros,"* 61–62.

307. MacVicar and Dillon, "Childhood and Adolescent Development," 154.

308. Gray, "Turning-Out I," 13, 125; Enablers, *Juvenile Prostitution,* 20.

309. James, *Entrance,* 78–79.

310. Ibid. James found that 82 percent were first involved in street prostitution, 5 percent in phone prostitution, 3 percent in bars, 2 percent in hotels/casinos, and 3 percent in several of these. When asked which form of prostitution they prefer, 46 percent of the respondents said streetwalking, 24 percent said phone prostitution, 4 percent said hotels or casinos, 3 percent said studio prostitution, and 5 percent said the bar scene. In the Enablers sample, 95 percent admit they are involved in streetwalking, 18 percent mentioned bars and hotels, 35 percent named private calls, and 18 percent cited sauna prostitution. Enablers, *Juvenile Prostitution,* 20. (Several individuals gave multiple responses to this question; percentages are based on the total number of responses.)

311. Gray, "Turning-Out I," 85.

312. Money is cited as the primary advantage in 94 percent of the cases in Silbert's study. Silbert, *Sexual Assault,* 56. Money and material goods are cited by 71 percent of James's respondents. James, *Entrance,* 80. Money is also the most frequently cited response by Gray's sample. Gray, "Turning-Out I," 104.

313. James, *Entrance,* 69.

314. Ibid., 70.

144 · *Children of the Night*

315. Pomeroy, "Some Aspects of Prostitution," 184.
316. Gray, "Turning-Out I," 104.
317. See Silbert, *Sexual Assault,* 56; James, *Entrance,* 80; Gray, "Turning-Out I," 105; Enablers, *Juvenile Prostitution,* 64.
318. When Silbert questioned her sample on the advantages and disadvantages of prostitution, respondents mentioned an average of 1.9 advantages and 6.2 disadvantages. Silbert, *Sexual Assault,* 56.
319. See Silbert, *Sexual Assault,* 56; James, *Entrance,* 80; Gray, "Turning-Out I," 105.
320. Ibid. See also Enablers, *Juvenile Prostitution,* 63.
321. Gray, "Turning-Out I," 105.
322. Silbert, *Sexual Assault,* 56. This was the fifth most commonly cited response in Silbert's mixed sample.
323. Harlan, Rodgers, and Slattery, *Male and Female,* 34.
324. Ibid., 35.
325. Silbert, *Sexual Assault,* 57.
326. Gray, "Turning-Out I," 159-60.
327. Gray, "Turning-Out II," 413.
328. Ibid.
329. Gray, "Turning-Out I," 161-62.
330. MacVicar and Dillon, "Childhood and Adolescent Development," 157.
331. Enablers, *Juvenile Prostitution,* 64.
332. Bracey, *"Baby-Pros,"* 51; James, *Entrance,* 31.
333. Bracey, *"Baby-Pros,"* 51.
334. Harlan, Rodgers, and Slattery, *Male and Female,* 35.
335. James, *Entrance,* 31.
336. Ibid.
337. Gray, "Turning-Out I," 48.
338. In comparing her data on juvenile prostitutes to data gathered by Kinsey on the population as a whole, Gray found that only 3 percent of the females in Kinsey's sample experienced coitus by age 15. Ibid., 49.
339. Mean age of first coitus is 12.8, and mean age for entry into prostitution is 14.7. Ibid., 53.
340. James, *Entrance,* 33, 46. Forty-seven percent of the prostitutes report that they had difficulties with their parents concerning their sexuality. The Huckleberry House project reports that slightly more than half of the females (52 percent) report hassles at home, at school, or with peers involving their sexuality. Harlan, Rodgers, and Slattery, *Male and Female,* 21.
341. James, *Entrance,* 33.
342. Ibid., 39.
343. Of juvenile prostitutes under age 18, 22.2 percent admit that they take no precautions against pregnancy. Enablers, *Juvenile Prostitution,* 87 (table 86).
344. James, *Entrance,* 35. See also John F. Kantner and Melvin Zelnick, "Sexual Experience of Young Unmarried Women in the United States," *Family Planning Perspectives* 4(1972): 9-18.
345. Of juvenile prostitutes under age 18, 35.6 percent report that they use the pill. Enablers, *Juvenile Prostitution,* 87.

346. James, *Entrance*, 35.

347. Ibid., 36.

348. Enablers, *Juvenile Prostitution*, 86 (table 85).

349. Ibid., 85.

350. Silbert, *Sexual Assault*, 58.

351. These statistics apply to prostitutes under age 18. Enablers, *Juvenile Prostitution*, 87 (table 87).

352. James, *Entrance*, 36.

353. Silbert, *Sexual Assault*, 44.

354. James, *Entrance*, 47.

355. Ibid., 37–38.

356. Gray, "Turning-Out I," 61.

357. Ibid., 62.

358. This is true of 4 percent of James's sample and 11 percent of Silbert's. James, *Entrance*, 46; Silbert, *Sexual Assault*, 57.

359. James found no women who defined themselves as exclusively gay. Silbert, however, reports that 72 percent state they are heterosexual, 14 percent homosexual or bisexual (combined), and 14 percent asexual. Silbert, *Sexual Assault*, 57. The Huckleberry House research reports that 67 percent of juveniles identify as heterosexual, 13 percent as gay, and 17 percent as bisexual. Harlan, Rodgers, and Slattery, *Male and Female*, 20.

360. Silbert, *Sexual Assault*, 57.

361. Ibid., 89.

362. Ibid., 90.

363. Karl Abraham, *Selected Papers of Karl Abraham* (London: Hogarth Press, 1948), 361; Frank S. Caprio, *Female Homosexuality* (New York: Citadel Press, 1954) 95–96, 101; Glover, "The Psychopathology of Prostitution."

364. Caprio, *Female Homosexuality*, 92–102; Glover, "Psychopathology."

365. Hollender, "Prostitution and Human Relatedness," 412.

366. Maerov, "Prostitution," 692.

367. Ibid., 686.

368. J.E. Exner, J. Wylie, A. Leura and T. Parrill, "Some Psychological Characteristics of Prostitutes," *Journal of Personality Assessment* 41(October 1977): 474–85.

369. Ibid.

370. Fields, "Parent–Child Relationships," 54.

371. Bracey, *"Baby-Pros,"* 62–63.

372. Ibid., 63.

373. Ibid.

374. Enablers, *Juvenile Prostitution*, 85.

375. Ibid.

376. Bracey, *"Baby-Pros,"* 63.

377. Gray, "Turning-Out I," 181.

378. James, *Entrance*, 48; Silbert, *Sexual Assault*, 50–54.

379. Ibid.

380. Ibid.

381. Ibid., 53.

382. Newman and Caplan, "Juvenile Female Prostitution," 131.

383. Ibid., 132.

384. MacVicar and Dillon, "Childhood and Adolescent Development," 146–47, 156.

385. Silbert, *Sexual Assault*, 80.

386. Only 6 percent of prostitutes under age 20 claim that they do not use drugs. Enablers, *Juvenile Prostitution*, 89.

387. Harlan, Rodgers, and Slattery, *Male and Female*, 22.

388. Crowley, "Female Runaway Behavior," 77.

389. Harlan, Rodgers, and Slattery, *Male and Female*, 22–23.

390. Ibid., 23.

391. Crowley, "Female Runaway Behavior," 80.

392. James, *Entrance*, 60.

393. Enablers, *Juvenile Prostitution*, 89 (17.9 percent); Silbert, *Sexual Assault*, 48 (58 percent).

394. Twenty percent feel that they have a drug problem and an additional 17 percent have mixed feelings about their drug use. Harlan, Rodgers, and Slattery, *Male and Female*, 23.

395. Silbert, *Sexual Assault*, 48.

396. Enablers, *Juvenile Prostitution*, 89 (19 percent); Silbert, *Sexual Assault*, 49 (two-thirds of a mixed sample of juveniles and adults).

397. Silbert, *Sexual Assault*, 50.

398. Ibid., 49.

399. Gray, "Turning-Out I," 135–36.

400. Bracey, *"Baby-Pros,"* 53.

401. Ibid., 53–54.

402. Ibid., 54.

403. James, *Entrance*, 89.

404. Ibid., 89.

405. Ibid.

406. Bracey, *"Baby-Pros,"* 36.

407. Enablers, *Juvenile Prostitution*, 97. Silbert also questioned juveniles on the positive features of the life they would like for themselves eventually. She found that most put having children first, having a good job second, and having a happy life third. Silbert, *Sexual Assault*, 80.

408. Enablers, *Juvenile Prostitution*, 96.

409. Ibid., 60–61.

410. Bracey, *"Baby-Pros,"* 48.

411. Silbert, *Sexual Assault*, 73.

412. Ibid., 80.

413. Ibid., 79.

414. Ibid.

415. See, for example, Steven H. Clarke, "Some Implications for North Carolina of Recent Research in Juvenile Delinquency," *Journal of Research in Crime and Delinquency* 12(1975): 51; Maynard L. Erickson, "Some Empirical Questions Concerning the Current Revolution in Juvenile Justice," in *The Future of Childhood and Juvenile Justice*, ed. LaMar T. Empey (Charlottesville: University Press of Virginia, 1979); Herbert A. Marra and Richard Sax, "Personality Patterns and Offense Histories of Status Offenders

and Delinquents," *Juvenile and Family Court Journal* 29(1978): 27; Dean G. Rojek and Maynard L. Erickson, "Delinquent Careers: A Test of the Career Escalation Model," *Criminology* 20(1982): 5; Charles P. Smith, David J. Berkman, Warren M. Fraser and John Sutton, *A Preliminary National Assessment of the Status Offender and the Juvenile Justice System: Role Conflicts, Constraints, and Information Gaps* (Washington, D.C.: U.S. Government Printing Office, 1980); Charles W. Thomas, "Are Status Offenders Really so Different? A Comparative and Longitudinal Assessment," *Crime and Delinquency* 22(1976): 438; Joseph G. Weis, Karleen Sakumoto, John Sederstrom and Carol Zeiss, *Jurisdiction and the Elusive Status Offender: A Comparison of Involvement in Delinquent Behavior and Status Offenses* (Washington, D.C.: U.S. Government Printing Office, 1980).

416. Enablers, *Juvenile Prostitution*, 102.

417. The Enablers collected data from police and court records on all juvenile females arrested for prostitution or loitering from 1972 through 1977 in Hennepin and Ramsey counties, Minnesota. Enablers, *Juvenile Prostitution*, 101–103. Both James's study and the Huckleberry House project relied on self-report data.

418. See Deborah K. Walker, *Runaway Youth: An Annotated Bibliography and Literature Overview*, Technical Analysis Paper No. 1 (Washington, D.C.: U.S. Department of Health, Education and Welfare, May 1975).

419. Newman and Caplan, "Juvenile Female Prostitution," 131.

420. Enablers, *Juvenile Prostitution*, 28.

421. Newman and Caplan, "Juvenile Female Prostitution," 131.

422. Silbert, *Sexual Assault*, 92.

423. James, *Entrance*, 50.

424. Gray, "Turning-Out II," 412.

425. Newman and Caplan, "Juvenile Female Prostitution," 131.

426. James, *Entrance*, 54.

427. Harlan, Rodgers, and Slattery, *Male and Female*, 29.

428. Enablers, *Juvenile Prostitution*, 29.

429. Silbert, *Sexual Assault*, 93.

430. Harlan, Rodgers, and Slattery, *Male and Female*, 29.

431. James, *Entrance*, 50.

432. Crowley, "Female Runaway Behavior," 86–87.

433. Harlan, Rodgers, and Slattery, *Male and Female*, 30.

434. Crowley, "Female Runaway Behavior," 88.

435. Ibid., 89 (table 20).

436. Harlan, Rodgers, and Slattery, *Male and Female*, 30.

437. Enablers, *Juvenile Prostitution*, 22.

438. Crowley, "Female Runaway Behavior," 84–85.

439. Enablers, *Juvenile Prostitution*, 106.

440. James, "Progress Report," 59.

441. Enablers, *Juvenile Prostitution*, 29.

442. Ibid.

443. Crowley, "Female Runaway Behavior," 83.

444. See, for example, Choisy, *Psychoanalysis of the Prostitute;* Davis, "The Prostitute"; Esselstyn, "Prostitution"; Greenwald, *Elegant Prostitute;* Maerov, "Prostitution."

445. Silbert, *Sexual Assault*, 25.

446. Crowley, "Female Runaway Behavior," 83.

447. Bracey, *"Baby-Pros,"* 41.

448. Silbert, *Sexual Assault,* 25.

449. Bracey, *"Baby-Pros,"* 40.

450. Ibid., 41.

451. This research falls in the second of the two theoretical orientations concerning the causes of runaway behavior. In the first view (the psychopathological model), the runaway's behavior is attributed to problems within the individual child (for example, lack of ego strength, poor impulse control, depression). The second view (the environmental context model) attributes runaway behavior to external factors, with running away as an adaptive response to situational pressures. Walker, *Runaway Youth,* 18.

452. Lillian Ambrosino, *Runaways* (Boston: Beacon Press, 1971), 3–4.

453. John Goldmeier and Robert D. Dean, "The Runaway: Person, Problem or Situation?" *Crime and Delinquency* 19, no. 4(1973): 542.

454. Von H. Regel and K.H. Parnitzke, "Entstehungsbedingungen des Fortlaufen bei Kindern" ("Causative Conditions of Running Away in Children"), *Psychiatrie Neurologie und Medizinische Psychologie* 19(1967): 282.

455. Kenneth Libertoff, "Runaway Children and Social Network Interaction," Paper delivered at the Annual Meeting of the American Psychological Association, Washington, D.C., 7 September 1976, cited in Silbert, *Sexual Assault,* 92.

456. Walker, *Runaway Youth,* 20.

457. See, for example, B.H. Balser, "A Behavior Problem—Runaway, *"Psychiatric Quarterly* 13(1939): 539–57; Goldmeier and Dean, "The Runaway"; Corneliz R. Keogh, "A Study of Runaways at a State Correctional School for Boys," *Journal of Juvenile Research* 19(1935): 45–61; Boris M. Levinson and Harry Mezei, "Self-Concepts and Ideal ʼSelf-Concepts of Runaway Youth: Counseling Implications, *Psychological Reports* 26, no. 3(1970): 775–83; George E. Outland, "Determinate Involved in Boy Transiency," *Journal of Educational Sociology* 11(1938): 360–72; George E. Outland, "The Home Situation as a Direct Cause of Boy Transiency," *Journal of Juvenile Research* 22(1938): 33–43; Robert Shellow, Juliana Schamp, Elliot Liebow and Elizabeth Unger, "Suburban Runaways of the 1960's," (Monographs of the Society for Research in Child Development, 1967), 32; Margaret Beyer, Susan A. Holt, Thomas A. Reid and Donald M. Quinlan, "Runaway Youths: Families in Conflict," Paper presented at the meeting of the Eastern Psychological Association, Washington, D.C., 1973; Margaret B. Saltonstall, *Runaways and Street Children in Massachusetts* (Boston: Massachusetts Committee on Children and Youth, 1973); Margaret Beyer, "The Psychological Problems of Adolescent Runaways," *Dissertation Abstracts International* 35(1974): 2420B–21B.

458. See, for example, Bibi Wein, *The Runaway Generation* (New York: McKay, 1970); Clairette P. Armstrong, "A Psychoneurotic Reaction of Delinquent Boys and Girls," *Journal of Abnormal and Social Psychology* 32(1937): 329–42; James A. Hildebrand, "Why Runaways Leave Home," *Journal of Criminal Law, Criminology, and Police Science* 54, no. 2(1963): 211–16; James A. Hildebrand, "Reasons for Runaways," *Crime and Delinquency* 14, no. 1(1968): 42–48.

459. See, for example, Jeffrey D. Blum and Judith E. Smith, *Nothing Left to Lose* (Boston: Beacon Press, 1972); Racco D'Angelo, *Families of Sand: A Report Concerning the Flight of Adolescents from Their Families* (Columbus: Ohio State University, School

of Social Work, 1974); Linda Blood and Racco D'Angelo, "A Progress Research Report on Value Issues in Conflict Between Runaways and Their Parents," *Journal of Marriage and the Family* 36(1974): 486–91; Donald S. Farrington, William Shelton, and James R. McKay, "Observations on Runaway Children from a Residential Setting," *Child Welfare* 42(1963): 286–91; Randall M. Foster, "Intrapsychic and Environmental Factors in Running Away from Home," *American Journal of Orthopsychiatry* 32(1962): 486–91; Nancy B. Green and T.S. Esselstyn, "The Beyond Control Girl," *Juvenile Justice* 23, no. 3(1972): 13–19; Mary C. Howell, E.B. Emmons, and D.A. Frank, "Reminiscences of Runaway Adolescents," *American Journal of Orthopsychiatry* 43, no. 5(1973): 840–53; Lawson G. Lowrey, "Runaways and Nomads," *American Journal of Orthopsychiatry* 11(1941): 775–82; Helm Stierlin, "A Family Perspective on Adolescent Runaways," *Archives of General Psychiatry* 29(1973): 56–62; Beyer et al., "Runaway Youths"; Tim Brennan, Fletcher Blanchard, Dave Huizinga and Delbert Elliott, *Final Report: The Incidence and Nature of Runaway Behavior* (Boulder: Behavioral Research and Evaluation Corporation, 1975); Saltonstall, *Runaways and Street Children*.

460. Walker, *Runaway Youth*, 20.

461. Libertoff, "Runaway Children." See also Lucy Olson, Elliot Liebow, Fortune V. Mannino and Milton F. Shore, "Runaway Children Twelve Years Later: A Follow-Up," *Journal of Family Issues* 1, no. 2(June 1980): 165–88, 177–78; Tim Brennan, "Mapping the Diversity Among Runaways: A Descriptive Multivariate Analysis of Selected Social Psychological Background Conditions," *Journal of Family Issues* 1, no. 2(June 1980): 189–209, 201; James D. Orten and Sharon K. Soll, "Runaway Children and Their Families: A Treatment Typology," *Journal of Family Issues* 1, no. 2(June 1980): 255.

462. Goldmeier and Dean, "The Runaway," 542.

463. Walker, *Runaway Youth*, 20. See also D'Angelo, *Families of Sand;* Armstrong, "A Psychoneurotic Reaction"; Green and Esselstyn, "The Beyond Control Girl"; Hildebrand, "Why Runaways Leave Home."

464. See James, *Entrance*, 51. Running away and truancy are examples of status offenses, which are noncriminal misbehavior that subjects the juvenile to the jurisdiction of the juvenile court, although such acts would not subject an adult to criminal sanctions.

465. Ibid.

466. Silbert places the percentage at 71 percent based on self-report data. The Huckleberry House project found that 73 percent of its sample (thirty juveniles aged 12 to 17) had been arrested at least once. Silbert, *Sexual Assault*, 46; Harlan, Rodgers, and Slattery, *Male and Female*, 26.

467. Gray, "Turning-Out I," 146.

468. James, *Entrance*, 51.

469. Silbert, *Sexual Assault*, 47.

470. Enablers, *Juvenile Prostitution*, 110. Also, according to court records, of eighty-two juvenile girls referred to juvenile courts in two counties, 62.2 percent had been arrested at least once before for some other nonprostitution offense.

471. James, *Entrance*, 51.

472. Enablers, *Juvenile Prostitution*, 112.

473. Ibid.

474. Ibid.

475. Ibid.
476. Ibid.
477. Ibid., 112–13
478. Ibid.
479. Ibid., 113.
480. James, *Entrance,* 49.
481. Ibid.
482. Ibid., 53.
483. Ibid., 58.
484. Gray, "Turning-Out I," 146.
485. Harlan, Rodgers, and Slattery, *Male and Female,* 26.
486. Enablers, *Juvenile Prostitution,* 114, 115 (table 106); total court records = 82 cases, total police records = 116 cases.
487. Ibid., 115 (table 106).
488. Gray, "Turning-Out I," 146.
489. Enablers, *Juvenile Prostitution,* 116 (table 107).
490. Ibid.
491. Gray, "Turning-Out I," 146.
492. Ibid., 147.
493. Enablers, *Juvenile Prostitution,* 121 (table 110).
494. Ninety-six percent of repeat offenders in Minneapolis are referred to court intake. Ibid.
495. See Enablers, *Juvenile Prostitution,* 121 (table 110).
496. Ibid., 118 (table 108).
497. Ibid.
498. Ibid.
499. Ibid.
500. Gray, "Turning-Out I," 148.
501. Ibid., 148–49.
502. Paul W. Tappan, *Delinquent Girls in Court: A Study of the Wayward Minor Court of New York* (New York: Columbia University Press, 1947), 147.
503. Gray, "Turning-Out I," 149–50.
504. Ibid., 150.
505. Ibid.
506. Ibid., 152.
507. See, generally, MacVicar and Dillon, "Childhood and Adolescent Development"; Newman and Caplan, "Juvenile Female Prostitution."
508. Enablers, *Juvenile Prostitution,* 49.
509. Ibid.
510. Ibid.
511. Ibid., 91.
512. Ibid.
513. Ibid., 92.
514. Ibid.
515. Ibid., 85.
516. Ibid.

517. Ibid.
518. Harlan, Rodgers, and Slattery, *Male and Female*, 41.
519. Ibid., 46.
520. Ibid., 47.
521. Ibid.
522. Ibid., 47–48.
523. Ibid., 49.
524. Ibid.
525. Ibid.
526. Silbert, *Sexual Assault*, 80.
527. Ibid., 80–81.
528. Harlan, Rodgers, and Slattery, *Male and Female*, 51.
529. Ibid., 52.
530. Ibid.

5

A Comparison of Female and Male Adolescent Prostitution

onsiderable research has been done recently on both male and female adolescent prostitution, but comparative studies are virtually nonexistent.[1] Therefore, an unanswered question remains: are male and female juvenile prostitution distinct or related phenomena? A review of the literature and the existing empirical data suggests that there are a number of major similarities between male and female adolescent prostitutes in regard to their demographic characteristics, family backgrounds, entrance into prostitution, prostitution lifestyles and experiences, juvenile justice involvement, and social service needs. Differences also exist, however.

Backgrounds and Family Characteristics

Age

Both female and male adolescent prostitutes range in age from 12 to 18,[2] and several researchers place the mean age for both at 16 years.[3] Studies that deal exclusively with juveniles and that contain detailed breakdowns of age distribution reveal that the modal age for juvenile prostitutes is 17 years.[4] Thus, it appears that the largest group of adolescent prostitutes consists of older adolescents.

Socioeconomic Status

Male and female adolescent prostitutes come from all socioeconomic backgrounds, but recent studies note the presence of a substantial number of youth from middle-class backgrounds. One study of juvenile boys, for example, notes that 38 percent characterize their homes as middle class and only 14 percent indicate that their family income is "very low."[5] These findings are consistent with other studies.[6] Studies of adolescent female prostitutes also reflect a large middle-class composition, and these studies also include a surprising number of affluent juveniles. Some juvenile girls have professional parents, and significant numbers have parents who are college-educated.[7] These findings contradict those in earlier studies, which characterized a majority of adolescent male and female prostitutes as lower class,[8] but the earlier findings undoubtedly reflect sample bias.

Race

The majority of both male and female adolescent prostitutes are Caucasian. Estimates on the percentage of adolescent male prostitutes who are Caucasian range from 53 percent to a high of 90 percent,[9] and the estimates for Caucasian females range from 50 percent to 80 percent.[10] Blacks comprise the second largest racial group for both male and female juvenile prostitutes.[11] Native American and Hispanic juveniles sometimes engage in prostitution,[12] but Asian youth rarely do.[13]

Family Composition

Studies of both male and female juvenile prostitutes reveal that an overwhelming number come from homes broken by separation or divorce. Research on juvenile females suggests that approximately 70 to 75 percent report the absence of one or both parents during part or all of their childhood.[14] Studies of juvenile male prostitutes report similar findings, with numerous researchers citing the high frequency of broken homes in the males' family backgrounds.[15] Estimates on the incidence of broken homes for juvenile males approximate those for juvenile girls,[16] and most studies note that the father more often is the absent parent.

Similarly, research on both juvenile males and females notes the juveniles' poor relationships with one or both parents.[17] These relationships are frequently characterized by parental absence, indifference, alcoholism, abuse, or hostility. In addition, some evidence reveals that a small percentage of both male and female juvenile prostitutes are raised by persons other than their parents,[18] generally relatives or institutional and foster caretakers. This signifies that some degree of caretaker instability exists in the early lives of both female and male juvenile prostitutes.

Physical and Sexual Abuse

Both physical abuse and sexual abuse characterize the childhood histories of male and female adolescent prostitutes, but more data are available on this variable for juvenile females than for juvenile males. Only a few recent studies focus on this issue in a juvenile male sample;[19] previous research on males mentions the existence of abusive family relations only in passing.[20] In contrast, physical abuse has been noted repeatedly as an etiological feature throughout much of the literature on adolescent female prostitution.[21]

A review of the literature suggests that female juveniles have a higher incidence of victimization, with several studies of female prostitutes noting that approximately two-thirds or more report being beaten by a family member.[22] This compares to a somewhat lower rate of victimization—34 to 47 percent—among adolescent males.[23]

Sexual abuse also appears to characterize the early life experiences of both male and female adolescent prostitutes. Estimates on the incidence of early intrafamilial sexual abuse among female prostitutes are high, ranging from 31 percent (Enablers) to 66.7 percent (Silbert).[24] Juvenile male prostitutes also report having been sexually abused by family members. For juvenile males, estimates of sexual abuse by family members range from 10 percent (Shick) to 29 percent (URSA).[25] One tentative conclusion that may be drawn from these incidence data is that juvenile females suffer more frequently from such victimization.

Entrance into Prostitution

Age

Both male and female adolescent prostitutes become involved in prostitution at an early age. For adolescent girls, the average age for the initial act of prostitution is 14,[26] and available data reveal the same mean age of entry into prostitution for adolescent males.[27]

Influence of Significant Others

The mode of entry into prostitution is similar for both male and female adolescents and is facilitated by numerous persons. Peer introduction is important in females' entrance into prostitution, but especially so for males. James reports that 13 percent of her respondents first learned of prostitution from a girlfriend,[28] and other studies note similar percentages of juvenile girls who learned about prostitution from their peers.[29]

On the other hand, most males learn about prostitution by peer introduction. Eighty percent of the Huckleberry House male sample learned about prostitution either from friends or from other youth on the street who engaged in prostitution,[30] and Allen also reports a large percentage of youth (70 percent) who are introduced through peers.[31] A typical peer introduction occurs, Allen notes, when a boy complains that he needs money and an older friend suggests that the youth can make quick money by prostitution. The older friend describes where and how prostitution is accomplished and usually accompanies the younger boy for at least the first experience.[32]

Other persons are also influential in adolescents' entry into prostitution. James reports that 23 percent of the girls in her study first learned of prostitution from a relative; 4 percent were with a family member at the time of their first act of prostitution.[33] Silbert also notes the influence of relatives in teaching juvenile girls about prostitution and in actually turning them out.[34] Family members also introduce some male youth to prostitution. For boys, these relatives usually are older brothers;[35] for girls, mothers and sisters-in-law have been noted as influential.[36]

Potential customers also influence both male and female juveniles to turn to prostitution by offering the youth money in return for sexual services. Studies of both male and female adolescent prostitutes reveal that some youth are introduced to prostitution by customers, but the research reports that higher percentages of males are introduced to prostitution in this manner. The Huckleberry House project reports that only 10 percent of female prostitutes are first propositioned by customers,[37] and Silbert notes an even smaller percentage of females introduced to prostitution in this manner.[38] In contrast, studies of young male prostitutes have found that significant numbers are initially propositioned by customers. Allen notes this method of introduction for twenty-nine of ninety-eight youth.[39] James found that 40.4 percent of the young men were first asked to prostitute by customers, and she reveals that this method is especially common for male prostitutes who identify as heterosexual. Whereas most homosexual prostitutes learn about prostitution from other prostitutes and from school peers, most heterosexual prostitutes learn about prostitution upon being propositioned.[40] This may constitute one important difference between males' and females' introduction to prostitution.

The most salient difference in the entry into prostitution of adolescent males and females, however, is the pimp. James notes that virtually all young female prostitutes have been approached at some time by a pimp and asked to prostitute,[41] and other studies similarly emphasize the role of the pimp in the girls' initial involvement in prostitution.[42] The pimp often sweet-talks the juvenile into entering prostitution, promising money, protection, and companionship.

In contrast, studies of young male prostitutes rarely mention the influence of a pimp in the youths' entry into prostitution. James reports that no male youth first learned of prostitution from pimps,[43] and only one youth in one other study specifically stated that he was introduced to prostitution by a pimp.[44] Although females are sometimes forced into prostitution against their will by the pimp,[45] the pimp plays a negligible role in juvenile male prostitution.

Several sources note that the transition from initial act to regular involvement in prostitution is rapid, generally taking less than a year. URSA found that 91 percent of male youth begin regular prostitution within 1 year of their first prostitution experience,[46] and Silbert reports an 8-month difference for females between the average age of starting prostitution and the average age of working regularly.[47]

Allen attributes the males' rapid drift into prostitution to several factors: acquisition of the knowledge of how to perform prostitution, a gradual loss of nervousness about what might happen, enjoyment of the sexual release, and appreciation of a source of quick "big" money. The drift is furthered by financial success, a lack of unpleasant experiences, little parental control, and sexual interest.[48]

James uses the concept of drift between conventional and deviant behavior, as described by Matza,[49] to explain the drift of adolescent females into prostitution. She theorizes that the drift is precipitated and maintained by events that occur in a linear process of (1) adaptation to a negative self-image; (2) acculturation to the expected behavior of that image, supported by informal labeling; (3) assimilation into the subculture and development of a deviant identity; and (4) formal labeling and self-identification as a prostitute, with subsequent commitment to prostitution as a lifestyle. The young girl initially discovers that, because of her promiscuity, her self-image is congruent with that of a deviant female, and this discovery is reinforced by labeling from her social network. Her response is to continue to behave in conformity with this deviant role. Societal reaction accompanied by periodic institutionalization complete her formal labeling as a prostitute, and this formal labeling forces her in the direction of further commitment to the lifestyle.[50]

Feelings upon Turning Out

Data on female juvenile prostitutes reveal that many have negative feelings about themselves at the time they first become involved in prostitution; many report feeling depressed, unhappy, lonely, or insecure just before their initial involvement.[51] Depression also characterizes the emotions of many young male prostitutes at the time of their first act of prostitution.[52] In addition, both female and male youth report feeling fearful, scared, and nervous during their first act of prostitution.[53]

Drug Use During Initial Involvement

Some youth cope with their introduction to prostitution by using drugs during the initial encounter. James found that 8 percent of juvenile females and 10.6 percent of juvenile males are high on drugs or alcohol at the time of their first act of prostitution.[54] These youth report that using drugs enables them to cope better with their nervousness and fear.

General Situations Prior to Starting Prostitution

Living Situations. A number of juvenile prostitutes have unstable living situations at the time they decide to engage in prostitution. Most juvenile females are not living at home when they start prostitution.[55] Data on the living situations of juvenile males prior to starting prostitution are not available. Some studies have inquired into the males' living situations prior to seeking services,[56] and into their living situations at the time of the interview,[57] but research has not inquired specifically into their living situations immediately prior to entrance into prostitution. Collection of such data would be valuable to add to the knowledge of the relationship between running away and prostitution.

Employment Histories. Most adolescent prostitutes have poor employment histories.[58] Research data are available on employment at two time periods: the time the youth first turn to prostitution and the time of the interview. Most girls are not working at the time they start prostitution,[59] and approximately the same percentage of boys are not otherwise employed.[60] Many youth have known long periods of unemployment. In Shick's sample, for example, 15 percent were unemployed for more than a year, and another 12 percent were unemployed between 7 months and 1 year. Eighteen percent had not been employed at all during the past 12 months, and an additional 52 percent had not been employed for at least half of the preceding 12 months. Moreover, of the forty subjects who were legally employed at some time during the month prior to the interview, 55 percent had been unemployed for 6 months or more during the preceding year.[61]

Although unemployment is high among adolescent prostitutes, most have prior work experience, either before leaving home or for short periods while on the run.[62] Few, however, have well-developed job skills. The type of work experience they acquire is usually short-term, part-time jobs in unskilled employment.[63] Frequently, in the crisis the youth face in being on their own, they are unable to find employment.[64]

Education. Both male and female juvenile prostitutes have poor school histories. Although most of these juveniles are of school age at the time of their involvement in prostitution, few are actually attending school.[65] Most adolescent prostitutes fail to complete high school; this is true of juvenile male prostitutes[66] as well as females.[67] At least half (and perhaps as many as three-fourths) are dropouts.[68] Among the dropouts, a surprising number have completed only the eighth grade.[69]

These youth experience many difficulties in school, and many are at least a year behind. Few of them have positive feelings about school, and many have totally negative feelings. Many have trouble getting along with their peers at school. A few have trouble in school because of drug or alcohol use.[70] Females are even more likely than males to have experienced difficulties with authority figures (teachers) and school regulations (truancy, fighting, rule violations). Also, females are more likely to report their peer relations to be poor. Males are more likely to have experienced school problems revolving around their sexuality; for example, some youth were suspended for being too publicly intimate with another boy, for making a pass at a male teacher, or for being vocal about gay relationships.[71]

Motivations for Entrance into Prostitution

Various research studies have examined the motivating factors leading to adolescent male and female prostitution. The literature on both male and female adolescent prostitutes mentions that socioeconomic factors are influential in the process of entrance into prostitution. Money is the primary motivating factor for males and females.[72] They desire money either for the material goods it can supply or, for some, out of economic necessity.

Other factors are also mentioned in the research. All studies emphasize the psychosocial background of male prostitutes as a predisposing factor, citing a high frequency of broken homes, lack of affection, indifferent or hostile mothers and fathers, hostile stepfathers, poor educational histories, deprived socioeconomic status, poor work histories, and few or no vocational skills.[73]

Information about motivations for entrance into adolescent male prostitution may also be drawn from research on adult entrance into male prostitution—which often took place during adolescence. The various authors of these adult studies suggest several theories. Craft, Doshay, and Jersild concur that poor background and chance play prominent roles.[74] Craft adds that parental attitudes are also motivating factors in that they prepare a child for misconduct—propelling him into situations of chance and influencing him to seek affection and money through prostitution.[75] MacNamara dismisses the psychological factors and describes the primary motivating factor as socioeconomic.[76] He claims that the youth drift into prostitution because they are ill-equipped educationally, vocationally, and by family conditioning to make their way in a complex competitive society. In prostitution, the youth find a "temporary and relatively satisfactory survival modus vivendi."[77]

In contrast, Ginsburg describes the motivating factors in psychological terms—as a neurotic acting-out of internal conflicts that are related to both a desire for affection and an antagonism toward men. He describes prostitution as solving the problem of relating to others rather than meeting a sexual need.[78] Coombs also attributes male prostitution to behavioral factors. Relying on opportunity theory, he theorizes that prostitution follows early sexual seduction by other males that is accompanied by an immediate reward (money or favors).[79] Russell suggests that prostitution of young males results from a combination of normal adolescent sex drive, an inhibited interest in women, a need for identification with older men, a withdrawal from family ties, and a competitive peer relationship.[80] Finally Caukins and Coombs cite a combination of socioeconomic, family background, and psychological factors that predispose young men toward prostitution: the promise of quick and easy money, loneliness, a need for acceptance, lack of vocational training, broken homes, unavailability of jobs, parental rejection, and the lack of psychological counseling.[81]

Theories on motivation for entrance into prostitution are similar for juvenile females. Some sources point to the females' impoverished family background, poor relationship with parents, and emotional deprivation.[82] Research also attributes prostitution to economic motivations—specifically, the financial problems that plague many females prior to their entrance into prostitution.[83] Additional research notes the influence of such factors as physical abuse,[84] and several studies note the influence of early negative sexual experiences.[85]

One central difference between males' and females' entrance into prostitution is the element of homosexuality. This factor is influential at various stages. First, the males' early negative sexual experiences are more likely than females' to be homosexual in nature.[86] James suggests that such early victimization may aggravate the youth's negative self-image.[87] The male victim's response to sexual assault also differs from the female's because of his sex-role conditioning—that men should be able to protect themselves, and he could not. Homosexuality is also influential at a subsequent stage. Especially for gay youth, the later decision to turn to prostitution may constitute an attempt to interact with gay persons.[88] The youth frequent prostitution locales and associate with persons at those locales, thereby hoping to discover whether or not they are homosexual and hoping to find acceptance within the gay community.[89]

Prostitution Lifestyles

Relationships with Pimps

One difference between female and male juvenile prostitutes as discussed earlier, is that male prostitutes are rarely introduced to prostitution by pimps and rarely work for pimps. The absence of pimps in male prostitution may be explained by gender differences. Young males tend to feel that they do not need pimps to provide protection and respect within the street subculture. Sex-role conditioning, the frequency of regular, ongoing relationships with customers, and physical size may combine to make males feel that they do not require pimps to care for them.[90] A few studies note that, occasionally, older male prostitutes may pimp for (derive support from) younger boys,[91] but such arrangements are generally short-lived.[92]

This absence of pimps results in several other differences between female and male adolescent prostitutes. Young men are not coerced into prostitution, as so many young women are. Furthermore, male prostitutes experience less physical abuse while working as prostitutes, since so much of the violence associated with female prostitution derives from the prostitute–pimp relationship.

Customers

Customers of juvenile male prostitutes tend to be 30 to 50 years old, usually Caucasian, and from a variety of social and occupational backgrounds.[93] In this regard, the customers of male and female adolescent prostitutes are similar,[94] except that the customers of male prostitutes manifest a desire for a same-sex prostitute and for homosexual acts. Acts of male prostitution usually occur in the customer's car or home. Use of the home as a location for prostitution activities also appears to differentiate male and female prostitution.[95] Male prostitutes will service a customer in his home, but female prostitutes prefer to remain close to the street or to use a hotel because of the possibility of physical danger from customers. Males are less likely to use a hotel, because an older man and a young boy entering a hotel room would raise suspicion.[96]

Some adolescent male prostitutes have a special relationship with a customer known as a "sugar daddy"—a male customer with whom the boy develops an ongoing relationship in which financial support is exchanged for sexual acts and companionship.[97] Being kept by a sugar daddy is a goal of many male prostitutes. It carries with it a modicum of prestige: "It is proof of one's lovability, approval, acceptance, desirability, and smart operating."[98] The sugar daddy performs functions for the male prostitute similar to those the pimp performs for the female prostitute. He provides a pseudo-family relationship and serves as an emotional and material resource.[99] Like the pimp–prostitute relationship, the sugar daddy relationship is often short-lived. Also, it is not uncommon for a youth to have several consecutive sugar daddies.[100] Such a relationship offers many advantages over regular street prostitution for the young male prostitute. It maximizes personal safety and financial security, and it lessens the psychological and physical demands of numerous anonymous sex partners.[101] Some prostitutes reject this type of relationship, however, perceiving it as threatening their independence and as too socially and sexually demanding.[102]

The norms of the prostitute–customer relationship for the peer-delinquent have been explored in Reiss's sociological classic.[103] The youth remains emotionally uninvolved and permits the customer to engage only in fellatio. Attempts at further sexual activity are likely to lead to violence. Homosexual prostitutes may be distinguished from Reiss's peer-delinquent types in terms of the nature of the sexual acts performed with the customer. Homosexual prostitutes generally are willing participants in fellatio as well as anal sexual activity, albeit the latter commands a higher fee.

The psychodynamics of the relationship in general have been explored by Caukins and Coombs and by Ginsburg.[104] Ginsburg explains that the male prostitute is enmeshed in a type of paradox. On the one hand, his interaction with the customer is characterized by a desire for affection and approval, which is often unadmitted and unrecognized. On the other hand, he feels considerable disdain and antagonism toward the men with whom he deals.[105] Caukins and Coombs maintain that the prostitute–customer relationship is held together by an unspoken agreement whereby each person allows the other to indulge his special sexual fantasy. Both prostitute and customer engage in elaborate role playing, and the sexual acts are heavily laden with fantasy and accompanied by considerable guilt.[106]

Violence

Much of the physical abuse associated with juvenile female prostitution derives from the relationship with the pimp.[107] The absence of pimps in juvenile male prostitution eliminates one major source of violence for young men, but assaultive behavior between prostitute and client occurs for both juvenile female and male prostitutes. Although more information is available on females' abuse by customers,[108] data suggest that juvenile male prostitutes also suffer violence by customers.[109] Furthermore, murders of both juvenile male and female prostitutes are not unknown.[110]

Violence by young prostitutes *toward* customers also has been noted. Instances of prostitutes beating customers are replete in the literature, and numerous researchers have found examples of prostitutes assaulting and/or robbing customers.[111] A number of studies point to the mutual hatred that exists between the prostitute and his customer.[112] Currents of subsurface hostility characterize the relationship. MacNamara suggests that the prostitute's hatred for the customer is really directed toward the prostitute's father.[113] Several studies mention juvenile delinquents who occasionally or frequently engage in prostitution as part of a plan of general criminal behavior.[114] They learn how to be picked up by a homosexual customer and then threaten, assault, or blackmail the customer, threatening to report him to the police if he does not cooperate; they frequently beat him up in any case.

The psychodynamics of the prostitute–customer relationship that give rise to this violence are explained by Caukins and Coombs. They found that the dependency relationship between prostitute and customer generates considerable hostility and that mutual hatred flows from the symbiotic nature of the relationship.[115]

Type of Prostitution

Most juvenile prostitutes, both female and male, are street hustlers. This is the type of prostitution to which they are first introduced, and it is also the type they prefer.[116] Some juvenile males, like some females, work as call boys.[117]

Those who have less difficulty being recognized as minors work in bars.[118] Adolescent male prostitutes engage in some types of prostitution that are not shared by their female counterparts. These tend to be contacts in locales either common to the gay subculture (such as steam baths) or otherwise known as meeting places for homosexual encounters with youth (such as public restrooms).[119]

Attitudes about Prostitution

Research on adolescent males and females has explored their attitudes toward prostitution. These studies have found that many adolescent prostitutes have negative feelings about prostitution. For many adolescent males (55 percent), prostitution is a negative experience or is positive only in terms of its financial possibilities, and even those who consider it positive as a way to make money point to its many drawbacks.[120] Some males feel that it damages their self-esteem or their health, and some feel that it physically endangers them but is a way to survive.[121] For some male prostitutes (30 percent), however, prostitution is a positive experience.[122] These youth note that the work is easy and glamorous. Also, some feel that the experience of being a prostitute makes them more mature and helps them learn to survive on their own.

Both negative and positive attitudes about prostitution are also expressed by adolescent girls. Many of the females believe prostitution to be an entirely negative experience.[123] The negative aspects of prostitution cited by female prostitutes include danger from customers, physical or sexual abuse, venereal disease, poor health, drug abuse, and arrest.[124] They also cite psychological costs, including lowered self-esteem and self-worth, feelings of shame and guilt, loss of respect, stigma, becoming negative toward men and sex, negative effects on family relationships, bad working conditions (for example, long hours), no future, and being controlled by pimps.[125] Pimps contribute to many of the females' negative attitudes about prostitution, causing the experience to be more frightening or damaging than it otherwise would be.[126]

One interesting difference between male and female prostitutes is that more females find prostitution to be an entirely negative experience.[127] As noted, one reason for this difference is the pimp,[128] who is responsible for much of the physical abuse that contributes to juveniles' negative feelings about prostitution. Another reason for the disparity in females' and males' attitudes about prostitution may be their different feelings about the sexual aspects of their employment. Whereas many young males indicate that sexual gratification is their primary reason for engaging in prostitution, few females enjoy prostitution for this reason.[129]

In her study of male youth, James suggests that attitudes toward prostitution change over time. Initially, the youth like the excitement, money, friends, and sense of freedom. They become disillusioned with street life, however, and they begin to find it more difficult to tolerate the sexual activity of prostitution. Then, only the money and a lack of alternatives explain their continued involvement.[130]

Money

Female and male juvenile prostitutes have similar habits and attitudes about money. They are well aware of their ability to earn large sums of money in their profession, and they tend to report high incomes and brag about their high fees and incomes to researchers. Sources suggest, however, that the reported incomes seem to be higher than they really are.[131]

Despite their ability to earn large sums of money, the youth rarely retain much of their earnings. Few accumulate any savings or substantial assets and most have no form of bank account.[132] Any earnings are expended quickly—on clothes, drugs and entertainment. In fact, the youth rarely have much money in their pockets. One researcher asked a group of young male prostitutes to count the money in their pockets at the time of the interview. More than half of the group had less than one dollar, and only seven boys possessed more than five dollars.[133] By the end of a week, the juvenile prostitutes rarely have much money left after paying expenses, and many have to depend on others, such as friends or customers, to provide them with places to sleep and free meals.

One difference between male and female adolescent prostitutes regarding money habits is that the females turn over much of their earnings to their pimps.[134] Even though the adolescent males are self-employed and thus do not have to turn over their earnings to pimps, however, they still are not able to retain any substantial portion of their earnings.

Sexuality

First Sexual Experience. For adolescent prostitutes, the first sexual experience tends to occur at an early age. Data on the first sexual experience of young male prostitutes are presented in three studies.[135] Allen notes a recurrent theme in the youth's background—growing up in an environment where sex is discussed, observed, encouraged (by peers, older siblings, older acquaintances), and experienced.[136] He finds that two-thirds of male prostitutes ($n = 98$) had their first sexual encounter with another male and one-third had it with a female. The age of the youth at the time of their first sexual experience with males ranges from 5 to 16 years, with an overall median of 13.5. The age range for their first sexual experience with a female is 8 to 15 years, with a median of 12.[137] In another study of young boys, the age at first sexual experience ranges from 3 to 17, with a slightly lower median than the Allen study—12 years.[138]

Similar conclusions can be drawn from James's data, which reveal that 44.7 percent of the young male prostitutes had their first sexual experience with another male—fathers or stepfathers (2.1 percent), other male relatives (12.8 percent), male acquaintances (21.3 percent), male strangers (2.1 percent), a parent's male lover or male friend (2.1 percent), or a male authority figure (4.3 percent).[139] An extrapolation from that data reveals a median age of 11 at the first sexual involvement.[140]

Allen and James also explored the method of introduction to the first sexual experience. For youth whose first sexual experience was with a female, 66 percent of the youth were seduced by older females and 34 percent initiated the sexual act. For youth whose first sexual experience was with a male, 56 percent were seduced, and 60 percent of this group received money or favors for their participation. The remainder of youth whose first sexual experience was with a male either initiated the sexual act or entered into it by mutual agreement.[141]

James points out that for many male youth, this first sexual experience was incestuous. For 25.6 percent of the prostitutes, their first sexual experience occurred with a relative. First sexual activity with a relative was reported more frequently by prostitutes who identify as homosexual than by those who identify as heterosexual.[142] James also found that a number of youth were physically forced to participate in this first sexual activity. In fact, 10.6 percent report being physically coerced and 12.8 percent felt emotionally coerced to participate.[143]

Allen concludes that adolescent male prostitutes have more frequent sexual experiences of all types than their nonprostitute cohorts. He also determines that, when compared to Kinsey's data for all males of similar educational background, adolescent prostitutes have a much lower incidence of sexual intercourse with females. By age 18, 100 percent of Allen's sample had had more than one sexual experience with a male, whereas only 35 percent had had sexual intercourse with a female. Allen contrasts this with Kinsey's data for all males of similar educational background, who had a 58 percent incidence of sexual intercourse with females by age 16.[144]

The early sexual experience of female prostitutes has received considerable attention in the literature. All studies concur that the women's first sexual experience occurred at a relatively young age. James compared this variable in a sample of adolescent prostitutes and nonprostitutes (delinquents who were not sexually labeled).[145] She found that the average age at first intercourse was 12.5 for the prostitutes and 13 for the nonprostitutes.[146] Other studies had similar findings.[147]

For many juvenile female prostitutes, coercion characterizes their first sexual intercourse. The Enablers report that for 21.7 percent of prostitutes under age 20, their first sexual intercourse was a rape.[148] For 66.7 percent of the juvenile sample, the first rape experienced took place by age 14 or younger.[149] James also found that first intercourse was coerced in many cases. She notes that about one-third of both the prostitute and delinquent nonprostitute subjects report being physically or emotionally coerced at first intercourse.[150] Regular intercourse followed shortly after first coitus, beginning at age 13.5 for prostitutes and age 14.5 for nonprostitutes.[151]

Gray, who also analyzed James's data, compared prostitutes' age at first coitus to Kinsey's data on the general population. Since only 3 percent of the females in Kinsey's sample had experienced intercourse by age 15, Gray concludes that adolescent female prostitutes experience first coitus considerably earlier than females in the general population.[152]

Like male prostitutes, females' first sexual experience in many cases was incest. James found that the first sexual partner for prostitutes was a relative in 10 percent of the cases (1 percent for nonprostitutes). Of the 37 percent of the prostitutes who were molested prior to their first intercourse by a person at least 10 years older, 17 percent were molested by a relative.[153] Another similarity in sexual victimization is the frequency of rape reported by male and female juveniles. Of the females, 47.1 percent have been raped and 4.4 percent have had a near-rape experience. Nearly half of the female prostitutes were raped more than once.[154] The frequency of rape for male prostitutes is also quite high: 36.2 percent have been raped once or more, and 27.7 percent have experienced an attempted rape. More homosexual prostitutes report being raped than male prostitutes who identify themselves as heterosexual. No rapes were reported by a control group of male nonprostitutes.[155]

Homosexuality. A central question in much of the research on male prostitutes is whether they are homosexual. Sources disagree on the extent to which male prostitutes are gay. Early studies noted that most young male prostitutes were not homosexual.[156] Several of these early sources noted that young prostitutes disavow homosexuality and vehemently insist that pecuniary gain is their sole interest. The researchers point out that the prostitutes often overcompensate by preserving a supermasculine image; they express contempt for customers and boast of conquests with women as evidence of their true sexual interest.[157]

Recent studies, however, criticize the earlier interpretations in the literature regarding homosexuality. James, for example, notes that homosexuality as an expression of pathology forms the basis of a great deal of prior research.[158] Studies on male prostitutes, she states, tend to accept the traditional definition of homosexual behavior as pathological. This bias of many researchers has led them to deny the homosexuality of male prostitutes and to explain their homosexual behavior as the product of internal flaws. James suggests that another explanation for the finding by prior researchers that few prostitutes are homosexual is that interviewers conveyed their biased attitudes toward homosexuality to the respondents, who were then less likely to admit their homosexual identity. She concludes that viewing homosexuality as indicative of internal flaws fails to advance our understanding of its relationship to prostitution.[159]

More recent research is based on a nonjudgmental perspective on homosexuality. These studies identify a youth as homosexual or not according to the youth's definition of the situation. In one research study in this tradition, it was found that nearly half of the adolescent prostitutes identify as homosexual (47 percent) and that only 16.5 percent identify themselves as heterosexual.[160] These findings are similar to those of the Huckleberry House study, which reveals that 57 percent of young male prostitutes identify themselves as homosexual and 20 percent identify as heterosexual.[161] Both the URSA and the Huckleberry House studies report similar percentages of youth who identify as bisexual (Huckleberry 23 percent, URSA 29 percent).[162] According to recent research, it appears that one striking difference between female and male adolescent prostitutes is their sexual identification. Whereas adolescent female prostitutes identify predominantly as heterosexual,[163] a significant number of young male prostitutes identify as homosexual.

Physical Health

Young male and female prostitutes have a number of health problems. The medical problems of young male prostitutes have merited attention by a number of physician-researchers.[164] The most complete data on the health of juvenile male prostitutes come from the Shick study, in which 23 percent of respondents report some current physical problem.[165] Suspected venereal disease is the most frequently reported health problem.[166]

Shick queried further about venereal disease history, finding that 34 percent of the youth sought treatment for venereal disease only once, 15 percent twice, and 16 percent three or more times. Of these cases, 70 to 80 percent were found to be positive.[167] Venereal disease is an occupational hazard that also plagues young female prostitutes; it is also their most prevalent health concern.[168]

Adolescent male prostitutes are troubled also by symptoms from colds and flu,[169] presumably because of their long hours working in inclement weather. Additional health complaints of male youth are (in rank order) skin problems, injuries from fights or violence, drug-related or sexually transmitted hepatitis, and suspected appendicitis.[170]

Mental Health

Comparative data are available on the psychological histories of both male and female juvenile prostitutes. Research reveals that adolescent male and female prostitutes have high rates of suicide, suicidal thoughts, and suicide attempts.[171] Approximately the same percentages of male and female juvenile prostitutes feel entirely negative about themselves.[172] Furthermore, most of the adolescent prostitutes have received psychological services in the past,[173] including about

13 percent of both males and females who have received in-patient treatment.[174] One gender-based difference emerges, however: significantly more female prostitutes than male prostitutes have attempted suicide.[175]

Shick's study reveals more details about the young men who have received psychiatric treatment. Approximately one-fifth of the youth have been hospitalized at least once in a psychiatric hospital, and half of these have been hospitalized more than once. One-third of those who have been hospitalized were first hospitalized in a psychiatric hospital before the age of 13, 27 percent were between 13 and 15, and 30 percent were between 16 and 18.[176]

Another difference between male and female juvenile prostitutes appears to be in their social networks. Juvenile females appear to have fewer social supports. They have few ties to individuals who can be relied on to provide emotional sustenance, assistance, and resources. Most female prostitutes report having no friends.[177] Therefore, in times of need, or in times of alienation from their pimps, there is no one to whom they can turn. A type of camaraderie appears to exist among young male prostitutes, however. Several studies mention the "street corner society" that prevails among the young men.[178] This suggests that young male prostitutes are more likely than their female counterparts to have a social support network available to them in times of need.

Drug and Alcohol Use

The use of drugs and alcohol appears to characterize young prostitutes' lives. In contrast to two early studies indicating that male prostitutes are not significantly involved in drug or alcohol abuse,[179] more recent in-depth studies indicate that adolescent males are frequent users of a variety of drugs. Allen found that 29 percent of his subjects are regular users of hard drugs, 42 percent are heavy drinkers, and more than half smoke marijuana as their only drug use (other than alcohol).[180] Full-time street and bar prostitutes, especially, have a high incidence of polydrug use, and about one-third are also involved in drug dealing.[181]

Considerable data on drug use were gathered by Shick, who found that the utilization of drugs other than marijuana and alcohol was confined to recreational, periodic use of sedative hypnotics, amphetamines, angel dust, or psychedelics—particularly over weekends or at parties. In his sample, 24 percent had tried at least one drug intravenously, and 10 to 15 percent were frequent users of a variety of intravenous drugs, commonly amphetamines and/or heroin. In terms of the frequency of usage, daily use was largely confined to marijuana and alcohol. Shick found relatively few daily users of drugs other than marijuana and alcohol.[182]

Female prostitutes are also frequent users of a large variety of drugs. Many are frequent users of marijuana and alcohol,[183] half have experimented with psychedelic drugs, and many have used narcotics at some time.[184] Significantly, more female than male prostitutes experiment with stimulants and narcotics, and more female than male prostitutes use psychedelics and depressants. Alcohol use, however, does not differ.[185]

A significant number of male prostitutes report at least one adverse reaction to drugs. Many of these adverse reactions (24 percent) were severe enough to require hospital treatment. Approximately half of these adverse reactions were intentional or accidental overdoses.[186]

Ironically, despite their frequent use of drugs, most prostitutes do not consider that they have a drug problem. In one sample, only 10 percent felt that they had a drug problem, but less than half of those desired help with their drug problem. Those who admit having a drug problem define their problem as excessive usage rather than being drug-dependent.[187] No significant difference appears in the self-assessment of drug abuse problems between males and females.[188]

Future Plans and Expectations

For the most part, juvenile prostitutes tend to be present-oriented; they live only for the moment.[189] They generally fail to make any plans for their future. Despite this present orientation, however, many youth do nurture hopes and expectations. Several studies have explored these adolescents' future plans and expectations. When queried about the type of life they want eventually, approximately half of the adolescent males mention a desire to get a good job or career or just to "get [themselves] together and get off the street."[190] The remaining youth (54 percent) manifest unrealistic expectations; they are interested in a glamorous life, characterized by fun, wealth, power, and success. Such dreams and hopes of attaining glamor and excitement often hold young men in prostitution, since few other occupations enable them to earn such high salaries.[191]

Adolescent female prostitutes appear to have more traditional goals than their male counterparts. A surprising percentage reveal a desire to marry and have children.[192] Many are thinking of the immediate future and want to be self-supporting and to live independently of their parents, and many mention a desire for a career or a good job.[193]

Exit from Prostitution

The career span of both male and female adolescent prostitutes is short. Age is the enemy. As the youth grow older, they lose the physical attractiveness that brings them customers. Speaking of the young male prostitute, Cory and LeRoy write: "They become the victims of the homosexual adoration of youthfulness as soon as their own youthfulness begins to fade. Unless he can keep himself unusually well preserved, the hustler is considered old by the time he reaches his mid-twenties."[194] Deisher et al. agree, stating:

By age 25 a hustler begins to lose his physical attractiveness and can no longer get clients. He then finds it very difficult to integrate himself into society and make a legitimate living. He has spent 5 to 10 crucial years on the streets instead of getting an education, work experience, or training in a marketable skill.[195]

Furthermore, clients constantly seek new faces; they desire the excitement of new sexual partners. As Raven notes:

In this world, change is the rule: clients would soon get bored even if the boys kept their looks, and they are far from doing that. Boys will be boys indeed, but not for long.[196]

Other factors are also associated with the termination of adolescent prostitutes' participation in prostitution. Some prostitutes exchange prostitution for other criminal activities. A surprisingly large number of young male prostitutes are in prison when follow-up studies are conducted.[197] Some prostitutes, both male and female, become quite heavily involved with drugs—and some become addicts.[198] Some prostitutes die young—either by accidental or intentional overdoses or by violence.[199] Also, perhaps ironically, some male prostitutes become the adult customers of younger prostitutes.[200]

On the positive side, some prostitutes find regular legitimate employment, attend college, and get married.[201] Still another route is open to young male prostitutes in urban settings, some of whom trade prostitution for the adult gay lifestyle. These youth often become employed in gay bars, gay baths, hair salons, or other gay-owned businesses.[202] Since follow-up data are limited, research in this area would be especially valuable. Given the mobility of the prostitute population, however, data undoubtedly would be difficult to gather.

Involvement with the Juvenile Justice System

Running Away

Age. A substantial number of adolescent prostitutes, both male and female, are runaways. Studies of adolescent males report that from one-third to as many as 85 percent have runaway histories.[203] Adolescent prostitutes generally begin their runaway careers at an early age, typically in the early adolescent years. Most adolescent female prostitutes first run away at age 13 or younger.[204] Speculations on gender differences can be made. It is possible that female prostitutes first leave home at an earlier age but that male prostitutes have more extensive runaway histories. Specifically, some research suggests that female prostitutes are likely to run away for the first time at age 13 or younger.[205]

Males appear to run away at a slightly older age; one study reports that half of the adolescent male prostitutes first ran away from home by age 14.[206] The mean age at which boys leave home for the first time is 14.8.[207]

Frequency of Running Away. Most adolescent prostitutes who are runaways have extensive runaway histories. Many boys have run away from home as many as three or more times.[208] The Huckleberry House project reports that the majority of their male adolescent prostitutes (77 percent) have run away three or more times,[209] compared to 63 percent of adolescent females who have run away three or more times.[210]

Criminal History

The extent of prostitutes' involvement with the juvenile justice system has not been as well-researched for males as for females. Both self-report and official record data exist for girls, but only self-report data exist for boys.[211] Findings based on self-report data must be viewed with caution, since many youth underreport the extent of their involvement in criminal acts. As a result, data on young males' juvenile justice involvement probably represent minimal frequencies.

Male prostitutes appear to have extensive involvement in criminal activities. Here, "criminal activity" refers to general criminal acts other than acts of prostitution (which will be discussed subsequently). A large percentage of young male prostitutes have been arrested for offenses other than prostitution: 43 percent of all males arrested were arrested for status offenses, such as running away from home; one-third were charged with property offenses (theft, trespassing); and a few were arrested on charges of assault or drug-related offenses.[212]

The extent of their criminal involvement is revealed by the number of times the youth are arrested. In one study, 76 percent of the male subjects report being arrested at least once (other than for minor traffic violations); 54 percent admit to being arrested more than once,[213] 11 percent admit to three arrests, 7 percent admit to four, 4 percent admit to five, and 15 percent claim to have been arrested ten or more times.[214] Another study reveals an even higher incidence of arrest: 19.1 percent report four arrests, 6.4 percent report five, and 27 7 percent report more than ten.[215]

Certain types of young male prostitutes may be less likely to be involved in criminal acts. Allen found that the majority of youth without criminal records are homosexual prostitutes, mostly full-time professional prostitutes who work as call boys or kept boys.[216] All those youth whom Allen classifies as "peer delinquents," however, reveal a history of criminal activity. Most of them are involved in major crimes, although a few are involved in minor delinquency.[217] James notes a similar difference between homosexual prostitutes and those who identify as heterosexual. Heterosexual prostitutes exhibit greater involvement in more serious criminal activity, including drinking, fighting, violence toward others, shoplifting, assault, robbery, nonnarcotic drug use, vandalism, and auto theft.[218]

The criminal activities of male and female juvenile prostitutes exhibit several similarities. Approximately the same number of females as males are arrested for status offenses, property offenses, and assault offenses, but slightly more girls than boys are arrested on drug-related charges.[219]

First Arrest

Some comparative data are available on the nature of the young prostitutes' first arrest and the age upon first arrest. Males' first arrest is most likely for shoplifting, followed by (in rank order) burglary, auto theft, and running away.[220] In contrast, females' first arrest is most likely to be for shoplifting or running away.[221] Since arrest for running away is significantly more common for young female prostitutes, as well as for nonprostitute delinquent females, this suggests that gender-based enforcement of status offender laws may be occurring.[222]

The mean age at first arrest for young female prostitutes is 14 years.[223] For young males, the mean age at first arrest appears to be one year earlier—13 years.[224] Although this may be a gender-based difference, further research is needed on this variable.

Subsequent Offense History

Some comparative data are available on young prostitutes' offense histories subsequent to first arrest. For males, the second arrest is most often for shoplifting, auto theft and running away, and the third arrest is most often for burglary and larceny.[225] Adolescent females' second arrest is most likely to be for running away, and their third arrest is most likely to be for prostitution.[226]

Prostitution Offenses

Many adolescent prostitutes have been arrested for prostitution. Some data suggest that significantly more juvenile females than males are arrested for prostitution. One study reports that 63.2 percent of juvenile female prostitutes are arrested for prostitution.[227] This compares to findings on young male prostitutes that reveal that only 5 percent have been arrested on charges of prostitution.[228]

Several factors suggest that the data on number of arrests for prostitution may not give an accurate picture. First, arrests for a number of other offenses may conceal prostitution-related acts, so that arrests for prostitution do not accurately reflect the number of subjects police apprehend on suspicion of prostitution. For example, loitering is a common charge for individuals suspected of prostitution when there is insufficient evidence of prostitution.[229] Futhermore, prostitution is a difficult charge to prove, unless a police officer poses as a patron. Prostitutes are particularly wary of this possibility and are careful to avoid clients whom they suspect may be police officers.[230] Shick's field observations suggest that some youths charged with possession of drugs, disorderly conduct, loitering, or running away from home are first stopped by police on suspicion of prostitution. When they are frisked, some are found to be holding drugs; or they put up a fight when they are stopped; or when their identification is checked, they are found to be runaways.[231] Thus, the official data on prostitution arrests undoubtedly do not reflect youths' actual involvement.

One apparent difference between male and female criminal involvement is that fewer males are arrested for prostitution activity.[232] One reason for this may be the manner in which prostitutes are arrested. Typically, an undercover police officer apprehends a prostitute who has propositioned the officer. It has been suggested that fewer male prostitutes are arrested because male police officers tend to be uncomfortable posing as homosexual customers of male prostitutes.[233] Male prostitutes are thus more likely than females to be arrested for other criminal acts (rather than for acts of prostitution), since evidence of prostitution by males is more difficult to obtain.

Dispositions

Some comparisons may be drawn on dispositions following the arrests of female and male juvenile prostitutes. James found that, for both females and males, the first arrest is disposed of most often by releasing the juvenile to his or her parents.[234] This was also the most common disposition following second arrest,[235] although slightly more females than males are likely to be detained in the youth center following the second offense.[236] Upon the third arrest, both females and males are likely to be detained in the youth center, but significantly more males than females receive this disposition.[237] This may result because the males' offenses are generally of a more serious nature; that is, the males' third arrest offense is most likely to be burglary or larceny.[238]

Another study of young male and female prostitutes also inquired about disposition. It did not explore disposition upon each arrest (that is, for first, then second, then third offense), but rather looked at dispositions in the aggregate. This study also found that, for both female and male juveniles, charges are often dismissed after they are detained or taken to juvenile hall.[239] Many youth are released to their parents or guardians.

These data support findings of prior research on gender differences in delinquency—that young girls are more likely than boys to be arrested for sexual delinquency, such as acts of prostitution. This is the females' third most frequent arrest offense.[240] Girls are certainly more visible on the streets than boys, and boys' acts while "hanging around together" late at night do not incur as much suspicion. Thus, males are more likely to be arrested for higher-visibility crimes, such as burglary and larceny.

Involvement with the Social Service Delivery System

Extent of Involvement

Data are limited on prostitutes' involvement with the social service delivery system. Until recently, published studies yielded some data on male and female respondents who approached psychologists or psychiatrists for care[241] and on male respondents interviewed by physician/researchers or psychologist/researchers,[242] but detailed discussions of the youth's involvement with these health personnel (or with other social service personnel, such as case workers and probation officers) are absent from these works. We are told, for example, that "most female and male prostitutes receive medical care at the fringe of the health care system; they are usually seen in free clinics, emergency rooms and juvenile detention infirmaries,"[243] but there are no empirical data to reveal the number of contacts with various health care delivery agents, the presenting problems, the treatment, or the youth's perceptions of service needs and responses to service delivery. An occasional article provides data (often via case histories) on psychiatric treatment of a small number of youth,[244] but the history and the extent of their involvement with the mental health delivery system is invariably lacking.

One reason for this paucity of material is that, until recently, rehabilitation programs have been virtually nonexistent.[245] As a result, social service agencies and public health authorities have failed to study this social problem. Recent unpublished studies, however, shed some light on the extent of youth's involvement with the social service delivery system.

Reasons for Referrals

There are several reasons that juvenile prostitutes contact social service personnel. In a study by a runaway center staff, the services most requested by adolescent prostitutes were crisis housing, employment counseling, and individual counseling.[246] In this regard, females' and males' primary service needs are identical.

After these most frequently requested services, the needs of juvenile females and males diverge. Medical services and school counseling are the next most frequently requested services by females upon agency intake, whereas food is the next most requested service for males, followed by school counseling.[247]

As the youth's contacts with the agency continue and they become more comfortable with the staff, the majority of prostitutes request additional services. These additional service requests consist of (1) services of a personal nature, i.e. services that require a level of trust in service providers; or (2) services that are not seen initially by the youth as a necessary component of their overall goals.[248] Services of the former type include family relationship counseling, peer relationship counseling, and sexuality counseling. Although the youth are initially unwilling to discuss these difficulties, they become more open as they develop a positive relationship with the staff. Services of the second type include alternative housing counseling, legal counseling, and medical services. These service requests only become apparent to the youth after their immediate needs (such as for crisis housing) are resolved.[249]

One difference between service requests by males and those by females is in placement information. More female than male prostitutes request placement counseling. Most are interested in foster home placement, either in households containing few other children or in single-female households. Placement is a special concern of the females, because many have already exhausted placement possibilities with their county social workers. Street youth are considered difficult to place in homes by most probation officers and social workers.[250] When the juvenile females are given information about available placements, many decide that they prefer independent living situations.

Another difference between female and male juvenile service requests is in sexually-related service requests. Whereas more males request sexuality counseling, more females request sexually-related medical services. The primary medical concerns of females involve birth control, abortion, pregnancy, and venereal disease.[251]

Finally, male prostitutes are more likely than females to request family counseling. This may result from female prostitutes' higher degrees of alienation from their families, stemming from longer-term, more severe family conflicts and a longer period of separation from their families.[252]

Differences Between Prostitutes and Nonprostitutes

The service requests of male and female juvenile prostitutes differ in several respects from those of a comparison group of adolescents. Significantly more male prostitutes request employment counseling and individual counseling to deal with their feelings. In comparison, more nonprostitute males request family counseling. This may be explained because considerably more male prostitutes intend to live independently, whereas more of the nonprostitute males plan to resolve their family difficulties and return home.[253]

In addition, significantly more of the male prostitutes than the nonprostitutes request crisis housing. The male prostitutes, who have been on their own for a long time before they request services, may be in a more intense crisis when they initially approach an agency. Furthermore, more male prostitutes than nonprostitutes request sexuality counseling, peer counseling, legal counseling, and medical services. Upon examining the total service needs, the agency study concludes:

> It is apparent that a program designed to meet the needs of male prostitutes needs to provide more of the following services than a program designed for the general population of adolescent males: employment counseling and referrals, including job placement and training programs; legal assistance, medical services and referrals; and counseling in the area of self-esteem, peer relationships, and sexuality, focusing especially on sexual identity and self-acceptance as a gay or bi-sexual person.[254]

Service needs of young female prostitutes also vary from other comparatively situated adolescent females. Female prostitutes need a wider variety of services than nonprostitute females. More female prostitutes than nonprostitutes request crisis housing and employment, medical services, and school counseling. As they remain in the program, the prostitutes tend to need more services than the nonprostitutes in all areas except family counseling. More of the female prostitutes make additional service requests in the areas of alternative housing, school counseling, medical counseling, legal assistance, individual counseling, and sexuality counseling. The agency study concludes that an agency serving adolescent female prostitutes must place greater emphasis on this group's needs for employment counseling, alternative housing, and school counseling. Needs that are especially important for an agency to provide to the female prostitutes compared to nonprostitutes are medical services, especially birth control and gynecological services, and crisis housing.[255]

Notes

1. For the two published comparative reports, see Debra K. Boyer and Jennifer James, "Prostitutes as Victims," in *Deviants: Victims or Victimizers?*, ed. Donal E.J. MacNamara and Andrew Karmen (Beverly Hills: Sage, 1983), 109–46; and Robert W. Deisher, Greg Robinson, and Debra Boyer, "The Adolescent Female and Male Prostitute," *Pediatric Annals* 11, no. 10(1982): 819–25.

2. Enablers, *Juvenile Prostitution in Minnesota: The Report of a Research Project* (St. Paul: The Enablers, 1978), 14; Sparky Harlan, Luanna L. Rodgers, and Brian Slattery, *Male and Female Adolescent Prostitution: Huckleberry House Sexual Minority Youth Services Project* (Washington, D.C.: U.S. Department of Health and Human Services, Youth Development Bureau, 1981)), 7; Jennifer James, *Entrance into Juvenile*

Prostitution (Washington, D.C.: National Institute of Mental Health, 1980), 17 [hereafter cited as James, *Entrance*]; Jennifer James, *Entrance into Juvenile Male Prostitution* (Washington, D.C.: National Institute of Mental Health, 1982), 17 [hereafter cited as James, *Male Prostitution*].

3. Donald M. Allen, "Young Male Prostitutes: A Psychosocial Study," *Archives of Sexual Behavior* 9, no. 5(1980): 407 (16.6 years for males); James, *Entrance*, 17 (16.2 for heterosexual prostitutes and 16.5 for homosexual prostitutes); Urban and Rural Systems Associates (URSA), *Report on Adolescent Male Prostitution* (Washington, D.C.: U.S. Department of Health and Human Services, Youth Development Bureau, 1982), 71 (16.96 years).

4. Enablers, *Juvenile Prostitution*, 18 (fifteen females in the juvenile sample are age 17); Harlan, Rodgers, and Slattery, *Male and Female*, 7 (37 percent of the juvenile females are age 17; 67 percent of the juvenile males are age 17).

5. URSA, *Report on Adolescent Male Prostitution*, 127.

6. Harlan, Rodgers, and Slattery, *Male and Female*, 12; James, *Male Prostitution*, 17, 23 (25.5 percent middle class, 36.2 percent upper class).

7. Enablers, *Juvenile Prostitution*, 21; James, *Entrance*, 18, 23; Mimi H. Silbert, *Sexual Assault of Prostitutes: Phase One* (Washington, D.C.: National Institute of Mental Health, National Center for the Prevention and Control of Rape, 1980), 15–16.

8. Dorothy H. Bracey, *"Baby-Pros": Preliminary Profiles of Juvenile Prostitutes* (New York: John Jay Press, 1979), 19; Patrick Gandy and Robert W. Deisher, "Young Male Prostitutes: The Physician's Role in Social Rehabilitation," *Journal of the American Medical Association* 212, no. 10(1970): 1662.

9. Robert W. Deisher, Victor Eisner, and Stephen I. Sulzbacher, "The Young Male Prostitute," *Pediatrics* 43, no. 6(1969): 939 (fifty-seven of sixty-three prostitutes, or 90 percent); Harlan, Rodgers, and Slattery, *Male and Female*, 7 (53 percent).

10. Maura G. Crowley, "Female Runaway Behavior and Its Relationship to Prostitution," Master's thesis, Sam Houston State University, Institute of Contemporary Corrections and Behavioral Sciences, 1977, 60; Enablers, *Juvenile Prostitution*, 18.

11. Different research samples include various proportions of black youth, ranging from a low of 3 percent to a high of 40 percent. Deisher, Eisner, and Sulzbacher, "Young Male Prostitute," 939 (9 percent); Gandy and Deisher, "Young Male Prostitutes," 1662 (6.7 percent); Harlan, Rodgers, and Slattery, *Male and Female*, 7 (40 percent); J.F.E. Shick, "Service Needs of Hustlers," Unpublished manuscript, Chicago, 1980 (3 percent); URSA, *Report on Adolescent Male Prostitution,*, 73 (24 percent). Estimates of black female juvenile prostitutes range from 10 to 52 percent. Crowley, "Female Runaway Behavior," 59, 60 (31 percent); Enablers, *Juvenile Prostitution*, 18 (12.1 percent); Diana Gray (Hilton), "Turning-Out: A Study of Teenage Prostitution," Master's thesis, University of Washington, 1971, 16 (52 percent) [hereafter cited as Gray, "Turning-Out I"]; Harlan, Rodgers, and Slattery, *Male and Female*, 7 (10 percent); James, *Entrance*, 19 (25 percent).

12. Enablers, *Juvenile Prostitution*, 18; Harlan, Rodgers, and Slattery, *Male and Female*, 7; James, *Entrance*, 19; James, *Male Prostitution*, 17; Silbert, *Sexual Assault*, 10; URSA, *Report on Adolescent Male Prostitution*, 71.

13. James and the Enablers report no Asians in their samples; only 1 percent of Silbert's sample was Asian; and Deisher notes the presence of only one Oriental male prostitute. Deisher, Eisner, and Sulzbacher, "Young Male Prostitute," 939; Enablers

Juvenile Prostitution, 18; Harlan, Rodgers, and Slattery, *Male and Female* 7; James, *Entrance,* 38; James, *Male Prostitution,* 17; Silbert, *Sexual Assault,* 10.

14. Crowley, "Female Runaway Behavior," 62–63; Enablers, *Juvenile Prostitution,* 22; Harlan, Rodgers, and Slattery, *Male and Female,* 14; James, *Entrance,* 88; Silbert, *Sexual Assault,* 95.

15. Allen, "Young Male Prostitutes," 401; William M. Butts, "Boy Prostitutes of the Metropolis," *Journal of Clinical Psychopathology* 8(1947): 676; Neil R. Coombs, "Male Prostitution: A Psychosocial View of Behavior," *American Journal of Orthopsychiatry* 44(1974): 782–89; Donald W. Cory and John P. LeRoy, *The Homosexual and His Society: A View from Within* (New York: Citadel Press, 1963); Kenneth N. Ginsburg, "The 'Meat-Rack': A Study of the Male Homosexual Prostitute," *American Journal of Psychotherapy* 21(1967): 179; Harlan, Rodgers and Slattery, *Male and Female,* 12; URSA, *Report on Adolescent Male Prostitution,* 77.

16. This finding is based on an extrapolation of data in several studies on the percentage of male prostitutes from intact families. Allen, for example, found that only eighteen of ninety-eight boys had intact nuclear families (thus, perhaps 80 percent originated from broken homes). URSA found that only 34 percent of male youth came from intact families (thus, approximately 66 percent originated from broken homes). Allen, "Young Male Prostitutes," 409; URSA, *Report on Adolescent Male Prostitution,* 77. Furthermore, James found that broken homes characterized the backgrounds of 83 percent of the young male prostitutes in her study. James, *Male Prostitution,* 28.

17. Allen, "Young Male Prostitutes," 409–10; Coombs, "Male Prostitution," 788; Crowley, "Female Runaway Behavior," 72–75; Enablers, *Juvenile Prostitution,* 22, 29; Ginsburg, "Meat-Rack," 179; Gray, "Turning-Out I," 25; Harlan, Rodgers, and Slattery, *Male and Female,* 15; James, *Entrance,* 18, 24; Silbert, *Sexual Assault,* 21– 25.

18. Bracey, *"Baby-Pros,"* 40; Enablers, *Juvenile Prostitution,* 22; Diana Gray, "Turning-Out: A Study of Teenage Prostitution," *Urban Life and Culture* 1(1973): 410 [hereafter cited as Gray, "Turning-Out II"]; Harlan, Rodgers and Slattery, *Male and Female,* 14; James, *Entrance,* 23; Silbert, *Sexual Assault,* 13; URSA, *Report on Adolescent Male Prostitution,* 77.

19. See, for example, Harlan, Rodgers, and Slattery, *Male and Female,* 19; James, *Male Prostitution,* 28, 32; URSA, *Report on Adolescent Male Prostitution,* 78–79.

20. See, for example, Allen, "Young Male Prostitutes," 409; D.E.J. MacNamara, "Male Prostitution in American Cities: A Socioeconomic or Pathological Phenomenon?" *American Journal of Orthopsychiatry* 35 (1965): 204.

21. Bracey, *"Baby-Pros,"* 44; Crowley, "Female Runaway Behavior," 63; Enablers, *Juvenile Prostitution,* 22–23, 29–33; Harlan, Rodgers and Slattery, *Male and Female,* 15; James, *Entrance,* 48; Silbert, *Sexual Assault,* 20.

22. Crowley, "Female Runaway Behavior," 63 (73 percent); Enablers, *Juvenile Prostitution,* 22 (two-thirds); James, *Entrance,* 48 (62 percent); Harlan, Rodgers, and Slattery, *Male and Female,* 15 (70 percent); Silbert, *Sexual Assault,* 20 (62 percent).

23. Harlan, Rodgers, and Slattery, *Male and Female,* 12 (47 percent); URSA, *Report on Adolescent Male Prostitution,* 78 (34 percent).

24. Enablers, *Juvenile Prostitution,* 22–23; Silbert, *Sexual Assault,* 26.

25. J.F.E. Shick, Personal communication, 11 May 1980; URSA, *Report on Adolescent Male Prostitution,* 78. James reports an intermediate percentage (17 percent) of juvenile male prostitutes who are victims of incest. James, *Male Prostitution,,* 56.

26. Most sources maintain that the average age for the females' first act of prostitution is 14. Enablers, *Juvenile Prostitution*, 52; James, *Entrance*, 29; Gray, "Turning-Out II," 412. Only one source reports an earlier mean age (age 13). Silbert, *Sexual Assault*, 39.

27. For males, Allen reports a mean age of 14.2 years; James found the average age at first prostitution to be 14.4 for homosexual prostitutes and 14.3 for heterosexual male prostitutes. URSA reports a mean age of 14.8. Allen, "Young Male Prostitutes," 408; James, *Male Prostitution*, 97; URSA, *Report on Adolescent Male Prostitution*, 79.

28. James, *Entrance*, 77.

29. Sixteen percent of the Enablers sample reported that, at the time they became involved in prostitution, they had friends who were already involved in prostitution. Enablers, *Juvenile Prostitution*, 53. The Huckleberry House project noted a similar percentage (19 percent) who learned about prostitution from friends or from other youth on the street. Harlan, Rodgers, and Slattery, *Male and Female*, 34. In addition, Silbert reports that 14 percent of prostitutes first hear about prostitution from friends and an additional 7 percent learn about it from "kids at school." Silbert, *Sexual Assault*, 39.

30. Harlan, Rodgers, and Slattery, *Male and Female*, 32. James found somewhat lower percentages; she states that male youth first learn of prostitution from other prostitutes (29.8 percent) and school peers (12.8 percent). James, *Male Prostitution*, 97.

31. Allen, "Young Male Prostitutes," 415 (table IX).

32. Ibid.

33. James, *Entrance*, 77, 82.

34. Silbert reports a smaller percentage of prostitutes who learn of prostitution from family members—13 percent compared to James's 23 percent. Silbert also notes, however, that 4 percent were actually turned out by a family member, which is similar to James's findings. Silbert, *Sexual Assault*, 39–40.

35. Allen, "Young Male Prostitutes," 415. James also notes the influence of family members but fails to specify their relationship to the youth. James, *Male Prostitution*, 97.

36. Kathryn Barclay and Johnny L. Gallemore, Jr., "The Family of the Prostitute," *Corrective Psychiatry and Journal of Social Therapy* 18(1972): 10–16; Gray, "Turning-Out II," 410; Katherine MacVicar and Marcia Dillon, "Childhood and Adolescent Development of Ten Female Prostitutes," *Journal of the American Academy of Child Psychiatry* 19(1980): 151–52.

37. Harlan, Rodgers, and Slattery, *Male and Female*, 32, 34.

38. Silbert, *Sexual Assault*, 40.

39. Allen, "Young Male Prostitutes," 415.

40. James, *Male Prostitution*, 97. Homosexual prostitutes learn about prostitution from prostitutes (36.4 percent) and school peers (18.2 percent); heterosexual prostitutes learn about prostitution after being propositioned (28.6 percent).

41. James, *Entrance*, 68.

42. See, for example, Bracey, *"Baby-Pros,"* 21– 24; Enablers, *Juvenile Prostitution*, 56; Harlan, Rodgers, and Slattery, *Male and Female*, 34; Silbert, *Sexual Assault*, 40.

43. James, *Male Prostitution*, 108, 110.

44. Harlan, Rodgers, and Slattery, *Male and Female*, 32.

45. See, for example, Harlan, Rodgers, and Slattery, *Male and Female*, 34. That study reports that 17 percent of the females were initially forced into prostitution by pimps.

46. URSA, *Report on Adolescent Male Prostitution*, 79.

47. Silbert, *Sexual Assault*, 39.

48. Allen, "Young Male Prostitutes," 415.

49. See David Matza, *Delinquency and Drift* (New York: Wiley, 1964); David Matza, *Becoming Deviant* (Englewood Cliffs, N. J.: Prentice-Hall, 1969).

50. James, *Entrance*, 118–25.

51. Enablers, *Juvenile Prostitution*, 53; Silbert, *Sexual Assault*, 41–42.

52. James, *Male Prostitution*, 114 (8.5 percent feel sad/depressed).

53. James, *Entrance*, 83; James, *Male Prostitution*, 114.

54. Ibid.

55. Enablers, *Juvenile Prostitution*, 52; Gray, "Turning-Out I," 88.

56. Harlan, Rogers, and Slattery, *Male and Female*, 9.

57. Shick, "Service Needs," 10.

58. Sivan E. Caukins and Neil R. Coombs, "The Psychodynamics of Male Prostitution," *American Journal of Psychotherapy* 30 (1976): 449; Coombs, "Male Prostitution," 784; Deisher, Eisner, and Sulzbacher, "Young Male Prostitute," 939–40; Gandy and Deisher, "Physician's Role," 1062; MacNamara, "Male Prostitution in American Cities," 204; James, *Entrance*, 79; Enablers, *Juvenile Prostitution in Minnesota*, 53.

59. Eighty-four percent of James's female sample and 73 percent of the Enablers sample were not working when they started prostitution. James, *Entrance*, 79; Enablers, *Juvenile Prostitution*, 53.

60. Shick reports that at the time of the interview, 78 percent (113) of the young males were unemployed. Similarly, Deisher et al. found that forty-five of sixty-three young men (or 71 percent) were not working at the time of the interview. James notes that 83 percent of young male prostitutes were not employed when they first prostituted. Shick, "Service Needs," 9; Deisher, Eisner, and Sulzbacher, "Young Male Prostitute," 939; James, *Male Prostitution*, 97.

61. Shick, "Service Needs," 9.

62. Harlan, Rodgers, and Slattery, *Male and Female*, 32, 36. This is true of 83 percent of juvenile females and 75 percent of juvenile males.

63. Juvenile female prostitutes often perform work such as babysitting or housecleaning while they are living at home. When they are on the run, some acquire the only types of jobs readily available to young runaways—modeling, dancing, and massage. Ibid., 36.

64. Juvenile males have employment experience primarily in yard work, painting, repair work, and in warehouse work. James, *Male Prostitution*, 38.

65. James, *Entrance*, 79; James, *Male Prostitution*, 97; Silbert, *Sexual Assault*, 32–33.

66. Allen, "Young Male Prostitutes," 407; Coombs, "Male Prostitution," 784; Deisher, Eisner, and Sulzbacher, "Young Male Prostitute," 938; MacNamara, "Male Prostitution in American Cities," 204; Shick, "Service Needs," 5–6; URSA, *Report on Adolescent Male Prostitution*, 73.

67. Enablers, *Juvenile Prostitution*, 52; James, *Entrance*, 79; Silbert, *Sexual Assault*, 32.

68. Harlan, Rodgers, and Slattery, *Male and Female,* 16, 18 (56 percent of the girls and 52 percent of the boys are recent dropouts); Shick, "Service Needs," 5–6 (three-fourths); URSA, *Report on Adolescent Male Prostitution,* 73 (more than 75 percent).

69. Allen, "Young Male Prostitutes," 407; Enablers, *Juvenile Prostitution,* 47; James, *Entrance,* 20 (20.6 per cent); URSA, *Report on Adolescent Male Prostitution,* 73.

70. Harlan, Rodgers, and Slattery, *Male and Female,* 17–19.

71. Ibid., 17.

72. Enablers, *Juvenile Prostitution,* 53; Harlan, Rodgers, and Slattery, *Male and Female,* 34; James, *Entrance,* 68–69; James, *Male Prostitution,* 97, 115; Silbert, *Sexual Assault,* 42; URSA, *Report on Adolescent Male Prostitution,* 82 (table 10) (87 percent cite this factor). In James's review of the predisposing factors that influence juveniles' entrance into prostitution, she notes that virtually all the literature on female prostitution cites money as a predisposing factor. Jennifer James, "Entrance into Juvenile Prostitution: Progress Report, June 1978," (Washington, D. C.: National Institute of Mental Health, 1978), 49–50 [hereafter cited as James, "Progress Report"].

73. This conclusion is reached by Allen in his review of the literature on motivation. Allen, "Young Male Prostitutes," 401.

74. Michael Craft, "Boy Prostitutes and Their Fate," *British Journal of Psychiatry* 112(1966), 1113; Lewis J. Doshay, *The Boy Sex Offender and His Later Criminal Career* (New York: Grune and Stratton, 1943); Jens Jersild, *Boy Prostitution* (Copenhagen: G.E.C. Gad, 1956).

75. Craft, "Boy Prostitutes," 1113.

76. MacNamara, "Male Prostitution in American Cities," 204: "It would be difficult indeed to label the group pathological. Nearly all were neurotic. Probably none was a psychotic or psychopath. Are they male prostitutes as a result of some neurotic, psychopathic or psychotic syndrome? Quite likely not."

77. Ibid.

78. Ginsburg, "Meat-Rack," 179.

79. Coombs, "Male Prostitution," 782.

80. Donald H. Russell, "From the Massachusetts Court Clinics: On the Psychopathology of Boy Prostitutes," *International Journal of Offender Therapy* 15 (1971), 49–52.

81. Caukins and Coombs, "Psychodynamics," 449.

82. See, for example, MacVicar and Dillon, "Childhood and Adolescent Development," 145–49; Frances Newman and Paula J. Caplan, "Juvenile Female Prostitution as a Gender Consistent Response to Early Deprivation," *International Journal of Women's Studies* 5, no. 2 (1981), 128–37.

83. See, for example, Harlan, Rodgers, and Slattery, *Male and Female,* 34; Silbert, *Sexual Assault,* 41.

84. See, for example, Enablers, *Juvenile Prostitution,* 22–23; Harlan, Rodgers, and Slattery, *Male and Female,* 15; James, *Entrance,* 48.

85. See, especially, Jennifer James and Jane Meyerding, "Early Sexual Experience as a Factor in Prostitution," *Archives of Sexual Behavior* 7, no.1(1977), 31–42; Jennifer James and Jane Meyerding, "Early Sexual Experience and Prostitution," *American Journal of Psychiatry* 134, no. 12 (December 1977), 1381–85; Mimi H. Silbert and Ayala M. Pines, "Sexual Child Abuse as an Antecedent to Prostitution," *Child Abuse and Neglect* 5, no. 4(1981), 407–11.

86. James, *Male Prostitution,* 43–47.

87. Ibid., 46.

88. Ibid., 100; URSA, *Report on Adolescent Male Prostitution,* 23–26.

89. James, *Male Prostitution,* 46.

90. Deisher, Robinson, and Boyer, "Adolescent Female and Male Prostitute," 823; James, *Male Prostitution,* 108.

91. Allen, "Young Male Prostitutes," 414; James, *Male Prostitution,* 108.

92. James, *Male Prostitution,* 108.

93. Ibid., 105.

94. Charles Winick and Paul M. Kinsie, *The Lively Commerce: Prostitution in the United States* (Chicago: Quadrangle Books, 1971), 186.

95. Deisher, Robinson, and Boyer, "Adolescent Female and Male Prostitute," 823.

96. James, *Male Prostitution,* 106.

97. Deisher, Robinson, and Boyer, "Adolescent Female and Male Prostitute," 823; Ginsburg, "Meat-Rack," 177.

98. Caukins and Coombs, "Psychodynamics," 445.

99. James, *Male Prostitution,* 106–107.

100. Ibid.

101. Allen, "Young Male Prostitutes," 406; Caukins and Coombs, "Psychodynamics," 445; Deisher, Robinson, and Boyer, "Adolescent Female and Male Prostitute," 823.

102. Ibid.

103. Albert J. Reiss, Jr., "The Social Integration of Queers and Peers," *Social Problems* 9, no. 2(1961): 102–20.

104. Caukins and Coombs, "Psychodynamics," 447–49; Ginsburg, "Meat-Rack," 179.

105. Ginsburg, "Meat-Rack," 179–81.

106. Caukins and Coombs, "Psychodynamics" 447–48.

107. Bracey, *"Baby-Pros,"* 37–39; Enablers, *Juvenile Prostitution,* 69–70; Gray, "Turning-Out II," 416–18; Harlan, Rodgers, and Slattery, *Male and Female,* 34–35; James, *Entrance* 48, 82; Silbert, *Sexual Assault,* 55, 60.

108. Bracey, *"Baby-Pros,"* 61–62; Enablers, *Juvenile Prostitution,* 75; Gray, "Turning-Out II," 421; Harlan, Rodgers, and Slattery, *Male and Female,* 40; James, *Entrance,* 48; Silbert, *Sexual Assault,* 59.

109. James, *Male Prostitution,* 106.

110. See, for example, two famous recent cases. Veronica Bronson, a 12–year-old prostitute, died in a fall from the tenth floor of a New York hotel. It was suggested that she was murdered by a pimp. Selwyn Raab, "Veronica's Short Sad Life—Prostitution at 11, Death at 12," *New York Times,* 3 October 1977; Sandra Johnson, *Cuppi: Circumstances Undetermined Pending Police Investigation* (New York: Delacorte, 1979). Donny Serefin was a 17-year-old prostitute who was allegedly murdered during a sadomasochistic sexual encounter with a customer. Peggy Townsend, "Cornett, Victim Were Together, Witness Says," *Santa Cruz Sentinel,* 10 September 1981; Peggy Townsend, "Handcuff Key Found in Murder Suspect's Car," *Santa Cruz Sentinel,* 15 September 1981; Peggy Townsend, "Noted Pathologist Testifies in Trial," *Santa Cruz Sentinel,* 5 October 1981; Peggy Townsend, "Murder Suspect's Wife Supports His Alibi," *Santa Cruz Sentinel,* 7

October 1981. See also Ted Morgan, "Little Ladies of the Night," *New York Times Magazine,* 16 November 1975. On the general topic of assaultive behavior between homosexual prostitutes and customers, see Park E. Dietz, "Medical Criminology Notes #5: Male Homosexual Prostitution," *Bulletin of the American Academy of Psychiatry and the Law,* 6, no. 4(1978), 468–71.

111. Caukins and Coombs, "Psychodynamics," 446–47; Cory and LeRoy, *Homosexual and His Society,* 97; Ginsburg, "Meat-Rack," 171; Reiss, "Social Integration" 112; H. L. Ross, "The 'Hustler' in Chicago," *Journal of Student Research* 1(1959), 13–19; Russell, "Psychopathology," 51; David Sonenschein, "Hustlers Viewed as Dangerous," *Sexual Behavior* 2 (1972), 20; David Sternberg, "Prostitutes as Victimizers," in *Deviants: Victims or Victimizers?,* ed. Donal E. J. MacNamara and Andrew Karmen (Beverly Hills: Sage, 1983), 79–83; George Westwood, *Society and the Homosexual* (New York: Dutton, 1952); Winick and Kinsie, *Lively Commerce,* 92.

112. Cory and Leroy, *Homosexual and His Society,* 98; Ginsburg, "Meat-Rack," 171; Westwood, *Society and the Homosexual.*

113. MacNamara, "Male Prostitution in American Cities," 204.

114. See, for example, Allen, "Young Male Prostitutes," 406–407; MacNamara, "Male Prostitution in American Cities"; Reiss, "Social Integration," 103; E. Sagarin, *Sex, Crime and the Law* (New York: Free Press, 1977), 142–49.

115. Caukins and Coombs, "Psychodynamics," 446.

116. Allen, "Young Male Prostitutes," 404, 406, 415; Enablers, *Juvenile Prostitution,* 20; Gray, "Turning-Out I," 13, 15; James, *Entrance,* 78–79; James, *Male Prostitution,* 97; URSA, *Report on Adolescent Male Prostitution,* 83.

117. Allen, "Young Male Prostitutes," 404–406; Enablers, *Juvenile Prostitution,* 20; James, *Entrance,* 78; James, *Male Prostitution,* 113, 117.

118. Enablers, *Juvenile Prostitution,* 20. James, *Entrance,* 78; URSA, *Report on Adolescent Male Prostitution,* 83.

119. James, *Male Prostitution,* 97. Also see, generally, Laud Humphreys, *Tearoom Trade: Impersonal Sex in Public Places* (Chicago: Aldine, 1970).

120. Harlan, Rodgers, and Slattery, *Male and Female,* 32.

121. Ibid.

122. Ibid. See also URSA, *Report on Adolescent Male Prostitution,* 80.

123. Forty-six percent of the adolescent female prostitutes in the Huckleberry House research voice this opinion. Harlan, Rodgers, and Slattery, *Male and Female,* 34.

124. Enablers, *Juvenile Prostitution,* 63–65; Gray, "Turning-Out I," 105; Harlan, Rodgers, and Slattery, *Male and Female,* 35; James, *Entrance,* 80; Silbert, *Sexual Assault,* 56.

125. Enablers, *Juvenile Prostitution,* 63–65; Gray, "Turning-Out I," 105; Harlan, Rodgers, and Slattery, *Male and Female,* 34; James, *Entrance,* 80; Silbert, *Sexual Assault,* 56.

126. Harlan, Rodgers, and Slattery, *Male and Female,* 34.

127. Ibid., 35; URSA, *Report on Adolescent Male Prostitution,* 80.

128. Harlan, Rodgers, and Slattery, *Male and Female,* 35.

129. Although more than one-fourth of males indicate this reason, only 2 percent of females choose prostitution for sexual gratification. Silbert, *Sexual Assault,* 56; URSA, *Report on Juvenile Male Prostitution,* 80.

130. James, *Male Prostitution,* 102–103.

131. Allen, "Young Male Prostitutes," 405; Deisher, Eisner, and Sulzbacher, "Young Male Prostitute," 940.

132. Allen, "Young Male Prostitutes," 405; Deisher, Eisner, and Sulzbacher, "Young Male Prostitute," 940; Gray, "Turning-Out I," 161–62; Gray, "Turning-Out II," 413.

133. Deisher, Eisner, and Sulzbacher, "Young Male Prostitute," 940.

134. Gray, "Turning-Out I," 161–62; Gray, "Turning-Out II," 413.

135. Allen, "Young Male Prostitutes," 411–12; James, *Male Prostitution,* 42–47; URSA, *Report on Adolescent Male Prostitution,* 79.

136. Allen, "Young Male Prostitutes," 412.

137. Ibid., 411–12.

138. URSA, *Report on Adolescent Male Prostitution,* 79 (table 8).

139. Based on data in James, *Male Prostitution,* 54.

140. Ibid.

141. Allen, "Young Male Prostitutes," 412.

142. James, *Male Prostitution,* 43.

143. Ibid., 44.

144. Allen, "Young Male Prostitutes," 412.

145. James, *Entrance,* 2. The sample included 136 juvenile female prostitutes and a control sample of 100 juvenile females who were categorized as delinquent but not sexually labeled. James notes that a number of the delinquent nonprostitutes later became involved in prostitution. Ibid., 29.

146. Ibid.

147. Davis reports a mean age of 13.6 years for prostitutes' first sexual experience. The Enablers note a mean age of 12.2 years. Gray reports 12.9 years. Nanette J. Davis, "The Prostitute: Developing a Deviant Identity," in *Studies in the Sociology of Sex,* ed. James M. Henslin (New York: Appleton-Century-Crofts, 1971), 301; Enablers, *Juvenile Prostitution,* 38; Gray, "Turning-Out II," 407.

148. Enablers, *Juvenile Prostitution,* 38.

149. Ibid.

150. James, *Entrance,* 29.

151. Ibid.

152. Gray, "Turning-Out I," 48–50

153. James, *Entrance,* 29.

154. Ibid.

155. James, *Male Prostitution,* 44.

156. Butts, "Boy Prostitutes of the Metropolis," 674; Coombs, "Male Prostitution," 783; Cory and LeRoy, *Homosexual and His Society,* 99; Simon Raven, "Boys Will Be Boys: The Male Prostitute in London," in *The Problem of Homosexuality in Modern Society,* ed. Hendrik M. Ruitenbek (New York: Dutton Paperback 1963); Reiss, "Social Integration," 103; Westwood, *Society and the Homosexual.*

157. Cory and LeRoy, *Homosexual and His Society,* 99; Coombs, "Male Prostitution," 783.

158. James, *Male Prostitution,* 7–8. See also Boyer and James, "Prostitutes as Victims," 119–21.

159. James, *Male Prostitution,* 7–8.

160. URSA, *Report on Adolescent Prostitution,* 76 (table 5).

161. Harlan, Rodgers, and Slattery, *Male and Female,* 19.

162. Ibid.; URSA, *Report on Adolescent Prostitution,* 76.

163. Silbert, *Sexual Assault,* 89 (only 8 percent of female prostitutes are homosexual).

164. Deisher, Eisner, and Sulzbacher, "Young Male Prostitute"; Deisher, Robinson, and Boyer, "Adolescent Female and Male Prostitute"; Shick, "Service Needs."

165. Shick, "Service Needs," 11.

166. Ibid., 12. See also Cory and LeRoy, *Homosexual and His Society,* 99: "During the course of his career, the hustler is likely to contract some form of venereal disease and spread it indiscriminately."

167. Shick, "Service Needs," 13.

168. Enablers, *Juvenile Prostitution,* 85.

169. Bracey, *"Baby-Pros,"* 63; Shick, "Service Needs," 12.

170. Shick, "Service Needs," 12.

171. Harlan, Rodgers and Slattery, *Male and Female,* 24. Sixty-four percent of male prostitutes either have thought about suicide or have attempted suicide, compared to 82 percent of female prostitutes. See also Deisher, Boyer, and Robinson, "Adolescent Female and Male Prostitute," 820; Deisher, Eisner, and Sulzbacher, "Young Male Prostitute," 940; Gray, "Turning-Out I," 181.

172. Ten percent of the young men reveal extremely low self-worth and feel entirely negative about themselves, compared to 13 percent of the females having entirely negative feelings. Harlan, Rodgers, and Slattery, *Male and Female,* 24.

173. Ibid., 25.

174. Ibid., 24, 25.

175. Ibid.

176. Shick, "Service Needs" 16.

177. James, *Entrance,* 48; Silbert, *Sexual Assault,* 50–54.

178. Harlan, Rodgers, and Slattery, *Male and Female,* 40; URSA, *Report on Adolescent Male Prostitution,* 80–81, 116.

179. Patrick Gandy, "Environmental and Psychological Factors in the Origin of the Young Male Prostitutite," Paper presented at the American Anthropological Association Meeting, New York, 20 November 1971; MacNamara, "Male Prostitution in American Cities," 204.

180. Allen, "Young Male Prostitutes," 416.

181. Ibid.

182. Shick, "Service Needs," 16–18.

183. Crowley, "Female Runaway Behavior," 77; Harlan, Rodgers, and Slattery, *Male and Female,* 22–23.

184. Harlan, Rodgers and Slattery, *Male and Female,* 23.

185. Ibid.

186. Shick, "Service Needs," 18.

187. Ibid.

188. Harlan, Rodgers, and Slattery, *Male and Female,* 23.

189. Bracey, *"Baby-Pros,"* 36; Butts, "Boy Prostitutes of the Metropolis," 678, 680, 681; Caukins and Coombs, "Psychodynamics," 445.

190. Harlan, Rodgers, and Slattery, *Male and Female,* 33.

191. Ibid.

192. Twenty-five percent of the Huckleberry House female subjects cite this hope. Ibid., 36. Similarly, the most frequent responses by the Enablers sample are having children (40 percent) and getting married (30 percent). Enablers, *Juvenile Prostitution,* 97. Silbert, too, found that having children is the most common hope. Silbert, *Sexual Assault,* 80.

193. Enablers, *Juvenile Prostitution,* 97; Harlan, Rodgers, and Slattery, *Male and Female,* 36; Silbert, *Sexual Assault,* 80. Getting a good job was the most frequent response by the Enablers sample but the second most frequent response by the Huckleberry House and Silbert samples (following getting married or having children).

194. Cory and LeRoy, *Homosexual and His Society,* 99.

195. Deisher, Eisner, and Sulzbacher, "Young Male Prostitute," 936–37.

196. Raven, "Boys Will Be Boys," 288.

197. Allen, "Young Male Prostitutes," 418; Craft, "Boy Prostitutes and Their Fate," 1112; Raven, "Boys Will Be Boys," 289. Offenses include robbery, burglary, and sex offenses.

198. James notes that potential addiction is indicated for the 30 percent of adolescent females who report that their drug use increased as a result of prostitution. James, *Entrance,* 89. See also Jennifer James, "Prostitution and Addiction: An Interdisciplinary Approach," *Addictive Diseases: An International Journal* 2, no. 4(1976), 601–18; Shick, Personal communication.

199. Shick, Personal communication; see also sources cited in note 110.

200. A frequently cited saying in the literature is "Today's trade is tomorrow's competition." Harry Benjamin and R.E.L. Masters, *Prostitution and Morality* (New York: Julian Press, 1964), 294; Ginsburg, "Meat-Rack," 182–83.

201. Allen, "Young Male Prostitutes," 418; Benjamin and Masters, *Prostitution and Morality,* 295; Craft, "Boy Prostitutes and Their Fate," 1112; Raven, "Boys Will Be Boys," 289; Shick, Personal communication.

202. Shick, Personal communication.

203. Allen, "Young Male Prostitutes," 410–11 (29 percent); Harlan, Rodgers, and Slattery, *Male and Female,* 31 (85 percent). URSA reports an intermediate percentage of 77 percent. URSA, *Report on Adolescent Male Prostitution,* 85.

204. Harlan, Rodgers, and Slattery, *Male and Female,* 29.

205. Ibid. (62 percent). James reports that 11 percent are involved in running away prior to age 12, 15.4 percent at age 12, and 23.5 percent at age 13. James, *Entrance,* 50.

206. Harlan, Rodgers, and Slattery, *Male and Female,* 27.

207. URSA, *Report on Adolescent Male Prostitution,* 85.

208. Harlan, Rodgers, and Slattery, *Male and Female,* 27.

209. Ibid (77 percent).

210. Ibid., 29.

211. Allen, "Young Male Prostitutes," 417; Harlan, Rodgers, and Slattery, *Male and Female,* 25–27; James, *Male Prostitution,* 73; Shick, "Service Needs," 13–15.

212. Harlan, Rodgers, and Slattery, *Male and Female,* 25.

213. Shick, "Service Needs," 13.

214. Ibid (table 4).

215. James, *Male Prostitution,* 82.

216. Allen, "Young Male Prostitutes," 417.

217. Ibid.

218. James, *Male Prostitution*, 73.

219. Harlan, Rodgers, and Slattery, *Male and Female*, 27.

220. James, *Male Prostitution*, 73.

221. Enablers, *Juvenile Prostitution*, 110; James, *Entrance*, 51; Silbert, *Assault*, 47.

222. On the gender-based application of status offense jurisdiction, see, generally, Gail Armstrong, "Females Under the Law—'Protected' but Unequal," *Crime and Delinquency* 23(1977), 109–20; Meda Chesney-Lind, "Judicial Enforcement of the Female Sex Role: The Family Court and the Juvenile Delinquent," *Issues in Criminology* 8(1973), 51–69; Allan Conway and Carol Bogdan, "Sexual Delinquency—The Persistence of a Double Standard," *Crime and Delinquency* 23(1977), 131–35.

223. Based on an analysis of data in James, *Entrance*, 51.

224. Based on an analysis of data in James, *Male Prostitution*, 75 (Table: Age at First Arrest).

225. Ibid., 76,77.

226. James, *Entrance*, 49.

227. Ibid., 58. Other data (though based on much smaller samples) suggest, however, that similar percentages of young males and females are arrested on charges of prostitution. The Huckleberry House project found that of young prostitutes arrested at least once, 29 percent of males were arrested for prostitution, compared to 27 percent of females. Harlan, Rodgers, and Slattery, *Male and Female*, 25, 26.

228. Shick, "Service Needs," 13.

229. Ibid., 13–14.

230. Ibid.

231. Ibid., 14.

232. Deisher, Robinson, and Boyer, "Adolescent Female and Male Prostitute," 823.

233. Ibid.

234. James, *Entrance*, 49; James, *Male Prostitution*, 76.

235. James, *Entrance*, 53; James, *Male Prostitution*, 77.

236. Sixteen percent of females are detained at the youth center, compared to 10.6 percent of males. James, *Entrance*, 53; James, *Male Prostitution*, 77.

237. Analysis of James's data shows that 27.7 percent of males are detained, compared to 13 percent of females. James, *Male Prostitution*, 78; James, *Entrance*, 54.

238. James, *Male Prostitution*, 77.

239. Harlan, Rodgers, and Slattery, *Male and Female*, 25.

240. James, *Entrance*, 53.

241. See, for example, Craft, "Boy Prostitutes and Their Fate"; MacVicar and Dillon, "Childhood and Adolescent Development"; Newman and Caplan, "Juvenile Female Prostitution."

242. See, for example, Allen, "Young Male Prostitutes"; Caukins and Coombs, "Psychodynamics"; Deisher, Eisner, and Sulzbacher, "Young Male Prostitute."

243. Deisher, Robinson, and Boyer, "Adolescent Female and Male Prostitute," 823.

244. See, for example, William F. Thorneloe and Eugene L. Crews, "Manic Depressive Illness Concomitant with Antisocial Personality Disorder: Six Case Reports and Review of the Literature," *Journal of Clinical Psychiatry* 42, no. 1(1981), 5–9.

245. See Gandy and Deisher, "Young Male Prostitutes," for a discussion of one of the few early intervention programs.

246. Harlan, Rodgers, and Slattery, *Male and Female,* 43, 46.

247. Ibid., 43.

248. Ibid., 44, 47.

249. Ibid., 44.

250. Ibid., 47–48, 50.

251. Ibid., 50.

252. Ibid.

253. Ibid., 45.

254. Ibid., 46.

255. Ibid., 49–50.

6
Federal and State Legislation on Juvenile Prostitution

A

lthough the term *prostitute* conjures up images of adult women loung-
ing in bars or on street corners on dark summer nights, a significant
proportion of prostitutes are juveniles.[1] Despite the numbers of juvenile females and males involved in prostitution throughout the country, however, surprisingly little attention has been devoted to juvenile prostitution in
the legal literature.[2]

This chapter examines the law's response to the problem of juvenile prostitution, exploring recent statutory reforms that address juvenile prostitution on
the federal and state levels. Dilemmas in the law's response to juvenile prostitution will be highlighted, with an eye to determining the extent to which this
legislation adequately addresses social reality. Finally, methods are suggested
by which the law could respond better to the problem of juvenile prostitution.

Federal Legislative Reform

Federal policy that addresses juvenile prostitution consists of four pieces of
legislation: (1) the Protection of Children Against Sexual Exploitation Act,[3] (2)
the Child Abuse Prevention and Treatment and Adoption Reform Act,[4] (3) the
Runaway and Homeless Youth Act,[5] and, (4) the Missing Children Act.[6] We
will now examine how this legislation deals with the problem of juvenile
prostitution.

Protection of Children Against Sexual Exploitation Act

The involvement of juveniles in prostitution became an object of widespread
national interest in the late 1970s. In response to increasing media attention
focusing on juvenile prostitution and child pornography, congressional hearings were held in 1977 on the subject of child sexual exploitation. After testimony by law enforcement officials, law professors, social workers, sociologists,
psychologists, journalists, and others, Congress enacted the Protection of

This chapter is a revised version of the author's article, "Children of the Night: The Adequacy of
Statutory Treatment of Juvenile Prostitution," in the *American Journal of Criminal Law* 12(March
1984), 1–67; © D. Kelly Weisberg.

Children Against Sexual Exploitation Act of 1977[7] [hereafter cited as the Sexual Exploitation Act].

The Sexual Exploitation Act was the culmination of considerable legislative activity in the 95th Congress. Numerous bills were introduced in both the House and the Senate,[8] and public hearings were held by two subcommittees in the House and one in the Senate.[9] These hearings concluded that new federal legislation was necessary. The resultant Sexual Exploitation Act was designed to fill gaps in federal law to protect children from sexual exploitation.

Prior to the enactment of the act, various federal agencies were involved in the federal effort to combat child sexual exploitation. These agencies (the Department of Justice, the Federal Bureau of Investigation, the Postal Service, and the Customs Service) were limited to the enforcement of five existing federal statutes, which prohibited mailing, importation, and interstate transportation of obscene material; broadcasts of obscenity;[10] and interstate transportation of females under age 18 for purposes of prostitution.[11]

The Sexual Exploitation Act addresses various forms of sexual exploitation of juveniles. Although much of the act pertains to the regulation of child pornography,[12] one provision addresses the problem of juvenile prostitution. Specifically, the legislation amends the White Slave Traffic Act [hereafter cited as the Mann Act] by expanding its scope to prohibit the interstate transportation of minor *males* for purposes of prostitution.[13]

The Sexual Exploitation Act was based primarily on Senate Bill 1585. This bill, introduced by Senators Mathias and Culver on May 23, 1977, was one of four Senate bills dealing with child sexual exploitation. As introduced, S. 1585 concentrated only on the production of materials depicting children in sexually explicit conduct. On June 9, however, Senators Mathias and Culver offered Amendment 380, which made minor revisions in their original bill and also included a new section revising the Mann Act.[14]

The amendment was a response to the May 27 hearings of the Subcommittee to Investigate Juvenile Delinquency, which uncovered several factors that led to the proposed amendment. First, the subcommittee learned of the interstate traffic in young boys and of a number of prostitution rings dealing in young men. Experts at the hearings also testified that child prostitution occurred on a nationwide scale and primarily consisted of young runaways. When the subcommittee realized that the existing Mann Act was applicable only to females, they felt that an amendment was necessary to remedy this gap.

Amendment 380 proposed several additions to S. 1585. First, it made the transportation provision gender-neutral. The former provision pertained only to a woman or girl under the age of 18, and at the time of the congressional hearings, no similar provision existed regarding the interstate transportation of males under the age of 18. Section 4(a) of S. 1585 remedied this gap by applying the general proscription to any person under 18 years of age.

In addition, Amendment 380 also attempted to clarify some vague and archaic language of the prior law. The existing provision of federal law prohibited the transportation across state lines of females under age 18 to engage in prostitution, debauchery, or other immoral acts. The proposed language prohibited the interstate transportation of a person under age 18 for purposes of engaging in, solely, prostitution.[15]

The committee also deleted the common carrier requirement. The previous Section 2423 required that the minor be transported in "a common carrier." By omitting this language, the committee intended the penalties for interstate transportation to apply regardless of the mode of transportation. Also, the Judiciary Committee chose not to define the term *prostitution*, which is also not defined statutorily in any provision of the Mann Act. This lack of definition enables prosecutions not to depend on whether the act of prostitution with a juvenile was illegal in the state to which the minor was transported. Similarly, since the term *prostitution* remained undefined, it retained the commonly understood meaning—the exchange of sexual favors for something of value. Finally, during committee consideration, the existing penalty provision (a maximum of $10,000 fine or 10 years' imprisonment, or both) was retained.[16]

On June 13, 1977, Senate Bill 1585 was referred jointly to the Subcommittee to Investigate Juvenile Delinquency and the Subcommittee on Criminal Laws and Procedures. After a joint hearing of these two subcommittees, the Subcommittee to Investigate Juvenile Delinquency reported out the bill, as amended by Amendment 380, by poll. Subsequently, after Senator McClellan, chairman of the Subcommittee on Criminal Laws and Procedures, indicated that his subcommittee did not plan to consider the legislation, the Juvenile Delinquency Subcommittee's report was considered by the full Judiciary Committee. On September 14, 1977, the committee unanimously agreed to report S. 1585 with an amendment in the nature of a substitute, with a recommendation that the amended bill pass.[17]

Meanwhile, legislation to combat sexual exploitation of children was being introduced in the House of Representatives. Thirty-nine bills were offered, with more than 100 cosponsors. The House Judiciary Committee and, ultimately, the House chose H.R. 8059, introduced by Representative Conyers on June 28, 1977, as their representative bill.[18]

Prior to the introduction of H.R. 8059, approximately half of the proposed bills were introduced as amendments to the Child Abuse and Prevention Treatment Act and were referred to the appropriate committee, the Committee on Education and Labor. The remaining bills were channeled to the House Judiciary Committee because of its jurisdiction over legislation to be placed in Title 18, the Criminal Code. Although they were working on a parallel course, the committees ultimately decided that criminal sanctions specifically imposed by the new legislation belonged in amendments to Title 18, to maintain consistency in the codification system.[19]

Support for inclusion of the Mann Act revision occurred at the joint hearing of the two House Subcommittees on Select Education and Crime on June 10, 1977. John C. Keeney, deputy assistant attorney general of the Criminal Division, Department of Justice, raised several potential constitutional conflicts inherent in some provisions of the then-pending pornography provisions. During his testimony (which occurred the day following and was influenced by the introduction of Amendment 380 in the Senate), Mr. Keeney supported, as an alternative approach, broadening the Mann Act to include within its scope, first, males and, second, other facilities of commerce in addition to common carriers. As introduced on June 28, 1977, H.R. 8059 incorporated both of these suggested provisions.

Following its introduction in the House, H.R. 8059 was channeled to the Subcommittee on Crime. During the subcommittee's markup of the bill, Representative Holtzman offered an amendment in the nature of a substitute. This amendment, which paralleled the Senate Judiciary Committee provision amending the Mann Act, was accepted, and vague and archaic language in the Mann Act was removed. Also, H.R. 8059 was made applicable not only to prostitution but also to any prohibited sexual conduct if commercially exploited.[20] After the adoption of one further amendment referring to pornography,[21] the Committee on the Judiciary favorably reported H.R. 8059, with amendments.

Although the Senate bill, S. 1585, and the House bill, H.R. 8059, were similar in many respects, differences needed to be resolved in the Conference Committee. Ultimately, the conferees chose the House version for the Mann Act revisions, with minor modifications, but selected the Senate language on child pornography. For the Mann Act revisions, the Conference Committee chose the language of H.R. 8059 rather than the Senate language, because of H.R. 8059's broader coverage and its more explicit terminology; that is, the House version, which was finally adopted, added "finances" and "facilitates the movement of any minor" to the more limited "transports" and "causing to be transported" language found in the Senate bill. The House version thus defines the act as more than mere transportation, to include financing the minors' transportation in whole or in part, as well as facilitating it in any manner.

Finally, the title of the House bill, "Transportation of Minors," was adopted rather than the Senate terminology, "Coercion or Enticement of Minors."[22] The new title, chosen in preference to the Senate language mirroring prior legislation, was selected as a more accurate reflection of the character of the new legislation.

Congress approved S. 1585 as reported out of the Conference Committee in the belief, first, that it would provide an effective tool for the federal agencies.

Second, the new legislation went as far as the federal government could, within constitutional limits, to eliminate child sexual exploitation. Unanimously approved by the House and approved on a voice vote by the Senate,[23] the legislation was signed into law on January 28, 1978, as P.L. 95–225, the Protection of Children Against Sexual Exploitation Act of 1977.

Child Abuse Prevention and Treatment Act

Federal legislation also addresses juvenile prostitution by means of statutory treatment of child abuse. In 1977, when Congress first considered legislation on sexual exploitation of children, a number of bills attempted to address the problem by proposing amendments to the Child Abuse Prevention and Treatment Act [hereafter cited as the Child Abuse Act].

Child sexual exploitation was addressed comprehensively on the federal level for the first time in 1977, but child abuse legislation had been enacted several years earlier, in 1974.[24] To assess the subsequent 1978 amendments to the Child Abuse Act as they pertain to juvenile prostitution, it is necessary to understand the nature of the original child abuse legislation. Prior to 1974, no coordinated federal effort addressed child abuse and neglect.[25] In 1973, in response to increasing public concern about battered children, Senator Mondale (D.-Minn.) introduced S. 1191. This legislation received tremendous bipartisan support and was ultimately enacted in 1974 as the Child Abuse Prevention and Treatment Act.

The act provided for several programs directed at the prevention and treatment of child abuse and neglect, including:

> (1) [t]he establishment of a National Center on Child Abuse and Neglect within the Department of Health, Education, and Welfare [now the Department of Health and Human Services]; (2) mandated programs for the collection and dissemination of information, including the incidence of child abuse and neglect; (3) a source of funding for basic research in the area of child abuse and neglect; (4) a source of funding for service delivery, resource, and innovative demonstration projects designed to prevent and/or treat child abuse and neglect; (5) an Advisory Board to assist the Secretary of Health, Education and Welfare in seeking to coordinate federal programs; and (6) encouragement to States by way of grants for the payment of expenses involved in developing, strengthening, and carrying out child abuse and neglect prevention and treatment programs.[26]

To qualify for federal funds, the states were required to meet a list of criteria specifying child abuse reporting procedures, a comprehensive uniform definition of child abuse and neglect, investigation of reports, and administrative procedures. Also required were the assurance of confidentiality of records and the appointment of guardians ad litem for children involved in child abuse or neglect judicial proceedings. For purposes of the act, the term *child abuse and neglect* was defined as "the physical or mental injury, sexual abuse, negligent treatment, or maltreatment of a child under the age of eighteen by a person who is responsible for the child's welfare under circumstances which indicate that the child's health or welfare is harmed or threatened thereby."[27]

When the Child Abuse Act was enacted in 1974, funds were appropriated for a 4-year period. Fifteen million dollars was appropriated for fiscal year 1974, $20 million for fiscal year 1975, $25 million for fiscal year 1976, and the same amount for the succeeding fiscal year. Upon termination of appropriations in 1977, the 95th Congress considered legislation to extend portions of the act dealing with child abuse. Simultaneously, the legislature also began to consider revisions of the act to include provisions dealing with the sexual exploitation of children.

The bills on sexual abuse of children introduced at the beginning of the 95th Congress (each entitled "Child Abuse Prevention Act") contained almost identical provisions, with one critical distinction. Some bills were intended to place increased criminal penalties for sexual abuse of children in Title 18 of the Criminal Code. Other bills proposed to place increased criminal penalties as amendments to the Child Abuse Act, located in Title 42.

Bills to amend Title 18 subsequently were referred for consideration to the Judiciary Committee, and the legislation proposing criminal penalties to amend the Child Abuse Act was referred to the Committee on Education and Labor. Although the two committees worked on a parallel course toward reporting the legislation, considerable debate ensued on whether the proposed federal legislation on sexual abuse should amend the Criminal Code or should be placed in the Child Abuse Act.

When hearings were held on proposed legislation before the House Subcommittee on Crime, primary among the issues considered was the potential location of the proposed legislation. Members of the House Subcommittee on Crime, as well as Judiciary Committee members, expressed the view that legislation imposing criminal penalties rightfully belonged in the federal Criminal Code. Members of the Judiciary Committee continued to espouse this viewpoint on later occasions and rejected any attempts to tie reauthorization legislation for the Child Abuse Act to state criminal laws on sexual abuse.[28]

A similar debate raged in the Senate when proposals to address child sexual exploitation by amending the Child Abuse Act were introduced. One such proposal was introduced by Senator Roth (S. 1011) and another by Senator Matsunaga (S. 1499). On June 13, 1977, the Matsunaga proposal, S. 1499, and two other bills on child sexual exploitation, Senator Roth's S. 1011 and the Mathias/Culver bill, S. 1585, were jointly referred to the Subcommittee to Investigate Juvenile Delinquency and the Subcommittee on Criminal Laws and Procedures. A joint hearing of the two subcommittees was held. Following testimony, the Subcommittee to Investigate Juvenile Delinquency reported out

S. 1585, with amendments, by poll[29]. (The Criminal Law Subcommittee did not consider the legislation.) Thus, the Matsunaga proposal (S. 1499) to amend the Child Abuse Act by providing criminal penalties for sexual exploitation died in the Subcommittee to Investigate Juvenile Delinquency. Instead, that subcommittee reported out S. 1585, which became the Protection of Children Against Sexual Exploitation Act. For this reason, the Senate bill extending the Child Abuse Prevention and Treatment Act contained no reference to criminal penalties for the sexual exploitation of children.

The Child Abuse Act amendments, as enacted, had several purposes. First, they authorized the act for 5 additional years, through the fiscal year ending September 30, 1982.[30] Second, they amended the act by the addition of a number of provisions. The most significant of these amendments in terms of juvenile prostitution was the expansion of the federal definition of child abuse and neglect. Specifically, the definition was amended to include sexual exploitation. By P.L. 95-266, Congress amended the Child Abuse Act to expand the definition of sexual abuse by the insertion of the phrase "or exploitation." Following this amendment, the definition of child abuse and neglect read:

> ... the physical or mental injury, *sexual abuse or exploitation,* negligent treatment, or maltreatment of a child under the age of eighteen, or the age specified by the child protection law of the State in question, by a person who is responsible for the child's welfare under circumstances which indicate that the child's health or welfare is harmed or threatened thereby.[31] [emphasis added]

In a later subsection of the act authorizing special state sexual abuse programs, it became clear that prostitution was one of the forms of sexual exploitation specifically addressed.[32] Unfortunately, when the act was reauthorized by the 97th Congress, this specific authorization section was deleted.[33] For a short time, then, the term *sexual exploitation* was left undefined in federal child abuse legislation. The current administration, however, issued new child abuse regulations that make specific reference to juvenile prostitution as a form of sexual exploitation. Final rules issued by the Department of Health and Human Services on January 26, 1983, state that for states to be eligible for funds under the Child Abuse Act, the statutory definition of child abuse in their mandatory reporting law must include the term *sexual exploitation.* That term is clearly defined in these rules to encompass "allowing, permitting, or encouraging a child to engage in prostitution, as defined by State law, by a person responsible for the child's welfare."[34] The issuance of these new regulations encourages states to address sexual exploitation, which is specifically defined to encompass juvenile prostitution.

Runaway and Homeless Youth Act

A third piece of federal legislation that addresses the problem of juvenile prostitution is the Juvenile Justice and Delinquency Prevention Act of 1974.[35]

Included as Title III of the act is the Runaway and Homeless Youth Act [hereafter cited as the RHYA]. The RHYA authorized the Secretary of Health, Education and Welfare (now the Secretary of Health and Human Services) to provide assistance to local groups for operating temporary shelter care facilities for runaways.[36]

In addressing the problems of runaway youth in general, the act also deals with the segment of the runaway population that consists of juvenile prostitutes. It is estimated that approximately one million young people run away from home each year.[37] Many of these youth turn to theft, robbery, or the sale of drugs to support themselves during their runaway episodes, and a significant percentage of these juvenile runaways, both male and female, turn to prostitution. Although exact figures are unknown, studies indicate that the number of runaways who become involved in prostitution varies from 10 to 90 percent.[38]

The RHYA authorized the availability of grants for the establishment or maintenance of runaway houses by states, localities, and nonprofit private agencies. To qualify for federal funding a runaway house, (1) must be located in an area accessible to such youth; (2) must have a maximum capacity of no more than twenty children, with an adequate staff-child ratio; (3) must develop adequate plans for contacting the child's parents or relatives and assuring the safe return of the child, for contacting local government officials, and for providing other appropriate alternative living arrangements; (4) must develop an adequate plan for assuring proper relations with law enforcement personnel, social service personnel, and welfare personnel and for the return of runaway youths from correctional institutions; (5) must develop an adequate plan for aftercare counseling of youth and their parents; (6) must keep adequate statistical records profiling the children and their parents, while assuring the confidentiality of these records; and (7) must submit annual reports and budget estimates to the Secretary of Health and Human Services.[39]

In contrast to halfway houses, runaway facilities shelter youth on a short-term rather than a long-term basis. Their primary function is to provide a place where runaways can find immediate assistance, including shelter, medical care, and counseling. Once a runaway is a resident of the runaway shelter, he or she is encouraged to contact home and to reestablish a permanent living arrangement.[40] The shelters are also equipped to provide aftercare counseling for both the runaway and the family after the runaway has moved to permanent living facilities, whether these facilities are the youth's own home or independent living arrangements. Community services, such as medical and psychological services, are often available to the clients of the runaway shelters. Although these shelters primarily serve runaway youth, many serve juvenile prostitutes as well.[41]

In 1980, Congress reenacted the Runaway Youth Act and broadened its scope. The act was renamed the Runaway and Homeless Youth Act,[42] and the amendment included recognition of the fact that many runaways do not leave home of their own volition—that many youth are "throwaways" rather than runaways. These "throwaways" leave home because their families have thrown them out or have disintegrated around them.

In addition, the 1980 amendments clarified the requirement that services provided by the shelters be available to the families of runaway and homeless youth as well as to the youth themselves.[43] Program authorities also were added for the development of model programs designed to assist chronic runaways.[44] As initially enacted in 1973, the act authorized specific appropriations of $10 million for the runaway programs for fiscal years 1975, 1976, and 1977. In 1977, the act was reauthorized for three additional years by adding provisions authorizing appropriations at the same level for fiscal years 1978, 1979, and 1980.[45]

The 1980 legislation extended the Juvenile Justice and Delinquency Prevention Act, including the Runaway and Homeless Youth Act, for four additional years and authorized appropriations for the act for the same period (1981–1984), increasing the amount to $25 million per year.[46] Considerable controversy ensued, however, regarding the appropriation of funds. Although it originally authorized appropriations for 1975–1977, Congress faced strong opposition from the Ford administration, which reduced the appropriation level. In fiscal years 1980 and 1981, only $11 million was actually appropriated.[47] The Reagan administration continued the opposition and, in 1982, proposed canceling the legislation and including the program, instead, in the Social Services Block Grant.[48] This proposal would have delegated the problem of runaway youth to the state governments.

Congressional resistance to the administration proposal in 1982 produced two results. First, Congress refused to include the RHYA in the block grant. Second, the fiscal year 1982 Continuing Resolution maintained the program at $11 million for one additional year; however, for fiscal year 1983, the administration proposed to reduce funding for the runaway youth program to $7 million, or a 36 percent reduction below prior funding levels. Furthermore, the administration proposal included, once again, delegation of the runaway program in 1984 to the states as part of the "new federalism" initiative.[49] Hearings were held on these proposals in July 1982. After considerable delay and debate, Congress appropriated $18 million to carry out the RHYA.[50]

Missing Children Act

A fourth piece of federal legislation that indirectly addresses the problem of runaway prostitutes was recently signed into law. The Missing Children Bill[51] was introduced in the 97th Congress to address the subject of missing persons, especially missing children. The existence of large numbers of missing children first came to public attention in 1981, and several well-publicized murders of children who were previously reported missing spurred national interest in this problem.[52]

The purpose of the proposed legislation was to facilitate the establishment of a special national clearinghouse of information to identify deceased persons and to help locate missing persons, especially missing children. This purpose was to be accomplished by amending Section 534 of Title 28, United States Code, to extend the Federal Bureau of Investigation's authority in regard to the National Crime Information Center (NCIC). The FBI maintains the NCIC, established in 1967, to collect and record data to assist in law enforcement. The NCIC, created under the authority granted to the attorney general, acquires, collects, classifies, and preserves identification, criminal identification, and other records and provides this information to authorized federal, state, and local officials.[53]

Two new tasks were imposed on the Justice Department, over and above the tasks previously mandated by Section 534. The first new task was to acquire, collect, classify, and preserve information that would assist in the identification, specifically, of deceased individuals as well as in the location of missing persons. Second, the legislation would facilitate intergovernmental cooperation by requiring that the Justice Department exchange this specific identifying information with state and local governments.

In May 1968, one year after the establishment of the NCIC, the NCIC Advisory Policy Board appointed a subcommittee to develop classifications of missing persons. At the 1969 Advisory Policy Board meeting, the subcommitte recommended two categories of persons who could be included in a special file on missing persons: (1) individuals under 18 years of age and (2) individuals over 18 years of age who suffer from senility or amnesia, who are mentally retarded or disturbed, or whose disappearance was not voluntary. The suggested categories were expanded to include other groups of missing persons. Among the categories added was the following: persons who are missing and declared unemancipated as defined by the law of the state of residence and who did not fall within the other categories which would include runaways.[54]

In 1973, while it was still formulating policy, the NCIC Advisory Policy Board suggested that rather than creating a separate missing persons locater file, the missing persons file should be placed in the existent wanted persons file. In so suggesting, the board requested the opinion of the FBI legal staff. The FBI, however, recommended against integrating these files and suggested also that the definition pertain to "unemancipated juveniles," among others.

The missing persons file classification was finally created in 1975. Although the file constitutes only a small proportion of the current NCIC computer databank, the creation of the classification is important in providing, for the first time, a database on missing juveniles. Since the establishment of the file classification in 1975, the records of approximately 780,000 missing persons, including 592,000 juveniles, have been entered in the file.[55]

Despite the creation of this file in 1975, several factors illuminated the need for additional federal legislation. First, few of the total number of children or adults actually missing were ever entered into the system. Although accurate statistics on missing children, including runaways, are unavailable, the Department of Health and Human Services estimates that 1.8 million children are missing from their homes each year. As of April 1, 1982, however, only about 24,000 persons, adults as well as juveniles, were listed on the NCIC computer.[56]

A second problem highlighting the need for federal legislation was the underutilization of the current system by state and local law enforcement agencies. Although estimates of the degree of underutilization varied, a survey conducted by the Subcommittee of Investigations and Oversight of the Senate Labor and Human Resources Committee showed that only 10 to 14 percent of missing children had been reported to the NCIC missing persons file.[57] One explanation is that many police departments do not regularly use the file to list children as missing. Several reasons have been suggested for their reluctance to enter missing children on the NCIC system, including (1) a feeling that missing children are a "domestic dispute," best handled on the local level; (2) a lack of awareness about the availability of the system; and (3) a reluctance to use limited manpower to update the NCIC files periodically.[58]

As a result of increasing activism by children's rights groups and law enforcement groups, demands were made for the federal government to play a larger role in the search for missing children. Public concern became manifest at a time when increasing attention was being paid to runaways and to their vulnerability to sexual exploitation.

The Missing Children Bill is based on S. 1701 and H.R. 6976, two bills among several pieces of legislation introduced in the 97th Congress. The primary sponsors of the legislation were Senator Paula Hawkins (R.-Fla.)[59] and Congressman Paul Simon (D.-Ill.). Congressman Simon introduced H.R. 3781 in the House on June 3, 1981.[60] In successive months, both Senator Hawkins and Congressman Simon introduced further legislation on the subject of missing children; Senator Hawkins introduced S. 1701 and Congressman Simon introduced H.R. 6976. Although they reflected the same purpose as the originally introduced legislation, S. 1701 and H.R. 6976 were different versions of the earlier bills. Both bills were referred to the Committee on the Judiciary of their respective houses. In the Senate, hearings were held on April 1, 1982,[61] and the Judiciary Committee reported out S. 1701 as amended on July 29, 1982.[62]

The bill chosen by the Senate Judiciary Committee, S. 1701, differed from S. 1355 in several respects, one of which was significant insofar as runaways were concerned. The two bills differed in their definition of the term *missing person*. Referring to "any missing child," S. 1355 classified into four categories the type of child subject to the protection of the new identification measures: (1) a child who has not attained 17 years of age; (2) a child who does not have a previous history of running away; (3) a child who, on the basis of available evidence, is not the victim of an abduction by a parent; and (4) a child who has been missing for at least 48 hours.[63] Thus, S. 1355 specifically excluded from the protected ambit of the proposed federal law juveniles with a history of running away.

The new bill, S. 1701, was not quite so restrictive. In referring to "any missing person," it defined the four classifications of protected persons differently, including any person (1) who is under proven physical or mental disability, making the person a danger to himself or others; (2) who is in the company of another person under circumstances indicating that his physical safety is in danger; (3) who is missing under circumstances indicating that the disappearance was not voluntary; or (4) who is unemancipated, as defined by the laws of his state of residence. Thus, missing children were protected as well as other missing persons; a 48-hour wait was not required prior to initiation of identification procedures; and unlike S. 1355, S. 1701 did not specifically exclude runaways.

In choosing S. 1701 as its representative bill, the Committee on the Judiciary made several amendments before reporting the bill. First, the committee added a broader definition of *missing person*. Rather than limiting the definition to the four categories originally proposed, the committee inserted more expansive phraseology, adding the phrase "including but not limited to ..."[64] to designate that even those missing persons who did not fall within the specified categories would be subject to identification assistance procedures. Second, the committee added an additional requirement to be fulfilled prior to the initiation of federal identification measures. To use the clearinghouse to help locate unemancipated minors, such minors' parents, legal guardians, or next of kin must first report the missing youth to the appropriate law enforcement agency with jurisdiction to investigate the the matter.[65] The parent, guardian, or next of kin could then directly request the FBI to make an entry into the NCIC. After thus amending S. 1701 and reporting it out of committee, the bill was cleared for floor action, and S. 1701 as amended passed the Senate on a voice vote on September 23, 1982.[66]

Meanwhile, the House Judiciary Committee considered legislation introduced in the House, among which were H.R. 3781 and H.R. 6976, both introduced by Representative Simon (D.-Ill.). Introduced on June 3, 1981, H.R. 3781 was the first legislation before Congress; H.R. 6976 was introduced almost a year later, on August 11, 1982. While the Senate bill, S. 1701, passed the Senate on a voice vote on September 23, 1982, the House was also taking action, selecting H.R. 6976 as its version of the Missing Children Act. That bill passed the House and was then sent to the Senate Judiciary Committee on September 22, 1982.[67]

After consideration by the Senate Judiciary Committee, H.R. 6976 was passed as amended by a voice vote on the Senate floor on September 28, 1982.[68] The House rejected the Senate amendment on September 29, 1982, however, and both Houses appointed conferees to meet jointly to settle the remaining issue that blocked passage of the Missing Children Act. The involvement of the FBI in the process of entering missing persons into the NCIC computer was the final point of contention.

Primarily influenced by a letter of September 29, 1982, from FBI Director William H. Webster, the Joint Conference reached a compromise. Director Webster expressed his preference for H.R. 6976, because S. 1701 would cause procedural problems for the FBI. Since S. 1701 required the FBI to make an entry into the computer of information regarding missing persons upon the direct request of that individual's parent, legal guardian, or next of kin, it thus bypassed the local or state law enforcement agency empowered to investigate the disappearance,[69] which was contrary to FBI policy.

Based on Director Webster's assurances of FBI cooperation, a compromise to the S. 1701 requirement was reached: parents, guardians, and next of kin could request *confirmation* of an entry. In the event that parents, legal guardians, or next of kin of missing persons, including unemancipated minors as defined by the jurisdiction of their disappearance, requested confirmation that information had been entered into the computer, the FBI was authorized (1) to verify such entry and (2) to enter such information if the appropriate state or local law enforcement agency refused to enter the missing child in the NCIC system.[70] The FBI would enter information upon the direct request of a parent or guardian only in cases where local police failed to enter such data. After being passed by both houses, H.R. 6976 as amended was signed by the president on October 12, 1982.[71]

The establishment of such a clearinghouse should better equip law enforcement officials to identify and find missing and runaway children and to return them to their parents. Particularly important is that such a nationwide clearinghouse could enable law enforcement officers to identify runaways more promptly so that they can intervene before such youth either turn to prostitution or become more entrenched in the occupation.

State Legislation

At the time of the congressional hearings on the protection of children from sexual exploitation in 1977, a wide range of state statutes addressed the issue of sexual abuse of minors. These statutes were available to prosecutors to punish individuals who engaged in child sexual exploitation, in general, and in prostitution with minors in particular. Some state statutes prohibited such offenses as carnal knowledge,[72] statutory rape,[73] indecent liberties,[74] and child molestation.[75] Others indirectly addressed the sexual conduct underlying juvenile prostitution by prohibiting certain forms of sexual contact between adults and minors, such as incest[76] and sodomy.[77] In many states, statutes that made it an offense to contribute to the delinquency of a minor[78] could also be utilized to penalize sexual misconduct involving such activities as pimping or patronizing a juvenile.

Still other state statutes addressed juvenile prostitution, again implicitly, by prohibiting the exploitation of children for certain purposes; for example, some laws prohibited the employment of children for illegal or immoral activities.[79] Although they did not specifically mention the employment of children for sexual activities, these laws were broad enough to permit prosecutions for acts of prostitution with juveniles.

State penal legislation had several limitations in its application to juvenile prostitution. Few states envisaged that the prostitute might be a juvenile, and criminal statutes in only a few jurisdictions[80] distinguished between participants involved with juvenile, as opposed to adult, prostitutes. Other statutes were discriminatory on their face, defining prostitution in gender-based terms to apply only to sexual acts with females,[81] and thus failing to prohibit prostitution involving juvenile males. Still other statutes prohibited sexual misconduct only with youth of certain ages,[82] failing to proscribe sexual acts (other than statutory rape) involving older adolescents. Finally, no statutory scheme prohibited the exchange of sexual services by a patron with a minor for a fee.[83]

At the time of the federal hearings on child sexual exploitation, few states had legislation directed at juvenile prostitution. Following the hearings in 1977, however, a wave of such legislation swept state legislatures. Numerous states have now enacted new criminal legislation or have revised existing legislation to address this social problem.[84]

Trends in Criminal Legislation

State statutory treatment of juvenile prostitution now encompasses both criminal and civil statutes. Criminal statutes are directed at punishing the adult actors engaged in acts of prostitution with juveniles, whereas civil statutes, in the form of revisions in state child abuse legislation, attempt to aid identification of juveniles engaged in prostitution to facilitate prevention and treatment. Several trends are apparent in state statutory treatment of juvenile prostitution.

Age-Based Lines. One trend in the criminal statutes is the enactment of age-based distinctions that reflect the different ages of the juveniles involved in prostitution. Specifically, many statutes increase the penalties for perpetrators according to the age of the juvenile involved. The targeted perpetrators are usually pimps and, in some states, patrons. Under statutory schemes with age-based lines, pimps and patrons of younger prostitutes are punished more severely than those involved with older prostitutes.

Some state statutes accomplish this objective of increased penalties by specifically proscribing prostitution offenses with "minors."[85] In these states, penalties for adult participants in prostitution vary according to the age of majority for juveniles, which is defined by reference to other statutes. Other states have enacted age-based distinctions by adding to their penal codes an offense incorporating various degrees—the degree determined by the age of the juvenile. These statutes typically proscribe an offense with two or more degrees. Washington, for example, has adopted the offense of promoting prostitution in the first degree if the prostitute is under 18 years old. In cases in which the prostitute is 18 or over, the Washington penal code sanctions an offense in the second degree, which carries a less severe penalty.[86]

Pimp-Focused Legislation. A second trend in recent legislation is the focus on pimps of juvenile prostitutes. These statutes fall into two general types. The first type punishes individuals who induce minors to become prostitutes. These statutes generally prohibit the "promotion" of prostitution and penalize the range of promotional activities commonly performed by pimps by means of the prohibition of such acts as "causing," "aiding", or "inducing" a minor to turn to prostitution. The second type of statute focuses on the profit element of pimping. These statutes prohibit such acts as "deriving support from child prostitution"[87] or "receiving profits derived from prostitution" by juveniles.[88]

Both types of statutes frequently incorporate the age-based distinctions discussed earlier. Some statutes define a separate offense, such as aggravated promotion, when the pimping activity involves a prostitute who is either under a specified age[89] or a minor.[90] Other statutes categorize the offense into several degrees according to the age of the prostitute. Penal codes utilizing this approach often classify promotion of juvenile prostitution as a first-degree felony, whereas promotion of adult prostitution is a felony of the second degree.[91] Other states have adopted a more complicated structure, including offenses with as many as three[92] or even four degrees.[93] Again, in either the aggravated offense or the two-plus-degree offense, penalties for pimps are increased according to the age of the juvenile.

Penalty Increases If Force Is Utilized. Recent statutes also reflect a legislative awareness of the coercion often used by pimps to induce minors to engage in prostitution. Several states have enacted prohibitions against inducing a juvenile to engage in prostitution through force, threats, or intimidation.[94] In some states, the prohibition includes compulsion by means of the use and/or withholding of drugs.[95] Offenses involving coercion carry especially severe penalties in all these jurisdictions.[96]

Punishment of Patrons. A fourth trend in recent legislation concerns punishment of the patrons of juvenile prostitutes. Several states have enacted provisions penalizing individuals who patronize, specifically, *juvenile* prostitutes. As is true for the offense of "promoting", some of these statutes incorporate age-based distinctions; that is, the lower the age of the juvenile prostitute, the greater the penalty is for the patron.[97] Although penalties for patrons are graduated, they tend to be less severe than those for pimps. Other states continue the double standard that is apparent in treatment of adult prostitution and fail to punish patrons of juvenile prostitutes.[98]

Severe Penalties. Another trend apparent in many state statutes is the increased severity of penalties meted out to adult actors engaged in acts of juvenile prostitution. The real target of these harsh penalties appears to be the pimp. Severity of punishment is apparent in two ways: (1) pimps are punished more severely than patrons of juveniles, and (2) pimps of juveniles are subject to more severe sanctions than pimps of adult prostitutes.

Such penalties reflect legislators' moral judgments about culpability. The sanctions illustrate the twin views that the individual who induces a juvenile to turn to prostitution is more culpable than the customer of a juvenile and that the pimp of a juvenile is more culpable than the pimp of an adult. These views of culpability are reflected differentially in the legislation. Some states handle it indirectly by punishing pimps but failing to punish patrons,[99] whereas other states deal with it more directly by legislating higher fines and longer periods of imprisonment for pimps than for patrons of juveniles.[100] Penalties for pimps of juveniles range up to 30 years[101] and $50,000 fine.[102]

This same philosophy of the aggravated culpability of pimps also explains the number of statutes that incorporate gradations in offenses for "promoting" (pimping) adolescent prostitution. These gradations, involving two, three, or four degrees, generally are not present in the various jurisdictions' statutory treatment of patrons of juveniles.

Statutes also punish pimps of juveniles much more severely than pimps of adult prostitutes. Thus, in Minnesota, for example, an individual who promotes the prostitution of an adult is subject to a penalty of 3 years or $3,000 fine, or both. In that same state, however, an individual who promotes child prostitution (specifically, prostitution of a juvenile under age 16) is subject to a penalty of 10 years or $10,000 fine, or both.[103] Some states have other stringent provisions in effect when juveniles are involved. One statute, for example, precludes probation and suspended sentences for perpetrators.[104] Such statutes also reflect widely held views of culpability for sexual misconduct with juveniles.

Third Parties. Another characteristic common to state statutory treatment of juvenile prostitution concerns the inclusion of third-party custodians. In many jurisdictions, third parties, such as parents or guardians, are subject to penalties for the roles they play in the prostitution of children or wards. Statutes now expressly punish persons who use a position of authority to solicit or induce an individual to practice prostitution[105] or who permit a minor under their custody or control to engage in prostitution,[106] or who, by abuse of any position of confidence or authority, procure another person for the purpose of prostitution.[107] Other statutes implicitly incorporate such proscriptions by broad statutory designation of perpetrators.[108] Such inclusion of third parties reflects an awareness of the influence of parents and significant others on some juveniles' entrance into prostitution.

Juvenile as Victim. Another trend in recent legislation is the treatment of juveniles as victims, rather than as criminals, which can be seen in the recently enacted state criminal statutes' failure to punish juvenile prostitutes. Most statutes simply omit any mention that the juvenile might be subject to sanctions, and some state statutes specifically exclude from liability the juveniles involved in prostitution.[109] Some juvenile prostitutes, of course, may be punished under juvenile delinquency statutes. It is significant, however, that punishment of the juvenile is absent in the wave of recent legislation. This view of the juvenile prostitute as victim is also reflected in recently enacted civil statutes (see later discussion), which treat juvenile prostitution as a form of child abuse.

Runaway Prostitutes. Another trend evident in recent legislation is the recognition of the interrelationship between runaway behavior and juvenile prostitution. Several state statutes address the link between runaway behavior and prostitution and penalize individuals who facilitate the transportation of minors for purposes of prostitution. Transportation may include movement into or through the jurisdiction. Minnesota, for example, defines *promoting* to include "transportation of persons for purposes of prostitution from one point within this state to another point either within or without this state, or bringing an individual into this state to aid the prostitution of that individual."[110] Similarly, California recently amended its penal code to prohibit transportation of juveniles for purposes of prostitution.[111]

Defenses. Many statutory schemes make certain defenses inapplicable to some persons who are prosecuted for involvement in juvenile prostitution. Such provisions are intended to facilitate prosecutions of adult perpetrators. Defenses that are specifically inapplicable include (1) that the persons involved are members of the same sex,[112] (2) that the juvenile did not actually engage in prostitution,[113] (3) that the juvenile previously prostituted,[114] and (4) that the juvenile consented to the acts of prostitution.[115] Such statutes have several effects: they facilitate prosecutions of male patrons of juvenile male prostitutes, and they facilitate prosecutions of adults in the characteristic situations in which juveniles are willing participants in the sexual acts.

Jurisdictions have taken different views toward the common mistake of age defense. Some states provide for a strict liability offense and do not permit the adult to argue ignorance of the juvenile's age,[116] whereas other states permit this defense. Some states allow the defense in prosecutions of patrons but not pimps,[117] and still other states allow the defense for offenses with older juveniles but not with younger juveniles.[118] In jurisdictions that permit the defense, a reasonable assumption that the juvenile is above the protected ages will enable the defendant either to escape liability or to incur a less severe penalty.

Exemptions. A final trend in state statutes is the provision for exemptions for some perpetrators. Several statutes accomplish a result similar to a defense by enabling certain defendants to escape liability. Minnesota, for example, exempts those who are related by blood, marriage, or adoption from the crime of receiving profit from prostitution.[119] This treatment is paradoxical in light of the trend in other states toward inclusion of such persons as parents or guardians as culpable parties. Some jurisdictions also exempt perpetrators who are similar in age to the juveniles;[120] this exemption attempts to eliminate prosecutions for mere sexual experimentation among juveniles.

Trends in Civil Legislation

Juvenile prostitution is also addressed by state statutory treatment of child abuse. All jurisdictions have child abuse and neglect reporting laws that mandate certain professionals to report suspected child abuse to appropriate state agencies. Each state defines the types of abuse that must be reported. Sexual abuse is often included in these definitional provisions, but until recently the term as defined in state laws included only, sexual contact between child and parent or caretaker. Juvenile prostitution, consisting of sexual contact between a child and a third party that is encouraged by a parent or caretaker, was not reportable.

Since 1978, states have been encouraged to incorporate the term *sexual exploitation,* clearly defined to include prostitution, as a form of child abuse that must be reported.[121] To date, fifteen states have revised their mandatory reporting laws to include the term *sexual exploitation* within their definitions of abuse and neglect,[122] and two of these fifteen statutes specifically refer to juvenile prostitution.[123]

These civil child abuse statutes reflect views previously noted in the discussion of the criminal treatment of juvenile prostitution. First, the civil statutes reflect an awareness that parents or guardians are occasionally involved in influencing the entrance of juveniles into prostitution. Second, they reflect the view that the juvenile prostitute should be treated as a victim of adult sexual misconduct, rather than as a youthful perpetrator of criminal acts.

The foregoing trends in criminal and civil legislation illustrate two themes that underlie recent legislative activity. The first theme is punitive—the intention to penalize severely individuals who engage in sexual exploitation of minors. The second theme, stemming from societal concern with child abuse, focuses on protecting the victim. In this view, the juvenile prostitute is a victim of adult conduct and is in need of intervention and protection by the legal system.

Legal Reality and Social Reality

Legislative policy on juvenile prostitution has been formulated only in the past decade. Similarly, social science research on the phenomenon has been conducted only recently. This poses a dilemma in that legislation has been enacted largely without the benefit of empirical knowledge. The question must be asked, therefore, whether the new legal policy comports with social reality— that is, whether federal and state legislation adequately addresses the many dimensions of this complex social problem. To answer this question, the effectiveness of both federal and state legislation must be explored.

Federal Legislation and Social Reality

Federal legislation addresses juvenile prostitution by several methods. First, summarizing the discussion earlier in this chapter, federal legislation prohibits the transportation of minors for purposes of prostitution. Second, by amendments to the Child Abuse Act, federal legislation defines juvenile prostitution as a form of child abuse. Third, by providing for the funding of runaway centers, federal legislation addresses the interrelationship between prostitution and runaway behavior. Finally, the Missing Children Act aids the identification and location of missing children, thereby facilitating intervention for some runaway prostitutes.

The effectiveness of these approaches, however, varies greatly. The federal prohibition against transportation of juveniles for prostitution appears to be only a partially effective response of the criminal justice system. Several problems are apparent in the application of this legislation. First, the effectiveness of the legislation appears to be gender-related. The Mann Act provisions are able to address the interstate aspects of prostitution in cases involving only juvenile females. Because the legislation is directed primarily at pimps, and because only female juvenile prostitutes have pimps, only female prostitution is affected.[124]

It is doubtful whether the legislation has any effect on juvenile male prostitution, because, as previously mentioned, research reveals that juvenile male prostitutes do not work for pimps; rather, they tend to work for themselves. It follows that no individual actually transports male youth across state lines; if juvenile males travel interstate for purposes of prostitution, they do so of their own volition and by means of their own resources. Thus, although neutral on their face, the Mann Act revisions appear to be gender-based in application. Sanctions directed at the transportation of juvenile male prostitutes appear to have only symbolic, rather than real, impact.

Even in cases involving juvenile females, however, the Mann Act appears to have limited effectiveness. The disparity between the number of convictions under the act and the considerable interstate travel involving prostitutes leads to disappointment with the Mann Act's effectiveness. In 1980, prosecutors achieved only fourteen convictions; there were only sixteen in 1981 and eight in the first nine months of 1982.[125]

Notwithstanding the low number of convictions, however, research data suggest that pimps facilitate considerable interstate travel involving juvenile female prostitutes. In one study of fifty-eight juvenile prostitutes, twenty-four states were mentioned by 60 percent of the juvenile prostitutes who were asked where they traveled for work.[126] These prostitutes indicated that the decision to travel frequently involves the pimp.[127] Thus, although the federal legislation is an important tool in the hands of law enforcement, it appears to be utilized effectively in only a small number of cases.

Another manner of addressing juvenile prostitution on the federal level is the Child Abuse Prevention and Treatment and Adoption Reform Act. As originally enacted, the act encourages states to adopt legislation requiring designated individuals to report child abuse. The 1978 amendments to this legislation define sexual exploitation, including juvenile prostitution, as a form of child abuse, and acts of prostitution involving parents or caretakers now constitute a form of abuse that must be reported to appropriate state agencies in many jurisdictions.

A major shortcoming of the legislation as applied to juvenile prostitution is its limitation to parents and caretakers. Only sexual exploitation perpetrated by parents, caretakers, or persons "responsible for the child's welfare" is a reportable condition.[128] Acts of prostitution promoted by any other family member, or by extrafamilial third parties such as pimps, are outside the scope of the reporting legislation.

The effectiveness of this provision depends on the extent of parents' or guardians' participation in acts of prostitution involving their children or wards. Occasional accounts of such misconduct do appear in the literature[129] and in case law,[130] but an analysis of empirical data suggests that parental involvement in juvenile prostitution is not a frequent occurrence.

Evidence on the incidence of parental or caretaker involvement may be deduced from data on the process of entrance into prostitution, which suggest that the persons who most often facilitate entrance into prostitution for girls are not their parents or caretakers. The pimp is the person most frequently named by female prostitutes as influencing their decision to turn out. Other persons who are influential in females' involvement in prostitution include women recruiting for a pimp, madams, other prostitutes, and customers.[131] Data on juvenile males suggest that friends are the most influential persons in their entrance into prostitution[132] Such evidence suggests that only in rare cases is the juvenile's entrance into prostitution facilitated by a parent or caretaker.

This hypothesis is supported further by data revealing that many adolescent prostitutes learn about prostitution only after they have run away from home[133] and that they make the decision to turn to prostitution when they are on the streets and in need of money to survive.[134] The timing of the youths' entrance into prostitution is an additional factor suggesting a lack of any significant correlation between parental involvement and juveniles' entrance into prostitution.[135]

These two factors (influential persons and the timing of entrance) lead to the tentative conclusion that parental involvement in prostitution is not widespread. Since the incidence of this problem appears to be small, the Child Abuse Act amendments on reporting of sexual exploitation by parents or caretakers appear to have limited utility in the identification of juvenile prostitutes.

This is not to suggest that federal child abuse legislation is totally ineffective in combating the problem. The legislation's primary contribution appears to be not identification but, rather, prevention of juvenile prostitution. The objective of the original legislation—to encourage reporting of physical abuse—is essential in the prevention of juvenile prostitution, since physical abuse is one of the primary factors contributing to juvenile prostitution. Not only do significant numbers of both male and female juvenile prostitutes come from abusive family backgrounds, but many prostitutes attribute their running away to such abuse. Thus, the federal child abuse legislation, through its efforts addressed to physical abuse, is an important weapon in the prevention of juvenile prostitution.

The third method of addressing juvenile prostitution on the federal level appears to be quite effective. The Runaway and Homeless Youth Act, which provides funding for runaway shelters nationwide, helps both male and female adolescent prostitutes who are runaways.[136] Several federally funded runaway shelters have exemplary programs that address the specific needs of adolescent prostitutes. Three such centers are Bridge over Troubled Waters in Boston, The Shelter in Seattle, and Huckleberry House in San Francisco.[137] Bridge was founded in Boston in 1970 to serve the needs of runaway youth. Located near the Boston Common (a setting for juvenile prostitution), the agency offers a broad range of services to runaway youth in general and specific services for juvenile prostitutes.

Providing shelter for homeless youth is one important service of Bridge. When a runaway approaches the agency, it first attempts family reunification. If this is neither possible nor advisable, the agency provides short-term residential care. Another component of the program is a mobile medical van that travels throughout Boston providing medical screening, treatment of simple disorders, and follow-up treatment. Venereal disease screening is an important medical service provided to juvenile prostitutes and other sexually active youth.

In addition, Bridge provides crisis intervention, ongoing personal counseling, and a 24–hour telephone crisis hotline. Family counseling is provided whenever possible. Bridge also provides training to help youth qualify for the high school graduation certificate—an important service for the many juvenile prostitutes who are high school dropouts. The agency also recently received funding for a youth employment program.

Seattle's The Shelter also offers services to juvenile prostitutes. The Shelter began in 1973 as a small, locally funded agency. After receiving federal funds in 1975, the agency increased its staff and services. It first estblished an emergency residential facility; then, after recognizing the incidence of juvenile prostitution in the greater Seattle area, The Shelter implemented an outreach street work project. Staffed by social work professionals and ex-street people, this street work program, called Project START (Street Transition Advocates Resource Team), features an intensive prevention and treatment effort.

Project START'S Judicial Advocates project has implemented an educational program about street life and prostitution in thirty-five city and county schools to increase community awareness and to prevent juveniles from turning to prostitution. In addition, street workers regularly visit sites frequented by street youth and young prostitutes to offer necessary services. The street outreach supervisor receives referrals of youth charged with prostitution from the prosecutor's office and the juvenile court. The supervisor, in conjunction with Judicial Advocates, has developed a counseling and educational program for these court-referred youth. To the extent that these youth desire to leave prostitution, referrals are made to a specialized employment and training program. In addition, one outreach worker coordinates housing resources for young prostitutes who desire to move away from the streets.

Huckleberry House in San Francisco also provides services to juvenile prostitutes and runaway youth. The agency provides crisis and short-term housing, employment counseling, training and job referrals, medical and legal assistance, educational assistance, food, and clothing. The agency facilitates independent living, out-of-home placements, and family reunification. In addition, youth can receive individual counseling in the areas of self-awareness and self-worth, sexuality and sexual identity, substance abuse, and peer relationships.

This agency initiated the Sexual Minority Youth Services Project in 1978 and the Sexual Minority Youth Employment Project in 1979 because of the increase in clients involved in prostitution as well as the numbers of clients identifying as gay or bisexual. These two projects offer special services to youth who identify as gay or bisexual. A large number of juvenile prostitutes are included among Huckleberry House's clients.

These and other centers funded by the Runaway Youth Act assist many juvenile prostitutes. Many centers are able to identify and provide specific services needed by these youth because of their aggressive outreach programs and because they are located in geographically accessible areas. The federally funded shelters provide both short-term and long-term services to youth in need.

The Runaway Youth Act furnishes funding that is essential to the operation of these facilities. The federal funds are used for services, for staff salaries, and to attract additional public and private funding. The services these facilities provide are necessary to prevent many runaways from turning to prostitution. They are also essential for youth who are already involved in prostitution because they fulfill the youth's survival needs by providing food and shelter, thereby decreasing dependence on pimps and patrons. In addition, by means of long-term services such as educational and vocational training, the centers provide the means by which these youth can change their lifestyles and eventually exit from prostitution.

The fourth method of addressing juvenile prostitution on the federal level is the Missing Children Act, which established a special national clearinghouse to facilitate identification of missing children, including runaways. This legislation has potential for helping juvenile prostitutes in several ways. First, it may facilitate location of runaways soon after they have departed from home, and such prompt identification of runaways might prevent some youth from turning to prostitution to meet their survival needs. Identification of runaway youth who already have entered prostitution also might yield positive outcomes. Intervention by local law enforcement authorities might lead to referrals to social service delivery systems that could facilitate the youth's exit from the profession or, at the least, provide needed services.

Despite its potential, however, the legislation faces several problems in addressing juvenile prostitution. First, the act's procedure is exceedingly cumbersome. Parents must first approach local law enforcement authorities and wait until they have completed an investigation. Only after local investigation—or local authorities' refusal to investigate—may parents approach the FBI. Parents may not place their children's names in the federal computer in the first instance, since only local authorities may do this; they may only *confirm* whether local authorities have entered a child's name. Only in egregious cases in which local authorities refuse to investigate may parents go over the heads of local authorities and request entry on the FBI computer. This cumbersome process requires that parents go back and forth numerous times between local and federal authorities. It thus places considerable responsibility on parents in times of stress and frequently results in intense frustration.

Problems also result because the effective functioning of the clearinghouse is premised on several assumptions. Initially, for the system to work effectively, parents must report a child as missing to local law enforcement authorities to commence an investigation that culminates in the entry of data into the national clearinghouse. Next, family reunification must be a viable objective. Finally, once apprehended, the runaways themselves must furnish accurate identifying information to law enforcement officials.

These assumptions generally do not apply to the juvenile prostitute for a number of reasons. First, some families may not report their child as missing, since the families of some juvenile prostitutes have disintegrated as a result of death, separation, or divorce. Other runaway prostitutes leave home because of family conflicts, and many are "throwaways," rather than runaways—that is their families have thrown them out and have told them not to return. Such families would be unlikely to report the adolescent's departure to local law enforcement officials.

Second, family reunification may not always be an appropriate solution. Many juvenile prostitutes come from abusive home situations, and reuniting the runaways with such families may not be desirable. Also, families who have rejected the youth because of family conflicts are not promising candidates for family reunification.

Finally, the successful functioning of the national clearinghouse depends not only on parental cooperation but also, to some extent, on the cooperation of the juveniles. A juvenile who has been taken into police custody must provide authorities with accurate identifying information, such as name, residence, and birthdate. This is essential to match data on the apprehended juvenile with data on a juvenile who was earlier reported missing. Juvenile prostitutes are especially prone to deception, however, and to the provision of false identification.[138] They are aware that they are committing illegal acts, and they frequently provide false information to prevent their families from learning of their offenses. Furthermore, some youth provide false information because they prefer not to return to an abusive family situation.

This is not to suggest that the legislation is of no avail. Rather, it suggests that the Missing Children Act has the potential to facilitate the location of very limited numbers of runaway prostitutes. Specifically, it offers hope for identifying those youth (1) who have a parent or parents remaining, (2) whose parents are sufficiently concerned about their children's disappearance to report them as missing, (3) whose parents desire the youth's return, and (4) who will cooperate with law enforcement officials by providing accurate identifying information.

State Legislation and Social Reality

State legislation suffers the same variation in effectiveness as federal legislation in addressing juvenile prostitution. One characteristic of many recent statutes is the use of age-based distinctions. Most statutes with age-based lines differentiate between offenses involving juveniles who are under 16 and those who are 16 and older. Some of these statutes make further distinctions in the 16-and-older category, treating separately offenses involving juveniles aged 16 through 18. This last group of statutes thus has three categories of offenses—with juveniles under 16, with those 16 through 18, and with those 18 and older.

The statutes that define offenses according to involvement of juveniles under age 16 appear to be well tailored to social reality. Although this age might have been incorporated in some statutes because it constitutes the age of consent,[139] nonetheless it comports well with empirical evidence on juvenile prostitution. Research data reveal that the median age of both male and female juvenile prostitutes is 16. Since half of juvenile prostitutes are younger than 16, age 16 is therefore an appropriate dividing line upon which to base sanctions.

A few statutes proscribe offenses with very young prostitutes, generally proscribing offenses with youth age 14 and under.[140] One jurisdiction penalizes offenses with juveniles under age 11.[141] These statutes do not accurately reflect social reality, however, since data reveal that juveniles younger than 14 rarely engage in prostitution on a regular basis.[142] Cases involving juveniles younger than 11 have never been reported in empirical studies. Although prostitution with youth of these ages certainly should be penalized, there appears to be little reason for a separate offense. Jurisdictions that penalize offenses with youth under age 16 adequately encompass these perpetrators.

State legislation also reflects a concern with penalizing the various aspects of pimping. This approach to juvenile prostitution appears to comport well with social reality. The pimp is a central feature of juvenile female prostitution and is especially deserving of punishment for two reasons: (1) he is actively involved in the juveniles' entrance into prostitution, and (2) much of the violence associated with prostitution stems from acts by pimps. As mentioned earlier, however, local and federal law enforcement of these penal statutes is woefully inadequate. Too frequently, police do not investigate or fail to press charges against pimps, because they believe that prostitutes will not testify against pimps. More vigorous efforts are necessary and can be successful. Our research with the staffs of a few law enforcement agencies suggests that patient police work with a prostitute may persuade her to testify.

Another problem in the enforcement mechanism of prosecuting pimps is its ineffectiveness regarding male prostitution. Since adolescent male prostitution is distinguishable from female prostitution by the absence of pimps, prosecution of pimps leaves juvenile male prostitution untouched. This characteristic of state legislation, similar to the federal Mann Act provisions, appears to be gender-based in application.

Another trend in some state statutes is punishment of customers of juvenile prostitutes. In theory, this appears to be an effective approach, since customers, like pimps, are committing criminal offenses, and some are violent toward the juveniles. In reality, however, prosecutions of customers are all but nonexistent. The focus of the law enforcement effort is the arrest of the prostitute, and few resources of local authorities are ever directed at the customer.

Still another characteristic of some recent state statutes is recognition of the link between runaway behavior and juvenile prostitution. These statutes prohibit the intrastate transportation of juveniles for purposes of prostitution, which appears to be an important method of addressing juvenile prostitution in light of the considerable transportation of juvenile prostitutes by pimps.

Nonetheless, as discussed in regard to the federal Mann Act revisions, these state statutes also appear to have gender-based application. Since only juvenile female prostitutes have pimps, the new state statutes still fail to address juvenile male prostitution. Young male prostitutes, if they travel within the state for purposes of prostitution, do so of their own volition. Furthermore, as previously discussed, enforcement of penal laws against pimps has been lax and ineffective even with respect to female prostitutes. Considerably more effort should be expended in this regard.

Several better ways of addressing juvenile prostitution should be suggested. Initially, state legislatures should address the underlying causes of running away, and adequate resources should be provided for the identification, prevention, and treatment of victims of physical and sexual abuse. Admittedly, the effectiveness of such measures may be crippled because resources are too often expended only on the more visible and egregious cases (and on the lower socioeconomic class). Nonetheless, this approach offers at least some hope of preventing future generations from turning to the streets.

Second, state legislatures should penalize the parental rejection that causes many youth to leave home as throwaways. Such acts of parental abandonment should be made criminal offenses; to date, however, only limited state remedies are available to punish or deter such conduct.[143] One important improvement in state legislation would be enforcement of parental support obligations. At the least, if parents refuse to readmit an adolescent to their home after a family conflict or a runaway episode, parents' support obligations should be enforced.[144] States furnishing support to these minors directly, or indirectly through state-funded runaway shelters, should be able to collect that support from these parents. This would enable youth to maintain themselves in shelter facilities and in independent living situations without turning to prostitution to meet their survival needs.

Third, better interstate and intrastate cooperation between agencies is essential to deal effectively with the problem of the runaway prostitute. Too often, an adolescent who leaves the state and is apprehended as a prostitute by authorities in another jurisdiction will be returned home without facing criminal charges and without notification to authorities in the home state.[145] As a consequence, social service agencies in neither state intervene, and in a short time, the juvenile runs away again and is working on the streets again. Law enforcement officials in one jurisdiction who apprehend and then release a runaway prostitute should notify social welfare authorities in the youth's home state before returning the juvenile home. Appropriate state agencies might then offer necessary services to the youth. In addition, if runaway juveniles are formally adjudicated on charges of running away and/or prostitution, the juveniles should be referred to appropriate social service agencies that might assist them. Police and juvenile court workers should be encouraged to make referrals to these agencies and to conduct follow-ups to assure that the youth receive adequate attention.

Finally, states should provide funding for the runaway programs in their jurisdictions, since these programs serve essential needs of the runaway prostitutes. Federal monies are simply not adequate to support the staff and many services of these runaway programs. Runaway shelters are one of the few effective resources with a proven record of dealing with this youth population, and they urgently need federal and state funds if they are to survive and continue to provide the services critically needed by these youth.

Conclusion

Juvenile prostitution is a complex social problem. Its complexity is due, in part, to its interrelationship with such other social problems as physical abuse, sexual abuse, and running away. It is a lifestyle that attracts both males and females, although differences exist between male and female juvenile prostitutes. These factors combine to make juvenile prostitution a difficult problem for policy-makers to address.

Recent state and federal legislation has taken a two-pronged approach to the problem: criminal statutes penalize adult participants who engage in or encourage prostitution with juveniles, and civil statutes attempt to identify the juvenile prostitutes more promptly to offer them necessary services. Several problems are apparent, however, in the federal and state statutory response to juvenile prostitution. One problem stems from assumptions about the best way to address juvenile prostitution. Such assumptions tend to be premised on knowledge about female prostitution, and the law's response to juvenile prostitution reflects little awareness of the nature and incidence of juvenile male prostitution. The recent Mann Act revisions—the only recent legislation to address juvenile male prostitution specifically—are hampered by the assumption that male and female juvenile prostitution are identical. State statutory treatment, primarily targeted at pimps, shares the same flaw.

Although they are similar in etiology, significant differences exist between female and male juvenile prostitution that require different responses by the legal system. Since legislative policy aimed at pimps generally will not affect juvenile male prostitutes, the efforts must be directed elsewhere. Statutes penalizing customers are one appropriate response, but effective enforcement of these statutes is essential. In addition, the effectiveness of many of these statutes is mitigated by the mistake-of-age defense, which allows customers to receive lighter sentences if they can prove that they were reasonably mistaken as to the age of the juvenile. Since patron statutes are the only criminal statutes that address the reality of juvenile male prostitution, it is important that more jurisdictions do not limit the effectiveness of the statutes by provision for this defense.

Statutes are only the initial stage, of course, in the law's response to male or female juvenile prostitution. The effectiveness of legislation depends on adequate enforcement. In terms of addressing juvenile female prostitution, the federal Mann Act should be enforced more vigorously. Similar criticisms have been levied that the enforcement of state prostitution laws is lax in regard to pimps.[146] Arrests and prosecutions of adult participants are necessary to combat the exploitation and violence associated with juvenile prostitution. Furthermore, law authorities must dispense with the double standard in enforcing statutes penalizing customers. To address juvenile male prostitution, such enforcement must be gender-neutral and must apply to customers of both male and female juveniles.

In addition, the application of the law to status offenders must also be gender-neutral. When legal officials apprehend runaways and juvenile prostitutes, attention must be directed toward both male and female juveniles. A "boys will be boys" philosophy will not help the males in this situation. Intervention must be assured to help runaway prostitutes of both sexes.

The legislative experience to date with juvenile prostitution has provided lessons that might improve future reform efforts. First, policymakers should take into account available social science research data. Only after examining empirical research findings will legislators be sufficiently aware of the nature of the problem and the best methods of addressing it. Ideally, legislators and social scientists should work together in determining effective methods of approaching the issues.

Second, before legislation is enacted, policy goals should be formulated. Alternative goals of prevention, punishment, and rehabilitation should be carefully explored to determine which goals best conform to the problem. In addressing a problem such as juvenile prostitution, it is simplistic to believe that punishment will eliminate the problem, since such an approach has failed with adult prostitution.

Too often, the legislative response to a social problem—especially one involving child victims—is enactment of harsher penalties for adult perpetrators; yet this approach ignores the plight of the victims. When addressing a social problem such as juvenile prostitution, an emphasis on prevention and treatment appears to be more effective if the goal is to assist the youth involved.

Lawmakers must realize that the best method of addressing juvenile prostitution is to reach into the public coffers to support programs in prevention and treatment. Stricter penalties for adult participants, though an easy response to the problem, have greater theoretical than real impact. Few services and programs exist that are targeted to juvenile prostitutes. The federal budget for runaway programs that provide important services for runaway prostitutes is woefully inadequate, and state resources for these runaway programs are similarly sparse.

The expenditure of adequate state and federal resources is necessary *before* juveniles become so entrenched in prostitution that they cannot leave the profession. Early intervention with runaways is the best approach. Juvenile prostitution needs to be addressed by means of increased services for these youth. If they do not address this issue, public policymakers are consigning these children of the night to continue walking the dark streets.

Notes

1. Sources at the Senate hearings on the Protection of Children Against Sexual Exploitation Act estimate that 600,000 juvenile females and 300,000 juvenile males are involved in prostitution. *Sexual Exploitation of Children: Hearings on H.R. 4571 Before the Subcomm. on Crime of the House Comm. on the Judiciary*, 95th Cong., 1st Sess. 347 (1977) [hereafter cited as *Hearings on H.R. 4571*].

2. For a rare article dealing in part with juvenile prostitution, see Comment, *Preying on Playgrounds: The Sexploitation of Children in Pornography and Prostitution*, 5 Pepperdine L. Rev. 809 (1978) [hereafter cited as *Playgrounds*]. See also David P. Shouvlin, *Preventing the Sexual Exploitation of Children: A Model Act*, 17 Wake Forest L. Rev. 535, 540-43 (1981) [hereafter cited as Shouvlin, *Model Act*].

3. 18 U.S.C. §§ 2251, 2252, 2253 (Supp. 1978).

4. 42 U.S.C. §§ 5101–5107 (Supp. 1978).

5. 42 U.S.C. §§ 5702, 5711–5713, 5715–5716, 5731–5741, 5751 (Supp. 1978).

6. 28 U.S.C. § 534 (1982).

7. 18 U.S.C. §§ 2251, 2253–2254 (1978). On January 24, 1978, the House demonstrated its unanimous support for the legislation by approving the act in a vote of 401–0. The Senate approved the measure on a voice vote. President Carter signed P.L. 95-225 into law on February 6, 1978.

8. In the first few months of the session, four bills addressing child sexual exploitation were introduced in the Senate. Three of these bills (S. 1011, S. 1499, and S. 1585) were referred to the Committee on the Judiciary. One bill (S. 1040) was referred to the Committee on Human Resources. On May 6, 1977, the Committee on Human Resources passed a resolution urging the Committee on the Judiciary to hold hearings at the earliest possible time, either singly or in conjunction with the Committee on Human Resources, to consider appropriate legislation. S. Rep. No. 438, 95th Cong., 2d Sess. 2, *reprinted in* [1978] U.S. Code Cong. & Ad. News 41 [hereafter cited as S. Rep. No. 438, with all cites to the U.S. Code Cong. & Ad. News].

9. Hearings were held by the Subcommittee on Crime of the House Committee on the Judiciary and the Subcommittee on Select Education, Committee on Education and Labor, in the House of Representatives. See, generally, *Hearings on H.R. 8059 Before the Subcomm. of Education and Labor of the House Comm. on the Judiciary*, 95th Cong., 1st Sess. (1977). Hearings were also held in the Senate by the Subcommittee to Investigate Juvenile Delinquency of the Committee on the Judiciary. See *Hearings on S. 1585 Before the Subcomm. to Investigate Juvenile Delinquency of the Senate Comm. on the Judiciary*, 95th Cong., 2d Sess. 41-42 (1978). This subcommittee has since been renamed Subcommittee on Juvenile Justice.

10. 18 U.S.C. § 1461 (1948) (1958 amendment provides for continuing offenses) [mailing]; 18 U.S.C. § 1462 (1948) [importation]; 18 U.S.C. § 1465 (1955) [interstate transportation of obscene material]; and 18 U.S.C. § 1464 (1948) [broadcasts].

11. 18 U.S.C. § 2423 (1948).

12. Prior to the Sexual Exploitation Act, federal law prohibited the sale, distribution, and importation of obscene materials. The act remedied a gap in existing federal law by adding a new offense to Title 18, § 2251, which prohibits the production of pornographic materials involving minors under age 16. See 18 U.S.C. § 2253(1). The act also increased the penalty provisions for the mailing (§ 1461), importation (§ 1462), and transportation for sale and distribution (§ 1465) of obscene materials involving children.

13. Ch. 395, 36 Stat. 825 (1910) (codified as amended at 18 U.S.C. §§ 2421-2424 (1976 & Supp. III 1979)).

14. S. Rep. No. 438 at 51.

15. *Id.* at 54.

16. *Id.* at 55.

17. *Id.* at 51.

18. H.R. Rep. No. 696, 95th Cong., 1st Sess. 2 (1977).

19. *Id.* at 5.

20. Section 2423(a)(2) prohibits any person from transporting, financing, or facilitating the interstate transportation of a minor with the intent that such minor engage in prohibited sexual conduct, if such person so transporting, financing, causing, or facilitating movement, knows or has reason to know that such prohibited sexual conduct will be commercially exploited by any person: "The purpose is to penalize persons who induce children to perform sexually explicit conduct not just for money but for any direct or indirect gain and at the same time to avoid penalizing a 16-year-old male who brings a female of the same age across State lines, with her consent or perhaps vice versa, to engage in sexual conduct." 123 Cong. Rec. 34,993 (1977).

21. H. Rep. No. 696, 95 Cong., 1st Sess. 10 (1977). Representative Ertel, a member of the Subcommittee on Crime, proposed an amendment to § 2251 to add the words "or if such film, photograph, negative, slide, book, magazine or other visual or print medium has actually been mailed or transported in interstate or foreign commerce." This amendment was adopted by the Judiciary Committee; however, only the "visual or print medium [which] has actually been mailed or transported" language was ultimately enacted as § 2251. See 18 U.S.C. § 2251 (1978).

22. This was the terminology of the Mann Act provision on minors. See 18 U.S.C. §§ 2421 *et seq.* (1910), amended as 18 U.S.C. § 2423 (1978).

23. 1978 U.S. Code Cong. & Ad. News 40, 57.

24. 42. U.S.C. §§ 5101-5106 (1974), *as amended by* Child Abuse Prevention and Treatment and Adoption Reform Act of 1978, Pub. L. No. 95-266, 92 Stat. 205 (1978). The act was retitled in 1978. Title I of the new act dealt with amendments to the earlier legislation; Title II focused on adoption and attempted to facilitate model adoption legislation and procedures. For the congressional hearings that led to the enactment of the 1974 legislation, see *Child Abuse Prevention and Treatment Act: Hearings on S. 1191 Before the Subcomm. on Children and Youth of the Senate Comm. on Labor and Public Welfare,* 93rd Cong., 1st Sess. (1973).

25. Limited federal support for child abuse prevention prior to the enactment of the Child Abuse Prevention and Treatment Act, Pub. L. No. 93-247, 88 Stat. (1974),

was available through Subchapter IV, Parts A and B, of the Social Security Act, 42 U.S.C. §§ 601-626 (1968), which authorizes social services to AFDC children and child welfare services including child protective services. The limited nature of earlier federal support can be seen in the funding of $46 million for the entire child welfare program in 1973. Of that $46 million, approximately $507,000 was spent on activities related to child abuse. S. Rep. No. 167, 95th Cong., 1st Sess. 27 (1977).

    26. See S. Rep. No. 167, 95th Cong., 1st Sess. 27 (1977).

    27. 42 U.S.C. § 5102 (1974).

    28. H.R. Rep. No. 696, 95th Cong., 1st Sess. 10 (1977).

    29. S. Rep. No. 438 at 5 (1977).

    30. H.R. Rep. No. 609, 95th Cong., 1st Sess. 1 (1977).

    31. 42 U.S.C. § 5102 (1977).

    32. The definition was contained in the section authorizing special state grants pertaining to sexual abuse. 42 U.S.C. § 5104(b)(3)(A)(1977). As used in this subsection, the term *sexual abuse* included:

> ... the obscene or pornographic photographing, filming, or depiction of children for commercial purposes, or the rape, molestation, incest, *prostitution,* or other such forms of sexual exploitation of children under circumstances which indicate that the child's health or welfare is harmed or threatened thereby .... [emphasis added] *Id.*

    33. Omnibus Reconciliation Act of 1981, Title VI, Ch. 7 §§ 609, 610. For further discussion of the history of this definition, see American Bar Association, *Child Sexual Exploitation: Background and Legal Analysis* (monograph by the National Legal Resource Center for Child Advocacy and Protection, April 1983), at 17-19 [hereafter cited as ABA, Sexual Exploitation Monograph, 2d ed.]

    34. 48 Fed. Reg. 3702, §1340.2

    35. Juvenile Justice and Delinquency Prevention Act of 1974, Pub. L. No. 93-415, 88 Stat. 1109-1143 (1974) (codified in scattered sections of 18 U.S.C. and 42 U.S.C.). The act consists of two separate measures, the Juvenile Justice and Delinquency Prevention Act of 1972 [42 U.S.C. § 5601 (Supp. 1975)] and the Runaway and Homeless Youth Act [42 U.S.C. §§ 5701-5702, 5711-5713, 5715-5716, 5731-5732, 5751 (Supp. II 1978)].

    36. Runaways are also dealt with by the legislation as a whole, which addresses juvenile court jurisdiction. The act defines runaways as juveniles who have left home without permission of their parents or guardians. Juvenile Justice Delinquency Prevention Act of 1974 § 312(a), 42 U.S.C. § 5712 (Supp. 1975).

    37. S. Rep. No. 165, 95th Cong., 1st Sess. 22 (1977).

    38. Research reveals that significant numbers of juvenile prostitutes are runaways. Prior studies suggest that from 75 to 100 percent of adolescent female prostitutes are runaways. Jennifer James, *Entrance into Juvenile Prostitution* (Washington, D.C.: National Institute of Mental Health, 1980), 51 [hereafter cited as James, *Entrance*]; Enablers, *Juvenile Prostitution in Minnesota: The Report of a Research Project* (St. Paul: The Enablers, 1978), 22, 28. Also, from 42 to 67 percent of adolescent male prostitutes are runaways. Sparky Harlan, Luanna L. Rodgers, and Brian Slattery, *Male and Female Adolescent Prostitution: Huckleberry House Sexual Minority Youth Services Project* (Washington, D.C.: Youth Development Bureau, Department of Health and Human Services, 1981), 27; Urban Rural Systems Associates (URSA), *A Report on Adolescent Male Prostitution* (Washington, D.C., Youth Development Bureau, Department of

Health and Human Services, July 1982), 85. Knowledge is more limited, however, on the percentage of runaways who turn to prostitution. Various unsubstantiated estimates have been suggested, ranging from 10 to 90 percent. See U.S. General Accounting Office, *Report to the Chairman, Subcommittee on Select Education, House Committee on Education and Labor, Pub. No. HRD-82-64, Sexual Exploitation of Children—A Problem of Unknown Magnitude* (April 20, 1982), at 46 [hereafter cited as *GAO Report*]. See also *Problems of Runaway Youth: Hearings Before the Subcomm. on Juvenile Justice of the Senate Comm. on the Judiciary,* 97th Cong., 2d Sess. 50–51 (1982) (testimony of Prof. D. Kelly Weisberg) [hereafter cited as *Hearings on Runaway Youth*].

39. 42 U.S.C §§ 5712(b)(3)–5712(b)(7) (Supp. 1981); Juvenile Justice Amendments of 1977, Pub. L. No. 95-115, 91 Stat. 1048 (1977).

40. The runaway shelter must contact the child's parents, if such action is required by state law, and assure the safe return of the child according to the best interests of the child. 42 U.S.C § 5712(b)(3) (Supp. 1981).

41. The GAO study reveals that some shelters exclusively serve juvenile prostitutes. Three such federally-funded shelters cited by the study include: New Bridge in Minneapolis, Minnesota, Chrysalis in Denver, Colorado, and Crossover in Milwaukee, Wisconsin. *GAO Report,* at 18–20. (New Bridge has ceased operation since the GAO study.) In addition, juvenile prostitutes also are included among youth generally who use runaway shelters. For more information on resources available to juvenile prostitutes nationwide, see, generally, Urban and Rural Systems Associates (URSA), *Juvenile Prostitution: A Resource Manual* (Washington, D.C.: Youth Development Bureau, Department of Health and Human Services, July 1982).

42. Pub. L. No. 96–509.

43. The 1980 amendment added the phrase "and their families" to the section authorizing grants and technical assistance to runaway youth. 42 U.S.C § 5711 (Supp. 1981).

44. *Id.*

45. Juvenile Justice Amendments of 1977, Pub. L. No. 95–115, 91 Stat. 1048 (1977).

46. 42 U.S.C. § 5751(a) (Supp. 1981).

47. See *Children's Defense Fund, A Children's Defense Budget: An Analysis of the President's Budget and Children* (1982), at 139.

48. *Id.*

49. *Id.*

50. See *Hearings on Runaway Youth,* and H. Rep. No. 914 at 24 (1982). This $18 million is still less than the $25 million per year authorized in 1980.

51. H.R. 6976, 97th Cong., 2d Sess. (1982).

52. Cases that attracted considerable notoriety involved the murders of twenty-nine black children in Atlanta and the death of 5-year-old Adam Walsh in Hollywood, Florida.

53. In 1975, a separate missing persons file was established to protect the appropriate privacy rights of affected individuals. H. Rep. No. 820, 97th Cong., 2d Sess. 3, *reprinted in* U.S. Code Cong. & Ad. News 2552–2554 (1982).

54. S. Rep. No. 583, 97th Cong., 2d Sess. 3 (1982).

55. *Id.*

56. *Id.*

57. *Id.*

58. *Id.* at 6.

59. 127 Cong. Rec. 6,115 (1981).

60. See *Missing Children Act: Hearings on H.R. 3781 Before the Subcomm. on Civil and Constitutional Rights of the House Comm. on the Judiciary,* 97th Cong., 1st Sess. (1981).

61. See *Hearings on S. 1701 Before the Subcomm. on Juvenile Justice of the Senate Judiciary Comm.,* 97th Cong., 1st Sess. (1982).

62. 128 Cong. Rec. 12,279 (1982); see S. Rep. No. 583, 97th Cong., 2d Sess. (1982).

63. S. 1355, 97th Cong., 1st Sess. (1981).

64. The committee inserted this language in proposed Sec. 2(a)(3). S. 1701, 97th Cong., 1st Sess. (1982). 128 Cong. Rec. 12,077 (1982).

65. The committee added this language in proposed Section 2(a)(3)(D). See S. 1701, 97th Cong., 1st Sess. (1982); 128 Cong. Rec. 12,077 (1982).

66. S. 1701, 97th Cong., 1st Sess. (1982); 128 Cong. Rec. 12,077 (1982).

67. 128 Cong. Rec. 11,998 (1982).

68. 128 Cong. Rec. 12,476 (1982). The House disagreed with the Senate amendments and agreed to a conference. 128 Cong. Rec. 7,953 (1982).

69. H. Rep. No. 911, 97th Cong, 2d Sess., *reprinted in* 128 Cong. Rec. 8,219 (1982).

70. See the letter from FBI Director William Webster to the Hon. Don Edwards, Chairman, Subcommittee on Civil and Constitutional Rights Before the House Judiciary Committee, 128 Cong. Rec. 8,219 (1982).

71. 128 Cong. Rec. 8,566 (1982).

72. See, for example, Miss. Code Ann. § 97-3-65 (1972 & Supp. 1983–84).

73. See, for example, Ga. Code § 16-6-3 (1982).

74. See, for example, Ill. Rev. Stat. Ch. 38, § 11-4 (1979 & Supp. 1982); Kan. Stat. Ann. §§ 21-3503, 21-3504 (1981), amend. 1983 Kan. Sess. Laws 109; Va. Code § 18.2-370 (1982).

75. See, for example, Ga. Code §§ 16-6-4, 16-6-5 (1982); Ind. Code §§ 35-42-4-3 (1979 & Supp. 1983–84). Another type of molestation statute involves the commission of lewd acts upon children, often on children under the age of 14. See, for example, S.C. Code Ann. § 16-15-140 (Law. Co-op. 1976); Okla. Stat. Ann. Title 21, § 1123 (1983).

76. See, for example, Kan. Stat. Ann. § 21-3506 (1981), amend. 1983 Kan. Sess. Laws 109.

77. See, for example, Kan. Stat. Ann. § 21-3606 (1981), amend. 1983 Kan. Sess. Laws 109; Va. Code §§ 18.2-361, 18.2-370 (1982).

78. See, for example, R.I. Gen. Laws § 11-9-4 (1981); Mich. Comp. Laws § 28.340 (1981); N.M. Stat. Ann. § 30-6-3 (1978); Ind. Code §§ 31-6-4-1, 35-46-1-8 (1979 & Supp. 1983–84).

79. See, for example, R.I. Gen. Laws §§ 11-9-1, 11-9-2 (1981).

80. See, for example, Ohio Rev. Code Ann. § 2907.21 (Page 1982) (effective January 1, 1974) [inducing or procuring a minor under 16 years of age to engage in sexual activity for hire]; Pa. Cons. Stat. Ann. § 5902(c)(1) (iii) (Purdon Supp. 1982) (effective December 4, 1978) [promoting prostitution of a child under 16]; Tex. Penal Code Ann. § 43.05 (Vernon 1974) [causing a person younger than 17 to commit

prostitution]; Wash. Rev. Code Ann. § 9A.88.070 (1977). Washington enacted its criminal legislation on juvenile prostitution in 1975, two years before the congressional hearings. The Washington legislation was enacted, in part, in response to empirical research on adolescent prostitution conducted by Jennifer James in Seattle.

81. ABA, Sexual Exploitation Monograph, 2d ed. Also, research conducted a few years before the 1977 sexual exploitation hearings explored the several prostitution statutes that were discriminatory on their face. See Charles Rosenbleet and Barbara J. Pariente, *The Prostitution of the Criminal Law*, 11 Am. Crim. L. Rev. 373, 422–27 (1973) [hereafter cited as Rosenbleet and Pariente].

82. See note 75.

83. The few state statutes existing at the time of the 1977 congressional hearings that penalized participants in juvenile prostitution were all directed at pimps, rather than patrons. See statutes cited in note 80.

84. See, for example, Ala. Code § 13A-12-110 to 13A-12-113 (1982); Alaska Stat. § 11.66.110 (1983); Colo. Rev. Stat. § 18-7-402 (Supp. 1983); Ill. Rev. Stat. Ch. 38, § 11-5.1 (1979 & Supp. 1983-84); Ind. Code §35-45-4-4 (1978 & Supp. 1983-84); Mass. Gen. Laws Ann. Ch. 272, §§ 4A, 4B (Supp. 1983-84); Minn. Stat. §§ 609.321- 609.323 (Supp. 1984); Mo. Rev. Stat. § 567.050 (Vernon 1977); N.J. Rev. Stat. § 2C:34-1 (1982); N.Y. Penal Law §§ 230.02-230.40 (McKinney 1980); S.D. Codified Laws Ann. § 22-23-2 (1979). One source estimates that, currrently, more than half the states have separate offenses for juvenile prostitution in their general prostitution statutes. ABA, Sexual Exploitation Monograph, 2d ed., 16.

85. This is the approach of Massachusetts and South Dakota, for example. The applicable offenses in Massachusetts referring to inducement with "minors" are "promoting child prostitution" and "deriving support from child prostitution." Mass. Gen. Laws Ann. Ch. 272, §§ 4A, 4B (West Supp. 1983-84). South Dakota prohibits promotion of "prostitution of a minor." S.D. Codified Laws Ann. § 22-23-2(2) (1979).

86. See Wash. Rev. Code Ann. §§ 9A.88.070, 9A.88.080, and § 9A.20.020 (1977 & Supp. 1983-84).

87. Mass. Gen. Laws Ann. Ch. 272, § 4B (West Supp. 1983-84).

88. Minn. Stat. § 609.323 (1982).

89. Me. Rev. Stat. Ann. Title 17-A, §§ 852 (1983).

90. Mass. Gen. Laws Ann. Ch. 272, § 4B (West Supp. 1983-84).

91. See, for example, Wash. Rev. Code Ann. § 9A.88.080 (1977 & Supp. 1983-84).

92. Minn. Stat. § 609.323 (1982).

93. N.Y. Penal Law §§ 70.00, 70.15, 80.00, 80.05, 230.20, 230.25, 230.30, 230.32 (McKinney 1980 & Supp. 1983-84).

94. Minn. Stat. § 609.322 (1982); Or. Rev. Stat. § 167.017 (1981). See also Cal. Penal Code § 266(i) (West 1970 & Supp. 1984).

95. See, for example, Me. Rev. Stat. Ann. Title 17A, § 852 (1983); Mo. Rev. Stat. § 567.050 (1979 & Supp. 1984).

96. The offense in Minnesota carries a maximum penalty of 10 years or a fine of up to $10,000, or both. In Oregon, the offense carries a penalty of 10 years or a fine of up to $100,000, or both. In Montana, aggravated promotion of prostitution—that is, compelling a person under age 18 to engage in prostitution—carries a maximum penalty of 20 years.

97. See, for example, N.Y. Penal Law §§ 230.02, 230.03, 230.04, 230.05 (McKinney 1980 & Supp. 1983–84), which penalize patronizing in the fourth degree when the prostitute is 17 or older, patronizing in the third degree when the juvenile is under 17, patronizing in the second degree when the juvenile is under 14, and patronizing in the first degree when the juvenile is under 11 years old.

98. The Massachusetts child prostitution statutes, for example, include no mention of patrons. For a discussion of the equal protection problems as applied to adult prostitutes, see Rosenbleet and Pariente, 381–411.

99. See, for example, Alaska Stat. § 11.66.110 (1978); Ky. Rev. Stat. Ann. § 529.040 (Baldwin 1981).

100. The following chart makes these differences apparent:

State	Penalty for Pimps	Penalty for Patrons
Maine	<18-year-old prostitute, class C felony	<18-year-old prostitute, class D felony
Minnesota	<16-year-old prostitute, 10 yrs. or $10,000, or both 16–18-year-old prostitute, 5 yrs. or $5,000, or both	<18-year-old prostitute, 5 yrs. or $5,000, or both
New York	<11-year-old prostitute, class B felony <16-year-old prostitute, class C felony <19-year-old prostitute, class D felony	<11-year-old prostitute, class D felony <14-year-old prostitute, class E felony <17-year-old prostitute, class A misdemeanor
Wisconsin	<18-year-old prostitute, class D felony	<18-year-old prostitute, class A misdemeanor

101. See, for example, Del. Code Ann. Title 11 § 1353 (1979) (class B felony carries a penalty of 3–30 years, as specified by Del. Code Ann. Title 11 § 4205).

102. See, for example, Mont. Code Ann. § 45-5-603 (1981).

103. Minn. Stat. §§ 609.322, 609.323(2) (1981).

104. Mass. Gen. Law Ann. Ch. 272, §§ 4A, 4B (West 1980). See also, Cal. Penal Code § 12303.065 (West 1982), which precludes probation and suspended sentences for violations of Cal. Penal Code § 311.4 (West 1970 & Supp. 1984).

105. A few criminal codes contained such provisions prior to the wave of legislation in the 1970s. Previous legislation derived from the era of concern with white slave traffic. For recent statutes evidencing this trend, see, for example, Minn. Stat. § 609.322 (1981).

106. See, for example, Ill. Rev. Stat. Ch. 38, § 11.18 (1979); Ind. Code Ann. § 35-45-4-3 (Burns 1979); Mo. Ann. Stat. § 567.030 (Vernon 1979).

107. Cal. Penal Code § 266(i)(e) (West 1970 & Supp. 1984).

108. Both the New York and the Washington statutes use the terms *aids* and *facilitates*. N.Y. Penal Law § 230.15 (McKinney 1980); Wash. Rev. Code Ann. § 9A.88.060 (1977). See, however, Minn. Stat. § 609.323 (1981), which specifically

precludes prosecution of relatives by blood, marriage, or adoption for receiving profit derived from prostitution (the preclusion does not apply to prosecutions for promoting prostitution).

109. See, for example, Ark. Stat. Ann. § 41-2004 (1977); Minn. Stat. §§ 609.322, 609.324 (1982). The statutes of Arkansas and Minnesota apply specifically to persons *other than* prostitutes.

110. Minn. Stat. § 609.321 (1982).

111. Cal. Penal Code § 266(j) (West Supp. 1984) applies to the transportation of a child under the age of 14 for the purpose of any lewd or lascivious act defined in Cal. Penal Code § 288 (West 1970 & Supp. 1984). It is thus applicable to more than acts of child prostitution.

112. Wash. Rev. Code Ann. § 9A.88.050 (1977); N.Y. Penal Law § 230.10 (McKinney 1980).

113. Minn. Stat. § 609.325 (1982).

114. *Id.*

115. *Id.*

116. See, for example, Colo. Rev. Stat. § 18-7-407 (Supp. 1983); Ill. Rev. Stat. Ch. 38, § 11-15.1 (1979 & Supp. 1982); Mont. Code Ann. § 45-5-603(b) 1983; N.Y. Penal Law § 230.07 (McKinney 1980).

117. See, for example, Minn. Stat. Ann. § 609.325(2)(1982) [mistake of age is no defense to prosecutions under code sections pertaining to promoting prostitution, implying that it *is* a defense for patronizing sections]; N.Y. Penal Law § 230.07 (1978) [mistake of age is a defense in prosecutions for patronizing in the first, second, or third degrees].

118. See, for example, Mo. Rev. Stat. § 566.020 (1978).

119. Minn. Stat. § 609.323 (1982).

120. New York exempts patrons under 21 years of age from the offense of patronizing in the third degree (patronizing a juvenile under 17 years old), and exempts patrons under 18 from the offense of patronizing in the second degree (patronizing a juvenile under 14 years old). N.Y. Penal Law §§ 230.04, 230.05 (McKinney 1980).

121. The encouragement first came in the form of proposed rules issued by the Department of Health and Human Services on May 27, 1980, which suggested that for states to be eligible for funds under the Child Abuse Prevention and Treatment and Adoption Reform Act, the statutory definition of child abuse in their reporting laws would have to include sexual exploitation. ABA, Sexual Exploitation Monograph, 1st ed., 1981, 17. These proposed rules specifically defined sexual exploitation as "allowing, permitting, or encouraging a child to engage in prostitution, as defined by State law, by a person responsible for the child's welfare." 45 Fed. Reg. 35794 (1980)(codified at 45 C.F.R. § 1340.2). This proposed regulation, however, which was intended to implement changes in the original act necessitated by the 1978 amendments, was never approved. *Id.* Nevertheless, it may well have served as a motivating force behind revisions in several jurisdictions. Final rules were issued by the Department of Health and Human Services on January 26, 1983. 48 Fed. Reg. 3698 (1983)(codified at 45 C.F.R. § 1340.2). The definition of sexual exploitation in these rules mirrored the proposed 1980 regulation.

122. Ala. Code § 26-14-1(1) (Supp. 1983); Ariz. Rev. Stat. § 8-546(A)(2) (Supp. 1983); Ark. Stat. Ann. § 42-807(b) (Supp. 1981); Colo. Rev. Stat. § 19-10-103 (Supp.

1980); Fla. Stat. § 827.07(2)(d)(3)(1977), amend., Ch. 83-75, 1983 Fla. Sess. Laws 592 (West 1983); Me. Rev. Stat., Title 22, § 4002(1) (Supp. 1983); Md. Code Ann., Art. 27, § 35A (Supp. 1980); Mich. Comp. Laws Ann. § 722.622(B) (West Supp. 1981); Mont. Rev. Code Ann. § 41-3-102 (3)(b)(1983); Nev. Rev. Stat. § 200.5011(1981); N.H. Rev. Stat. Ann. § 169-C:3 (Supp. 1983); N.M. Stat. Ann. § 32-1-3 (M)(2)(b) (1981); Utah Code Ann. § 78-38-2(Supp. 1983); Va. Code § 63.1-248.2(A)(4)(Supp. 1983); Wash. Rev. Code Ann. § 26.44.020(12) (1981).

123. Colo. Rev. Stat. § 19-10-103(1)(Supp. 1983); N.M. Stat. Ann. § 32-1-3(M) (1983).

124. See Jennifer James, *Entrance into Juvenile Male Prostitution* (Washington, D.C.: National Institute of Mental Health, 1982), 108.

125. Telephone interview with Calvin Shosida, Federal Bureau of Investigation, September 24, 1982.

126. Enablers, *Juvenile Prostitution,* 78, 80 (extrapolated from data in table 77). Confirming the existence of the "Minnesota pipeline" (the name given to the prostitution route between Minnesota and New York), ten of forty-four women in the Enablers study (age 17 or younger) said they had traveled to New York City for business. *Id.* at 78. See also Marlin Bree, "Obsessed with Faith: The Minnesota Connection," *Saturday Evening Post* 28(March 1979), 28–31; and Al Palmquist and John Stone, *The Minnesota Connection* (New York: Warner Books, 1978).

127. Enablers, *Juvenile Prostitution,* 82. For the prostitutes under 20 ($n = 41$), 32.6 percent of the respondents explained the decision to travel as a mutual decision with the pimp; 6.1 percent said it was the pimp's decision. *Id.*

128. 42 U.S.C. § 5102 (1978).

129. One journalist mentions an account in an article about the runaway center Covenant House. The center's director of residential services told about a juvenile who came to the shelter having been beaten from head to toe with an extension cord by her mother, who wanted the girl to work the streets. Cited in *Hearings on Exploitation of Children,* at 43. See also Kathryn Barclay and Johnny L. Gallemore, Jr., "The Family of the Prostitute," *Corrective Psychiatry and the Journal of Social Therapy* 18(1972), 10; Katherine MacVicar and Marcia Dillon, "Childhood and Adolescent Development of Ten Female Prostitutes," *Journal of the American Academy of Child Psychiatry,* 19, no. 1(1980), 151–52.

130. See, for example, State v. Shipp, 93 Wash.2d 510, 610 P. 2d 1322 (1980).

131. In Silbert's study, 20 percent of these other persons were women recruiting for a pimp or were madams, 7 percent were other prostitutes, and 3 percent were customers. Mimi H. Silbert, *Sexual Assault of Prostitutes: Phase One* (Washington, D.C.: National Center for the Prevention and Control of Rape, National Institute of Mental Health, 1980).

132. The Huckleberry House research reveals that 80 percent of juvenile male prostitutes learn about prostitution from friends or other street youth. Harlan, Rodgers, and Slattery, *Male and Female,* 32.

133. James notes, "In our interviews of 135 adolescent prostitutes many had learned about prostitution after they had run away, been on the streets and had become involved with the juvenile rehabilitation system. Juvenile prostitutes learn the fundamentals of prostitution from other adolescents with prostitution and pimping experience on the street, in juvenile detention, and in foster, group and receiving homes." James,

Entrance, 68. See also Harlan, Rodgers, and Slattery, *Male and Female*, 34; URSA, *Report on Adolescent Male Prostitution*, 79–81.

134. Harlan, Rodgers, and Slattery, *Male and Female*, 34.

135. This is not to suggest that parents are never perpetrators of sexual abuse on their children—only that few parents engage in this particular form of sexual abuse, the prostitution of their children.

136. The Runaway and Homeless Youth Act, as amended, supports 169 runaway and homeless youth centers in all 50 states, the District of Columbia and Puerto Rico. *Hearings on Runaway Youth, supra* note 38 at 42. For descriptions of these programs, see *Runaway Youth Program Directory*, Office of Juvenile Justice and Delinquency Prevention (August 1979).

137. For a discussion of these and other federally funded runaway shelters, see *Runaway Youth Directory* and URSA, *Resource Manual*.

138. URSA, *Resource Manual*, 63. This proclivity to deception is apparent in the following account by a juvenile prostitute:

> I was sitting in this police station and a cop asks me, "What's your name?" So I said [to myself] "What can I use?" I used "Paul Philip Shannon." I looked out the window— you could see out the window—they had the roll-out windows with the bars. I looked out the window and I saw this [sign] "Shannon Bail Bondsman Company." Then I see the chain link fence at the outside of the windows and it said, "Phillip Fence Company." So that's where I got my name.

Interview with Larry (conducted by Urban and Rural Systems Associates), 7 August 1980.

139. The commentator to the revised Missouri legislation notes: "The age of 16 was chosen as the dividing line in subsection 1(2) because that is the 'age of consent' in the Sexual Offenses Chapter." Mo. Rev. Stat. § 567.050 (Vernon 1977)(commentary). Subsection 1(2) refers to "Promoting Prostitution in the first degree."

140. See, for example, Cal. Penal Code § 266(i) (West Supp. 1984)[person under 14 years old]; Hawaii Rev. Stat. § 712-1202 (1976)[person under 14 years old)]; N.Y. Penal Law § 230.05 (McKinney 1980)[patronizing person under 14].

141. N.Y. Penal Law § 230.06 [patronizing person under 11]; 230.32 (McKinney 1980)[promoting person under 11].

142. Although some prostitutes under age 14 have been reported, two samples (Enablers and URSA) found no juveniles younger than age 14. See Enablers, *Juvenile Prostitution*, 18, table 1; Harlan, Rodgers, and Slattery, *Male and Female*, 7; James, *Entrance*, 17; URSA, *Report on Adolescent Male Prostitution*, 71, figure 1.

143. This was the conclusion of a study conducted by Commissioner Hodges, Administration for Children, Youth and Families, which was solicited by Senator Specter, chairperson of the Subcommittee on Juvenile Justice during the RHYA oversight hearings. *Hearings on Runaway Youth*, 6.

144. By statute, both parents generally have a responsibility to support their children. See, for example, Fla. Civ. Code § 196 (1979). Statutes also provide that a state furnishing support has the right to seek reimbursement for that support where possible. See, for example, Fla. Civ. Proc. Code § 1671 (1979).

145. This appears to be the traditional response of law enforcement authorities to runaway juvenile prostitutes, as is evident from the congressional testimony of a

detective in one metropolitan police department. See *Hearings on Runaway Youth,* 44.

146. Data for 1970 for the state of California, for example, reveal that only twenty-five males were convicted of either pimping or pandering. Of the twenty-five, only four were sentenced to state prison. Cited in Ann W. Burgess and Lynda L. Holmstrom, *Rape: Crisis and Recovery,* 2d. ed. (Bowie, Md.: Robert J. Brady Co., 1979), 402.

7

Community and Program Responses to Adolescent Prostitution

D. Kelly Weisberg and
*Bruce Fisher**

S,everal traditional approaches are used by communities to address the problem of prostitution. The two most longstanding responses to juvenile prostitution stem from the legal system and the medical profession. The most recent development, runaway shelters, dates to the early 1970s with the discovery of the problem of runaway youth. Following the enactment of the Runaway Youth Act in 1974,[1] federal funding was provided to various local, community and state organizations and institutions to enable them to furnish services to runaway and homeless youth. These different community and program approaches to juvenile prostitution will now be explored in further detail.

The Law Enforcement Response to Adolescent Prostitution

The traditional approach to adolescent prostitution in most communities stems from the criminal justice system, with several divisions of law enforcement responding to different aspects of child sexual exploitation. In most communities, the juvenile division is assigned to cases of child abuse and neglect, including intrafamilial sexual abuse.[2] The juvenile division often works closely with child protective services units, and in some communities, teams of police and social workers investigate reports of child abuse and neglect. In contrast, cases involving extrafamilial sexual exploitation, including molestation, child pornography, and adolescent prostitution, are most often handled by the vice division of the police department. This delegation to the vice division occurs because the vice squad is traditionally responsible for *adult* prostitution.

In cases handled by the vice division that involve juveniles, the juveniles are usually referred to juvenile court. At that point, the juvenile division may

*Bruce Fisher, J.D., is a partner in the San Francisco-based consulting firm, Urban and Rural Systems Associates (URSA), and acted as Project Director of a recent national study of juvenile prostitution.

become involved in the case. In some communities, however, juvenile probation has intake responsibility for juvenile prostitutes, and the juvenile division
may not be involved at all.

The fact that different divisions within the police department deal with
child sexual exploitation poses several problems. Having several different units
and several police officers involved in cases of juvenile prostitutes leads to a lack
of a coordinated response; only recently have some police vice divisions organized specialized units to deal with child sexual exploitation. In addition, the
several police units have different areas of expertise and different philosophies
regarding treatment of the problem; for example, the vice division represents a
punitive approach, and the juvenile division represents a rehabilitative approach. Vice officers involved in prostitution tend to view juvenile prostitutes
as offenders, rather than as victims. This view results because most members of
the juvenile street population are involved in illegal activities, including petty
theft, pickpocketing, parking meter looting, and drug dealing, as well as prostitution. Also, many of these youth, with their backgrounds of abuse and neglect
and their "streetwise" behavior, appear to the police as troublemakers. Thus,
police intervention by vice officers concentrates on arrest and/or harassment of
these youth to force them off the streets on which they are prostituting.

The juvenile division, which is more familiar with community resources
and treatment programs than the vice division, is able to play a more useful role
in handling the cases of juvenile prostitutes. Regrettably, however, juvenile
officers' knowledge of community resources that provide services to adolescent
prostitutes may never be utilized in cases handled by the vice squad. Many vice
squad officers are unaware of the nature and extent of community resources for
youth involved in prostitution, so their response is to arrest the youth and not
to be concerned about rehabilitation and treatment.

Moreover, the traditional police response by the vice division does not
involve a long-term resolution of the youth's problems. According to interviews
with Kenneth Lanning of the FBI Academy and John Rabun, director of the
Exploitative and Missing Child Unit (EMCU) of the Louisville, Kentucky,
Police Department, only if police officers view these youth as victims, rather
than as offenders, can they concentrate on the best way to deliver services to
these youth.

Another problem that lessens the effectiveness of police intervention is law
enforcement's sense of pessimism. Some police who have dealt with cases of
adolescent prostitutes are aware of the youth's child abuse and neglect histories,
parental rejection, and runaway histories, and many police are concerned that
the courts and the rehabilitation agencies will probably be unsuccessful in
short-term and long-term resolution of the youth's problems. Many law
enforcement officers believe that the treatment programs (whether traditional
mental health programs or community-based runaway centers) generally have
not been effective in resolving the youth's problems and keeping them off the

street, because, even after participation in a program, many youth return to involvement in prostitution. Police fail to recognize that these youth need months, if not years, of therapeutic intervention before their behavior can be altered.

Police also express their frustration regarding the deinstitutionalization of status offenders. Deinstitutionalization results in the provision of nonsecure facilities for status offenders, such as runaways and truants. Police often arrest suspected juvenile prostitutes on a status offense charge (such as running away)—sometimes because the status offense is the only charge they can substantiate, and other times because the police do not want to stigmatize the youth with the label of "prostitute." Officers are frustrated when, after they have arrested a suspected prostitute on a charge such as running away, the youth is released immediately after being brought to juvenile hall. Because of the policy of deinstitutionalization and juvenile hall's nonsecure facilities, the youth is told he or she may leave whenever he or she desires. One officer's experience epitomizes this frustration: he complained that he arrested one adolescent prostitute on four separate occasions during one day, and each time the youth immediately returned to the street.

When they are questioned as to whether incarceration of status offenders (including incarceration of suspected prostitutes) is effective, many police believe that the answer is no. The institutional stay for status offenders and/or juvenile prostitutes is often quite short, and the youth soon return to the streets.

Another problem that militates against police effectiveness in dealing with adolescent prostitution is the focus of most police agencies on female prostitution. Police concentrate their efforts on arresting females involved in prostitution—often using undercover officers to solicit the prostitutes. The use of undercover agents poses a problem for police, however. This method is expensive; it requires the use of many different officers since, inevitably, the prostitutes begin to identify the undercover officers.

In addition, arrests of the pimps who promote both adult and juvenile female prostitution are difficult to accomplish. To arrest a pimp, a victim (that is, a prostitute) must be willing to testify in court, but most victims (adults and juveniles) are unwilling to testify. They view the pimp as a friend and a source of support, and they are also afraid of the consequences. Some progressive police departments address this problem by providing emotional and residential support services to prostitutes, as well as providing protection from the pimp. Police officers in Seattle and Minneapolis, as well as EMCU's John Rabun, suggest that when the police take time to be supportive to female prostitutes, they are more willing to testify. Police in Seattle admit, however, that efforts to provide protective custody to juveniles, in particular, are inadequate, because the juveniles are so fearful and the pimps are so effective.

Furthermore, many police agencies are unsuccessful in arresting the customers of juvenile female prostitutes, which may be attributed to a failure to concentrate efforts on this area and to a longstanding policy of nonenforcement of prostitution laws against customers. Successful prosecutions of customers require either observation of a criminal act in the officer's presence or persuasion of the victim to testify against the customer, both of which are difficult to accomplish. Our research suggests that the latter approach can be successful if police take time to work with the victim and to identify and persuade other victims to testify against a particular customer.

The response of law enforcement to adolescent male prostitution is also problematic. Police intervention in cases of adolescent male prostitution, in particular, appears minimal. Many police respondents indicate that they fail to expend much effort on this problem. This appears to result from several factors. First, somewhat surprisingly, some police officers fail to perceive the existence of juvenile male prostitution—it is an "invisible" social problem to some law enforcement agencies. Police indifference to adolescent male prostitution may also stem from a certain attitude toward these youth—that boys are more independent and less vulnerable than girls and therefore merit less official attention. Furthermore, some police view these youth as gay and consider their prostitution part of the gay subculture. Some police prefer to ignore problems within the homosexual subculture unless violent criminal acts are perpetrated. In addition, many police agencies do not have male police officers who are willing to pose as customers for adolescent male prostitutes. Officers prefer to avoid the potential stigma, personal discomfort, and casual touching associated with the act of hiring a male prostitute, and they are reluctant to be employed in this fashion. If they must work in the vice division, they are more comfortable soliciting female prostitutes.

Police report additional problems in dealing with juvenile prostitutes, since many juvenile prostitutes present false identification, claiming that they are over 18. Other juvenile prostitutes do not carry any identification, but if arrested they adamantly state they are adults. Police have considerable difficulty in identifying juveniles in these cases. If the prostitutes are charged as adults, they are soon released in accordance with normal processing of adults. Bail for prostitutes is relatively low, and some prostitutes are released on their own recognizance. Sentences are usually short, so punishment is seldom a deterrent to further acts of prostitution.

Problems exist even if the suspected prostitutes admit they are juveniles. If youth are processed as juveniles, considerable paperwork is involved in referring prostitutes to juvenile court. In addition to this paperwork, juveniles must be transported from police headquarters to a different facility for juveniles. One law enforcement official complained that an arrest of a juvenile ties up the officer for two hours, keeping him off the street for that time period and preventing the performance of other duties. According to our research, some police often release a first-time offender just to avoid the inordinate trouble involved in processing a juvenile.

In a few police agencies across the country, special units are being created to deal with child sexual exploitation. Several such units have been created within the police departments of Indianapolis, Los Angeles, Seattle, and Washington, D.C. Two such specialized units that have received considerable attention recently are the Washington, D.C., Metropolitan Police Juvenile Prostitution Unit and the Exploited and Missing Child Unit (EMCU) in Louisville, Kentucky.

Washington, D.C.

The Washington, D.C. Metropolitan Police Juvenile Prostitution Unit, created in 1976, was located in the Third District headquarters' prostitution section. The unit originally was staffed by Sergeant Edward A. Smith, chief of the special section, and by Sergeant Harry Anderson and Detective Gerald Robertson. Nightly, two officers patrol the 14th Street "prostitution strip," located only three blocks from the White House. Sergeant Anderson has noted that "juveniles run as high as 45 percent [of those on the strip] some nights."[3] Statistics for Washington, D.C., indicate that 104 youth were arrested by police for prostitution in 1977. By the next year, the statistics had doubled.[4]

The officers search for underage juveniles who may be runaway prostitutes. When they encounter a juvenile working "on the strip" whom they suspect is a runaway, they question her. Either on the street or at headquarters, they attempt to determine her name, age, and residence; often the juveniles assert they are adults. After persistent questioning, the officers are sometimes able to establish the prostitute's identity as a juvenile. If so, they take her to the juvenile division (a 15–minute ride from headquarters), where further identification checks are made. Typically, the juvenile is logged in as a status offender—as a runaway. "We don't like to charge them as prostitutes," said Captain George Henry, assistant commander of the youth division, "because we're not interested in this division in stigma."[5]

Detective Robertson notes how difficult it is to "crack the lies" of runaways. Sometimes he and his partner pick up and question a juvenile numerous times over a several-month period before they are able to discover her real name and age.[6] If they do discover a juvenile's real name, they can sometimes trace her residence by using the National Crime Information Center if she has been listed as a missing person. Once the juvenile has been identified as a runaway and has been taken to the juvenile division, the family division of Superior Court handles the case. There, the decision is made to return the juvenile to the juvenile facility or to release her to her family.

The unit later broadened its focus and became the Juvenile Sexual Exploitation Unit. On October 1, 1981, however, the Metropolitan Police Department underwent a reduction in force. Staff was cut, and the department was forced to eliminate the specialized unit. As of March 1984, a recommendation was made to restaff the specialized unit. After consideration by the Chief of Police and an ad hoc committee, that proposal resulted in the designation of a six-month trial effort, beginning in September 1984, to accomplish the following departmental goals using existing manpower:

1. to start a Child Protection Initiative;
2. to become a clearinghouse for all information relating to juvenile sexual exploitation;
3. to train officers in the department and other persons on the issue of juvenile sexual exploitation; and
4. to provide investigative support to the Sex Offense Branch and the Morals Division in cases of commercial sexual activity, including juvenile prostitution.

At the termination of the six-month period, the Office of Finance and Management will review the manpower needs of the Youth Division with respect to this special function.

Louisville, Kentucky

Another unusual program that specializes in the problem of child sexual exploitation is the Exploited and Missing Child Unit (EMCU) in Louisville, Kentucky—a division of the Louisville Police Department and Department of Human Services, with jurisdiction over all aspects of child sexual exploitation and juvenile prostitution. The first director of the EMCU, John Rabun, was a social worker; the unit includes both social workers from the County Department of Human Services and police officers. The EMCU investigates cases by using teams composed of one police officer and one social worker. The unit originated in conjunction with a citywide task force that was convened to explore the problems of exploited and missing children. Rabun suggests that the EMCU's success derives, in large part, from its willingness to view the youth as victims. Thus, its efforts are concentrated on providing support services to these victims and developing investigations leading to the arrest and conviction of perpetrators.

In an effort to view the youth as victims, the EMCU does not use the terms *runaway* or *juvenile prostitute,* because these terms are perjorative and assess blame on the youth rather than on the perpetrator. Instead, the terms *exploited child* and *missing child* are used. Rabun is also concerned that the deinstitutionalization of status offenders has undermined police efforts in this area; however, he does not believe that secure placements or institutional placements are appropriate either. He describes the experience in Louisville as a better alternative:

When we first started the program we brought youth to the county children's group homes. At first many kids did run away from the shelters, oftentimes because their pimps came to get them. In order to combat this problem, our staff began to take shifts around the clock at the group homes. After winning the trust of the victims, the victim signed statements to us that in fact the visitor was a pimp, we arranged for our police officers to box the pimp in and make an arrest at that time. Word soon got out that it was unsafe for pimps to come around the group homes. At the same time, the youth realized that the support services of the entire unit were at their disposal and tended to allow our teams to try to arrange for appropriate placement for them, rather than running back to the street.[7]

Rabun also suggests other reasons why the Louisville program has been successful in prosecuting customers and pimps. In cases of offenders with multiple victims, the program patiently works with these youth and often is able to identify three or four victims of an individual offender. With sworn statements by three or four youth incriminating a particular offender, the EMCU is able to obtain an arrest warrant. This approach has been effective in the arrest and prosecution of customers as well as pimps.

When Mr. Rabun departed in April 1984 to become the Deputy Director of the National Center for Missing and Exploited Children in Washington, D.C., a number of changes were instituted in the EMCU. Earl Dunlap became the new administrator of the unit, with Lieutenant Marvin Wilson serving as the police administrator. Instead of the three former teams of social workers and police officers, the unit now has six teams. It has added supervisory personnel for the social workers and also has added 24–hour investigative coverage.[8]

Summary

The experience of these and other law enforcement agencies reveals that the police response to adolescent prostitution is, indeed, a serious problem, for which we offer several recommendations. First, coordination within police departments needs to be improved, and increased communication between community agencies and local law enforcement is important. In many cities, police and social service agency staffs note the absence of dialogue between the agencies. The police are not familiar with social service resources available in their city for adolescent prostitutes, and many social service programs have little knowledge of the specific division of responsibility within the police department for handling juvenile prostitution. Meetings could be held between the directors of the various social service agencies and the juvenile division and vice squad of local police departments.

In addition, relationships between police and agencies serving youth by outreach efforts could be improved. If police are familiar with the street workers and can identify them, they are able better to assist the workers if the need arises. Police agencies also could establish procedures with the social service programs that would encourage police referrals to these particular agencies.

Police and social service providers should develop appropriate procedures for protecting clients of emergency shelter programs. Such voluntary programs must prevent pimps from gaining access to female clients, and supervision and monitoring procedures should also be developed to minimize a client's ability or desire to run away from these voluntary placements.

Social service programs should provide feedback to law enforcement in cases of referrals to the agency by the police. This would enable police to acquire a sense of program accountability. Protocols should be established to enable police to secure follow-up information about individual youth, but these procedures should protect the confidentiality of the service provider–youth relationship when possible.

Furthermore, training for police should include material on child sexual exploitation, including adolescent prostitution. Such training would focus on the nature of adolescent prostitution and its etiology, giving police a better understanding of the difficulties involved in successful intervention with these youth.

In addition, police should focus their resources on younger prostitutes, especially those under 16, who appear to be the most vulnerable population. These youth appear to be most needy of services and especially subject to exploitation by customers and pimps.

Police efforts, as well as those of social service programs, must also focus greater resources on the identification and successful prosecution of pimps and customers of juvenile prostitutes. The notion that prostitution is a victimless crime is not applicable when the victim is a juvenile.

The Medical Profession's Response to Juvenile Prostitution

Most female and male juvenile prostitutes have a number of health problems. Physical problems primarily involve venereal disease and other sexually transmitted diseases; hepatitis (drug-related or sexually transmitted); pregnancies (for female prostitutes); sore throats, colds and flu; and treatment for drug problems. Mental health problems involve depression, suicidal thoughts, and suicidal attempts. Many of these maladies stem from the youth's general lack of concern for their physical health as well as from the inevitable consequences of their street lifestyle.

Street youth and juvenile prostitutes occasionally consult medical personnel for treatment of physical and mental conditions. Case studies are reported in the literature of prostitutes who consult physicians for treatment of syphilis and gonorrhea[9] and those who consult psychologists or psychiatrists for a variety of mental health conditions.[10] They sometimes approach medical personnel on their own initiative and sometimes are referred by the criminal justice system. In addition, a number of physicians have conducted research on the problems of adolescent prostitutes, and several of these physicians have provided medical and/or social services to the youth in the course of their research.[11]

Traditionally, adolescent prostitutes approach medical facilities and physicians with considerable hesitation. According to Robert W̃. Deisher, M.D. and his colleagues, the reason for this hesitation is that "[t]hey perceive medical personnel as authority figures representing general societal values which conflict with their personal characteristics and experiences on the street."[12]

Medical personnel who deal with the problems associated with juvenile prostitution face several difficulties in providing services. First, the youth may be reluctant to obtain services at traditional treatment centers. Shick, for example, reports that many male prostitutes are hesitant to seek treatment for venereal disease at their local public health facility. The youth are aware that the site of infection might require their disclosure of homosexual contact, and they fear that the clinic staff would uncover their prostitution activities (by queries about their sexual partners) and would require reporting of partners, who would then be contacted.[13] Youth who do seek medical attention may not disclose their complete medical histories because of the stigma they fear from disclosure of their occupation.

In addition, juveniles involved in prostitution may lack the knowledge necessary to seek appropriate services; they may not be aware of an appropriate medical facility and its location or hours. J. Fred Shick, M.D., for example, notes that in Chicago, the one local gay venereal disease treatment center frequently was unknown to many youth.[14] Also, these juveniles may not be aware of the extent of their problems or may not understand the significance of their symptoms. Deisher notes that a major mistake in working with adolescents involved in prostitution is "the assumption that sexual activity equates with an understanding of sexuality, venereal disease and birth control."[15]

Another problem is that these youth possess limited information on sexuality. Many juvenile prostitutes left home and school at an early age. Consequently, their sexual education may be incomplete, and much of their information originates from other street youth. They are likely to be unaware, for example, of the subtle forms venereal disease can take, so many will not seek medical attention unless they have more recognizable and more serious symptoms of the disease.[16]

The juveniles' limited knowledge about sexuality also poses other problems. Females' knowledge of contraceptive practices is woefully inadequate, and myths and false beliefs abound.[17] Few juvenile females have consistent access to reliable forms of birth control or use birth control on a regular basis. Furthermore, juvenile males possess a lack of awareness of the variety of homosexual-related sexually transmitted diseases.

One significant problem in addressing the medical and mental health needs of juvenile prostitutes is the difficulty in developing rapport. A difficulty that arises in collecting medical histories from heterosexual male prostitutes, for example, is that many are hesitant to disclose their involvement in homosexual activity.[18] Professionals must work to establish trust with these youth. Gay and bisexual youth are especially sensitive about self-disclosure. In general, the use of non-gender-specific nouns, such as "lover" or "sexual partner" (rather than "boyfriend" or "girlfriend") is useful. Direct, nonjudgemental questions regarding the youth's sexual orientation and practices are recommended to gather better medical histories.[19]

Another recommendation concerning medical services involves an understanding of the psychological makeup of many street youth, which may inhibit medical treatment. Many street youth are not conscientious enough to take proper daily dosages of medication.[20] Also, many youth are present-oriented, which results in their failure to keep previously scheduled appointments (either initial appointments or follow-up examinations).[21] An understanding of these problems would enable physicians to give simpler directions to youth and to obtain names of caseworkers and outreach workers who are likely to have continued contact with the adolescents if ongoing treatment is necessary. This would result in better medical treatment for these youth.

Some alternative medical facilities exist that address the needs of adolescent prostitutes. In the late 1960s and early 1970s, free clinics were established to serve the health needs of street prople. With the decline of the hippie movement, a number of these clinics altered their focus to address specific needs of the street population. Many of these clinics currently provide drug counseling and detoxification services, venereal disease screening and treatment, and sometimes dental care, nutrition, and prevention services. Such clinics also serve as an entry point into the social service system for many prostitutes. Clinic staffs who recognize the special social service needs of their prostitute-clients are able to provide referrals to other service providers.

Several service programs have medical service components that are especially targeted to street youth and juvenile prostitutes. Some of these programs are Bridge Over Troubled Waters in Boston, Covenant House in New York City, and the Gay and Lesbian Community Services Center in Los Angeles. Two other clinics also have significant contact with juvenile prostitutes: the Red Door Clinic in Minneapolis and the Pioneer Square Youth Services Clinic in Seattle.

The Red Door is an alternative public health facility that provides, among other services, screening and treatment for sexually transmittable diseases. One staff nurse, who was himself a street prostitute for five years in Minneapolis, has publicized the program to the male prostitute population. His interaction with young prostitutes, though focused on health care, also provides him an opportunity to counsel prostitutes about the risks of street life and the alternatives to it.

Pioneer Square Youth Services operates a free medical clinic for young people in downtown Seattle. Its director, Dr. Robert Deisher, who was one of the early researchers on adolescent male prostitution, helped establish the program in 1974 as a component of the Pioneer Square Medical Clinic. The most common problems presented by clients are pregnancy and venereal disease. Besides providing medical services and individual counseling, the clinic also sponsors a seminar series for youth and youth workers on a wide range of subjects, including adolescent pregnancy, prostitution, transsexuality, and drug and alcohol abuse. Operating under the auspices of the University of Washington, the clinic is a volunteer effort, staffed one night per week by two doctors and four to six medical students from the University's Adolescent Medicine Program. The clinic makes referrals to local social service providers when necessary. Although the clinic's weekly turnout is large, indicating a need to expand services, the volunteer nature of the operation has limited its growth.

Such clinics are a valuable resource for serving the health needs of adolescent prostitutes. With clinic staff members who are knowledgeable about the problems of juvenile prostitutes, these clinics can serve as an important entry point into the social service delivery system, enabling youth to receive necessary services.

Runaway Youth Shelters

Following the discovery of the problem of runaway youth in the late 1960s and early 1970s, a number of programs developed to deal with the needs of this population. After the enactment of the Runaway Youth Act in 1974, federal funding was made available for some of these programs. Runaway shelters for troubled youth exist in several communities throughout the country, a significant number of which receive federal funding through the Youth Development Bureau (YDB) within the Department of Health and Human Services (HHS), which is charged with administering the Runaway and Homeless Youth Act (RHYA). These shelters provide crisis counseling and emergency shelter, and most offer additional services, such as medical services, vocational training, and hotlines. Many of these shelters provide crisis counseling not only for the adolescent but also for parents and the entire family.

Although runaway shelters attempt to serve street youth, they face difficulties in reaching this population. Some runaway youth programs are located outside the downtown metropolitan areas where street youth congregate. In addition, many street youth are distrustful of social service programs and often will not avail themselves of their services. They fear that contacts with a social service program will result in their being sent back to their family or in referral to the police for their involvement in illegal activities. Also, most street youth know that runaway programs provide only temporary shelter and are unable to supply long-term solutions. Furthermore, many female prostitutes are reluctant to utilize shelters, since these facilities are not "safe houses"; they fear that their pimps will discover their whereabouts and retaliate. Finally, many gay-identified prostitutes are hesitant to avail themselves of runaway youth shelters for fear they will be stigmatized because of their sexual identity.

Despite these handicaps, however, runaway youth shelters are an invaluable resource for street youth; they are one of the few sources of support for this population. Over time, the staffs have developed expertise in dealing with troubled adolescents. In addition to their counseling skills, most programs have developed considerable referral networks. Many programs also have a component encompassing outreach and street work to identify the runaway youth in their locales and to make it easier for the youth to seek services.

During the last several years, a number of communities have begun programs that serve street youth in general and juvenile prostitutes in particular. Many programs have received assistance from federal demonstration grants. Among these are The Shelter, Seattle, Washington; Project Luck, Tri-County Youth Services Consortium, Portland, Oregon; Hospitality House and Huckleberry House, San Francisco, California; Daymark, Charleston, West Virginia; and the Street Intervention and Diversion of Juvenile Prostitutes Program within the Human Resources Administration, New York City. In addition to these federally funded programs, a number of other programs have recently begun, including Children of the Night, Los Angeles, California; the Homeless Youth Project of the Los Angeles Free Clinic; Chrysalis, Denver, Colorado; the Minneapolis Youth Diversion Program and North Star, Minneapolis, Minnesota; and the Transitional Living Program, Chicago, Illinois.

The unique aspect of many of these prostitution-specific programs is their location near the "sex-trade zones" of the major cities and their ability to do outreach to this population. Most have developed a street work or outreach component that allows them to develop trust with the street population and to serve as a referral resource. Such programs struggle constantly to obtain sufficient funding to provide comprehensive services to street youth. Many do not have their own residential placement program but must rely on existing group homes or foster homes. As more attention focuses on the problem of juvenile prostitution, these programs are beginning to receive more private funding, city funding, and volunteer support, but funding continues to be a serious and perpetual problem.

Service Approaches to Juvenile Prostitution

Runaway programs and others offer a number of different services to runaway and homeless youth involved in prostitution—and the needs of runaway and homeless youth involved in prostitution are many. Besides being homeless, these youth are often abused, unskilled, and uneducated. They usually are abusing drugs and alcohol and are often in trouble with the law. They have few family resources to rely on, and they often are confused about their sexuality. In addition, this population is particularly difficult to reach. These youth see the lure of the streets as a pull toward involvement in a "romantic" lifestyle, but most of them are caught in a "failure syndrome"; that is, they have a history of failure and are therefore resistant to involvement with social service programs. Most lack an ability to follow through on any service plan, and most distrust traditional systems that attempt to work with them. Many have forged a deep sense of isolation, often as a result of physical, sexual, and emotional abuse. They also have low self-esteem; consequently, many of the females become dependent on pimps, and the males depend on the street peer support group.

Ten primary services are especially needed by these youth: prevention; outreach and street work; crisis intervention (including crisis counseling and short-term shelter); family reunification and/or individual and group counseling; long-term shelter; long-term counseling (including drug abuse, alcohol abuse, sexual and physical abuse counseling); vocational training and job placement; independent living skills training; legal and medical services; and friendship and support services.

Prevention

Research on juvenile prostitutes now suggests a correlation between abuse, neglect, and runaway behavior as factors contributing to juvenile prostitution. Research on adolescent male prostitution also suggests a relationship between intrafamily conflict over sexual identification and family breakdown, which contribute to the youth's involvement in prostitution. Thus, prevention services aimed at preserving families and improving family system dynamics would be an effective long-term solution to the problems of runaway and homeless youth.

A variety of prevention activities exist in many communities. Programs directly related to juvenile prostitution, including those dealing with intrafamilial child abuse and neglect, range from mandatory reporting laws to public awareness campaigns. In addition, some of these programs include runaway shelters whose staffs conduct some family work with high-risk families. They also include parenting classes and sexual abuse education classes.

One cannot overemphasize the importance of prevention programs. Many social service staff respondents in our study of juvenile prostitution indicated that, once a youth has lived on the street, it is difficult to change his lifestyle. Since most of these youth run away to escape childhood sexual or physical abuse, until the cycle is ended, we shall continue to see young people running away and trying to survive on the street.

Outreach and Street Work

Aggressive outreach activities are necessary for programs serving adolescent prostitutes, since street work appears to be an effective method of reaching young prostitutes. Researchers and social service delivery staff constantly emphasize the difficulty of reaching the street population. These youth are fearful of any intervention, and they have learned to distrust adults. Many are afraid they will be sent home or jailed, and gay-identified youth often fear rejection by insensitive agency staff or physical assault by other, nongay, youth. To reach this difficult population, many community programs have determined they must incorporate outreach components.

Street work refers to service delivery on the streets where these youth are located. Trained street workers mingle on the streets of the "sex-trade zones" in the evening hours and meet the youth who are involved in prostitution; over time, they develop rapport. The street worker may buy a youth coffee or donuts and sit and listen to the youth's problems, but only gradually will the youth trust the worker and ask for assistance. Most street workers suggest that their constant presence and availability is the primary method by which they are able to help these youth leave the streets. Street workers also suggest that the best opportunities for successful intervention are either within one or two weeks of the youth's arrival on the street or at some subsequent time when the youth is involved in a crisis, such as a drug overdose, the disappearance and/or killing of a prostitute friend, an arrest, or depression. Because these youth have a difficult time following through on referrals, the street workers are also available to assist the youth in following through on a referral for services. This might mean transporting the youth to an emergency shelter or to emergency medical services.

Another effective means of outreach is to maintain a drop-in center within walking distance of the center of street prostitution. Such drop-in centers are usually open until the late hours of the evening or on a 24–hour basis, and they have simple intake procedures. Drop-in centers often provide some recreational services as well as immediate crisis and referral assistance. A few drop-in shelters, such as Covenant House in New York City, also offer emergency overnight shelter.

Covenant House is one of the largest programs dealing with street youth. Founded in 1968 by the Reverend Bruce Ritter, a Franciscan priest and former Manhattan College professor in medieval theology, Covenant House operates the Under 21 crisis center in the Times Square area of New York City. The program has grown to become the largest single agency serving homeless street youth in the nation. Recently, it has expanded its Under 21 crisis centers to Houston, Toronto, Boston, and Guatemala. In addition to its residential services, Covenant House also offers medical and legal services, vocational training, educational services, family counseling, and general social services. Covenant House maintains a full-time staff of more than 200 professionals.

Medical Clinics

Medical clinics located near the areas of juvenile prostitution are also an effective method of reaching this population. Such clinics have been established in downtown areas of Seattle, San Francisco, Minneapolis, New York City, and Boston. Some medical programs also have outreach components. These programs emphasize venereal disease screening and treatment, and treatment for drug abuse.

Crisis Intervention Services

Many street youth who seek services do so at a time of crisis. These crises range from emotional distress and depression to drug overdoses, criminal arrest, and the murder of a friend. Programs serving juvenile prostitutes report that crisis counseling and emergency shelter are two crucial services, but the identification of emergency shelter beds has been a primary problem for programs serving street youth. Such shelters need to be located near the area where prostitution occurs so that they are accessible to youth who need shelter late in the evening. Emergency shelter may constitute one night or up to two weeks of shelter, although most program staffs suggest that longer-term shelter should be outside the area of street prostitution to facilitate the youth's exit from street life.

Individual and Group Counseling

Whether or not family reunification is feasible in a particular case, youth workers stress the need to provide individual and group counseling to this street population on a long-term basis. Such counseling may include family system issues, even if no plan exists to reunite the youth with their families. Practitioners suggest that the youth will always be working through family issues while attempting to deal with independent living; therefore, therapy based on family system and other family therapy modes is suggested.

Long-Term Shelter

Long-term shelter is one of the most difficult services to provide for street youth. Most of these youth, as previously noted, are age 16 or over, and placements for older adolescents are scarce. Placement of street youth who have been involved in prostitution, drugs, and other illicit street activities is even more difficult. Some programs have experimented with the development of specialized foster homes for such youth, particularly those aged 14, 15, or 16. Other programs spend time attempting to teach independent living skills to their client population so that these youth can maintain themselves in their own apartments. Partially because they lack alternative placements, many youth find themselves in residential institutions pursuant to juvenile court placements.

A few programs have experimented with the establishment of long-term group homes operated by the youth agency itself. Funding for such long-term placement is problematic, however, and often involves lengthy procedures with state and local regulatory agencies, concerning such issues as licensing and location. Some programs have explored the idea of long-term placements for female prostitutes in cities other than those in which the girls have been involved in prostitution. This has been considered necessary to remove them from the influence of and intimidation by pimps. To date, no formal network exists for such out-of-town placements. Regrettably, such placements pose significant financial problems, since the host cities would be asked to fund residential treatment programs for nonresidential youth.

Long-term residential facilities must be closely monitored and must have specialized staffs. Clients are often destructive and failure-prone, and most programs dealing with street youth emphasize the importance of patience when working with this population. This sometimes conflicts with residential program philosophies, which emphasize strict regulations forbidding a youth who runs away from the program to return. It has also been noted that some youth in residential placements have returned to their involvement in prostitution while continuing to reside in the shelters. Programs vary in their reaction to this problem: some insist that such behavior is unacceptable and prohibit further agency contact; other programs are aware that street youth will continue to test the agency and to be attracted to the allure of the street. Programs with this latter philosophy usually allow the youth to return to the shelter program.

Programs also have been clear in insisting that, as a paramount agency rule, agency staff must have absolutely no sexual contact with residential clients. This has been a problem in an occasional runaway program and treatment facility, but for the most part, programs have been able to maintain this strict prohibition.

Long-Term Counseling

Street youth are often individuals with low self-esteem. Since they come from backgrounds of abuse or neglect and disrupted homes, their emotional problems are severe. For such youth, short-term intervention is not likely to be successful in combatting prior life experiences. Even the notion of rehabilitation may be inappropriate in the context of street youth, since it suggests a *return* to a state of positive mental health. Many of these youth must be helped in developing such basic concepts as self-respect, self-discipline, and hope.

Many programs that provide services to street youth focus on short-term services, such as emergency and crisis-related services, and are not staffed to provide long-term therapeutic intervention. As a result, it is necessary for such programs to develop links with mental health providers who are able to work on long-term issues. The youth's high rate of failure, however, militates against success. Therefore, referrals for long-term counseling must be closely monitored and must allow for temporary setbacks. Traditional mental health agencies that insist upon scheduled appointments and have poor follow-up procedures undoubtedly will be ineffective.

Most programs agree that issues of sexuality are important in long-term counseling with the young prostitute. Many juvenile female prostitutes have a negative attitude toward sex in general. Most have been victims of sexual abuse at home and from pimps or clients, and counseling must address these experiences. Most young male prostitutes also have conflicts regarding their sexual identification and their involvement in homosexual experiences. Therefore, counselors must offer a supportive context in which the youth can explore issues of sexuality and sexual preference.

Long-term counseling must also focus on family issues, even if family reunification is not feasible. Some programs attempt to provide a sense of family through group discussions and counseling sessions. Some programs also attempt to establish support groups with parents of troubled or runaway children to provide support to the adolescents and to their parents.

Vocational Training and Job Placement

Other necessary services for young prostitutes are job development, education, and job placement. To offer youth an alternative to street life, such resources must be developed to enable them to become self-sufficient.

A few programs have developed innovative education and job development programs. One of the most extensive is at Covenant House in New York City. Through PS 106-M (Under 21's accredited school that encompasses grades one through twelve), young people at Under 21 in New York have the opportunity to remedy their educational gaps. The staff members first test many of the youth to determine the source of their learning difficulties, and counseling follows this testing. When education seems a viable alternative, PS 106-M enables students to continue their studies until they are ready for placement in a school. This education also focuses on independent living skills. Many youth have not acquired the traits of punctuality, reliability, and good grooming, which are necessary if they are to obtain employment. Furthermore, once they find a job, these youth have trouble developing a good rapport with supervisors, co-workers, and customers. They also must learn to budget and to perform such tasks as establishing a bank account and obtaining a driver's license or identification. As part of its vocational program, Covenant House has developed a youth employment program called Dove Messenger Service. Dove enables older youth from Under 21 to be trained, not merely as messengers, but also as office workers and managers. The youth learn how to take calls and how to handle billing and petty cash. In addition, they are taught basic skills in typing and bookkeeping.

A number of other programs attempt to provide independent living and job development training within their agencies. Huckleberry House in San Francisco has had a CETA-funded job developer for a number of years, and the Seattle program has developed an extensive program in job training and placement, including a full carpentry program on-site at the Orion Street Center.

The provision of job development and independent living skills is problematic for a number of reasons. Unemployment among adults and youth is a problem in many communities. Since even qualified youth have difficulty finding jobs, it is a dilemma to find employment for youth with little experience and minimal skills and education. The problem is exacerbated by the inability of most street youth to hold a full-time job. Part-time jobs are especially needed. An innovative approach is the Seattle job training program, which tries to find youth part-time, one-day-only job placements. This allows the youth to work occasionally, and over time, they develop an ability for regular employment.

Although, by some accounts, juvenile prostitutes earn significant amounts of money and are unwilling to exchange street life for traditional employment, many observers feel this is not the case. Both male and female prostitutes occasionally earn significant sums, but their overall economic situation is bleak. Job placement and vocational training is therefore an important component of any social service program targeted to adolescent prostitutes.

Independent Living Skills Training

Independent living skills refers to training in such basic matters as learning to rent an apartment, establishing a bank account, applying for a driver's license, managing a budget, and obtaining valid identification. Many program staffs believe that independent living skills training is a prerequisite to a successful vocational training and job development component; that is, if the youth have not learned to survive on their own and to manage their lives in a disciplined manner, job placement is unlikely to succeed. Independent living skills training has been developed by many youth service programs, including most runaway youth agencies. A few programs even maintain apartment units where they can provide a supervised independent living experience for their clients. Although these programs report a high success rate in developing independent living skills, they are expensive to operate. Moreover, they require funding sources that allow monies to be used for such purposes as the lease of an apartment. Such a solution, however, may well answer some of the basic needs of runaway street youth.

Legal Services

Most youth involved in juvenile prostitution have a number of legal problems. Many have been arrested recently, and even when they are involved in a service program, many are arrested and require legal assistance. An advocacy program that is able to accompany the youth to the juvenile court (or, at times, to the adult court) is a useful aspect of any service program. Legal resources are scarce for this population. A few legal aid offices provide ad hoc services to runaway and other youth-serving programs, and some city and county bar associations maintain lists of volunteer attorneys who provide assistance. A few programs have been established to serve the needs of children and youth directly. In San Francisco, for example, Legal Services for Children has a staff of attorneys and social workers who provide services exclusively to youth. In some other communities, the public defenders association has undertaken responsibility for providing legal services to this population, especially to those who are arrested and brought into juvenile court.

Legal services are also necessary in a number of civil matters. Many youth, for example, are in need of legal emancipation if they are unable to return home. Legal emancipation allows them to enter into contracts on their own and to qualify for some county-funded services. In addition, some youth who want to enter county-funded job training programs or special education programs have legal obstacles to overcome. Legal aid attorneys and/or volunteer attorneys are an essential resource for programs attempting to provide comprehensive services to this population.

Support and Friendship

However trite it may seem, one of the most valuable services that programs provide is emotional support. Most of these youth come from unstable backgrounds, and many have never experienced consistent friendship. To the extent that a program can provide intensive one-to-one support services, it will be more successful with this population. Some programs experiment with Big Brother/Big Sister-type programs to fulfill this need, either utilizing those agencies directly or developing their own lay counselor/aide programs with volunteers.

Summary

Respondents from law enforcement agencies, the courts, social service programs, and the medical profession emphasize the neediness of adolescent prostitutes. They also note, however, that any interventions appear doomed to fail. The value of street work programs, in particular, seems to lie in the ability of the street workers to establish trust with the youth over a period of weeks or months. It is this relationship that encourages the youth to participate in other, more traditional services. Success stories, albeit few and far between, indicate that once a youth has developed trust with a worker, the relationship will continue for a number of years. It is not uncommon for some programs to employ ex-clients who have left the street to provide the friendship that other youth are seeking.

Case Studies

Seattle, Washington

Seattle is currently one of five cities selected for HHS federal demonstration grants for dealing with juvenile prostitution. The Seattle project is a collaboration of nine local organizations under the leadership of The Shelter, an established program for runaway and homeless youth. Other members of the project are Catholic Community Services, University of Washington Medical Clinic, the Learning Center (Seattle public schools), Downtown YMCA, Public Defenders, Committee for Children, Southwest Youth Service Bureau, and Urban Policy Research (evaluator). The project has established a downtown multiservice center from which most project services are provided and from which a six-person street work team operates. (In a recent visit by HHS Secretary Margaret Heckler, it was announced that the project was selected for a second year of funding in fiscal year 1984–85.)

Seattle has been active for several years in service delivery to sexually abused children, including juvenile prostitutes. This early awareness results from the work of two researchers: Robert W. Deisher, M.D., of the University of Washington Medical School, who conducted early research on the incidence and etiology of male prostitution, and Dr. Jennifer James, also of the University of Washington, who directed several National Institute of Health–funded studies of juvenile prostitution.

The Shelter has operated a six-bed facility for runaway youth for a number of years. When public awareness focused on the problem of juvenile street prostitution in the First and Pike area of downtown Seattle (across from the entrance to the Pike Place Farmers' Market), The Shelter received a city grant to establish a CETA outreach team. It later received support from the State of Washington Division of Law and Justice Planning to conduct Project START, which added employment, prevention, and emergency downtown housing to the outreach program. In the last three years, the program has gained a national reputation as a model service provider to street youth involved in prostitution. It also has enlisted the support of a variety of agencies and sponsors in Seattle and has developed into a multiagency, multidisciplinary consortium providing a range of services and conducting community education campaigns.

The collaboration project is managed by a multidisciplinary team of eight members, each representing a key agency in the consortium. To the extent that each agency participates in project design and management, greater coordination within the consortium results. The theoretical model for the project emphasizes a coordinated response, with careful case monitoring. The response system addresses prevention and intervention at four primary points: (1) before the youth are involved in street life; (2) during the early "romance" phase of street life; (3) during the transition phase, in which youth begin to make efforts to leave the streets; and (4) during the phase in which the youth leave the streets and are in need of supportive services to stabilize new nonstreet lifestyles.

The project components include a new multiservice facility for street youth in downtown Seattle, the Orion Street Center; an in-school sexual abuse prevention curriculum designed to reach more than 5,000 students; a client health program that includes 5,160 hot meals for street youth at the center as well as a medical outpatient program for at least 400 youth per year; a street outreach program that delivers 6,900 hours per year of outreach client contact (street work) and provides intensive counseling and case management services for more than 600 youth; an employment and educational component that provides drop-in educational services to 75 youth per year, GED-oriented transitional education services to at least 15 youth per school year on-site at the center, and employment training to at least 185 youth per year; and a housing component consisting of 600 bed-nights of overnight emergency housing, short-term residential care to a minimum of 84 youth per year, and long-term professional foster care to 6 youth per year.

One of the special features of the Orion Street Center is its employment program. The provider, Southwest Youth Service Bureau, hopes to provide training for at least 185 youth during the project year. The project is designed to employ and train youth in in-house revenue-generating industries, in preparation for eventual transition to unsubsidized employment. A woodworking shop and a small retail storefront will be developed in the downtown facility for the manufacture and sale of youth-produced goods. To date, the employment program has been nearly self-sufficient.

Since many street youth quickly fail traditional employment referrals and return to prostitution for survival, the employment program will emphasize a half-day labor placement. Staff members believe that this approach will allow quick rewards to the youth and will provide them with the incentive to continue job involvement. The half-day schedule also allows sufficient flexibility for the youth to develop the discipline necessary to maintain a full-time job. Half-day labor is being offered in the woodworking shop at the Orion Center or at on-job sites arranged by the employment director. The program also offers on-the-job training in an agency-sponsored print shop and construction crew, through involvement in the facility's retail storefront, or through a public OJP program. The program also includes traditional employment counseling and independent living skills preparation courses that are often a component of job training and job development programs.

Boston, Massachusetts

The Bridge Over Troubled Waters was founded in 1970, when hippies were first coming to national attention. A central figure in the development of Bridge was Paul Shanley, a Roman Catholic priest, who was concerned about the problems of the youth who were flocking to Boston. Many of these youth gravitated to the Boston Common. Few had places to live, and many experienced drug problems or medical crises.

Bridge is located in downtown Boston, one block from the Boston Common and Park Street Station, the central connecting point for the greater Boston subway system. Over the past 14 years, Bridge has become a multiservice agency and has served approximately 3,000 troubled youth per year.

Staffed by 26 paid employees and 150 volunteers, Bridge works with youth from ages 14 to 21. Its clients include runaways, street youth, drug and alcohol abusers, pregnant girls, delinquent youth, formerly institutionalized youth, and many female and male prostitutes. Bridge's client population has changed over the years. In the early 1970s, the hippies and flower children disappeared and were replaced by a needier, younger client population composed of many runaways and youth who were alienated from their families.

The focus of Bridge changed with the shift in its client population. It now offers a broad range of youth services. One of its primary efforts is a street-based outreach program for runaways and homeless youth. Bridge street workers tour the streets in areas where youth gather, focusing particularly on the region near the bus station, which is a center for both street youth and juvenile prostitutes.

Outreach workers are assigned to specific locations within the city so that they become familiar to their clients. Whenever possible, Bridge assigns a gay-identified outreach worker to gay neighborhoods to facilitate client contact. Five street workers, supervised by a street work coordinator, bring the agency and its services to the clients. Their work day lasts from late afternoon to 11 p.m.—times when youth in need are on the street. The street workers give information and advice to youth and provide referrals.

A major component of the program is the medical van, a well-equipped mobile medical clinic. The van, staffed by medical personnel, travels to different neighborhoods of Boston each evening. Street workers accompany the medical van into the areas to which they are assigned. Medical services are available to anyone who requests them at no charge. Services provided through the van include medical screening, treatment of simple disorders, and follow-up treatment. One important function of the medical van is venereal disease screening—an essential service for this sexually active population. Because many of the youth who avail themselves of the medical services may be involved in homosexual activity, medical personnel are sensitive to the needs of these youth for medical screening in all three at-risk areas: urethral, anal, and pharangeal. In addition to the medical van, the Bridge offers dental services at its downtown location. Bridge considers dental hygiene crucial for youth who are seeking employment.

Bridge has a comprehensive housing program to provide for the housing needs of its client population. When Boston-area youth approach the agency, reconciliation with the family is attempted immediately, because the staff believes that housing the youth can unnecessarily reinforce their break with the home. The staff recognizes, however, that for youth from outside the area or for youth escaping abusive home situations, housing is sometimes necessary.

Bridge has established a network of residential facilities, including a number of volunteer hosts who provide short-term residential care for youth. Staff members pride themselves on their process of screening, orienting, training, and supervising the volunteers—not only to protect the hosts but also to protect the youth. Generally, only one youth at a time is placed with a volunteer host. Thus, when youth arrive at the agency in pairs, they are often separated. This serves two functions: it reduces the burden on the host and it dilutes the influence that one youth may exert on another.

In addition to these services, Bridge offers crisis intervention and ongoing counseling, family counseling, and a telephone hotline. The agency also provides training to prepare youth for the graduate equivalency diploma and offers occasional workshops in the development of specific job skills. The agency recently received funding for a youth employment program that employs ten youth to work within the agency to learn job skills in preparation for finding legitimate employment.

Services to street youth and adolescent prostitutes are also provided in Boston by Place Runaway House, which provides residential services to youth under the age of 18. It offers family counseling and a 24–hour hotline. Since 1975, Bridge Over Troubled Waters, in collaboration with Place Runaway House, has received a federal Runaway and Homeless Youth Program grant. Like many other federally funded runaway centers, however, funding for these programs is a constant problem. According to the present director of Bridge, sister Barbara Whelan, "the level of federal funding is clearly insufficient for the numbers of youth served ... "[22]

San Francisco, California

The San Francisco project is similar in some respects to The Shelter project in Seattle. It is also a multiagency consortium that provides several services and has established a new multiservice street center for homeless and runaway youth. The San Francisco program is sponsored by Youth Advocates/Huckleberry House, an established runaway agency in the city. Other participants include Hospitality House, a social service program in the Tenderloin area of San Francisco; Catholic Social Services; and the Urban and Rural Systems Associates (URSA) Institute. The consortium project focuses on early intervention with homeless street youth and juvenile prostitutes. Its services include outreach and street work, crisis intervention, a 24–hour hotline, counseling, temporary shelter, food, clothing, medical and legal aid, family reunification, educational and vocational assistance, and independent living skills training.

The program relies on volunteers and on financial assistance from the city of San Francisco.

Some of the more unusual aspects of the San Francisco program are (1) its primary focus on young prostitutes, since this is the major street population in San Francisco; and (2) its focus on early intervention, as opposed to treatment. This focus on early intervention is manifested by eligibility guidelines within the program that give priority to youth who have been on the street less than two months.

Although San Francisco has been active in recent years in the issues of runaway youth and the sexual abuse of children, significant communitywide activities have only recently focused on juvenile prostitution. As in Seattle, a number of separate activities that took place in the city formed the backdrop of this coordinated project: a survey of runaway youth involved in prostitution conducted by Huckleberry House, the local runaway youth center; the funding of a street outreach project at Hospitality House, focusing on street work with juvenile prostitutes in the Tenderloin area; a national study of juvenile prostitution with a focus on adolescent male prostitution, conducted by the URSA Institute; a study of juvenile females involved in prostitution, funded by the National Institute of Mental Health and conducted by Delancey Street Foundation (a drug treatment program in the San Francisco area); and a grant to the School of Medicine of the University of California–San Francisco from the Robert Wood Johnson Foundation, focusing on medical services to high-risk youth.

Another factor in the community effort to deal with the runaway youth population in San Francisco is the Mayor's Task Force on the Homeless, which was created in December 1982. As a result of the efforts of advocates for youth services in San Francisco, that task force, created to deal with the adult homeless population, led to the development of a subcommittee to focus on services for runaway youth.

The San Francisco Juvenile Prostitution Project focuses on outreach and street work as well as counseling and job development services. A major problem in the early phase of the project was that services were being provided from three different locations: Hospitality House in the Tenderloin, Huckleberry House in the Haight-Ashbury district, and Catholic Social Services in the Castro Street area. The consortium realized that one ingredient to project success—that is, a multiservice facility in the Polk Street area, where much adolescent male prostitution occurs—was missing. As a result of their efforts, the City of San Francisco awarded a $70,000 grant to the project to lease space and to provide some staff in the Polk Street area.

San Francisco opened a new multiservice center, the Larkin Street Youth Center in January 1984. At the same time, Catholic Social Services opened a crisis shelter in a church basement located in the Castro area. Simultaneously, the city contracted for a new emergency receiving shelter for referrals of status offenders in San Francisco. The emergency shelter replaced the Youth Guidance Center as the location for temporary placement of status offenders.

At present, the San Francisco program is developing its services component. Outreach teams have begun working on the street and counselors are beginning to see clients on a longer-term basis. The model for the program calls for initial contacts with street youth to be conducted by the street work team and for that team to meet with the youth once or twice at the Larkin Street Youth Center. Once a youth expresses a desire to leave the street and demonstrates a commitment to do so, the case is assigned to a counselor. Counselors focus on the delivery of support services to the youth, including mental health services. They also provide, by means of referrals, medical services, job placements and training services, and education services. The program has attracted a number of volunteers. Currently, volunteer training is being conducted with approximately forty volunteers, who are expected to staff clerical positions at the Larkin Street Youth Center and to serve as "big brothers and big sisters" to the clients. Volunteers may also be used in the street work and outreach efforts.

The San Francisco program is intended to be a citywide program; it attempts to reach street youth throughout the prostitution areas of San Francisco. Since San Francisco has several prostitution areas and homosexual neighborhoods, it is necessary to do outreach in the Tenderloin area, the Polk Street area, the Castro area, and the Union Square area. To address this challenge, the project adapted a satellite office in the Tenderloin to supplement the Larkin Street Youth Center. Another problem facing the San Francisco program is the ability to provide services to adolescent males involved in prostitution, as well as females. Since many of these males are gay-identified and are involved in the gay subculture, the project must be staffed by individuals who are comfortable with issues of sexuality and are able to relate to young men who are exploring issues of homosexuality.

Although the social service agencies in San Francisco have developed a coordinated response to the provision of services, the coalition has yet to establish protocols with law enforcement. Because the city established the project in part, problems have arisen concerning parental notification and police notification. Negotiations have been conducted between the juvenile division and the juvenile court and the project's consortium, and pursuant to a city attorney's opinion and an agreement by the juvenile court judge, the established policy is to notify parents and the Department of Social Services of individuals placed in overnight shelter programs within 72 hours of the commencement of such placement. In addition, San Francisco police have expressed concern over the ability of the program to prevent street youth, particularly younger youth, from leaving the Larkin Street Youth Center and returning to street life. The program is organized as a voluntary program and thus does not have coercive or police powers to detain these youth. It is feared that if the program appeared coercive, it would destroy its credibility with the juvenile street population and it therefore would not be able to attract clients.

Whether or not the San Francisco program will be successful remains to be seen. It is generally admitted by law enforcement and social service staffs that New York and San Francisco have the most difficult street populations with which to work. It is unclear whether the program will be successful in early intervention with youth who are newly arrived in San Francisco. Mayor Diane Feinstein, in announcing the grant to the project, expressed reservations regarding the ability of the program to succeed, and she also expressed some concern that the development of comprehensive services might serve as a "magnet" for youth to come to San Francisco. Thus far, the project has experienced moderate success in mobilizing a coordinated effort among many agencies and establishing a task force to coordinate services—the Youth Emergency Services Task Force (YES).

Minneapolis, Minnesota

Minneapolis has a nontraditional approach to prostitution as well as a long-standing involvement in the area of female juvenile prostitution. In 1978, the Minnesota legislature enacted legislation on the mandatory reporting of maltreatment of minors that treated prostitutes as victims, rather than as criminals.[23] In the same year, Minneapolis became the site for a federal demonstration project for female juvenile prostitutes. Minneapolis also has a Youth Diversion Program, a nonprofit organization that monitors youth channeled through the juvenile justice system. Despite Minneapolis' involvement in female juvenile prostitution, however, juvenile male prostitutes have not received much attention from the city's law enforcement agencies or social service programs.

Weather permitting, both young male and young female prostitutes can be seen prostituting within a few blocks of a thriving downtown commercial center of Minneapolis along Hennepin Avenue. During the cold winter months, some of the youth operate inside the enclosed skyways that connect the downtown area to commercial centers. It appears to be a singular aspect of adolescent prostitution in Minneapolis that male and female prostitutes work alongside each other. (In other communities, males and females tend to operate in different geographic locations.)

The traditional criminal justice approach to juvenile prostitution, as mentioned earlier, is to treat youth as law violators, but the Minnesota legislature rejected this approach in 1978. The 1978 legislation defines young prostitutes as victims, rather than as criminals, and defines pimps and customers as victimizers. Minneapolis is one of the few cities that has had and continues to have a range of services targeted specifically to adolescent prostitutes. Service providers believe this results from the shift from the traditional criminal justice approach to a more service-oriented approach.

The Minnesota legislative response was due, in part, to the work of a large coalition of youth workers and to the recommendations of a research project conducted by a nonprofit group, The Enablers, Inc. In 1976, The Enablers, Inc. was funded to conduct research on female prostitutes, with a special emphasis on adolescent prostitution.[24] The Enablers study concluded that young females involved in prostitution have a number of characteristics in common, including dysfunctional families and parents with chemical dependency, extensive histories of physical and sexual abuse, poor self-images, and extensive runaway histories.

Even before the Enablers study and the 1978 legislation, Minneapolis had a variety of programs serving youth. One such Minneapolis program, The Bridge for Runaway Youth, Inc. (The Bridge), was founded in 1970. Originally developed as a crisis center and shelter for young people, it continues to provide these services. Currently, The Bridge operates a runaway program—a fourteen-bed shelter for youth that provides counseling, advocacy, and referral services. It also has a family-counseling program. From August 1978 until July 1981, The Bridge also had a residential program specifically for adolescent female prostitutes, New Bridge. This program, the first in the country, was a demonstration project initially funded in part by the Youth Development Bureau of HHS and in part by private corporations. It provided both short-term and long-term shelter to young females involved in prostitution and to adolescent girls from dysfunctional families who had few job skills and incomplete high school educations and were at risk of becoming prostitutes. Since so many clients were involved with pimps, New Bridge had to be a "safe house." It had an elaborate alarm system hooked into the police station; if the alarm was triggered and was not turned off within 15 seconds, the police responded.

New Bridge provided shelter for up to three months in its residential facility (ten beds), individual and group counseling, education classes, a 24-hour hotline, an in-house medical clinic, and outreach and aftercare programs. Unfortunately, in 1981 the board of The Bridge decided to discontinue the program, partly because of organizational and funding problems.

Another program in Minneapolis is the Minneapolis Youth Diversion Program (MYDP), a private nonprofit agency founded in 1970. Its purpose is to prevent Minneapolis youth from entering the juvenile justice system. Funded by county government and other public and private funds, it accommodates eleven youth and their families. The MYDP is an integral part of the Minneapolis juvenile justice system and receives many referrals from the juvenile court. The youth who receive services present such problems as truancy, shoplifting, separation and loss problems, and running away. One youth worker is assigned specifically to work with adolescent female prostitutes. The MYDP also has a residential treatment program for juvenile female prostitutes, North Star. North Star opened its doors on November 9, 1982, in the same facility that housed the New Bridge program. Youth come to North Star via referrals from the juvenile court, referrals from other youth-serving agencies, or on their own initiative. The philosophy of the program is that exit from prostitution is a process and that the stay at North Star is one step in that process.

The program is designed as a short-term residential facility. Residents in the program stay from six to twelve weeks. During this time, they receive extensive counseling concerning prostitution, including participation in an adolescent prostitute group cosponsored by the MYDP and Minneapolis Family and Children's Services. Medical needs are addressed and other counseling needs—such as those not necessarily related to prostitution behavior—are assessed. When the client leaves the program, she has an individually tailored treatment program. North Star has an extensive aftercare program that facilitates continuation in the treatment program. Family counseling is available and encouraged but is not forced upon the prostitute or her family.

North Star can house eight prostitutes at one time, almost all of whom are runaways. The program has local clients as well as clients from all over Minnesota and some from out of state, since there is no residency requirement. If the program is full when a prostitute needs to be admitted, North Star workers find an alternative; no one is sent back to the street.

The MYDP also has a nonresidental program for female prostitutes, the Outreach Program. Youth involved in this program receive counseling and advocacy services in a nonresidential setting. The types of youth using this service include those who were at North Star but disliked the residential program; youth who want to be at North Star but cannot because of a waiting list; youth who live at home; youth who live in other group homes; North Star graduates; and youth who are at high risk for but not actively involved in prostitution.

Louisville, Jefferson County, Kentucky

In recent years, Jefferson County, Kentucky, has demonstrated a commitment to working with sexually exploited and missing children. Jefferson County's involvement in this area was initiated by Jefferson County Judge/Executive Mitchell McConnell, who called for an investigation of allegations that Louisville was a recruiting center for child prostitutes. Subsequently, a local interagency, intergovernmental task force on child prostitution and pornography was formed. The Exploited and Missing Child Unit (EMCU) was created to work under the direction of the local task force.

Because the problem of sexual exploitation was not merely local, a statewide task force (the Task Force on Exploited and Missing Children) was also established. The statewide task force was a multidisciplinary group, including representatives from education, law enforcement, medicine, government, and private industry, as well as other individuals and organizations. The task force held public hearings thoughout the state and formulated findings and recommendations.

On the local level in Jefferson County, the local task force and the EMCU have two primary purposes. The first is to identify and arrest adult perpetrators and, at the same time, to find victims at the early stage and protect them from further exploitation. To achieve this purpose, more than three dozen arrests were made and successfully prosecuted in the first three years of the task force's existence. Work on arrests and convictions are divided between the EMCU, which investigates the sexually exploited child cases, and the Jefferson County Police Department Youth Bureau, which investigates intrafamilial sexual child abuse cases. Several of the convictions involved both child prostitution and pornography.

The second purpose of the task force is to make the public aware of the problem of exploited children. To achieve this purpose, the task force established and publicizes a 24–hour hotline for people to call with information regarding instances of child pornography or prostitution. The task force meets with school officials, church groups, and community organizations. These efforts resulted in more than 2,000 calls during the first three years.

Louisville also has a residential program for runaway youth, Shelter House, which has been in existence since 1974. It provides both short- and long-term housing for more than 600 youth per year. The Shelter is managed and supported by the YMCA and houses an average of twenty youth per night at a cost of about $40 per child per night. Most clients leave the shelter to enter approved placements.

The Louisville, Kentucky, statewide task force made a number of recommendations that are now incorporated in a bill before the Kentucky legislature. The bill recommends that the state establish and fund local prevention programs; require local police to report all cases of missing children to a state clearinghouse; clarify that child victims may claim compensation from the Crime Victim's Compensation Board; allow the use as evidence of pretrial videotaped testimony from child victims; upgrade offenses involving unlawful transactions with a minor to a felony rather than a misdemeanor; and establish that sentences for certain sexual offenses against children cannot be probation or suspended.

Conclusion

Programs such as those described here are essential to improve the situation of street people and young runaways. Moreover, they offer hope that these youth will eventually be able to exit from a life of prostitution. A number of suggestions may be made for program personnel who serve clients with a past or current history of adolescent prostitution.

Aggressive outreach activities are necessary.

Outreach is an essential component of any program hoping to serve these youth. Many young prostitutes are reluctant to seek assistance from social service providers and all programs must somehow bridge the distance between their service delivery headquarters and the street milieu where the young prostitute lives and works. Outreach is a necessary prerequisite in order for the youth's needs to be identified and addressed.

Street work (the provision of street workers who work in prostitution settings) appears to be the most effective method of reaching young hustlers. Different programs have developed a number of techniques to reach prostitutes, including: the employment of street workers during late night and weekend hours when youth are likely to be on the streets; the use of staff members who are comfortable spending time "hanging out" with street youth; staff members who know that patience is the key to building relationships with these youth; the establishment of information networks with known prostitutes and other street youth to monitor new arrivals on the street as well as those youth undergoing crisis; and the dissemination of information (by means of easily retained wallet-sized materials, for example) regarding available resources for youth in need. Some programs ensure that the street workers also serve as clients' case workers. This serves to guarantee continuity of care and also helps ease the youth's transition into the program.

Program staff report that street work appears to be more productive in reaching adolescent male prostitutes than female prostitutes. The presence of pimps often makes young women inaccessible to street workers or poses a threat of violence to staff members who approach them. This suggests that law enforcement rather than social service providers may be more effective in making initial contact with young female prostitutes.

Programs must develop agency referral systems.

The points at which juvenile prostitutes first interact with the social service delivery system vary, and when youth do contact social service providers they reveal many service needs. Consequently, programs must develop an adequate referral system in order to meet these diverse needs. For example, some youth reveal they are prostitutes upon seeking assistance for substance abuse, or when they approach a runaway program for shelter. Personnel at such "entry points" need to be aware of the various programs and services within their community which deal with the problems of juvenile prostitutes so that they may promptly refer the youth to these programs for assistance. Police who arrest young prostitutes should also be cognizant of available resources should they desire to utilize an alternative to arrest. Establishing referral linkages often demands considerable patience and perseverance on the part of program staff.

Cooperation and coordination of the entire service delivery system in the community is essential.

Since there is usually a variety of services within a community which address a prostitute's problems, some coordination among agencies needs to be maintained. Personnel of these programs should meet with staff of other agencies on a regular basis, sharing their knowledge of the needs of the youth and the most effective treatment approaches. Without such inter-agency cooperation, youth tend to be shuffled back and forth between programs without their needs being met.

Establishment of rapport with clients is essential in working with the juvenile prostitute.

Many young prostitutes have had prior negative experiences with traditional social service providers, and are often reluctant to interact with program staff for fear of stigma and embarrassment. Staffing, then, becomes a critical issue for programs desiring to serve adolescent prostitutes. Staff members of effective programs tend to have professional training in therapeutic interventions, adolescent development, social work and psychology. Many members receive specialized training in crisis intervention.

To intervene successfully, programs also need staff who are able to establish rapport with the prostitute. In order to establish a positive helping relationship with the adolescent, the counselor must be a person to whom the client can relate. Successful counselors are often individuals who themselves have had comparable experiences; some programs have found that ex-prostitutes, ex-alcoholics or ex-drug addicts are especially effective counselors. Such experiences give staff credibility and also facilitate efforts to encourage change in the clients. Of course, staff personnel must have achieved sufficient distance from their prior experiences.

Some programs have found that gay-identified staff may more quickly establish rapport with some clients. These staff members are effective counselors for several reasons. First, they serve as role models with whom the youth can identify. Second, they can better understand the problems the youth are experiencing, especially regarding sexuality and sexual conflicts, and can better help the youth to understand these problems.

Staff effectiveness increases with efforts to deal with worker "burnout."

Counselor burnout is an occupational hazard in youth work, especially when the clients are troubled street youth. Personal and program efforts to deal with burnout are essential to the provision of services and help avoid considerable staff turnover. Several programs have tried innovative approaches to preventing burnout. For example, Steppingstone in Los Angeles has adopted a team counseling approach in which a youth is assigned to two counselors; the counselors work together on a case, sharing insights and providing support to each other. Counselors report that this technique inhibits manipulation of counselors by youth and also facilitates effective casework.

Central City Hospitality House in San Francisco has adopted other measures to improve staff morale and to reduce turnover. This program provides staff members with six weeks paid vacation to help offset the long hours, low pay and stressful conditions of youth work. A number of other programs hold weekly staff meetings during which members share problems and concerns. These meetings address case management, problems with individual clients, program administration, personnel policies, as well as individual staff performance. Such meetings tend to promote a cohesiveness which reduces staff burnout.

Programs must perform an adequate assessment of the needs of the young prostitute and determine the appropriate services to meet those needs.

Adolescent prostitutes have numerous service needs, thus program responses must include an intake and assessment component that identifies specific needs, determines eligibility, and screens potential clients. Such a service assessment must be performed by staff who understand the range of problems commonly faced by these adolescents. Intake and needs assessment not only serves as a critical source of information on specific clients, but also provides valuable data on the general client population and its changing needs for services. These data can then be used for program evaluation and service development.

Because of the nature of adolescent prostitution, the intake process may involve sensitive questions about the youth's sexuality and family history of abuse, neglect, and runaway behavior. Such information is vital to assessing the youth's need for services and treatment, and must be solicited by staff who are comfortable discussing these problem areas. The information obtained can have a significant effect on subsequent referral. For example, traditional resources such as foster care or family counseling may be inappropriate for these youth due to their conflict-laden family background, and program staff may be required to find and utilize more non-traditional resources within the community.

Intervention with young prostitutes must address the different levels of the youth's service needs.

Four different levels of service needs of young prostitutes may be delineated. These include: (1) immediate needs, (2) proximate needs, (3) ancillary needs and (4) remote needs. Immediate needs constitute the most essential area for intervention. Such needs are often precipitated by crisis and are the basic survival needs: food, housing, and money. Intervention at this stage, especially for runaway prostitutes and new arrivals on the streets, has the best prognosis for success.

Proximate needs are those that emerge after the youth's immediate needs are met. They include the acquisition of basic skills for independent living, such as obtaining a checking account, an apartment, and a social security card. Ancillary needs, which also must be addressed, are occasional needs based on a youth's particular circumstances. They include such services as legal advocacy, medical care, dental care, and drug and/or alcohol treatment.

Only after immediate, proximate, and ancillary needs have been met can the youth's more remote needs—emotional and psychological needs—be addressed. Since many young prostitutes come from abusive family backgrounds, psychological counseling is essential. Often, these youth require long-term counseling to help them learn to deal better with their daily problems and understand their own motivations. Because this long-term counseling can often not be provided by community-based mental health programs, referral networks should include a number of mental health professionals, such as volunteer psychiatrists and psychologists and other local mental health practitioners, who will treat clients and provide training and technical assistance on individual cases.

An understanding of these different levels of needs of adolescent prostitutes by social service delivery providers and by law enforcement officials is essential to addressing juvenile prostitution. This understanding, coupled with an awareness of the many problems which beset service providers, will improve community and program responses to this social problem.

Notes

1. Runaway and Homeless Youth Act, 42 U.S.C. §§ 5701–5702, 5711–5713, 5715–5716, 5731–5732, 5751 (Supp. 1978).

2. For several excellent legal reference works on the prosecution of intrafamilial child sexual abuse, see *Child Sexual Abuse and the Law,* Report of the American Bar Association, National Legal Resource Center for Child Advocacy and Protection, 2d ed. (February 1982); and *Innovations in the Prosecution of Child Sexual Abuse Cases,* Report of the American Bar Association, National Legal Resource Center for Child Advocacy and Protection (November 1981).

3. Louise Sweeney, "Get These Children Off the Streets," *Christian Science Monitor,* 22 August 1978, B5.

4. Ibid., B18.

5. Ibid., B5.

6. See also "Problems of Runaway Youth," *Hearings Before the Subcommittee on Juvenile Justice of the Committee on the Judiciary U.S. Senate,* 97th Cong., 2d Sess., July 22, 1982 (testimony of Gerald Robertson, detective, D.C. Metropolitan Police Department), 43–47 [hereafter cited as "Problems of Runaway Youth," *Senate Hearings*].

7. Interview with John Rabun, Exploited and Missing Child Unit, Louisville, Kentucky (now Deputy Director, National Center for Missing and Exploited Children).

8. Interview with Leo D. Hobbs, Social Work Supervisor, Exploited and Missing Child Unit.

9. See, for example, A.J. Jones and Lee Janis, "Primary Syphilis of the Rectum and Gonorrhea of the Anus in a Male Homosexual Playing the Role of a Female Prostitute," *American Journal of Syphilis, Gonorrhea and Venereal Diseases* 28(1944): 453-57.

10. See, for example, Kathryn Barclay and Johnny L. Gallemore, Jr., "The Family of the Prostitute," *Corrective Psychiatry and Journal of Social Therapy* 18, no. 4(1972): 10-16; Michael Craft, "Boy Prostitutes and Their Fate," *British Journal of Psychiatry* 112, no. 492(November 1966): 1111-14; Katherine MacVicar and Marcia Dillon, "Childhood and Adolescent Development of Ten Female Prostitutes," *Journal of the American Academy of Child Psychiatry* 19(1980): 145-59; Frances Newman and Paula J. Caplan, "Juvenile Female Prostitution as a Gender Consistent Response to Early Deprivation," *International Journal of Women's Studies* 5, no. 2(1981): 128-37; Donald H. Russell, "From the Massachusetts Court Clinics: On the Psychopathology of Boy Prostitutes," *International Journal of Offender Therapy* 15(1971): 49-52; William F. Thorneloe and Eugene L. Crews, "Manic Depressive Illness Concomitant with Antisocial Personality Disorder: Six Case Reports and Review of the Literature," *Journal of Clinical Psychiatry* 42, no. 1(January 1981): 5-9.

11. J. Fred E. Shick, M.D., provided services in the diagnosis and treatment of venereal disease in the course of his research in Chicago during 1975-1976. Robert W. Deisher, M.D., provided vocational rehabilitation to prostitutes in the course of research in Seattle from December 1967 to February 1969. See, generally, J. Fred E. Shick, "Service Needs of Hustlers," Unpublished manuscript, Chicago, 1980; Patrick Gandy and Robert W. Deisher, "Young Male Prostitutes: The Physician's Role in Social Rehabilitation," *Journal of the American Medical Association* 212, no. 10(1970): 1661-66. Deisher is currently director of the Pioneer Square Youth Services' medical program, established in downtown Seattle in 1974 to address the medical needs of street youth and adolescent prostitutes.

12. Robert W. Deisher, Greg Robinson, and Debra Boyer, "The Adolescent Female and Male Prostitute," *Pediatric Annals* 11, no. 10(1982), 823.

13. Shick, "Service Needs," 12.

14. Ibid.

15. Deisher, Robinson, and Boyer, "Adolescent Female and Male Prostitute," 825.

16. Ibid.

17. Jennifer James, *Entrance into Female Prostitution* (Washington, D.C.: National Institute of Mental Health, 1980), 35-38.

18. Deisher, Robinson and Boyer, "Adolescent Female and Male Prostitute," 825.

19. Ibid.

20. Ibid.

21. Ibid.; see also Shick, "Service Needs," 26.

22. "Problems of Runaway Youth," *Senate Hearings* (prepared statement of Sister Barbara Whelan, Director, Bridge Over Troubled Waters), 77. Other data about this runaway shelter and about the other programs in these case studies were collected by URSA field research staff.

23. Minn. Stat. Ann. § 626.556 (West 1982 & Supp. 1984).

24. Enablers, *Juvenile Prostitution in Minneapolis: The Report of a Research Project* (St. Paul: The Enablers, 1978).

Appendix: State Statutes

State	Offense Description	Protected Age
Alabama ALA. CODE §13A-12-111 and §13A-12-112 (Supp. 1983)	promoting prostitution= (1) causes by force or intimidation, or profits from such conduct by another; (2) causes person under 16; (3) receives benefit from; --- advances or profits from prostitution of person under 18	under 16 --- under 18
Alaska ALASKA STAT. §11.66.110 (1983)	promoting prostitution= 1) causes by force 2) causes person under 16 3) causes person in legal custody to engage in prostitution	person under 16 years of age
Arizona no specific statute	---	---

Arkansas
ARK. STAT. ANN.
§41-3004 (Supp. 1981)
	promoting prostitution=
	1) compels by force or profits from
	   coercive conduct
	2) advances prostitution or profits from
	   prostitution of person less than 18
		person less than 18 years of age

California CAL. PENAL CODE §266, §266(h), §266(i), §266(j), §267 (Deering Supp. 1984)	§266--inveigles, entices for prostitution or procures, or aids §266(h)--lives or derives support in part or in whole from proceeds of prostitution §266(i)--procuring by any device §266(j)--intentionally offers or procures, transports, provides a child 14, or causes, induces child to engage in act of prostitu- tion with another person §267--taking person under 18 away from parents, etc., without consent of prostitute	§266--unmarried female of previously chaste character under 18 years of age §266(h)--person under 14 years §267--person under 18
Colorado COLO. REV. STAT. §18-7-401 to §18-7-406 (Supp. 1983)	18-7-402--solicits, arranges, offers to arrange prostitution of child for another (soliciting) 18-7-403--for value induces, arranges, offers to arrange situation (pandering) 18-7-403.5--intentionally gives, transports, makes available a child for purposes of prostitution, (or offers to do so) (procuring)	person under 18
Connecticut CONN. GEN. STAT. §53a-86, §53a-87 (West 1972)	promoting prostitution= §53a-86--compels by force or profits from conduct; advances, profits from prostitution of person less than 16 years old §53a-87--connected with prostitution enterprise; advances, profits from prostitution of person less than 18 years	§53a-86--person less than 16 years §53a-87--person less than 18 years

Targets of Legislation			Penalties	Special Defenses/ Exemptions
Pimps/ Customers	Parents	Other Persons		
pimp			2-20 years imprisonment, and up to $10,000 fine	none
pimp			1 year and a day-10 years imprisonment, and up to $5,000 fine	
promoter (pimp)	legal custody (parents)	---------------	class B felony: §12.55.125--not more than 10 years §11.05.145--1 year minimum §12.55.040--fine no more than $50,000	none §11.66.110(3)(b)-- mistake of age is no defense
pimps promoters			Class D felony: §41-901--not to exceed 5 years imprisonment §41-1101--fine not to exceed $10,000	none
pimps (procurer, abductor		§266(g)- husband	§266--jail not exceeding 1 year and/or $2,000 maximum fine §266(h)(i)(j)--state prison for 3, 6, 8, years. §267--imprisonment in state prison and $1,000 maximum fine	none
both		owner of premises; middleman	class 3 felony: 4-8 years imprisonment and 1 year parole	none
pimps promotors		under §53a-85 middleman, owner of premises, financer etc.	§53a-86--class B felony §53a-87--class C felony §53a-35a--imprisonment B--1-20 years C--1-10 years §53a-41 --fines B--$10,000 maximum C--$ 5,000 maximum	none §53a-84--female customers and homosexual conduct are not exempt

State	Offense Description	Protected Age
Delaware DEL. CODE ANN. tit. 11 §1352, §1353 (1979)	promoting prostitution— §1352--same as Conn. §53a-87 §1353--same as Conn. §53a-86	§1352--person less than 18 years §1353--person less than 16 years
District of Columbia D.C. CODE ANN. §22-2704, §22-2705 (1981)	§22-2704--a) persuading, enticing, forcibly abducting female from home or from custody of parents b) knowingly and/or secretly, harbors such female §22-2705--parent or person with legal custody who consents to taking or detention of female for purpose of prostitution	female under 16 ------------------------
Florida FLA. STAT. ANN. §796.03 (West Supp. 1984	procuring for prostitution or causing person less than 16 years to be prostituted	person less than 16 years of age
Georgia GA. CODE ANN. §26-2018, §26-2019, §26-2020 (1983)	§26-2018--statutory rape - intercourse with female under 14, not spouse §26-2019--child molestation - immoral or indecent act, to or in presence of child with intent to arouse or satisfy sexual desires of the child or the person §26-2020--enticing child for indecent purposes - solicits, entices, or takes child to place for purpose of child molestation or indecent acts	under 14 under 14 under 14
Hawaii HAWAII REV. STAT. §712-1202, §712-1203 (1976)	§712-1202--compelling by force or promotes; profits from or advances prostitution of person less than 14 years of age §712-1203--managing, supervising, controlling or owning, alone or in association with others, a house of prostitution or prostitution business involving prostitution of person less than 18 years old	§712-1202--person less than 14 years §712-1203--person less than 18 years

Targets of Legislation			Penalties	Special Defenses/ Exemptions
Pimps/ Customers	Parents	Other Persons		
pimps promoters	-------------	under §1355-56 middleman, owner of premises, manager, etc.	§1352--class D felony §1353--class B felony tit. 11 §4203-- D--10 years B--3-30 years and fine or other conditions that court may impose	none ------------------- §1344--female customers and homosexual relations are not exempt
pimps if procurer	-------------	abductor	imprisonment for no less than: (a) 2 years nor more than 20 (b) not more than 8 years	none
no	yes	guardian or other person having legal custody	imprisonment - not more than 5 years, fine not more than $1,000	
pimps (also under §796.05) customers §796.07	-------------	procurers; §796.01- keeper of prostitution; §796.06- owner of premises;	§796.01--1st misdemeanor - up to 1 year imprisonment, up to $1,000 fine §796.03--2nd degree felony - up to 15 years imprisonment, up to $10,000 fine §796.06 and §796.07= 2nd degree misdemeanor up to 60 days imprisonment, up to 500 fine	none
----------	yes, if applicable	yes, if applicable	§26-2018--1-20 years §26-2019--1-20 years §26-2020--1-20 years	none
pimps promoters	-------------	owners, lessors, of property and small scale promoters of prostitution	§712-1202--class B felony §712-1203--class C felony §706--imprisonment B--not exceeding 10 years C--not exceeding 5 years	none

State	Offense Description	Protected Age
Idaho IDAHO CODE §18-5609 (Supp. 1984)	§18-5609--inviegles or entices or aids, assists in the enticing into house of ill-fame or illicit carnal connections also §18-5610--abducting from person having legal charge	§5609--unmarried person under 18 of previously chaste character §5610--any person under 18
Illinois ILL. REV. STAT. ch. 38 §11-15.1 (1979 & Supp. 1983-84)	§11-15.1--soliciting, arranging meeting, or directing to place for purpose of prostitution §11-19.1--juvenile pimping - receiving money, property from activity §11-19.2--exploitation of a child - confining, threatening, coercing or drugging person under 16 and - 1) compelling child to become a prostitute; 2) arranging situation; 3) receiving money or property from child with knowledge it was earned from prostitution	§11-15.1--person under 16 years §11-19.1--person under 16 years §11-19.2--person under 16 years
Indiana IND. CODE §35-45-4-4 (1978 and Supp. 1983-84)	promoting prostitution= 1) enticing, compelling prostitution 2) procures or offers to 3) permits use of premises 4) receives money, property from 5) directs another to place for prostitution purposes (all knowingly, intentionally)	person under 18 years (applies to (1) only)
Iowa no specific statute, but cross reference to IOWA CODE ANN. §233.1 (West Supp. 1983)	contributing to delinquency - to send or cause to be sent any child into a house of prostitution; to knowingly permit, encourage or cause such child to be guilty of any vicious or immoral conduct	under 18

Targets of Legislation			Penalties	Special Defenses/
Pimps/ Customers	Parents	Other Persons		Exemptions
pimp/ promoter under §18-5607	parents under §18-5611 for allowing or putting in prostitution house/room	§18-5604-- procurer §18-5608-- harborers, involved in business	§5609--in state prison, term not to exceed 5 years; in county jail not to exceed 1 year; and/or fine $1,000 maximum §5610--in state prison 5 years and/or $1,000 fine	§5609--by implica- tion if married or unchaste, statute would not apply §5610--if parents consent, by impli- cation would not apply
§11.15= solicitors inducing customers §11.18= patrons §11.19= pimps	-------------	§11.17-- controller of premises	both §11-15.1 and §11-19.1 class 1 felonies ----------------------- ch. 38 §1005-8-1 4-15 years imprisonment ch. 38 §1005-9-1 $10,000 maximum fine ----------------------- §11-19.2 class X felony, 6-30 years imprisonment, $10,000 maximum fine	§11-15.1 and §11-19.1--reason- able belief that 16 or over serves as a defense §11-19.2--none
pimps/ procurers patrons under §35-45-4-3	-------------	controller of premises	class B felony: §35-50-2-5--fixed term 10 years with not more than 10 years added 4 years subtracted for aggravat- ing, mitigating, circum- stances and no more than $10,000 fine	none
----------	-------------	---------------	fine - not exceeding $100, and/or imprisonment in county jail not exceeding 30 days	none

State	Offense Description	Protected Age
Kansas no specific statute, but see: KAN. STAT. ANN. §21-3503, §21-3509, §21-3510, §21-3511 (Supp. 1983)	§21-3503--indecent liberties with a child - sexual intercourse or lewd fondling or touching	§21-3503--under 16
	§21-3509--enticement of a child - inviting, pursuading child to enter place with intent to commit unlawful sexual act on or with child	§21-3509--under 16
	§21-3510--indecent solicitation of a child - enticing, soliciting, accosting child to commit or submit to unlawful sexual act	§21-3510--under 16
	§21-3511--aggravated indecent solicitation of a child - same as §21-3510 but with child under 12	§21-3511--under 12
Kentucky KY. REV. STAT. ANN. §529.030, §529.040 (Baldwin 1981)	promoting prostitution 1st degree= advances, profits from prostitution of person less than 16 years old	under 16
	promoting prostitution 2nd degree= advances, profits from prostitution of person less than 18 years old	under 18
Louisiana LA. REV. STAT. ANN. §14:86 (West Supp. 1984)	enticing persons into prostitution= persuading, placing or causing entrance of person under 21 into the practice of prostitution by force, threats, promises or any device or scheme	person under 21 years of age
Maine ME. REV. STAT. ANN. tit. 17A, §852 (1983)	§852--aggravated promotion 1) compels person to engage in prostitution 2) promotes prostitution of person less than 18	person less than 18
	§855--patronizing prostitution of minor (18 years)	

Targets of Legislation			Penalties	Special Defenses/
Pimps/ Customers	Parents	Other Persons		Exemptions
----------	-------------	solicitor, offender	§21-3503--class C felony 1-20 years imprisonment, and/or up to $10,000 fine §21-3509--class D felony 1-10 years imprisonment, and/or up to $5,000 fine §21-3510--class A misdemeanor up to 1 year imprisonment in county jail, and/or up to $2,500 fine §21-3511--class E felony 1-5 years imprisonment, and/or up to $2,500 fine	§21-3503= defense if child is spouse
pimp/ promoter	-------------	---------------	§529.030 class C felony 5-10 years imprisonment, fine up to $10,000 or 2x the amount gained by committing the offense, whichever is more §529.040 class D felony 1-5 years imprisonment	§529.060-- sex of prostitute is immaterial; no defense that both persons were same sex or that customer was female
pimps (also under §14:84)	§14:84-- pandering if consent by parent or tutor	§14:84-- transporter, maintaining of place §14:83-- solicitor §14:85-- lessor	imprisonment with or without hard labor for 2-10 years	none --------------------- §14:86--mistake of age is no defense
pimps/ promoters (also under §851)	-------------	lessor or transporter or engaged in business operations §851	§852--class C crime §855--class D crime ------------------------- §1252--imprisonment C--not to exceed 5 years D--less than 1 year §1301--fines C--$2,500 maximum D--$1,000 maximum	none

State	Offense Description	Protected Age
Maryland MD. ANN. CODE art. 27, §1 (1982)	abducting, pursuading, enticing, holding or knowingly secreting person under 16 for purposes of prostitution or concubinage	under 16
Massachusetts MASS. GEN. LAWS ANN. ch. 272, §4A, §4B (West Supp. 1983-84)	§4A--promoting child prostitution - induces, aids or abets such inducement §4B--profits from child prostitution - lives or derives support, in whole or in part, from minor's prostitution, knowing proceeds are so desired	under 18
Michigan no specific statute but see, MICH. STAT. ANN. §28.341 (Callaghan 1981)	accosting, enticing, soliciting child with intent to force or induce said child to commit or submit to immoral act or act of gross indecency or act of sexual inter-course	under 16
Minnesota MINN. STAT. §609.322, §609.323, §609.324 (Supp. 1984)	§609.322(1)--solicits, promotes or induces an individual under 16 to practice prostitu-tion	under 16
	§609.322(2)--solicits, promotes or induces an individual at least 16 but less than 18 to practice prostitution	at least 16 but under 18
	§609.323(1)--receives profit, knowing it to be derived from prostitution or promotion of prostitution of individual under 16	under 16
	§609.323(2)--receives profit, knowing it to be derived from prostitution or promotion of prostitution of individual at least 16 but not 18	at least 16 but under 18
	§609.324--engages in prostitution with, hires, offers or agrees to hire individual under 18 to engage in prostitution	under 18
Mississippi no specific statute, but cross reference to MISS. CODE ANN. §97-5-5 (1972)	wilfully, fraudulently leads, takes, carries or entices away any child under 14 for pur-poses of prostitution or concubinage	under 14
Missouri MO. ANN. STAT. §567.050 (Vernon 1979)	promoting▪ 1) compelling person to engage in prostitu-tion 2) promotes person less than 16 §567.010--promotes, causes, aids to engage in procuring, soliciting, operating	person less than 16 years old

Targets of Legislation			Penalties	Special Defenses/ Exemptions
Pimps/ Customers	Parents	Other Persons		
abductor/ pimp	-------------	accessories	up to 8 years imprisonment	none
pimps/ promoters	-------------	---------------	§4A--3-5 years imprison- ment, 3 years manda- tory - no parole or probation - $5,000 fine §4B--5 year minimum imprisonment, no parole or probation - $5,000 fine	none
solicitor	-------------	---------------	imprisonment in county jail for up to 1 year	none
pimps/ patrons	-------------	owners of premises, lessors, trans- porters	§609.322(1)--not more than 10 years imprisonment, and/or not more than $10,000 fine §609.322(2)--not more than 5 years imprisonment, and/or not more than $5,000 fine §609.323(1)--up to 5 years imprisonment and/or $5,000 fine §609.323(2)--up to 3 years imprisonment and/or up to $3,000 fine §609.324--up to 5 years imprisonment and/or $5,000 fine	§609.325--no defense that prostitution was merely solicited or promoted and did not occur mistake of age or consent are not defenses under §609.322 or §609.323 (implying mistake of age is a defense under §609.324)
enticer	-------------	---------------	imprisoned in penitentiary not more than 10 years, or imprisoned in county jail not more than 1 year, and/or fined not more than $1,000	none
pimp- §567.010 customer- §567.030	-------------	business operator or owner; premise owner §567.010	class B felony: §558.011--5-15 years (too serious crime for imposi- tion of fines alone)	none ------------------- §567.040 specifi- cally excludes sex of parties

State	Offense Description	Protected Age
Montana MONT. CODE ANN. §45-5-603 (1983)	aggravated promotion= 1) compels to engage in 2) promotes prostitution of person less than 18 3) promotes prostitution of spouse, child, ward, or any person for whose care, protection and support he is responsible	child under 18 years
Nebraska no specific statute, but see NEB. REV. STAT. §28-805 (1979)	debauching a minor= 1) inducing a minor to carnally know another person 2) soliciting minor to visit house of prostitution for purposes of prostitution 3) arranging or assisting in arranging meeting between minor and male or female of dissolute character 4) arranging, aiding or assisting in arranging meeting between minor and any other person for purpose of sexual penetration	under age 17
Nevada NEV. REV. STAT. §201.360 (1979)	placing person in house of prostitution or permitting, consenting, conniving for person to be in house of prostitution	person under 18 years
New Hampshire N.H. REV. STAT. ANN. §645:2 (1974 & Supp. 1983)	a) soliciting, engaging in sexual contacts or penetration for fee b) induces c) transports d) supported by proceeds e) allows place to be used	person under 18 years
New Jersey N.J. REV. STAT. §2C:34-1(b)(1982)	promoting prostitution= 1) owning, managing business 2) procuring inmate of house 3) inducing to be prostitute 4) soliciting to patronize 5) transport or pay for transportation	child under 16 years or spouse, child, ward
New Mexico no specific statute	--	-----------------------

Targets of Legislation			Penalties	Special Defenses/ Exemptions
Pimps/ Customers	Parents	Other Persons		
pimp (also under §45-5-602)	parents (support) but under §45-5-602(h) it is not promoting to live off prostitutes income, if dependant is incapable of self-support	husband §45-5-602 procurer, transporter backer, premises owner	imprisonment in state prison for maximum of 20 years and/or fined a maximum of $50,000	none ------------------ §45-5-603(b)-- mistake of age is no defense
pimp/ panderers	--------------	----------------	up to one year imprisonment and/or $1,000 fine	none
pimps	parents	----------------	felony: 1-10 years and/or $10,000 fine if physical force, if no force, threat 1-6 years and/or $5,000 fine	none
pimps/ customers	--------------	transporter, premise owner	class B felony: §651:2= maximum term of 7 years and/or fine $2,000 maximum	sex of persons involved is not relevant
pimps under (b), (c), and (d) customers (e)	parents under (c)(4)	spouse (c)(4) business (b)(1) transporter (b)(6) premise owner (b)(7)	3rd degree crime: §20:43-6= term 3-5 years §20:43-3= fines not to exceed $7,500	2C:34-1(c)(3)-- mistake of age is no defense homosexual activity is specifically covered
----------	--------------	----------------	-------------------------	-------------------

State	Offense Description	Protected Age
New York N.Y. PENAL LAW §230.02 to §230.35 (McKinney 1980 & Supp. 1983-84)	§230.02-10 patronizing a prostitute: §230.04--3rd degree - patron over 21, prostitute under 17	under 17
	§230.05--2nd degree - patron over 18, prostitute under 14	under 14
	§230.06--1st degree - prostitute under 11	under 11
	§230.15-35 promoting prostitution: §230.25--3rd degree - advances or profits from prostitution of person under 19	under 19
	§230.30--2nd degree - advances or profits from prostitution of person under 16	under 16
	§230.32--1st degree - advances or profits from prostitution of person under 11	under 11
North Carolina no specific statute	---	-----------------------
North Dakota N.D. CENT. CODE §12.1-29-02 (1983)	facilitating prostitution= a) knowingly soliciting b) knowingly procuring c) knowingly leases premises for d) knowingly induces, intentionally causes another to remain a prostitute	person less than 16 years (wife, child also)
Ohio OHIO REV. CODE ANN. §2907.21, §2907.22 (Page 1982)	§2907.21= 1) compelling another to engage in sexual activity for hire 2) inducing, procuring minor to engage in sexual activity for hire	minor under 16 years of age
	§2907.22= 1) establish, control brothel 2) supervise, manage activities of prostitute 3) transport or cause to be transported to facilitate prostitution	minor under 16
Oklahoma no specific statute	---	-----------------------

| Targets of Legislation | | | Penalties | Special Defenses/ Exemptions |
Pimps/ Customers	Parents	Other Persons		
§230.02-.10 patrons	--------------	----------------	§230.04 class A misde-meanor - up to 1 year imprisonment and/or up to $1,000 fine	§230.04--patron under 21 not liable
			§230.05 class E felony - up to 4 years imprisonment	§230.05--patron under 18 not liable
			§230.06 class D felony - up to 7 years imprisonment	§230.07--in prose-cution under §230.04, .05, .06,
			§230.15-35 if defendant has gained money or property through commis-sion of a crime, the court may impose a fine up to 2x the value gained	mistake of age is no defense §230.10--sex of the parties involved is irrelevant
			§230.25 class D felony - up to 7 years imprisonment	
			§230.30 class C felony - up to 15 years imprison-ment	
			§230.32 class B felony - up to 25 years imprison-ment	
----------	--------------	----------------	-------------------------	-------------------
pimps (also under §12.1-29-01)	parents or person respon-sible for support, care protection who facilitate prostitution	husband, premise owner	class C felony: §12.1-32-01--5 years imprisonment maximum and/or fine $5,000 maximum	none
pimps §2907.22 (also applies to minor under 16)	--------------	business operator §2937.22 transporter §2907.22	3rd degree felony: §2929.11--minimum of 1 year, 18 months, 2 years or 3 years and maximum 10 years and/or fine $5,000 maximum	§2907.21--mistake of age is no defense §2907.22--mistake of age is no defense
----------	--------------	----------------	-------------------------	-------------------

State	Offense Description	Protected Age
Oregon OR. REV. STAT. §167.017 (1983)	compelling prostitution if knowingly: a) uses force, intimidation b) induces person under 18 c) induces spouse, child, stepchild to engage in prostitution	person under 18 ------------------------ spouse, child, stepchild
Pennsylvania 18 PA. CONS. STAT. ANN. §5902 (Purdon 1973 & Supp. 1983)	promoting: 1) involved in prostitution business 2) procuring inmate for house 3) inducing to become prostitute 4) soliciting to patronize 5) procuring for patron 6) transporting, or financing transportation 7) leasing premises	(c)(iii)-child under 16 (c)(iv)-wife, child
Rhode Island Cross reference to R.I. GEN. LAWS §11-9-1(c), §11-9-2 (1981)	§11-9-1(c)--exploitation for commercial or immoral purposes - exhibit, use, employ child for purpose of prostitution §11-9-2--employment of children for unlawful purposes - take, employ or cause to be taken, employed any child for purposes prohibited in §11-9-1	under 18 under 16
South Carolina Cross reference to S.C. CODE ANN. §16-17-490 (Law Co-op. 1983)	contributing to the delinquency of a minor - encourage, aid, cause or influence minor to: 1) violate law 2) engage in occupation which is in violation of law 3) associate with immoral or vicious persons 4) frequent any place the existence of which is in violation of law	under 18
South Dakota S.D. CODIFIED LAWS ANN. §22-23-2 (1979)	procuring, promoting prostitution= 1) encouraging, procuring, causing to become, remain prostitute 2) promoting prostitution of minor 3) promoting prostitution of spouse, child, ward, etc.	minor §26-1-1--natural male or female persons under 18 years of age

Targets of Legislation			Penalties	Special Defenses/ Exemptions
Pimps/ Customers	Parents	Other Persons		
pimps (also under §167.012) customers §167.007	parents §167.017(b)	spouse §167.017(c) business operator §167.012	class B felony: §161.605--term 10 years maximum §161.625--fine not to exceed $100,000 or double amount of gain from commission	none
pimps (procurer solicitor) customer under (e)	(c)(iv) parents or person respon- sible for support who promotes pros- titution	a) business participant transporter, premise owner b) spouse	felony of 3rd degree: §106--term maximum 7 years §1101--$5,000 maximum fine	§5902(c)(iii)-- mistake of age is no defense ------------------- §5902(d)--prosti- tute's minor child or other legal dependent incapable of self-support is exempt from promot- ing
pimp- §11-9-1 employer/ customer pimp §11-9-2	yes	----------------	§11-9-1(c)--up to 20 years imprisonment, and/or up to $20,000 fine §11-9-2--misdemeanor	none
----------	--------------	----------------	up to 3 years imprisonment and/or up to $3,000 fine	none
pimps (also under §22-23-8) customers under §22-23-9	parents (wards)	spouse §22-23-8 premise owner, transporter	class 5 felony: §22-6-1--maximum term of 5 years in state peniten- tiary, fine of $5,000 may also be imposed	none

State	Offense Description	Protected Age
Tennessee TENN. CODE ANN. §39-2-635 (1982)	soliciting, procuring, aiding, abetting prostitution or assignation, receiving money or other things of value from procuring	females: a) less than 18 years b) less than 16 years
Texas TEX. PENAL CODE ANN. §43.05 (Vernon 1974)	knowingly causes by force, threat or fraud to commit prostitution or causes by any means a person younger than 17 to commit prostitution	person younger than 17
Utah UTAH CODE ANN. §76-10-1306 (1978)	aggravated exploitation= a) using force, threat b) person procured, transported, persuaded or with whom shares proceeds is under 18 or wife of the actor note = exploiting prostitution defined under §1305	person under 18 years of wife
Vermont no specific statute	-------------------------------------	---------------------
Virginia Cross reference to VA. CODE §18.2-48, §18.2-355 (Supp. 1983)	§18.2-48--abduction or attempt of female for purpose of concubinage or prostitution ------------------------------------- §18.2-355(3)--parent or guardian consenting to person being taken or detained for purpose of prostitution or unlawful sexual intercourse is guilty of pandering	under 16 --------------------- person in custody of parent or guardian
Washington WASH. REV. CODE ANN. §9A.88.070, §9A.44.100 (1977 & Supp. 1983-84)	§9A.88.070--promoting prostitution – 1st degree – advances or profits from prostitution of person less than 18 years old ------------------------------------- §9A.44.100--indecent liberties – knowingly causes person (not spouse), to have sexual contact with him or another	under 18 --------------------- under 14
West Virginia no specific statute	-------------------------------------	---------------------
Wisconsin WIS. STAT. ANN. §944.32 (West 1982)	intentionally soliciting or causing person to practice prostitution or establishing person in place of prostitution	person under 18 years
Wyoming WYO. STAT. ANN. §6-4-103 (1983)	promoting prostitution= 1) knowingly entices or compels another person to become a prostitute	under 19

Targets of Legislation			Penalties	Special Defenses/ Exemptions
Pimps/ Customers	Parents	Other Persons		
pimps (procurer)	-------------	---------------	a) imprisonment for 2-5 years b) imprisonment for 3-10 years	none
pimps (§43.03 also) customers (§43.02)	-------------	business participant (§43.04)	felony of 2nd degree: penal code §12.33-- confinement in Texas Dept. of Corrections for 2 to 20 years	commentary follow- ing §43.02 indi- cates that both homosexual and heterosexual pros- titution are covered
pimps (procurer or inducer) §76-10-1305 customer §76-10-1303	-------------	§76-10-1305 transporter, business participant §76-10-1304 premise owner §76-10-1306 husband	2nd degree felony: §76-3-203--not less than 1 year no more than 15 years imprisonment §76-3-301--fine of $10,000 maximum	none
----------	-------------	---------------	------------------------	------------------
---------- ----------	------------- yes	abductor guardian, legal custodian	class 2 felony: imprisonment for life, or any term not less than 20 years class 4 felony: 2-10 years imprisonment	none
pimps	-------------	owner of premises who 'permits' pros- titution §9A.88.090	§9A.88.070--class B felony: imprisonment up to 10 years, and/or fine up to $20,000 §9A.44.100--class B felony	§9A.88.050--no defense that persons were of same sex
----------	-------------	---------------	------------------------	------------------
pimp 944.33 customer §944.31	-------------	§944.34- premise owner business participant	class C felony: §939.50--fine of $10,000 maximum and/or term of 10 years maximum	none
pimps customers under §6-4-102	-------------	---------------	up to 5 years imprison- ment, and/or up to $5,000 fine	none

Selected Bibliography

Adolescent and Adult Male Prostitution

Allen, Donald M. "Young Male Prostitutes: A Psychosocial Study." *Archives of Sexual Behavior* 9, no. 5 (October 1980), 399–426.

Benjamin, Harry, and Masters, R.E.L. "Homosexual Prostitution." In Harry Benjamin and R.E.L. Masters, *Prostitution and Morality.* New York: Julian Press, 1964.

Boyer, Debra K., and James, Jennifer. "Prostitutes as Victims." In Donal E. J. MacNamara and Andrew Karmen, eds., *Deviants: Victims or Victimizers?* Beverly Hills: Sage, 1983.

Butts, William M. "Boy Prostitutes of the Metropolis." *Journal of Clinical Psychopathology* 8 (1947), 674–81.

Caukins, Sivan E., and Coombs, Neil R. "The Psychodynamics of Male Prostitution," *American Journal of Psychotherapy* 30 (July 1976), 441–51.

Coombs, Neil R. "Male Prostitution: A Psychosocial View of Behavior." *American Journal of Orthopsychiatry* 44, no. 5 (1974), 782–89.

Cory, Donald W. and LeRoy, John P. "The Hustlers." In Donald W. Cory and John P. LeRoy, *The Homosexual and His Society: A View from Within.* New York: Citadel Press, 1963, 92–104.

Craft, Michael. "Boy Prostitutes and Their Fate." *British Journal of Psychiatry* 112, no. 492 November 1966, 1111–14.

Davidson, Michael. *Some Boys.* London: David Bruce, 1970.

Deisher, Robert W.; Eisner, Victor; and Sulzbacher, Stephen I. "The Young Male Prostitute." *Pediatrics* 43, no. 6 (1967), 936–41.

Deisher, Robert W.; Robinson, Greg; and Boyer, Debra. "The Adolescent Female and Male Prostitute." *Pediatric Annals* 11, no. 10(1982), 819–25.

Dietz, Park E. "Medical Criminology Notes #5: Male Homosexual Prostitution." *Bulletin of the American Academy of Psychiatry and the Law* 6, no. 4(1978), 468–71.

Doshay, Lewis J. *The Boy Sex Offender and His Later Criminal Career.* New York: Grune & Stratton, 1943.

Drew, Dennis, and Drake, Jonathan. *Boys for Sale: A Sociological Study of Boy Prostitution.* New York: Brown Books, 1969.

Gandy, Patrick, and Deisher, Robert. "Young Male Prostitutes: The Physician's Role in Social Rehabilitation." *Journal of the American Medical Association* 212, no. 10(1970), 1661–66.

Gerassi, John. *The Boys of Boise.* New York: Macmillan, 1966.

Ginsburg, Kenneth. "The 'Meat-Rack': A Study of the Male Homosexual Prostitute," *American Journal of Psychotherapy* 21, no. 2(April 1967), 170–85.

Harlan, Sparky; Rodgers, Luanna L.; and Slattery, Brian. *Male and Female Adolescent Prostitution: Huckleberry House Sexual Minority Youth Services Project.* Washington, D.C.: Youth Development Bureau, U. S. Department of Health and Human Services, 1981.

Harris, M. *The Dilly Boys: The Game of Male Prostitution in Picadilly.* Rockville, Md.: New Perspectives, 1973.

Hauser, Richard. "Homosexual Prostitutes." In Richard Hauser, *The Homosexual Society.* London: Bodley Head, 1962.

Hoffman, Martin. "The Male Prostitute." *Sexual Behavior* 2(August 1972), 16–21.

Humphreys, Laud. *Tearoom Trade: Impersonal Sex in Public Places.* Chicago: Aldine, 1970.

———. "Dollars Take Priority Over Love." *Sexual Behavior* 2(August 1972), 19.

———. "New Styles in Homosexual Manliness." In John H. Gagnon and William Simon, eds., *The Sexual Scene.* New Brunswick, N.J.: Transaction Books, 1973.

James, Jennifer. *Entrance into Juvenile Male Prostitution.* Washington, D.C.: National Institute of Mental Health, 1982.

Jersild, Jens. *Boy Prostitution.* Copenhagen: C.E.C. Gad, 1956.

Lloyd, Robin. *For Money or Love: Boy Prostitution in America.* New York: Vanguard, 1976.

MacNamara, D.E.J. "Male Prostitution in American Cities: A Socioeconomic or Pathological Phenomenon?" *American Journal of Orthopsychiatry* 35(1965), 204.

Marlowe, Kenneth. "The Life of the Homosexual Prostitute." *Sexology* 31(1964), 24–27.

O'Day, John and Loway, Leonard A. *Confessions of a Male Prostitute.* Los Angeles: Sherbourne Press, 1964.

Ollendorf, Robert. *The Juvenile Homosexual Experience.* New York: Julian Press, 1966.

Pieper, R. "Identity Management in Adolescent Male Prostitution in West Germany." *International Review of Modern Sociology* 2(1979), 239–59.

Pittman, David J. "The Male House of Prostitution." *Trans-Action* 8(March–April, 1971), 21–27.

Raven, Simon. "Boys Will Be Boys: The Male Prostitute in London." In Hendrik M. Ruitenbeek, ed., *The Problem of Homosexuality in Modern Society.* New York: Dutton Paperback, 1963.

Rechy, John. *City of Night.* New York: Grove Press, 1962.

———. *The Sexual Outlaw: A Documentary.* New York: Grove Press, 1977.

Reiss, Albert J., Jr. "The Social Integration of Queers and Peers." *Social Problems* 9, no. 2(1961), 102–20.

Rossman, Parker, "The Pederasts." In Erich Goode et al., eds., *Sexual Deviance and Sexual Deviants.* New York: William Morrow, 1974.

———. *Sexual Experience Between Men and Boys.* New York: Association Press, 1976.

Russell, Donald H. "From the Massachusetts Court Clinics: On the Psychopathology of Boy Prostitutes." *International Journal of Offender Therapy* 15(1971), 49–52.

Sonenschein, David. "Hustlers Viewed as Dangerous." *Sexual Behavior* 2(August 1972), 20.

Southwell, Margaret. "Counseling the Young Prison Prostitute." *Journal of Psychiatric Nursing and Mental Health Services* 19, no. 5(1981), 25–26.

Thorneloe, William F., and Crews, Eugene L. "Manic Depressive Illness Concomitant with Antisocial Personality Disorder: Six Case Reports and Review of the Literature." *Journal of Clinical Psychiatry* 42, no.1(1–81), 5–9.

Tindall, Ralph H. "The Male Adolescent Involved with a Pederast Becomes an Adult." *Journal of Homosexuality* 3, no. 4(Summer 1978), 373–82.

Urban and Rural Systems Associates (URSA). *An Annotated Bibliography on Adolescent Male and Female Prostitution and Related Topics.* Washington, D.C.: Youth Development Bureau, U.S. Department of Health and Human Services, October 1981.

———. *A Report on Adolescent Male Prostitution.* Washington, D.C.: Youth Development Bureau, U.S. Department of Health and Human Services, April 1982.

———. *Juvenile Prostitution: A Resource Manual.* Washington, D.C.: Youth Development Bureau, U.S. Department of Health and Human Services, July 1982.

Weeks, Jeffrey. "Inverts, Perverts, and Mary-Annes: Male Prostitution and The Regulation of Homosexuality in England in the Nineteenth and Early Twentieth Centuries." *Journal of Homosexuality* 6, nos. 1 and 2(1980–81), 113–34.

Weinberg, Martin. "Labels Don't Apply." *Sexual Behavior* 2(August 1972), 18.

Weisberg, D. Kelly. "Children of the Night: The Adequacy of Statutory Treatment of Juvenile Prostitution." *American Journal of Criminal Law* 12(March 1984), 1–67.

Westwood, Gordon. *A Minority.* London: Longmans, Green, 1960.

Winick, Charles, and Kinsie, Paul M. "Male Homosexual Prostitution," In Charles Winick and Paul M. Kinsie, *The Lively Commerce: Prostitution in the United States.* Chicago: Quadrangle Books, 1971.

Adolescent Female Prostitution

Baizerman, Michael; Thompson, Jacquelyn; Stafford-White, Kimaka; and An Old Young Friend. "Adolescent Prostitution." *Children Today* 8, no. 5(September-October, 1979), 20–24.

Barclay, Kathryn, and Gallemore, Johnny L., Jr. "The Family of the Prostitute." *Corrective Psychiatry and the Journal of Social Therapy* 18, no. 4(1972), 10–16.

Bell, Robert R. "Prostitution." In Robert R. Bell, *Social Deviance: A Substantive Analysis.* Homewood, Ill.: Dorsey Press, 1971.

Boyer, Debra K., and James, Jennifer. "Easy Money: Adolescent Involvement in Prostitution." In Sue Davidson, ed., *Justice for Young Women: Close-Up on Critical Issues.* Tucson: New Directions for Young Women, 1982.

———. "Juvenile Prostitution." In Curt Taylor Griffiths and Margit Nance, eds., *The Female Offender.* Selected papers from an International Symposium. Vancouver, Canada. Simon Fraser University: Criminology Research Center, 1979.

———. "Prostitutes as Victims." In Donal E.J. MacNamara and Andrew Karmen, eds., *Deviants: Victims or Victimizers?* Beverly Hills: Sage, 1983.

Bracey, Dorothy H. *"Baby-Pros": Preliminary Profiles of Juvenile Prostitutes.* New York: John Jay Press, 1979.

Bracey, Dorothy H; Marden, F.; and Jefferson, K. "Juvenile Prostitution in Midtown Manhattan." New York: John Jay College of Criminal Justice, 1977.

Bree, Marlin. "Obsessed with Faith: The Minnesota Connection." *Saturday Evening Post,* March 1979, 28–31.

Brenton, Myron. "Runaways." *Today's Education* 66(March 1977), 64–66.

Brown, Marjorie E. "Teenage Prostitution." *Adolescence* 14, no. 56(Winter 1979), 665–80.

Bryan, James H. "Apprenticeships in Prostitution." In E. Rubington, ed., *Deviance: The Interactionist Perspective,* 2nd ed. New York: Macmillan, 1973.

Budgen, Mark. "Selling Teen Sex Off Trendy Street." *Macleans* 93 (12 June 1980), 29.

Chaplin, G. "Heartbreak Kids." *Washington Post Magazine,* 12 November 1978, 10–13, 15–16.

Crowley, Maura G. "Female Runaway Behavior and Its Relationship to Prostitution." Master's thesis, Sam Houston State University, Institute of Contemporary Corrections and Behavioral Sciences, 1977.

Debenham, A. "Adolescent Prostitutes." In Marien Dreyer, *The Innocent Victims; A Warning to Parents, A Textbook of Crimes Committed by and Against Children.* Sydney, Australia: Edwards & Shaw, 1969.

Deisher, Robert W.; Robinson, Greg; and Boyer, Debra. "The Adolescent Male and Female Prostitute." *Pediatric Annals* 11, no. 10(1982), 819–25.

Densen-Gerber, Judianne. *Medical, Legal and Societal Problems Involving Children: Child Prostitution, Child Pornography and Drug-Related Abuse: Recommended Legislation.* Baltimore: University Park Press, 1978.

Enablers, *Juvenile Prostitution in Minnesota: The Report of a Research Project.* St. Paul: The Enablers, 1978.

Fields, Pamela. "Parent–Child Relationships, Childhood Sex Abuse and Adult Interpersonal Behavior in Female Prostitutes." Ph.D Dissertation, California School of Professional Psychology, 1980.

Foster, Henry H. "The Devil's Advocate." *Bulletin of the American Academy of Psychiatry and the Law* 5, no. 4(1977), 470–73.

Freudenberger, Herbert J. "A Patient in Need of Mothering." *Psychoanalytic Review* 11(1973); 7–14.

Gibbens, T.C.N. "Juvenile Prostitution." *British Journal of Delinquency* 8, no. 1(July 1957), 3–12.

———. "Certain Aspects of Prostitution." *Revue de Science Criminelle et de Droit Penal Compare* (Paris) 4(1971), 907–17.

Gordon, J.S. "Runaways—Changing Perspectives and New Challenges." In James S. Gordon, *Caring for Youth—Essays on Alternative Services.* Washington, D.C.: U.S. Department of Health, Education and Welfare, 1978.

Gray, Diana (Hilton). "Turning-Out: A Study of Teen-Age Prostitution." Master's thesis, University of Washington, 1971.

———. "Turning-Out: A Study of Teenage Prostitution." *Urban Life and Culture* 1, no. 4(1973), 401–25.

Gray, W. "System Specifics in Offender Therapy." *International Journal of Offender Therapy and Comparative Criminology* 22, no. 1(1978), 56–67.

Harlan, Sparky; Rodgers, Luanna L., and Slattery, Brian. *Male and Female Adolescent Prostitution: Huckleberry House Sexual Minority Youth Services Project.* Washington, D.C.: Youth Development Bureau, U.S. Department of Health and Human Services, 1981.

Hogg, James A. "Female Adolescent Prostitution—A Humanistic Model for Intervention and Therapy." Master's thesis, University of Oregon, 1979.

James, Jennifer. *Entrance into Juvenile Prostitution.* Washington, D.C.: National Institute of Mental Health, 1980.

———. "Motivations for Entrance into Prostitution." In Laura Crites, ed., *The Female Offender.* Lexington, Mass.: Lexington Books, 1976.

James, Jennifer and Meyerding, Jane. "Early Sexual Experience as a Factor in Prostitution." *Archives of Sexual Behavior* 7, no. 1 (1977), 31–42.

———. "Early Sexual Experience and Prostitution." *American Journal of Psychiatry* 134, no. 12(December 1977), 1381–85.

Johnson, Sandra. *CUPPI: Circumstances Undetermined Pending Police Investigation.* New York: Delacorte, 1979; Dell Paperback, 1980.

Kagan, Herman. "Prostitution and Sexual Promiscuity Among Adolescent Female Offenders." Ph.D. dissertation, University of Arizona, 1969.

Kosof, A. "Runaways." Danbury, Conn.: Franklin Watts, 1977.

Lindsay, Mary K. "Prostitution—Delinquency's Time Bomb." *Crime and Delinquency* 16, no. 2 (April 1970), 151–57.

MacLeod, Celeste. "Street Girls of the '70s." *The Nation,* 20 April 1974, 486–88.

MacVicar, Katherine, and Dillon, Marcia. "Childhood and Adolescent Development of Ten Female Prostitutes." *Journal of the American Academy of Child Psychiatry* 19, no. 1(1980), 145–59.

"Minors and the Public Streets of Paris." *Liaisons* 231(May–June 1977), 2–6.

Morgan, Ted. "Little Ladies of the Night." *New York Times Magazine,* 16 November 1975, 34+.

Newman, Frances, and Caplan, Paula J. "Juvenile Female Prostitution as a Gender Consistent Response to Early Deprivation." *International Journal of Women's Studies* 5, no. 2(1981), 128–37.

Padilla-Pimentel, Manuela de Jesus. "Prostitution in Adolescence: La Prostitucion en la Adolescencia." *Revista de la Clinica de la Conducta* (Mexico) 6, no. 13(1963), 10–18.

Patil, B.R. "Devadasis and Other Social Evils." *Social Defence* (New Delhi) 9, no. 34(1973), 24–33.

Raab, Selwyn. "Veronica's Short Sad Life—Prostitution at 11, Death at 12." *New York Times,* 3 October 1977, 1.

Remsberg, Charles, and Remsberg, Bonnie. "What Happens to Teen Runaways." *Seventeen* 35(June 1976), 114–15+.

Roberts, Robert E.; Abrams, Laurence; and Finch, John R. "'Delinquent' Sexual Behavior Among Adolescents." *Medical Aspects of Human Sexuality* 7, no. 1(1973), 162–83.

Saffold, Carolyn. *A Street Perspective of Prostitution: Police, Prostitutes and the Public.* Washington, D.C.: National Council on Crime and Delinquency, 1977.

Sato, Yasuko; Hasimoto, Juzaburo; and Sato, Noriko. "An Investigation of the Process by Which Girls Fall into Prostitution." *Homu Sogo Kenkyusho, Kenkyu Kiyo* (Tokyo) 1(1969), 102–106.

Schafer, S., and Knudten, Richard D. "Professional Delinquency." In S. Schafer, *Juvenile Delinquency: An Introduction,* vol. 1. New York, Random House, 1970.

Schorr, Mark. "Blood Stewart's End." *New York Magazine,* 27 March 1978, 53–58.

Silbert, Mimi H. *Sexual Assault of Prostitutes: Phase One.* Washington, D.C.: National Center for the Prevention and Control of Rape, National Institute of Mental Health, 1980.

Silbert, Mimi H., and Pines, Ayala M. "Sexual Child Abuse as an Antecedent to Prostitution." *Child Abuse and Neglect* 5, no. 4(1981), 407–11.

Singh, Indrajit. "Juvenile Subculture in Varansi City." *Journal of Social Research* 12(September 1969), 86–91.

Taylor, A.J.W. "Prediction for Parole—A Pilot Study with Delinquent Girls." *British Journal of Criminology* 7, no. 4(1967), 418–24.

"Teen-age Prostitutes." *Society* 17, no. 3 (November–December 1979), 3.

U.S. Congress, Senate Subcommittee to Investigate Juvenile Delinquency. "Protection of Children Against Sexual Exploitation," Hearings before the Senate Subcommittee to Investigate Juvenile Delinquency, 95th Congress, 1st Session. Washington, D.C.: U.S. Government Printing Office, 1978.

U.S. Congress, House Subcommittee on Crime. "Sexual Exploitation of Children," Hearings before the Subcommittee on Crime, 95th Congress, 1st Session, May 23, 25, June 10, and September 20, 1977.

Vitaliano, Peter P.; Boyer, Debra; and James, Jennifer. "Perceptions of Juvenile Experience: Females Involved in Prostitution versus Property Offenses." *Criminal Justice and Behavior* 8, no. 3(1981), 324–42.

Vitaliano, Peter P.; James, Jennifer; and Boyer, Debra. "Sexuality of Deviant Females: Adolescent and Adult Correlates." *Social Work* 26, no. 6(1981), 468–72.

Weisberg, D. Kelly. "Children of the Night: The Adequacy of Statutory Treatment of Juvenile Prostitution." *American Journal of Criminal Law* 12(March 1984), 1–67.

"White Slavery, 1972." *Time,* 5 June 1972, 24.

Wilson, V.W. "A Psychological Study of Juvenile Prostitutes." *International Journal of Social Psychiatry* 5, no. 1(Summer 1959), 61–73

Winick, Charles, and Kinsie, Paul M. *The Lively Commerce: Prostitution in the United States.* Chicago: Quadrangle Books, 1971.

"Youth for Sale on the Streets." *Time,* 28 November 1977, 23.

Index

298 · *Children of the Night*

About the Author

D. Kelly Weisberg is associate professor of law at Hastings College of the Law, University of California, San Francisco. She received the Ph.D. in sociology from Brandeis University and the J.D. from the University of California at Berkeley. She teaches courses in family law and children and the law and specializes in research on the sexual abuse of children. She is the editor of *Women and the Law: The Social-Historical Perspective,* Vols. I and II (Cambridge, Mass.: Schenkman, 1982). In addition to her publications dealing with children and the law and women and the law, she recently testified on the problems of runaway youth before the Senate Subcommittee on Juvenile Justice, Committee on the Judiciary.